Financial Literacy

Financial Literacy: Implications for Retirement Security and the Financial Marketplace

EDITED BY

Olivia S. Mitchell
and Annamaria Lusardi

OXFORD
UNIVERSITY PRESS

OXFORD
UNIVERSITY PRESS

Great Clarendon Street, Oxford OX2 6DP
United Kingdom

Oxford University Press is a department of the University of Oxford.
It furthers the University's objective of excellence in research, scholarship,
and education by publishing worldwide. Oxford is a registered trade mark of
Oxford University Press in the UK and in certain other countries

First published 2011
Reprinted 2013

Published in the United States of America by Oxford University Press
198 Madison Avenue, New York, NY 10016, United States of America

British Library Cataloguing in Publication Data
Data available

Library of Congress Cataloging in Publication Data
Data available

ISBN 978-0-19-969681-9

Preface

In the wake of the global financial crisis and the ensuing recession, a wide variety of stakeholders—households, plan sponsors, financial service firms, and governments—is now searching for more effective ways to manage financial risk. Nowhere is this more important than in the arena of planning and saving for retirement, where widespread evidence of financial illiteracy is spurring a rich variety of new projects on how to best enhance financial knowledge and tools for decision-making. Accordingly, we are proud to present our newest Pension Research Council/Boettner Center volume exploring lessons for financial literacy in the wake of the crisis, as we work to identify how to help decision-makers in making more informed economic choices.

In the process of preparing this book, several key people and institutions played essential roles. Excellent editorial help was provided by my co-editor Annamaria Lusardi, a valued colleague in financial literacy research. On behalf of the Council, I thank her, along with all the contributors to the book, the reviewers who helped bring this work to fruition, and the Council's Advisory Board on whom we rely for guidance. A key supporter of important research and development in the US financial literacy arena is the Social Security Administration's Financial Literacy Research Center, with which both Lusardi and I work closely. We are also grateful for the intellectual and financial sustenance provided by our Senior Partners and the Institutional Members of the Pension Research Council, listed elsewhere in this volume. The Wharton School graciously provided access to conference facilities and more through its Impact Conference funding. Additional financial support was received from the Pension Research Council, the Boettner Center for Pensions and Retirement Research, and the Ralph H. Blanchard Memorial Endowment at the Wharton School of the University of Pennsylvania. We also offer our appreciation to Oxford University Press, who hosts the Pension Research Council series of books on retirement security. This book was expertly prepared and carefully edited by Matthew Rosen with assistance from Andrew Gallagher.

Our work at the Pension Research Council and the Boettner Center for Pensions and Retirement Security of the Wharton School of the University of Pennsylvania has focused on aspects of pensions and retirement well-being for over half a century. This fine volume will be a welcome addition to all concerned with the future of financial literacy and retirement security.

Olivia S. Mitchell
Executive Director, Pension Research Council
Director, Boettner Center for Pensions and Retirement Research
The Wharton School, University of Pennsylvania

Contents

List of Figures   ix
List of Tables   x
Notes on Contributors   xiii
Abbreviations   xix

1. The Outlook for Financial Literacy   1
   Annamaria Lusardi and Olivia S. Mitchell

Part I. Financial Literacy and Financial Decision-Making

2. Financial Literacy and Planning: Implications for
   Retirement Well-being   17
   Annamaria Lusardi and Olivia S. Mitchell

3. Pension Plan Distributions: The Importance of
   Financial Literacy   40
   Robert L. Clark, Melinda S. Morrill, and Steven G. Allen

4. Financial Literacy and 401(k) Loans   59
   Stephen P. Utkus and Jean A. Young

5. Financial Illiteracy and Stock Market Participation:
   Evidence from the RAND American Life Panel   76
   Joanne Yoong

Part II. Evaluating Financial Literacy Interventions

6. Fees, Framing, and Financial Literacy in the Choice
   of Pension Manager   101
   Justine Hastings, Olivia S. Mitchell, and Eric Chyn

7. Investor Knowledge and Experience with Investment
   Advisers and Broker-Dealers   116
   Angela A. Hung, Noreen Clancy, and Jeff Dominitz

8. Pecuniary Mistakes? Payday Borrowing by Credit
   Union Members   145
   Susan P. Carter, Paige M. Skiba, and Jeremy Tobacman

9. Annuities, Financial Literacy, and Information Overload   158
   Julie Agnew and Lisa Szykman

Part III. Shaping the Financial Literacy Environment

10. Financial Counseling, Financial Literacy,
    and Household Decision-Making   181
    *Sumit Agarwal, Gene Amromin, Itzhak Ben-David, Souphala
    Chomsisengphet, and Douglas D. Evanoff*

11. Time Perception and Retirement Saving: Lessons
    from Behavioral Decision Research   206
    Gal Zauberman and B. Kyu Kim

12. Making Savers Winners: An Overview of Prize-Linked
    Saving Products   218
    Melissa S. Kearney, Peter Tufano, Jonathan Guryan, and Erik Hurst

13. How to Improve Financial Literacy: Some Successful Strategies 241
    Diana Crossan

14. Bringing Financial Literacy and Education to Low- and
    Middle-Income Countries   255
    Robert Holzmann

15. Improving Financial Literacy: The Role of Nonprofit Providers 268
    J. Michael Collins

End Pages   288
Index   293

List of Figures

2.1   Distribution of survey responses across race. Panel A:
      interest rate; Panel B: inflation; Panel C: stock risk   22
2.2   Distribution of survey responses across education. Panel A:
      interest rate; Panel B: inflation; Panel C: stock risk   24
2.3   Distribution of survey responses across gender   26
3.1   How learning affects plans for disposition of
      employer-provided pensions   46
3.2   How learning affects plans for 401(k) disposition choice   47
4.1   Full model marginal effects predicting an outstanding loan 69
7.1   Types of firms that employ individual professionals   125
7.2   Types of firms used that are not associated with
      individual professionals   126
7.3   Methods of payment to individual professionals
      for financial services   127
7.4   Methods of payment to firms for professional services   129
8.1   Liquidity over time   150
8.2   Histogram of pecuniary losses   151
8.3   Payday borrowing as a function of credit scores   153
8A.1 Distribution of credit union members' credit score   154
12.1 Breadth of Premium Bond ownership in the UK from
      2005 to 2006   230
13.1 Components of personal financial well-being   244
13.2 Introducing financial education into New Zealand schools   248

List of Tables

2.1 Financial literacy patterns in the Health and
Retirement Study 21

2.2 Prevalence of retirement planning calculations in
the Health and Retirement Study 27

2.3 Links between planning tools, planning success,
and financial literacy in the Health and Retirement Study 29

2.4 Planning and wealth holdings in the Health and
Retirement Study (US$ 2004) 30

2.5 Probit analysis of Simple, Serious, and Successful
Planners in the Health and Retirement Study
(marginal effects reported) 31

2.6 Wealth accumulation and financial literacy in the
Health and Retirement Study 33

3.1 Disposition choices by respondent characteristics (%) 45

3.2 Disposition choices for defined benefit and defined
contribution plans 48

3A.1 Respondents' descriptive statistics 53

3A.2 Dependent variable definitions 54

3A.3 Key covariate definitions 54

3A.4 Knowledge score questions 55

4.1 Descriptive statistics (%) 61

4.2 Financial literacy questions 63

4.3 Financial literacy scores (%) 64

4.4 Financial literacy score by various characteristics (%) 65

4.5 Logistic estimation of the probability of a loan outstanding 67

4.6 Reported use of loan proceeds (%) 71

5.1 American Life Panel sample summary statistics 79

5.2 Financial literacy assessment questions (%) 81

5.3 Multivariate OLS estimates: individual financial literacy
questions and stock market participation 84

5.4 Probit estimates: individual financial literacy questions
and stock market participation 85

5.5	OLS/probit estimates: stock market illiteracy and participation	86
5.6	OLS estimates: stock market illiteracy, beliefs, and participation	87
5.7	Testing for valid instrumental variables (IV)	89
5.8	Split-sample analysis with and without a planner	92
6.1	Financial literacy and other characteristics of 2009 EPS interviewees	106
6.2	Financial literacy responses and respondent characteristics of AFP participants	106
6.3	Logit analysis of reasons for AFP choice and other controls (odds ratios reported)	108
6.4	Factors associated with respondent ranking the lowest-cost AFP the best (AFP participants)	109
6.5	Logit analysis of factors associated with respondent ranking the lowest-cost AFP the best (odds ratios reported)	111
7.1	Respondent beliefs about financial service professionals (%)	122
7.2	Respondents who use financial professionals by respondent characteristics (%)	123
7.3	Professional titles most commonly reported by respondents	124
7.4	Methods of locating individual professionals (%)	130
7.5	Methods of locating financial service firms (%)	130
7.6	Length of time with same individual professional and customer satisfaction (%)	131
7.7	Length of time with same firm and customer satisfaction (%)	132
7.8	Reasons given for not using a financial professional (%)	133
7.9	Inclination to seek future services from investment advisers and brokers (%)	134
7.10	Participants' beliefs about financial service professionals (%)	140
8.1	Summary statistics	148
8.2	Predictors of pecuniary losses from payday borrowing	152
8A.1	Regression discontinuity	155
9.1	Financial literacy questions	164
9.2	Accuracy of responses to financial literacy questions	165
9.3	Financial literacy raw scores	165
9.4	Demographics and financial literacy (%)	166
9.5	Accuracy of self-assessed financial literacy score	167

9.6	Marginal effects from multivariate probit analysis of tested financial literacy	168
9.7	Overload measures	169
9.8	Marginal effects from multivariate probit analysis of cognitive and emotional overload	170
9.9	Marginal effects from multivariate probit analysis of decision to pick the annuity	171
9.10	Marginal effect for multivariate probit analysis of confidence and satisfaction	173
12.1	Prize-linked saving products	224
12.2	Families holding UK Premium Bonds by income quintiles (%)	229
15.1	GuideStar records for tax-exempt organizations by National Taxonomy of Exempt Entities—Core Codes (2007–9)	277
15.2	GuideStar records for tax-exempt organizations by program category (ten most frequent, 2007–9)	277
15.3	Financial literacy extract from GuideStar records by IRS tax status (2007–9)	278
15.4	Financial literacy GuideStar records median dollar value of reported revenue, expenses, and administrative cost to total expenses ratio by organization category (2007–9)	279

Notes on Contributors

Sumit Agarwal is a Senior Financial Economist in the research department at the Federal Reserve Bank of Chicago. His research interests include issues relating to household finance, as well as financial institutions and behavioral finance. He is also Visiting Associate Professor in the Department of Finance at the Indian School of Business. He received his Ph.D. from the University of Wisconsin-Milwaukee.

Julie Agnew is Associate Professor of Finance and Economics and Co-Director of the Center for Interdisciplinary Behavioral Finance Research at the Mason School of Business at the College of William and Mary. Her research focuses on behavioral finance and its relationship to decisions made in individuals' retirement plans. She is a TIAA-CREF Institute Fellow, a member of the Defined Contribution Plans Advisory Committee for the Virginia Retirement System, and a Research Associate for the Center for Retirement Research at Boston College. She received her Ph.D. in Finance from Boston College.

Steven G. Allen is Associate Dean for Graduate Programs and Research in the College of Management at North Carolina State University, where he holds appointments in the Departments of Economics and Management. He is also a Research Associate of the National Bureau of Economic Research and a fellow of the Employee Benefits Research Institute. His research has focused on absenteeism, employee benefits, labor turnover, productivity, retirement, unions, technological change, and wage determination. He received his Ph.D. from Harvard University.

Gene Amromin is a Senior Financial Economist in the financial markets group at the Federal Reserve Bank of Chicago. His research interests include household financial decision-making, taxation and corporate finance, and retirement savings. He also serves as adjunct faculty at the Kellogg Graduate School of Business. He earned his Ph.D. in Economics from the University of Chicago.

Itzhak Ben-David is an Assistant Professor of Finance at the Fisher College of Business at the Ohio State University. His research focuses on household finance (real estate, financial counseling) and limited arbitrage in financial markets. He received an MBA and a Ph.D. in Finance from the University of Chicago.

Susan P. Carter is a Ph.D. student in the Economics Department at Vanderbilt University. Her areas of interest include applied microeconomics, consumer finance, behavioral economics, and bankruptcy law. She received her BS in Mathematical Economics from Wake Forest University.

Souphala Chomsisengphet is a Senior Financial Economist in the Credit Risk Analysis Division at the Office of the Comptroller of the Currency (OCC). She conducts research on issues related to household finance, real estate finance, banking and financial institutions. Prior to joining the OCC, she was an Economist at the Federal Housing Finance Agency. She earned her Ph.D. in Economics from the University of Wisconsin-Milwaukee.

Eric Chyn is a Research Assistant at the National Bureau of Economic Research (NBER). He is pursuing his MS in Economics from American University.

Noreen Clancy currently conducts policy research and program assessments at RAND, where she works on hedge funds and their role in capital markets, as well as associated policy and regulatory issues. She received her MS from Johns Hopkins University.

Robert L. Clark is Professor of Management, Innovation, and Entrepreneurship, and Professor of Economics, North Carolina State University. His research examines retirement decisions, the choice between defined benefit and defined contribution plans, the impact of pension conversions to defined contribution and cash balance plans, the role of information and communications on 401(k) contributions, government regulation of pensions, and Social Security. He is a Member of the Advisory Board of the Pension Research Council, a Fellow of the Employee Benefit Research Institute, a Fellow of the TIAA-CREF Institute, a member of the American Economic Association, the Gerontological Society of America, the International Union for the Scientific Study of Population, and the National Academy of Social Insurance. He received his Ph.D. from Duke University.

J. Michael Collins is an Assistant Professor in Consumer Science at the University of Wisconsin-Madison and a specialist with the Wisconsin Cooperative Extension in the area of financial education. His research focuses on consumer decision-making in the financial marketplace, including the role of public policy in influencing credit, savings, and investment choices. He is the faculty director of the Center for Financial Security, and co-director of the Social Security Administration Financial Literacy Research Consortium. He received his Ph.D. from Cornell University.

Diana Crossan is the Retirement Commissioner of New Zealand, where she is responsible for increasing the financial knowledge of New Zealanders and providing advice to the Government regarding New Zealand's retirement income policies, and overseeing legislation regarding retirement villages. She graduated from Otago University and the University of Wales.

Jeff Dominitz is Director of Statistics for the Philadelphia Eagles. Previously, he was Senior Economist at RAND, where he served as co-director of the Center on Financial Decision Making and survey director of the American Life Panel. He has also taught economics and public policy at Carnegie Mellon University. He received his Ph.D. in Economics from the University of Wisconsin-Madison.

Douglas D. Evanoff is a Senior Financial Economist and Vice President in the Economic Research Department of the Federal Reserve Bank of Chicago. As Director of the Financial Studies Group, he oversees the research activities concerning financial markets and regulation. Previously, he taught at St Cloud State University and Southern Illinois University. He is currently an adjunct faculty member at DePaul University. He earned his Ph.D. in Economics from Southern Illinois University.

Jonathan Guryan is an Associate Professor of Economics at the University of Chicago's Booth School of Business, a faculty research fellow of the National Bureau of Economic Research, and a member of the University of Chicago Crime Lab. His research investigates patterns in the demand for lottery tickets, race and discrimination in schools and labor markets, the effects of racial prejudice on the wages earned by blacks, and the causes of black–white differences in cognitive test scores. He received his Ph.D. in Economics from the Massachusetts Institute of Technology.

Justine Hastings is an Associate Professor in the Economics Department at Yale University and a Faculty Research Fellow at the NBER. Her primary research interests include applied industrial organization and public economics, examining consumer behavior and how it interacts with firm strategy, and regulation to shape market outcomes in private and publicly funded markets. She received her Ph.D. in Economics from the University of California at Berkeley.

Robert Holzmann is Research Director and Senior Advisor of the Labor Mobility Program at the Marseille Center for Mediterranean Integration and the Financial Literacy & Education Program at the Russia Trust Fund of the World Bank. Previously, he was World Bank Sector Director and Head of the Social Protection Department of the Human Development Network. He has also been Professor of Economics and Director of the

European Institute at the University of Saarland; Professor of Economics at the University of Vienna; and Senior Economist at the IMF and OECD. He received a Ph.D. from the University of Vienna.

Angela A. Hung is Senior Economist and Director of RAND Center for Financial and Economic Decision Making. Previously, she taught at the Heinz School of Public Policy and Management at Carnegie Mellon University, where her research focused on behavioral economics. She received her Ph.D. in Social Science from the California Institute of Technology.

Erik Hurst is the V. Duane Rath Professor of Economics and the Neubauer Family Faculty Fellow at the University of Chicago's Booth School of Business. He is a Research Associate at the National Bureau of Economic Research and his research focuses on macroeconomic policy, household consumption behavior, time use, housing markets, entrepreneurship, and household financial behavior broadly defined. He received his Ph.D. in Economics from the University of Michigan.

Melissa S. Kearney is an Associate Professor in the Department of Economics at the University of Maryland and a Research Associate of the National Bureau of Economic Research. Previously, she was a Brookings Institution Fellow and Assistant Professor at Wellesley College. Her research focuses on public finance and labor, with special interests in social policy issues and government programs relevant to low-income populations. She earned her Ph.D. from the Massachusetts Institute of Technology.

B. Kyu Kim is completing his Ph.D. degree in Marketing at the Wharton School of the University of Pennsylvania, and he will soon join the Marshall School of Business at the University of Southern California as an Assistant Professor of Marketing. His research focuses on the measurement of subjective time perception and its implication to various time-related decisions. He received his MBA in Marketing at Seoul National University, Korea.

Annamaria Lusardi is the Joel Z. and Susan Hyatt Professor of Economics at Dartmouth College and a Research Associate at the National Bureau of Economic Research. She has taught at Dartmouth College, Princeton University, and the University of Chicago's Harris School of Public Policy and Booth School of Business. She is the Director of the new Financial Literacy Center, a joint consortium with the Rand Corporation, Dartmouth College, and the Wharton School of the University of Pennsylvania, with the support of the Social Security Administration. She received her Ph.D. in Economics from Princeton University.

Olivia S. Mitchell is the International Foundation of Employee Benefit Plans Professor of Insurance and Risk Management, Department Chair of the same department, and Director of the Pension Research Council, all at the Wharton School, University of Pennsylvania. Her main areas of interest are private and public insurance, risk management, public finance, labor markets, compensation, and pensions, with both a US and an international focus. She is a Research Associate of the NBER and she earned her Ph.D. in Economics from the University of Wisconsin-Madison.

Melinda S. Morrill is a Research Assistant Professor in the Department of Economics at North Carolina State University, where she studies labor economics and economic demography, as well as pre-retirement financial literacy and education. She received her Ph.D. from the University of Maryland, College Park.

Paige M. Skiba is an Assistant Professor of Law at Vanderbilt Law School, where she teaches in the Ph.D. in Law and Economics Program. Professor Skiba conducts innovative research on the ways in which behavioral biases affect financial decision-making. Most recently she has studied payday loans, pawnshops, consumer bankruptcy, lottery playing behavior, and the links between credit card default and crime. She earned her Ph.D. in Economics from the University of California at Berkeley.

Lisa Szykman is Associate Professor of Marketing and Co-Director of the Center for Interdisciplinary Behavioral Finance Research at the Mason School of Business at the College of William and Mary. She serves on the editorial review board of the *Journal of Public Policy and Marketing*. She earned the MBA from Villanova University and the Ph.D. in Marketing from the University of North Carolina at Chapel Hill.

Jeremy Tobacman is Assistant Professor at the Wharton School of the University of Pennsylvania, where he studies behavioral economics and household finance in developed and developing countries. Previously, he was a Postdoctoral Research Fellow in the Department of Economics at Nuffield College, University of Oxford. He received his Ph.D. in Economics from Harvard University.

Peter Tufano is the Sylvan C. Coleman Professor of Financial Management at Harvard Business School, where he also serves as Senior Associate Dean for Planning and University Affairs. His research and teaching address consumer finance issues focusing on saving, payments, credit, and financial capabilities. He is the Co-Founder and Chair of Doorways to Dreams Fund, a nonprofit organization fund that designs and tests new financial products and services to serve low- to moderate-income consumers. He received his Ph.D. in Economics from Harvard University.

Stephen P. Utkus is the director of the Vanguard Center for Retirement Research, where he conducts and sponsors research on retirement savings and retirement benefits. He is a member of the Advisory Board of Wharton's Pension Research Council, and he is currently Visiting Scholar at The Wharton School of the University of Pennsylvania. He earned his MBA in Finance from The Wharton School of the University of Pennsylvania.

Joanne Yoong is an Associate Economist at RAND, where her research focuses on individual decision-making with an emphasis on finance and health in vulnerable populations. Previously, she was a credit derivatives research analyst in the Fixed Income, Commodities, and Currencies Division of Goldman Sachs in New York and London. She received her Ph.D. in Economics from Stanford University.

Jean A. Young is a Senior Research Analyst at the Vanguard Center for Retirement Research, where she focuses on research that assists employers, consultants, policymakers, and the media in understanding developments in the US retirement system. She received her MS in Taxation from Widener University.

Gal Zauberman is Associate Professor of Marketing at The Wharton School of the University of Pennsylvania, where his research focuses on consumer behavior, time in judgment and decision-making, and memory for emotions and choice. He earned his Ph.D. in Marketing from Duke University.

Abbreviations

ADD	American Dream Demonstration
AFI	Assets for Independence
AFP	Asociación de Fondos de Pensiones
ALP	American Life Panel
AMEX	American Express Company
ANZ	Australia and New Zealand Banking Group
ARM	adjustable rate mortgage
BD	Becton, Dickinson and Company
BLS	Bureau of Labor Statistics
CCT	conditional cash transfer
CD	certificate of deposit
CFA	Consumer Federation of America
CRRA	constant relative risk aversion
D2D	Doorways to Dreams
DB	defined benefit
DC	defined contribution
DHS	DNB Household Survey
DK	don't know
DWPUK	Department of Works and Pensions United Kingdom
EBRI	Employee Benefits Research Institute
EPS	Encuesta de Protección Social
FDIC	Federal Deposit Insurance Corporation
FLE	financial literacy and education
FNB	First National Bank
FRS	Family Resource Survey
FSA	Financial Saving Authority
GMM	generalized-methods-of-moments
GNI	Gross National Income
HIC	high-income country
HRS	Health and Retirement Study

HUD	Department of Housing and Urban Development
IBRD	International Bank for Reconstruction and Development
IDA	Individual Development Account
INHP	Indianapolis Neighborhood Housing Partnership
IRA	Individual Retirement Account
IRS	Internal Revenue Service
IV	instrumental variables
LIC	low-income country
MaMA	Million-a-Month Account
MDC	Matching defined contributions
MIC	middle-income country
MMA	money-market accounts
MRRC	Michigan Retirement Research Center
MS	Monthly Surveys
NASPL	North American Association of State and Provincial Lotteries
NCEE	National Council on Economic Education
NFCC	National Foundation for Credit Counseling
NGO	nongovernment organization
NIA/NIH	National Institute on Aging/National Institute of Health
NORC	National Opinion Research Council
NSAI	National Savings and Investments
NTEE-CC	National Taxonomy of Exempt Entities Core Codes
OECD	Organisation for Economic Co-operation and Development
OLS	ordinary least squares
PARS	Participants Attending Retirement Seminars
PCA	principal components analysis
PISA	Program for International Student Assessment
PLS	prize-linked saving
PSRA	Princeton Survey Research Associates
RHS	Retirement History Survey
RRC	Retirement Research Consortium
SCA	Survey of Consumer Attitudes
SCF	Survey of Consumer Finances
SEC	Securities and Exchange Commission

SHARE	Survey of Health, Ageing, and Retirement in Europe
SRC	Survey Research Center
SRO	self-regulating organization
SSA	Social Security Administration
TF	Trust Fund
USDOL	United States Department of Labor
USGAO	United States Government Accountability Office
ZAG	Zero Alpha Group

Chapter 1

The Outlook for Financial Literacy

Annamaria Lusardi and Olivia S. Mitchell

As financial markets grow more complex and integrated, individuals and their families are increasingly faced with making highly sophisticated and all-too-often irreversible economic decisions. Nowhere is this more evident than with regard to retirement decision-making: a half-century ago, traditional defined benefit (DB) pension schemes were the norm in the United States, Japan, Australia, and much of Europe, but these have now been largely replaced with defined contribution (DC) pensions. In the process, employer and government judgment regarding how much to save and where to invest has been replaced by individuals having to make these choices on their own (perhaps assisted by advisers they also select on their own). Additionally, participants in DC plans must also decide how to spend down their pension assets and determine whether to annuitize or take their benefits in a single lump sum. The trend toward increased individual responsibility and greater financial complexity extends into other realms of life as well, for example regarding decisions over credit cards, adjustable rate mortgages, and when to claim retirement benefits (Campbell, 2006; Ferguson Jr, 2010). Moreover, given the demographic forces at work and the structure of the labor markets, where workers change jobs and employers many times before retiring, the increase in individual responsibility with regard to financial security after retirement will continue to be a feature of many economies around the world.

A larger array of sophisticated financial instruments does offer new opportunities for more tailored financial plans than available in the past, but these can also make poor decision-making more costly to the ill-informed investors. Indeed, recent events surrounding the global crisis that began in 2008 show that, when people and institutions make grievous financial errors, poor financial decision-making can have substantial costs, not only for individuals but also for society at large.[1] This volume focuses on key lessons for financial decision-making in the wake of that crisis, exploring how financial literacy can enhance peoples' skills and abilities to make more informed economic choices. The chapters that follow draw on cutting-edge research by prominent researchers and practitioners engaged in examining how financial knowledge can shape cost-effective financial planning and behavior. The research reported in the volume suggests several main findings. First, financial literacy determines how well people make and execute financial decisions, including saving, investing, borrowing from one's retirement account, and planning for retirement. Second, new evidence is reported on the extent of financial knowledge (or lack thereof), drawing from several surveys; financial literacy's effects on financial decision-making extend above and beyond the effects of education, sex, race, income, and other factors previously found to be associated with gaps in financial knowledge. Third, researchers acknowledge and address directly the all-important causal question, namely, whether financial literacy drives saving and wealth accumulation, or whether the causal mechanism is the reverse, from wealth to financial literacy. For instance, people might invest in financial knowledge, so they then learn about complex assets, in which case the positive association of literacy and wealth would not imply that knowledge causes investing. But conversely, lack of knowledge might prevent people from investing, or alternatively those with no money may fail to learn about financial markets. Accordingly, several of the researchers represented in this volume develop controlled settings in which they try to disentangle these causal links. And this work shows, we believe quite convincingly, that financial education programs do indeed enhance financial decision-making and asset accumulation.

The work presented in this volume will be of interest not only to researchers and teachers, but also to policymakers from all over the world engaged in financial reforms in the wake of the financial crisis, as well as providers of financial advice and financial services. Global awareness is growing on the need to improve retirement security via increasing financial literacy. For instance, the US President's Advisory Council on Financial Literacy (PACFL, 2008) noted that: 'While the crisis has many causes, it is undeniable that financial illiteracy is one of the root causes...Sadly, far too many Americans do not have the basic financial skills necessary to develop and maintain a budget, to understand credit, to understand investment vehicles, or to take advantage of our banking system. It is essential to provide basic financial education that allows people to better navigate an economic crisis such as this one.' Many other groups concur, including the Organisation for Economic Co-operation and Development in Europe, a leader in recognizing the importance of financial literacy, which recently announced a major initiative to 'identify individuals who are most in need of financial education and the best ways to improve that education' (OECD, 2010); the Reserve Bank of India, which launched an initiative to establish financial counseling centers throughout the country; and the Russian Federation, which is implementing, with the World Bank, a major initiative to build consumer financial sophistication (The Financial, 2010). Countries covered in this volume, such as New Zealand, had also undertaken major initiatives to address the problem of financial illiteracy. These initiatives, developed after collecting thorough information on the financial capability of the individuals in those countries, offer important suggestions to other countries as well.

The research presented in this volume can also be helpful to those seeking ways to help individuals and their families as they embark gingerly into the modern financial system, sometimes after substantial missteps. In what follows, we briefly outline themes and highlight salient lessons.

Financial literacy and financial decision-making

In our own prior work (Lusardi and Mitchell, 2007*a*, 2007*b*, 2007*c*, 2008, 2009), as well as in this volume (Lusardi and Mitchell, 2011), we examine how many different groups understand basic financial concepts and plan for retirement. Our chapter in this volume explores how older Americans make financial plans, collect the information needed to make these plans, and implement the plans. Moreover, we show how financial literacy affects retirement planning.

We show that financial illiteracy is widespread, particularly when it comes to understanding calculations related to interest rates and the effects of inflation, along with the more nuanced concept of risk diversification. Only half of all respondents in the survey can correctly answer two simple questions regarding interest rates and inflation, and only one-third correctly answer these two questions plus a question on risk diversification. Financial illiteracy is widespread among older Americans, but shortfalls are particularly concentrated among women, minorities, and the least educated. Furthermore, the financially savvy are more likely to plan and to succeed in their planning, and they tend to rely on formal methods such as retirement calculators, retirement seminars, and financial experts, instead of family/relatives or coworkers. We argue that targeted financial education efforts are likely to be most effective in filling these knowledge gaps.

The workplace is an important source of financial education, particularly as workers approach retirement. In a study by Robert L. Clark et al. (2011), the authors investigate the role of employer-sponsored retirement planning sessions in shaping retirement planning. Drawing on case studies, they examine seminars offered to individuals with mandatory DB plans and voluntary DC plans. In these seminars, employees learn about retirement planning, as well as details of their own benefits and pension distribution rules. To see how the seminars work, participants are asked about their retirement intentions *prior to* and *after* the sessions, to determine whether the seminar is associated with any change in retirement intentions and plans.

The authors conclude that a third of those who originally indicated they would probably take the DB lump-sum payment before the seminar decided afterwards not to take that option. Of those who originally planned not to take the lump sum, almost half changed their minds post-seminar. As for annuitizing DC plans, almost half changed their plans and decided not to annuitize following the information session, compared to one-fifth who decided to annuitize after learning more about their retirement options. Those who indicated they would take the lump sum tend to have more knowledge about retirement-related finance. In this sense, many people who indicated that they would not take the lump-sum distribution actually did not know they had that option, prior to the seminar. The survey also reflects only stated intentions rather than actual behavior, but when it comes time to actually make a final decision, the authors show that some two-thirds of employees do opt for the lump-sum distribution. Overall, this research shows that workers are not well informed about their pensions, and also that the provision of information and knowledge can shape workers' behavior.

Another way in which pension accruals are utilized includes plan loans, particularly in the US 401(k) environment. Steve Utkus and Jean Young (2011) explore how borrowing from one's DC plan is linked to financial literacy and report that almost one-fifth of 401(k) participants had loans outstanding at any given time, with the loans averaging 16 percent of plan balances. The authors also find that lower levels of financial literacy are linked to pension borrowing; that is, those with lower literacy test scores are also more likely to take the loans. A surprising result of the study is that higher-income people are also more likely to borrow from their 401(k) accounts. In sum, financial literacy is related to pension borrowing, but this behavior should not be viewed in isolation from the household's overall balance sheet.

Financial literacy also plays a key role in influencing decision-making regarding stock market investment, as demonstrated in Joanne Yoong's study (2011) linking lack of understanding about equity markets and investment in stocks. She employs the American Life Panel (ALP), an internet survey, to study stock market behavior. She first shows that avoiding stock investments is not associated with mistaken financial beliefs or other important variables, such as risk aversion and income. She further shows that people tend to shy away from the stock market, primarily because they do not understand it. Thus, even if employers design pension plans to 'default' people into portfolios containing equity investments, investors would still benefit from learning about how financial markets work in order to make sensible investment choices.

Evaluating financial literacy interventions

It is not surprising that uneducated consumers fail to make good choices when faced with complex decisions, risk, and lengthy time horizons, and there is at least the chance that financial literacy can help inform the decision process. Accordingly, the volume next covers various methods of assessing how to improve financial literacy. The chapter by Justine Hastings et al. (2011) explores how to present fees and charges in pension choice, focusing on the national mandatory DC scheme in Chile, where workers elect which of five pension funds they invest their mandatory contributions in. Using a nationally representative individual-level survey, the researchers examine respondents' financial literacy and link it to how they select from among five fund managers available to handle their retirement investments. People respond that the top three factors they use in choosing a fund are recommendations from a friend, fund profitability, and to help a salesman (perhaps because the salesman would, in turn, do a favor for, or provide some sort of gift to, the participant). The empirical analysis shows that better-educated and higher-income respondents are more likely to select fund managers generating highest returns. This group is also more likely than others to turn to their employers for recommendations on fund managers. Lower-income respondents rely more on advertising and recommendations from friends. This suggests that the less educated are more susceptible to how information is framed, implying that it may be important to monitor information and plan design as a protective measure for the least literate.

To the extent that people can hire advisers, they may not need to have financial information themselves; nevertheless, many are confused about where to find it and whom to trust to deliver it. This is the topic of the chapter by Angela Hung et al. (2011), who study investor knowledge and experience with advisers and broker-dealers. In the United States, broker-dealers and investment advisors have distinctly different roles: brokers conduct security transactions, dealers buy and sell securities for others, investment advisors provide financial planning services and advice regarding securities, and consultants simply provide advice. However, in practice, the lines may blur, so to gain a better sense of how well consumers understand these distinctions, the researchers surveyed members of the ALP and, in addition, conducted focus groups. They show that many people seem to understand how broker-dealers and investment advisors differ, but few can distinguish between financial advisors and financial consultants. Furthermore, people who have worked with financial professionals tend to have long-term relationships with them involving trust. Nevertheless, many respondents believe they cannot use these services due to insufficient assets. A key challenge for the financial industry is to find ways to provide unbiased, experienced, and high-quality investment advice for low cost, and to serve people with widely varying financial situations and needs.

A more detailed examination of how individuals with limited assets use the financial system is the subject of the study by Susan Carter et al. (2011). In some subpopulations, alternative financial providers play a key role, including payday loan offices and pawn shops offering much-needed cash but often at a heavy price. Those who use these financing sources take out small and short-term loans, typically about $300 for a term of two weeks, carrying very high rates. To better understand payday loans, the authors compare credit union members having an electronic debit charge to a payday lender versus other credit union members. Unexpectedly, those taking out payday loans had higher credit scores, higher inferred income, and smaller loan amounts than did their counterparts. Also these borrowers had higher initial account balances, relative to others, and half could have used their checking or saving accounts, or cheaper lines of credit, instead of the more expensive payday loans. These findings show that it is important to examine all the financial pathways that influence long-term financial security.

Another risk to which consumers are exposed is the possibility that they may outlive their retirement wealth, and this too may be related to financial literacy. The study by Julie Agnew and Lisa Szykman (2011) explores why many workers seem reluctant to annuitize their retirement wealth, even when relatively low-cost annuities provide much-needed protection against longevity risk. In an experimental setting, the researchers first administer a short test to participants to assess their financial literacy levels. Next, participants play a game simulating investment versus annuitization decisions that might unfold for someone leading up to and through retirement. The experiment is structured to make the annuity choice simple, permitting the comparison of participant financial literacy to self-reported levels of cognitive and emotional overload, confidence, and satisfaction. The analysts find that individuals with higher levels of financial literacy are more likely to pick the investment option, while those reporting emotional overload tend to select the annuity. One implication is that plan sponsors would do well to simplify decisions about retirement plans if they are concerned about helping to protect against retirement insecurity. As in the case of Chile, it is important to evaluate how a retirement scheme might unwittingly drive participants into a 'path of least resistance' that is contrary to their best interests, particularly in the case of the less financially literate.

Financial illiteracy can be costly not only to individuals but also to society, which suggests that programs could be designed to help consumers and plan providers better achieve retirement security goals. This topic is taken up by Sumit Agarwal et al. (2011), in their exploration of how counseling can influence mortgage demand patterns. The authors examine two programs: a mandatory two-hour review of mortgage offers in Chicago, and a voluntary two-year counseling program in Indiana. In the former case, the State of Illinois required borrowers in ten zip codes to submit mortgage offers for review by HUD (Department of Housing and Urban Development)-certified counselors, over a four-month period. Borrowers electing risky mortgage products or who had a low credit score were required to attend counseling. The researchers show that, to avoid counseling, small lenders with loose lending criteria and consumers with low borrowing capability dropped out of the market; other potential borrowers chose less risky products so as to avoid the counseling requirement. In other words, it appears that the program may have achieved its goals without actually providing the counseling. Under the latter voluntary program, participants could learn about credit and budgeting, develop a financial plan, and meet with counselors one-on-one each month. If they remained on track with their financial plan, they were entitled to receive loans from partner lenders. In this second case, the evidence suggests that loans made to program graduates performed much better than those of a control group. Nevertheless, there remain questions of causality about the second example, as those who participated may have also been more likely to be particularly motivated to succeed in the program.

Shaping the financial literacy environment

Understanding retirement saving shortfalls may also be due, in part, to problems with time perception, as discussed by Gal Zauberman and B. Kyu Kim (2011). Their work suggests that people often tend to weigh the present more heavily than the future, even when they know their short-term decisions will interfere with important long-term goals, such as saving for retirement. The authors characterize this psychological pattern with the term 'resource slack', defined as the notion that one's preference for something today versus sometime in the future depends on the amount of resources available now versus later. The researchers point out that time is often viewed in economic models as a limited resource, but in experimental settings people claim they will have more time in the future than they actually do, which helps explain why they put off tasks, such as retirement saving, today. A related finding, playing into the apparent disconnect in the ability to save now for future benefits, is a lack of understanding about time itself. The authors argue that people perceive time as being expansive in the present, but it is telescoped in the future. Thus, if retirement is twenty, thirty, or forty years away, it all seems equally far away, as the future is compressed. In addition to believing that they have more time to save in the future than they actually do, people think they will have more money in the future than they do now, which further prompts them to put off saving for retirement. More generally, much psychological research shows that people often fail to grasp the linear nature of time and hence develop hyperbolic rates of future discounting.

One way to reduce the effect of time misperception on retirement saving is to design programs based on precommitment. Accordingly, some have tried to tie retirement saving to the annual tax filing process, so as to make saving automatic. This, in turn, prompts discussion of whether it is better to use behavioral approaches to encourage saving, for example by defaulting workers into pensions, or whether it is preferable to construct mandates that require people to adequately fund their own retirement. This is a theme which runs throughout the volume, emerging in several of the chapters.

An intriguing prize-based model designed to encourage retirement saving is the focus of work by Melissa Kearney et al. (2011), who illustrate how a lottery-like system can harness the popularity of low-probability, high-reward schemes to build retirement saving. The approach has been demonstrated to appeal to those favoring low odds to 'win big', including on their retirement saving, while preserving initial capital. For instance, the so-called Million Adventure bonds were sold in the United Kingdom to finance war debt in the 1690s, with exactly this structure. Again after World War II, the United Kingdom launched prize-based Premium Bonds with the slogan 'Savings with a Thrill!'. This program today has more than 20 million bondholders. Similarly, in South Africa, a privately run plan, sponsored by the First National Bank and called the 'Million a Month Account' plan, enjoyed a take-up rate higher than any other bank product.

The authors helped initiate a prize-based saving program operated by a US credit union, called the 'Save to Win'. This program attracted many participants before it was closed down by authorities, who viewed it as competition to the state lottery. Nevertheless, this initiative provides insight about how to engage certain segments of the population who are hard to reach by traditional saving programs.

We also seek to expand understanding about financial literacy efforts underway around the world. In the case of New Zealand, Diana Crossan (2011) described the work the Retirement Commission has done to design a national strategy for financial literacy, along with numerous private-sector and nongovernment partnerships. Specifically, the national strategy to improve retirement readiness involved working with banks and other organizations to help assess needs and develop programs to improve financial literacy and retirement saving adequacy. A key role is assigned to a well-designed and informative website for all citizens, young and old; to date over one-third of the country's population has consulted and used calculators on the national website. In addition, the author highlights how the government integrated financial education in schools and in tertiary educational institutions.

In addition, nongovernmental organizations are also taking on an increasingly salient role around the world to improve financial literacy in poor populations. Robert Holzmann (2011) from the World Bank correctly advocates for programs to be tailored to meet the attributes of low- and middle-income countries, rather than exporting lessons from developed nations. For instance, many people in low-income countries lack access to basic financial services, and day-to-day needs become priorities, rather than long-term planning. The rural nature of poor countries is also an important factor inasmuch as, in these nations, assets are likely to be seeds or cattle, rather than homes or investment accounts. Moreover, poor countries have far greater numbers of people working in the informal economy, curtailing the reach of organized interventions to develop *financial capability*, a concept that not only encompasses financial knowledge but also looks at financial behavior. Finally, risk in the developing-country context may be more complex and more personal than in richer nations, further hampering incentives to develop long-term financial capability. Accordingly, the author proposes that policymakers do more to monitor and evaluate programs that work. Moreover, he favors direct approaches to change behavior, including social marketing approaches that have worked in other capacities, for instance in improving health outcomes (particularly for those with HIV/AIDS). These tactics could also be used to improve financial capability in low- and middle-income nations.

The role of nonprofit organizations in the United States is the focus of the chapter by J. Michael Collins (2011), who notes that nonprofit organizations may enjoy more public trust as these institutions are not designed to benefit other stakeholders. In addition, nonprofits are often viewed as a force for pluralism, because they are able to reach underserved populations. The author reviews tax filings of tax-exempt organizations using the terms 'credit counseling' or 'financial education', and he concludes that these organizations tend to be small and very diverse. Some are small, community-based organizations with volunteer educators, while others are large agencies with professional staff providing multiple services. He finds it noteworthy that few nonprofit organizations were specifically set up to deliver financial literacy programs; rather, many began to offer financial education programs as part of some other activity. For instance, the US HUD housing counseling program has financed over one thousand nonprofits geared to financial counseling related to housing. In addition, the US Treasury Community Development Financial Institutions Fund has launched a financial education and counseling pilot program to provide grants to nonprofits focusing on financial literacy. After examining what the nonprofit programs offer, the author concludes that low-income clients do receive basic help on goal-setting and budgeting. As the organizations increase in sophistication, they then tend to move into offering credit management, help with access to financial institutions, and provide assistance with income tax filing and saving strategies. Although some may believe that nonprofits are a less expensive source of financial education than private advisers, the author can detect little evidence that nonprofits are any more or less efficient in providing financial literacy services.

Conclusion

Widespread financial illiteracy makes it increasingly challenging for ordinary consumers and their families to cope in an ever-more complex economic environment. This is a problem not only for those who live in developed countries, where it might be surmised that people *should* have a minimal command over simple numeracy, inflation, and risk, but also in middle- and low-income nations, where financial challenges are perhaps more likely to bring hardship than in richer nations. Further, financial illiteracy undermines not only individual retirement security but, indeed, the stability of the global financial system more generally. Indeed, in a recent statement, US President Barack Obama argued that the 'economic crisis was the result of both irresponsible actions on Wall Street, and everyday choices on Main Street....[M]any Americans took out loans they could not afford or signed contracts without fully understanding the terms. Ensuring this crisis never happens again will require new rules to protect consumers and better information to empower them' (Alarkon, 2010).

For all of these reasons, boosting financial literacy skills is likely to be critically important for economic and social welfare—not only for this generation, but also for those to come. Finding out which sorts of programs and financial decision-making structures are most effective (as well as least costly) is a task of supreme importance. This task is best informed with carefully designed experiments and evidence-based research with solid evaluation efforts, many of which we report in this volume. Although much remains to be done to enhance financial literacy, we do know who is likely to be most positively affected; as described in several chapters in this volume, the least educated, those with low incomes, and women are more likely to display low financial literacy. Increased financial knowledge will help people make better lifetime financial decisions, thus better protecting them from financial hardship and an insecure old age.

Endnote

[1] For instance, Bergstresser and Beshears (2009), Gerardi et al. (2010), and Bucks and Pence (2008) show that the least financially literate are also most likely to fail to understand mortgage terms, take out complex mortgages, and fall behind on their housing payments. These mistakes can result in welfare transfers and other transfer payments that increase the public in addition to the private costs of financial illiteracy.

References

Agarwal, S., G. Amromin, I. Ben-David, S. Chomsisengphet, and D. D. Evanoff (2011). 'Financial Counseling, Financial Literacy, and Household Decision-Making,' in O. S. Mitchell and A. Lusardi, eds, *Financial Literacy: Implications for Retirement Security and the Financial Marketplace*. Oxford, UK: Oxford University Press.

Agnew, J. and L. Szykman (2011). 'Annuities, Financial Literacy and Information Overload,' in O. S. Mitchell and A. Lusardi, eds, *Financial Literacy: Implications for Retirement Security and the Financial Marketplace*. Oxford, UK: Oxford University Press.

Alarkon, W. (2010). 'Obama Names April National Financial Literacy Month,' *On The Money*, April 4. http://thehill.com/blogs/on-the-money/801-economy/90435-obama-names-april-national-financial-literacy-month

Bergstresser, D. and J. Beshears (2009). 'Who Selected Adjustable-Rate Mortgages? Evidence from Surveys of Consumer Finances,' Harvard Business School Working Paper No. 10-083. Cambridge, MA: Harvard University.

Bucks, B. and K. Pence (2008). 'Do Borrowers Know their Mortgage Terms?' *Journal of Urban Economics*, 64: 218–33.

Campbell, J. (2006). 'Household Finance,' *Journal of Finance*, 61: 1553–604.

Carter, S. P., P. M. Skiba, and J. Tobacman (2011). 'Pecuniary Mistakes? Payday Borrowing by Credit Union Members,' in O. S. Mitchell and A. Lusardi, eds, *Financial Literacy: Implications for Retirement Security and the Financial Marketplace*. Oxford, UK: Oxford University Press.

Clark, R. L., M. S. Morrill, and S. G. Allen (2011). 'Pension Plan Distributions: The Importance of Financial Literacy,' in O. S. Mitchell and A. Lusardi, eds, *Financial Literacy: Implications for Retirement Security and the Financial Marketplace*. Oxford, UK: Oxford University Press.

Crossan, D. (2011). 'How to Improve Financial Literacy: Some Successful Strategies,' in O. S. Mitchell and A. Lusardi, eds, *Financial Literacy: Implications for Retirement Security and the Financial Marketplace*. Oxford, UK: Oxford University Press.

Collins, J. M. (2011). 'Improving Financial Literacy: The Role of Nonprofit Providers,' in O. S. Mitchell and A. Lusardi, eds, *Financial Literacy: Implications for Retirement Security and the Financial Marketplace*. Oxford, UK: Oxford University Press.

Ferguson Jr, R. W. (2010). *The 2010 Martin Feldstein Lecture—National Bureau of Economic Research*. Cambridge, MA: NBER. http://www.tiaacref.org/public/about/news/gen1007_229.html

Gerardi, K., L. Goette, and S. Meier (2010). 'Financial Literacy and Subprime Mortgage Delinquency: Evidence from a Survey Matched to Administrative Data,' Federal Reserve Bank of Atlanta Working Paper No. 2010–10. Atlanta, GA: Federal Reserve Bank of Atlanta.

Hastings, J., O. S. Mitchell, and E. Chyn (2011). 'Fees, Framing, and Financial Literacy in the Choice of Pension Manager,' in O. S. Mitchell and A. Lusardi, eds, *Financial Literacy: Implications for Retirement Security and the Financial Marketplace*. Oxford, UK: Oxford University Press.

Holzmann, R. (2011). 'Bringing Financial Literacy and Education to Low- and Middle-Income Countries,' in O. S. Mitchell and A. Lusardi, eds, *Financial Literacy: Implications for Retirement Security and the Financial Marketplace*. Oxford, UK: Oxford University Press.

Hung, A. A., N. Clancy, and J. Dominitz (2011). 'Investor Knowledge and Experience with Investment Advisers and Broker-Dealers,' in O. S. Mitchell and A. Lusardi, eds, *Financial Literacy: Implications for Retirement Security and the Financial Marketplace*. Oxford, UK: Oxford University Press.

Kearney, M. S., P. Tufano, J. Guryan, and E. Hurst (2011). 'Making Savers Winners: An Overview of Prize-Linked Saving Products,' in O. S. Mitchell and A. Lusardi, eds, *Financial Literacy: Implications for Retirement Security and the Financial Marketplace*. Oxford, UK: Oxford University Press.

Lusardi, A. and O. S. Mitchell (2007*a*). 'Baby Boomer Retirement Security: The Roles of Planning, Financial Literacy, and Housing Wealth,' *Journal of Monetary Economics*, 54: 205–24.

—— —— (2007*b*). 'Financial Literacy and Retirement Planning: New Evidence from the RAND American Life Panel,' Pension Research Council Working Paper No. 2007-33. Philadelphia, PA: Pension Research Council.

—— —— (2007*c*). 'Financial Literacy and Retirement Preparedness: Evidence and Implications for Financial Education.' *Business Economics*, 42: 35–44.

—— —— (2008). 'Planning and Financial Literacy: How Do Women Fare?' *American Economic Review Papers and Proceedings*, 98: 413–17.

—— —— (2009). 'How Ordinary Consumers Make Complex Economic Decisions: Financial Literacy and Retirement Readiness,' NBER Working Paper No. 15350. Cambridge, MA: National Bureau of Economic Research.

—— —— (2011). 'Implications for Retirement Wellbeing of Financial Literacy and Planning,' in O. S. Mitchell and A. Lusardi, eds, *Financial Literacy: Implications for Retirement Security and the Financial Marketplace*. Oxford, UK: Oxford University Press.

Organisation for Economic Co-operation and Development (OECD) (2010). *Financial Education*. Paris, France: Directorate for Financial and Enterprise Affairs. http://www.oecd.org/department/0,3355,en_2649_15251491_1_1_1_1_1,00.html

President's Advisory Committee on Financial Literacy (PACFL) (2008). *Annual Report to the President: Executive Summary*. Washington, DC: PACFL. http://www.ustreas.gov/offices/domestic-finance/financial-institution/fin-education/council/exec_sum.pdf

The Financial (2010). 'The World Bank Supports Russia's Government Efforts to Improve Financial Literacy, Education,' *The Financial*, August 12. http://goldenbrand. finchannel.com/Main_News/Business/77063_The_World_Bank_Supports_Russia% E2%80%99s_Government_Efforts_to_Improve_Financial_Literacy,_Education/

Utkus, S. P. and J. A. Young (2011). 'Financial Literacy and 401(k) Loans,' in O. S. Mitchell and A. Lusardi, eds, *Financial Literacy: Implications for Retirement Security and the Financial Marketplace*. Oxford, UK: Oxford University Press.

Yoong, J. (2011). 'Financial Illiteracy and Stock Market Participation: Evidence from the RAND American Life Panel,' in O. S. Mitchell and A. Lusardi, eds, *Financial Literacy: Implications for Retirement Security and the Financial Marketplace*. Oxford, UK: Oxford University Press.

Zauberman, G. and B. K. Kim (2011). 'Time Perception and Retirement Saving: Lessons from Behavioral Decision Research,' in O. S. Mitchell and A. Lusardi, eds, *Financial Literacy: Implications for Retirement Security and the Financial Marketplace*. Oxford, UK: Oxford University Press.

Part I
Financial Literacy and Financial Decision-Making

Chapter 2

Financial Literacy and Planning: Implications for Retirement Well-being

Annamaria Lusardi and Olivia S. Mitchell

Most older Americans are not at all confident about the efficacy of their efforts to save for retirement, and in fact one-third of adults in their 50s have failed to develop any kind of retirement saving plan at all (Lusardi, 1999, 2003; Yakoboski and Dickemper, 1997). What explains this low level of retirement preparedness? Why do people do such a poor job when it comes to designing and carrying out retirement saving plans? In this chapter, we explore the hypothesis that poor planning may be a primary result of financial illiteracy. That is, we evaluate whether those who report that they are unable to plan for retirement and/or who cannot carry out their retirement saving plans are also those who are least aware of fundamental economic concepts driving economic well-being over the life cycle.

While several prior studies offer suggestions about why people fail to plan for retirement, few examine the roles that planning and information costs might play in affecting retirement saving decisions. Others have offered evidence on related topics; for instance Calvert et al. (2007) show that more sophisticated households are more likely to buy equities and invest more efficiently,[1] and Hilgert et al. (2003) and Lusardi and Mitchell (2009) demonstrate strong links between financial knowledge and financial behavior. Our contribution reports on a special module on planning and financial literacy we designed for the 2004 Health and Retirement Study (HRS), which allows us to investigate how workers make their saving decisions, how they collect the information for making these decisions, and whether they possess the financial literacy needed to make these decisions. Using the responses to this survey, we argue that lack of literacy is critical because it has important consequences for lifetime well-being.

Methods and data

The conventional economic framework used to model consumption and saving decisions posits that rational and foresighted consumers derive utility from consumption and leisure over the lifetime. In its simplest format, the consumer's problem is modeled in terms of lifetime expected utility or the expected value of the sum of per-period utility $U(c_j)$ discounted to the present (with discount factor β), multiplied by the probability of survival p_j from the worker's current age j to the oldest possible lifetime D:

$$E\left[\sum_{j=s}^{D} \beta^{j-s} U(c_j)\right].$$

Per-period assets and consumption (a_j and c_j) are determined endogenously by maximizing this function subject to an intertemporal budget constraint; here e_j is labor earnings, ra_j represents the household's returns on assets a_j, and SS and PP represent the household's Social Security benefits and pensions, which depend on the worker's retirement (R) age:

$$y_j = e_j + ra_j, \quad j \in \{s, ..., R-1)\}$$

and

$$y_j = SS_j(R) + PP_j(R) + ra_j, \qquad j \in [R, ..., D].$$

Furthermore, consumption depends on income, assets, and benefits so that:[2]

$$c_j + a_{j+1} = y_j + a_j, \qquad j \in [S, ..., R-1] \text{ before retirement}(R)$$

and

$$c_j + a_{j+1} = y_j + a_j, \quad j \in [R, ..., D] \text{ from retirement to death } (D).$$

In other words, the economic model posits that the consumer holds expectations regarding prospective survival probabilities, discount rates, investment returns, earnings, pensions, Social Security benefits, and inflation. Further, the consumer is assumed to use that information to formulate and execute optimal consumption and saving plans.

This formulation makes it clear that saving for retirement requires substantial information and financial literacy, as well as the tools to plan and implement retirement saving plans. But whether 'real people' can meet this challenge is a topic of substantial current interest, and it is particularly important in view of the trend of workers taking responsibility to save, manage their pension investments, and draw down their retirement assets in a self-managed retirement environment. To further investigate the links between the sources of information on which households rely and financial literacy and planning, we designed a special module on retirement planning to assess levels of financial literacy along with consumers' efforts to budget, calculate, and develop retirement saving plans. We implement this in the context of the HRS, a nationally representative longitudinal dataset of Americans over the age of 50. This survey, conducted every two years since 1992, is designed to address these questions by tracking health, assets, liabilities, and patterns of well-being in older households. The core survey consists of a 90-minute core questionnaire administered to age-eligible respondents and their spouses. In addition, our special financial literacy and planning module included three questions on financial literacy, as follows:

- Suppose you had $100 in a savings account and the interest rate was 2 percent per year. After five years, how much do you think you would have in the account if you left the money to grow: more than $102, exactly $102, less than $102? I do not know; I refuse to answer.
- Imagine that the interest rate on your savings account was 1 percent per year and inflation was 2 percent per year. After one year, would you be able to buy more than, exactly the same as, or less than today with the money in this account? I do not know; I refuse to answer.
- Do you think that the following statement is true or false? 'Buying a single company stock usually provides a safer return than a stock mutual fund.' I do not know; I refuse to answer.

The first two questions we refer to as the 'Interest Rate' and 'Inflation' items, and they indicate whether respondents command key economic concepts fundamental to saving. The third question, which we dub 'Stock Risk', evaluates knowledge of risk diversification, crucial to informed investment decisions.

We also ask respondents how they calculate retirement saving needs. To do so, we replicate a question on whether people plan for retirement asked by Employee Benefits Research Institute (EBRI) in its Retirement Confidence Survey and in TIAA-CREF surveys (Ameriks et al., 2003; EBRI, 1996, 2001). We also ask whether people ever assessed their retirement saving needs and what followed from such assessment. The three HRS modular questions on retirement planning are as follows:

- Have you ever tried to figure out how much your household would need to save for retirement?
- Did you develop a plan for retirement saving?
- How often were you able to stick to this plan: would you say always, mostly, rarely, or never?

Last, we assess what tools people use to devise and carry out their retirement saving plans. Specifically, we inquire whether respondents contact friends, relatives, or experts, and whether they use retirement calculators. Further, we ask whether respondents track their spending and set spending budgets. The specific planning tools questions are as follows:

- Tell me about the ways you tried to figure out how much your household would need.
  - Did you talk to family and relatives?
  - Did you talk to coworkers or friends?
  - Did you use calculators or worksheets that are computer- or Internet-based?
  - Did you consult a financial planner or advisor or an accountant?
- How often do you keep track of your actual spending: would you say always, mostly, rarely, or never?
- How often do you set budget targets for your spending: would you say always, mostly, rarely, or never?

Using respondents' answers to these questions, along with information of their socio-demographic characteristics, we can assess the prevalence of financial literacy, retirement calculations, and the planning tools people deploy to devise and execute their plans. In addition, we determine whether those who lack knowledge of basic economic concepts also seem to be those who have particular difficulty devising plans and carrying them out in practice. In what follows, we offer both tabular and multivariate analysis of the data, so as to evaluate whether those who are more financially literate are also more likely to plan and be successful planners.

Financial literacy results

Our first set of findings on financial literacy among this sample of older Americans is reported in Panel 1 of Table 2.1, where we see that only two-thirds of the respondents can do simple calculations related to interest rates.[3] This is a discouraging finding inasmuch as this generation in its 50s and 60s has made many important financial decisions over its lifetime. More of the respondents—three-quarters—can answer the inflation question correctly and understand they would be able to buy less after a year if the interest rate was 1 percent and inflation 2 percent. Yet only half of the respondents know that holding a single company stock implies a riskier return than a stock mutual fund. It is also of interest to distinguish between those who can give a correct answer, versus those giving either an incorrect answer or saying they 'don't know' (DK). Interestingly, the proportion of

TABLE 2.1 Financial literacy patterns in the Health and Retirement Study

	Correct	Incorrect	Don't know	Refuse
Panel 1: Distribution of responses on financial literacy questions (%)				
Interest rate	67.1	22.2	9.4	1.3
Inflation	75.2	13.4	9.9	1.5
Stock risk	52.3	13.2	33.7	0.9
Panel 2: Joint probabilities of being correct on financial literacy questions (%)				
	All three responses correct	Only two responses correct	Only one response correct	No responses correct
Proportion	34.3	35.8	16.3	9.9

Source: Authors' calculations based on unweighted data from the 2004 Health and Retirement Study, Planning Module; see text.

incorrect/DK responses varies according to the question. For example, only 9 percent did not know about interest rate calculations, but more than one-fifth (22 percent) gave an incorrect answer. On the inflation question, 10 percent did not know, while 13 percent gave a wrong answer. The question about stock risk elicited the most DKs: one-third (34 percent) of the sample did not know, while a smaller fraction (13 percent) gave a wrong answer.

Inasmuch as the first two questions are crucial to financial numeracy, it is disturbing that only slightly over half (56 percent) of the sample gets *both* questions right. Also disturbing is the fact that only one-third (34 percent) of respondents can correctly answer all three questions and 36 percent can answer only two questions correctly (see Panel 2). Another interesting finding is that the 'DK' responses are highly correlated: that is, financial illiteracy is systematic across areas examined. For instance, there is a 70 per cent correlation between those who cannot answer both the interest rate question and the inflation question. Erroneous answers are more scattered, with mistakes having a correlation of only 11 percent.[4]

These results reinforce other US findings on older respondents (cf. Bernheim, 1995, 1998; Hogarth and Hilgert, 2002; Moore, 2003; Lusardi and Mitchell, 2007*b*, 2007*c*). These authors tend to concur that such individuals often fail to understand key financial concepts, particularly relating to bonds, stocks, mutual funds, and the working of compound interest; they also report that these people often do not understand loans (and in particular, mortgages).[5] The same is true of younger Americans: the National Council on Economic Education (NCEE, 2005) study of high-school students and working-age adults in 2005 revealed a widespread lack of knowledge of fundamental economic concepts. Similar results for US high school students are reported by Mandell (2004) and for young adults by Lusardi et al. (2010).[6] Clearly, the news is far from positive: Americans' financial literacy levels are low.

Who is financially literate? Next we evaluate the extent of heterogeneity in financial knowledge across demographic groups. Specifically, we are interested in whether knowledge patterns differ by race/ethnicity and education, as depicted in Figure 2.1. A first point to note is the differences in knowledge between Whites, Blacks, and Hispanics.[7] Specifically, fewer than half of the Hispanics can answer correctly the interest rate question, and a sizable fraction of the remainder stated they did not know the answer. This is a potentially important result in view of the fact that many Hispanics tend to be unbanked and do not hold checking accounts (Hogarth et al., 2004). A similar pattern emerges with the question about inflation, where again Hispanics are least likely to answer correctly. As far as risk diversification is concerned, Hispanics and Blacks both display difficulty answering this question: only one-third (37 percent) of the Blacks responded correctly, and over 40 percent did not know the answer to this question. This may shed further light on why so many Blacks do not hold stocks (Haliassos and Bertaut, 1995).

Differences in financial knowledge across education groups are represented in Figure 2.2, and the patterns confirm expectations that financial literacy is highly and positively correlated with schooling. Most importantly, financial illiteracy is most acute for those with less than a high school

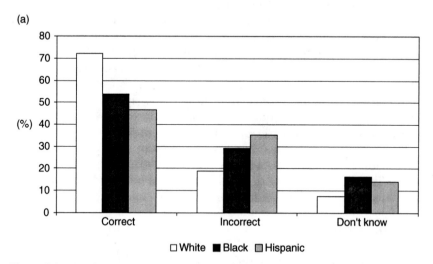

Figure 2.1 Distribution of survey responses across race. Panel A: interest rate

Source: Authors' calculations based on unweighted data from the 2004 Health and Retirement Study, Planning Module; see text.

(b)

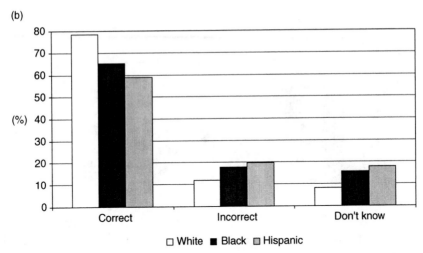

Figure 2.1 Distribution of survey responses across race. Panel B: inflation

Source: Authors' calculations based on unweighted data from the 2004 Health and Retirement Study, Planning Module; see text.

(c)

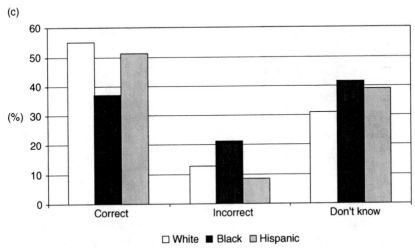

Figure 2.1 Distribution of survey responses across race. Panel C: stock risk

Source: Authors' calculations based on unweighted data from the 2004 Health and Retirement Study, Planning Module; see text.

(a)

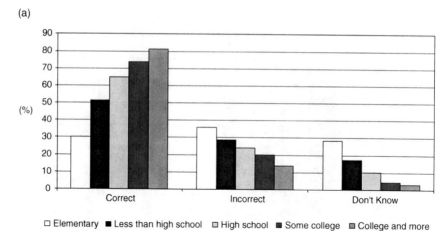

□ Elementary ■ Less than high school ▢ High school ■ Some college ▨ College and more

Figure 2.2 Distribution of survey responses across education. Panel A: interest rate
Source: Authors' calculations based on unweighted data from the 2004 Health and
Retirement Study, Planning Module; see text.

(b)

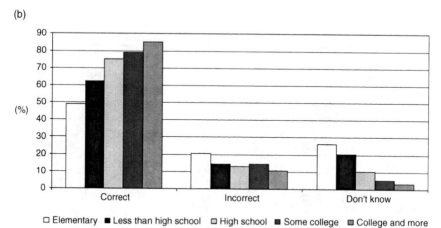

□ Elementary ■ Less than high school ▢ High school ■ Some college ▨ College and more

Figure 2.2 Distribution of survey responses across education. Panel B: inflation
Source: Authors' calculations based on unweighted data from the 2004 Health and
Retirement Study, Planning Module; see text.

(c)

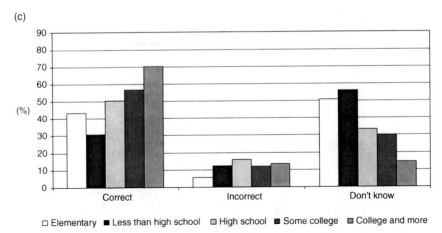

Figure 2.2 Distribution of survey responses across education. Panel C: stock risk
Source: Authors' calculations based on unweighted data from the 2004 Health and Retirement Study, Planning Module; see text.

degree, and less than one-third of respondents with only elementary education could correctly answer the question about interest rates (another one-third did not know). The prevalence of correct answers to the interest rate question rises with education, while the proportion of both incorrect answers and DKs falls. A similar pattern characterizes answers to the inflation question, where those lacking a high school education are much more often incorrect or cannot answer the question. Turning to the risk diversification question, only those with at least a college degree display a high proportion of correct answers, though even here, almost one-third of these did not know the answer or answered incorrectly to this question. Among the less educated, the proportion of DK was particularly high; over half of those with less than high school education reported they did not know the answer to these questions.

Figure 2.3 reveals response patterns by sex, where the results confirm that women are generally less financially knowledgeable than men (cf. Lusardi and Mitchell, 2008). Concerning risk diversification, women are less likely to respond correctly to the question compared to men, and are more likely to not know the answer, rather than answering incorrectly. Also fewer women can answer all questions correctly compared to men.

For brevity, we merely summarize other financial literacy results along other dimensions. Findings worth highlighting include the fact that the leading edge of the Baby-Boomers (age 51–56 in 2004) was not very knowledgeable about inflation, perhaps a result of their limited historical

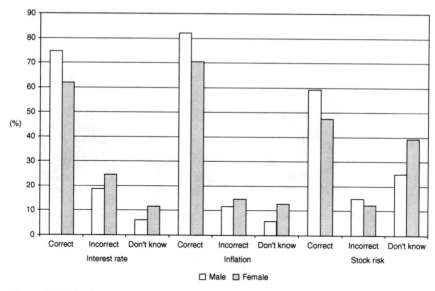

Figure 2.3 Distribution of survey responses across gender

Source: Authors' calculations based on unweighted data from the 2004 Health and Retirement Study, Planning Module; see text.

exposure to inflation or the fact they were in their 20s in the high inflation period during the 1970s and early 1980s. Moreover, financial literacy decreases sharply at an old age (for older cohorts). While it is not possible to distinguish between age and cohort effects in a single cross-section, older individuals/generations display lower financial knowledge than individuals in their 50s.

Findings for retirement planning

Next, we turn to an assessment of some of the other predictions of the canonic economic model, including the hypothesis that people look ahead and calculate how much they need to save for retirement. To this end, our HRS modules ask respondents whether they ever tried to figure out how much they need to save for retirement, and Table 2.2 reports the results. Somewhat discouragingly, less than one-third of the sample respondents (31 percent) indicated that they actually attempted to do a retirement saving calculation; these we call the *Simple Planners*. The small size of this group confirms summaries of older HRS waves, where many people indicated they had given little thought to retirement, even when they were just a

TABLE 2.2 Prevalence of retirement planning calculations in the Health and Retirement Study

Question	Response				
Panel 1: Proportion of planners in respective subgroups (%)					
	Yes	No	Refuse/ Don't know		
Did you try to figure out how much to save for retirement?	31.3	67.8	0.9		
	Yes	More or less	No	Refuse/ Don't know	
Did you develop a plan?	58.4	9.0	32.0	0.6	
	Always	Mostly	Rarely	Never	Refuse/ Don't know
Were you able to stick to the plan?	37.7	50.0	8.0	2.6	1.0
Panel 2: Proportion of planners in the full sample (%)					
	Yes				
Simple Planners: Did you try to figure out how much to save for retirement?	31.3				
	Yes or more or less				
Serious Planners: Did you develop a plan?	21.1				
	Always or mostly				
Successful Planners: Were you able to stick to the plan?	18.5				

Source: Authors' calculations based on unweighted data from the 2004 Health and Retirement Study, Planning Module; see text.

few years away from leaving the workforce (Lusardi, 1999, 2002, 2003). Our results also confirm a widespread lack of retirement planning, even among the educated (Yakoboski and Dickemper, 1997; Ameriks et al., 2004). It is also consistent with work by Mitchell (1988) and Gustman and Steinmeier (1999), who found that workers seem to know very little about their Social Security and pension benefits, two of the most important components of retirement wealth. In fact, close to half of workers in the HRS analyzed by Gustman and Steinmeier (2004) could not report their type of pension plan, and an even larger portion was ignorant of future Social Security benefits.[8]

A key advantage of our module, compared to previous core HRS questions and other surveys, is that we probe further to inquire about the outcomes associated with undertaking planning and related calculations. Panel 1 of Table 2.2 indicates that only 58 percent of those who tried to develop a plan actually did so, while a small group 'more or less' developed a plan (9 percent). Both of these groups we refer to later as the *Serious Planners*. The high failure rate, so far as developing a plan is concerned, underscores the fact that retirement projections are difficult to do. If we consider those who responded positively to the question, as many as half of Simple Planners did not succeed in developing a plan, another disappointing finding. Furthermore, of the subset of Serious Planners, only one-third (38 percent) were always able to stick to their plan, while half were 'mostly' able to stick to their plans (later we call these respondents *Successful Planners*). In the sample as a whole, this represents a meager 19 percent rate of successful planning. Of course, households may face unexpected shocks, making them deviate from plans, but the fact remains that few respondents do what the economic models suggest that they should. In other words, planning for retirement is difficult, few do it, and fewer still think they get it right.

To further evaluate what planning means and what people actually do when planning for retirement, we also asked respondents to indicate which tools they used in the process. It is possible that those who used crude or inaccurate tools were also those who had low planning success. In fact, respondents used a wide variety of tools to calculate their retirement needs (see Panel 1 of Table 2.3; note that these questions were asked only to those who reported they attempted retirement saving calculations). Results show that between one-quarter and one-fifth of respondents talked to family/relatives or coworkers/friends, while one-third or more used formal means such as retirement calculators, retirement seminars, or financial experts. *Successful Planners* were more likely to use formal means (over 40 percent), whereas *Simple Planners*—some of whom tried and failed—tended to rely on less formal approaches. The table also shows that financial literacy is correlated with planning tools, although unevenly. The list of tools does not exhaust what people might do; in fact, as many as one-quarter of the self-reported planners indicated that they did not use any of the listed tools.

Those who were correct regarding interest rate and inflation were more likely to have attended a retirement seminar, suggesting that such seminars may provide information (without further control variables we cannot hold constant other background variables). Those knowledgeable about risk diversification also tend to use formal rather than informal tools for planning. Panel 2 of Table 2.3 also reveals what the correlations were between planners' levels of financial literacy and the tools they used in their planning efforts. Those who used more sophisticated tools were always more likely to get the literacy questions right, as compared to

TABLE 2.3 Links between planning tools, planning success, and financial literacy in the Health and Retirement Study

Link	Response

Panel 1: Tools planners report using (% and correlation)

	Simple Planners ($n = 397$)	Successful Planners ($n = 235$)
Talk to family or friends	21.1 (0.409)	17.4 (0.380)
Talk to coworkers or friends	24.7 (0.432)	21.3 (0.410)
Attend retirement seminar	35.3 (0.479)	40.4 (0.492)
Use calculator or worksheet	37.8 (0.485)	43.4 (0.497)
Consult financial planner	39.0 (0.488)	49.4 (0.501)

Panel 2: Correlation between planning, tools used, and financial literacy (%)

	Simple Planners ($n = 397$)	Talk to family or friends ($n = 84$)	Talk to coworkers or friends ($n = 98$)	Attend retirement seminar ($n = 140$)	Use Calculator or worksheet ($n = 150$)	Consult financial planner ($n = 155$)
Correct on interest rate	75.3	65.5	69.4	77.9	83.3	80.6
Correct on inflation	84.4	82.1	88.8	88.6	89.3	86.5
Correct on stock risk	52.2	65.5	71.4	80.0	79.3	73.5

Panel 3: Budgeting questions: all respondents (%)

	Always	Mostly	Rarely	Never	Refuse/ Don't know
Track spending	43.2	30.8	14.7	11.0	0.3
Set spending budget	23.6	27.6	22.4	26.0	0.5

Source: Authors' calculations based on unweighted data from the 2004 Health and Retirement Study, Planning Module; see text.

TABLE 2.4 Planning and wealth holdings in the Health and Retirement Study (US$ 2004)

	Nonplanners	Simple Planners	Serious Planners	Successful Planners
25th percentile	30,400	107,750	171,000	197,500
Median	122,000	307,750	370,000	410,000
75th percentile	334,500	641,000	715,000	781,500
Mean	338,418	742,843	910,382	1,002,975

Notes: This table reports the distribution of total net worth across different planning types. 'Simple' Planners are those who tried to calculate how much they need to save for retirement; 'Serious' Planners are those who were able to develop a saving plan; and 'Successful' Planners are those who were able to stick to their saving plan. The total number of observations is 1,269. *Source:* Authors' calculations based on unweighted data from the 2004 Health and Retirement Study, Planning Module; see text.

those who relied on personal communications; furthermore, the knowledge gap was relatively the greatest for the interest rate question. Panel 3 shows that a very large segment—almost three-quarters (74 percent) of the respondent pool—indicates that it always or mostly tracks its spending, and over half (51 percent) always or mostly tries to set spending budget targets. This is impressive, given the low level of planning for retirement. It is unclear whether those undertaking the spending budget efforts did so simply to get through the month without running out of money, or whether these efforts indicate a greater sensitivity of retirement saving needs and plans.

Prior work has established that planning has important implications for wealth accumulation (Lusardi and Mitchell, 2007*a*, 2007*b*). To this end, we report the distribution of total net worth across different planning types in Table 2.4, and emphasize that, at the median, planners accumulate three times the amount of wealth than nonplanners. Moreover, the amount of planning also matters: those who are able to develop a plan and those who can stick to the plan accumulate much more wealth than Simple Planners.

Linking financial literacy and planning

One reason people fail to plan for retirement, or do so unsuccessfully, may be because they are financially illiterate. In this case, they may fail to appreciate the role of (or may have a hard time solving problems with) interest rate calculations, inflation, and risk diversification. Table 2.5 sheds light on the importance of financial literacy and its relationship with planning in a multivariate Probit analysis of three dependent variables:

TABLE 2.5 Probit analysis of Simple, Serious, and Successful Planners in the Health and Retirement Study (marginal effects reported)

	Simple Planners ($n = 1,269$)			Serious Planners ($n = 1,269$)			Successful Planners ($n = 1,269$)		
	I	II	III	I	II	III	I	II	III
Correct on interest rate	0.068** (0.028)	0.032 (0.031)	0.024 (0.032)	0.064** (0.024)	0.037 (0.025)	0.004 (0.027)	0.061** (0.022)	0.037 (0.024)	0.007 (0.024)
Correct on inflation	0.104*** (0.03)	0.079** (0.035)	0.053 (0.037)	0.073*** (0.026)	0.057* (0.029)	0.038 (0.030)	0.072*** (0.024)	0.062** (0.027)	0.043 (0.027)
Correct on stock risk	0.165*** (0.026)	0.109*** (0.038)	0.094** (0.038)	0.155*** (0.022)	0.101*** (0.032)	0.086*** (0.032)	0.137*** (0.021)	0.088*** (0.031)	0.067*** (0.029)
Don't know interest rate		-0.171** (0.056)	-0.162*** (0.056)		-0.138** (0.042)	-0.127** (0.040)		-0.130** (0.036)	-0.117** (0.032)
Don't know inflation		0.025 (0.080)	0.035 (0.081)		0.036 (0.077)	0.047 (0.078)		0.057 (0.078)	0.068 (0.079)
Don't know stock risk		-0.071* (0.042)	-0.044 (0.043)		-0.070* (0.035)	-0.044 (0.036)		-0.064* (0.033)	-0.038 (0.33)
Demographics	No	No	Yes	No	No	Yes	No	No	Yes
Pseudo R^2	0.048	0.056	0.107	0.060	0.069	0.133	0.060	0.069	0.142

* Estimated coefficient significant at the 10 percent level.
** Estimated coefficient significant at the 5 percent level.
*** Estimated coefficient significant at the 1 percent level.

Source: Authors' calculations based on unweighted data from the 2004 Health and Retirement Study, Planning Module; see text.

who was a planner, who developed a plan, and who was able to stick to a plan.[9] Column I in each case takes on a value of 1 if the respondent was correct regarding the literacy variables (0 otherwise); Column II adds an indicator equal to 1 if the respondent indicated he or she did not know the answer to the question (0 otherwise); and Column III has the same dependent variable, but adds controls for demographics and specifically age, race, gender, educational attainment, and a dummy for being a Baby-Boomer (the table reports marginal effects).

The reported estimates are interesting along several dimensions. First, financial literacy is strongly and positively associated with planning, and the results are statistically significant at conventional levels. That is, planners of all types are much more likely to give a correct answer to our financial literacy questions (Column I). Second, knowledge about risk diversification best differentiates between sophisticated and unsophisticated respondents. Not only does it have a much larger estimated marginal effect than being able to correctly answer the interest and the inflation questions, but it also remains statistically significant, even after accounting for the demographic characteristics of the respondent. Third, lack of knowledge also matters. Even with respect to those answering incorrectly, those who cannot answer the questions are much less likely to plan and to succeed in their planning effort (Column II). What appears most crucial is a lack of knowledge about the interest rate, which makes sense, as basic numeracy is crucial for doing calculations about retirement saving. Column III reports estimates after controlling for demographic characteristics, and some indicators of financial literacy remain statistically significant even after we account for these factors. For example, financial literacy is clearly linked to planning above and beyond the effect of education. Accordingly, the information provided in the financial literacy variables may prove very useful in explaining the differences we observe among households in their behavior toward retirement wealth accumulation, to which we now turn.

Wealth accumulation and financial literacy

If financial illiteracy leads to poor or no planning, it may also affect wealth accumulation. Lusardi (2003) finds that those who plan accumulate more wealth before retirement and are more likely to invest in stocks. Moreover, planners are more likely to experience a satisfying retirement, perhaps because they have higher financial resources to rely on after they stop working. In Table 2.6 (Panel 1), we report estimates from a simple regression of total net worth on the three dummies measuring financial literacy and a set of demographic characteristics. Here, wealth is defined as the sum of checking and saving accounts, certificate of deposits and other short-

TABLE 2.6 Wealth accumulation and financial literacy in the Health and Retirement Study

	Total sample	1st quartile	Median	3rd quartile
Panel 1: OLS and quantile regressions				
Correct on interest rate	40.85 (25.66)	19.72 (16.91)	29.18*** (10.43)	21.29 (27.28)
Correct on inflation	31.23 (27.71)	3.44 (7.54)	17.96 (11.28)	34.51 (29.39)
Correct on stock risk	11.68 (23.79)	19.39*** (6.44)	26.95*** (9.67)	20.73 (26.31)
Demographics	Yes	Yes	Yes	Yes
Pseudo R^2	0.32	0.14	0.20	0.24
Panel 2: Probit analysis of stock ownership				
	Total sample	Low education	High education	
Correct on interest rate	0.064** (0.030)	0.041 (0.030)	0.101* (0.051)	
Correct on inflation	0.035 (0.033)	0.001 (0.037)	0.027 (0.057)	
Correct on stock risk	0.121*** (0.027)	0.077** (0.032)	0.202*** (0.042)	
Demographics and wealth	Yes	Yes	Yes	
Pseudo R^2	0.173	0.257	0.168	

* Estimated coefficient significant at the 10 percent level.
** Estimated coefficient significant at the 5 percent level.
*** Estimated coefficient significant at the 1 percent level.

Source: Authors' calculations based on unweighted data from the 2004 Health and Retirement Study, Planning Module; see text.

terms assets, bonds, stocks, other assets, housing equity, other real estate, IRAs and Keoghs, business equity, and vehicles minus all debts.[10] Controls include age, sex, race, education attainment, marital status, place of birth, and income. We estimate the model in both the full sample and also for quartiles of the wealth distribution.

The results indicate that financial illiteracy is particularly pronounced among those with low income, low education, and low wealth holdings. Further, financial literacy is positively correlated with wealth at the bottom of the wealth distribution, which suggests that those who have basic financial knowledge are better able to save. Those having a command of basic numeracy and who understand risk diversification also have higher wealth holdings, something of a remarkable result, given that we control for several of the demographic characteristics that elsewhere have been linked to low financial literacy (race, gender, and low income); we also account for educational attainment.

Panel 2 of Table 2.6 reports estimates from a Probit model of stock ownership. The hypothesis here is that financial literacy will be influential over portfolio choice: if investors do not understand interest rate, inflation, or risk diversification, they are less likely to invest in complex assets such as stocks. We control for the socio-demographics listed earlier and additionally add total net worth. The findings indicate a strong positive correlation between stock ownership and knowledge of risk diversification, for both the total sample and across education groups. Basic numeracy (interest rate calculations) also plays a role, but mostly for those with high education (defined as having more than a high school degree); this is true even after accounting for education and total net worth. These findings may help explain the 'puzzle' of why so few households hold stocks (Haliassos and Bertaut, 1995). Moreover, they may shed light on another puzzling finding in household surveys such as the Survey of Consumer Finances. When asked how much risk respondents are willing to take, a large majority (more than 60 percent) state they are unwilling to take any financial risk. This may be due not only to strong risk aversion but also to the fact that many respondents do not understand risk diversification.

Conclusion

As more individuals approach and cross over the retirement threshold, it is crucial to ascertain whether they actually know how to plan for retirement and whether they seem able to execute these plans effectively. Our HRS module is informative in this regard, as it asks about people's basic financial literacy in terms of their comprehension of interest rate and inflation, along with the more nuanced concept of risk diversification. It is disturbing that only half of the respondents can correctly answer questions regarding interest rate calculations and inflation, and only one-third can correctly answer both of those two questions and a question about risk diversification. This suggests widespread financial illiteracy among older Americans. When we examine whether people tried to figure out how much they need to save for retirement, whether they devised a plan, and whether they succeeded at the plan, the news is also not good. Less than one-third of this cohort on the verge of retirement had ever tried to come up with a retirement plan, and only two-thirds of these succeeded. In the sample as a whole, less than one in five of these older Americans engaged in successful retirement planning.

Furthermore, we show that financial knowledge and planning are clearly interrelated, and keeping track of spending and budgeting appears conducive to retirement saving. Finally, we evaluate the planning tools people use. It is interesting that the respondents who did plan were *less* likely to talk to family/relatives or coworkers/friends, and more likely to use formal means such as retirement calculators, retirement seminars, or financial experts. Inasmuch as planning is an important predictor of saving and investment success, we may have uncovered an important explanation for why household wealth holdings differ, and why some people enter retirement with very low wealth (Mitchell and Moore, 1998; Lusardi, 1999; Moore and Mitchell, 2000; Venti and Wise, 2001). The empirical analysis here suggests that financial literacy can play a key role on both saving and portfolio choice.

Our work has relevance for policy in several directions. First, there has been a long-term growth in financial planning products and service providers (Hung et al., 2011). Further, governments and nonprofits have sponsored programs to spur financial education, and employers are increasingly offering retirement seminars to their workers as well (Clark and D'Ambrosio, 2008; Clark et al., 2011; Collins, 2011). While some researchers suggest that such programs will have only minimal effects on saving, our work suggests that this may be due to the lack of well-targeted content. For example, if financial illiteracy is widespread among particular subsets of employees, a one-time financial education lesson may be insufficient to influence planning and saving decisions. Conversely, education programs targeted specifically to particular subgroups may be better suited to address substantial differences in preferences and saving needs.

Acknowledgments

The research reported herein was pursuant to a grant from the US Social Security Administration (SSA) funded as part of the Retirement Research Consortium (RRC) and the Pension Research Council/Boettner Center at the Wharton School. Without implicating them, we are grateful for comments provided by Alberto Alesina, Rob Alessie, Maristella Botticini, John Campbell, Andrew Caplin, Sewin Chan, Gary Engelhardt, Alan Gustman, Mike Hurd, Arie Kapteyn, Mauro Mastrogiacomo, Mary Beth Ofstedal, William Rodgers, Chris Snyder, Maarten van Rooij, Arthur van Soest, and Steve Utkus. Helpful suggestions were offered by participants at conference at Dartmouth, Harvard, Rand, the NBER, the RRC, the Dutch Central Bank, and the American Economic Association. Mark Christman and Jason Beeler provided excellent research assistance. Opinions and errors are solely those of the authors, and not of the institutions with whom the authors are affiliated. Findings and conclusions do not represent the views of the SSA, any agency of the Federal Government, or the RRC.

Endnotes

[1] See Campbell (2006) for an excellent discussion of the myriad problems households face when making financial decisions.

[2] In conventional economic models, assets in the last period of life will not exceed zero and the consumer does not die in debt.

[3] Note that these data are derived from an experimental module of the 2004 HRS sample of persons age 50 and older.

[4] For brevity, these tables are not reported.

[5] Other surveys also find similar results concerning knowledge regarding properties of bonds, stocks, and mutual funds (see Agnew and Szykman, 2005).

[6] Similar findings are found internationally; for instance, Miles (2004) shows that UK borrowers also display poor understanding of mortgages and interest rates, and Christelis et al. (2010) use SHARE surveys from several European countries to show that these respondents also score low on financial numeracy and literacy scales.

[7] For brevity, we exclude other minority groups and exclude those who do not answer the questions (a small group).

[8] There is also evidence that knowledge about pensions and Social Security affects retirement decisions; see Chan and Stevens (2003), Duflo and Saez (2003, 2004), and Mastrobuoni (2005).

[9] It is possible that causality may also go the other way: that is, those who plan may also become more financially literate and develop the ability to do retirement calculations; for discussion of endogeneity considerations, see Lusardi and Mitchell (2007*a*).

[10] The analysis herein uses the 2004 wealth data, which included imputes for those who did not report assets or debt.

References

Agnew, J. and L. Szykman (2005). 'Asset Allocation and Information Overload: The Influence of Information Display, Asset Choice and Investor Experience,' *Journal of Behavioral Finance*, 6: 57–70.

Ameriks, J., A. Caplin, and J. Leahy (2003). 'Wealth Accumulation and the Propensity to Plan,' *Quarterly Journal of Economics*, 68: 1007–47.

———— (2004). 'The Absent-Minded Consumer,' NBER Working Paper No. 10216. Cambridge, MA: National Bureau of Economic Research.

Bernheim, D. (1995). 'Do Households Appreciate their Financial Vulnerabilities? An Analysis of Actions, Perceptions, and Public Policy,' in *Tax Policy and Economic Growth*. Washington, DC: American Council for Capital Formation, pp. 1–30.

—— (1998). 'Financial Illiteracy, Education, and Retirement Saving,' in O. S. Mitchell and S. Schieber, eds, *Living with Defined Contribution Pensions*. Philadelphia, PA: University of Pennsylvania Press, pp. 38–68.

Calvert, L., J. Campbell, and P. Sodini (2007). 'Down or Out: Assessing the Welfare Costs of Household Investment Mistakes,' *Journal of Political Economy*, 115: 707–47.

Campbell, J. (2006). 'Household Finance,' *Journal of Finance*, 61(4): 1553–604.

Chan, S. and A. H. Stevens (2003). 'What You Don't Know Can't Help You: Knowledge and Retirement Decision Making.' *The Review of Economics*, 90(2): 253–66.

Christelis, D., T. Jappelli, and M. Padula (2010). 'Cognitive Abilities and Portfolio Choice.' *European Economic Review*, 54: 18–38.

Clark, R. and M. D'Ambrosio (2008), 'Adjusting Retirement Goals and Saving Behavior: The Role of Financial Education,' in A. Lusardi, ed., *Overcoming the Saving Slump: How to Increase the Effectiveness of Financial Education and Saving Programs*. Chicago, IL: Chicago University Press, pp. 237–56.

——M. S. Morrill, and S. G. Allen (2011). 'Pension Plan Distributions: The Importance of Financial Literacy,' in O. S. Mitchell and A. Lusardi, eds, *Financial Literacy: Implications for Retirement Security and the Financial Marketplace*. Oxford, UK: Oxford University Press.

Collins, J. M. (2011). 'Improving Financial Literacy: The Role of Nonprofit Providers,' in O. S. Mitchell and A. Lusardi, eds, *Financial Literacy: Implications for Retirement Security and the Financial Marketplace*. Oxford, UK: Oxford University Press.

Duflo, E. and E. Saez (2003). 'The Role of Information and Social Interactions in Retirement Plan Decisions: Evidence from a Randomized Experiment,' *Quarterly Journal of Economics*, 118: 815–42.

——————(2004). 'Implications of Pension Plan Features, Information, and Social Interactions for Retirement Saving Decisions,' in O. S. Mitchell and S. Utkus, eds, *Pension Design and Structure: New Lessons from Behavioral Finance*. Oxford, UK: Oxford University Press, pp. 137–53.

Employee Benefits Research Institute (EBRI) (1996). 'Participant Education: Actions and Outcomes,' *EBRI Issue Brief* 169. Washington, DC: Employee Benefit Research Institute.

——(2001). 'Retirement Confidence Survey (RCS), Minority RCS, and Small Employer Retirement Survey,' *EBRI Issue Brief* 234. Washington, DC: Employee Benefit Research Institute.

Gustman, A. and T. Steinmeier (1999). 'Effects of Pensions on Savings: Analysis with Data from the Health and Retirement Study,' *Carnegie-Rochester Conference Series on Public Policy*, 50: 271–324.

——————(2004). 'What People Don't Know about their Pensions and Social Security,' in W. Gale, J. Shoven and M. Warshawsky, eds, *Private Pensions and Public Policies*. Washington, DC: The Brookings Institution, pp. 57–125.

Haliassos, M. and C. Bertaut (1995). 'Why Do So Few Hold Stocks?,' *Economic Journal*, 105: 1110–29.

Hilgert, M., J. Hogarth, and S. Beverly (2003). 'Household Financial Management: The Connection between Knowledge and Behavior,' *Federal Reserve Bulletin*, July: 309–22.

Hogarth, J. and M. Hilgert (2002). 'Financial Knowledge, Experience and Learning Preferences: Preliminary Results from a New Survey on Financial Literacy,' *Consumer Interest Annual*, 48(1): 1–7.

Hogarth, J., C. Anguelov, and J. Lee (2004). 'Why Don't Households Have a Checking Account?,' *The Journal of Consumer Affairs*, 38: 1–34.

Hung, A., N. Clancy, and J. Dominitz (2011). 'Investor Knowledge and Experience with Investment Advisers and Broker-Dealers,' in O. S. Mitchell and A. Lusardi, eds, *Financial Literacy: Implications for Retirement Security and the Financial Marketplace*. Oxford, UK: Oxford University Press.

Lusardi, A. (1999). 'Information, Expectations, and Savings for Retirement,' in H. Aaron, ed., *Behavioral Dimensions of Retirement Economics*. Washington, DC: Brookings Institution Press and Russell Sage Foundation, pp. 81–116.

——(2002). 'Preparing for Retirement: The Importance of Planning Costs,' *National Tax Association Proceedings*, 2002: 148–54.

——(2003). 'Planning and Saving for Retirement,' Dartmouth College Working Paper. Hanover, NH: Dartmouth College.

——and O. S. Mitchell (2007*a*). 'Baby Boomer Retirement Security: The Roles of Planning, Financial Literacy, and Housing Wealth,' *Journal of Monetary Economics*, 54(1): 205–24.

————(2007*b*). 'Financial Literacy and Retirement Planning: New Evidence from the RAND American Life Panel,' Pension Research Council Working Paper No. 2007-33. Philadelphia, PA: Pension Research Council.

————(2007*c*). 'Financial Literacy and Retirement Preparedness: Evidence and Implications for Financial Education,' *Business Economics*, 42: 35–44.

————(2008). 'Planning and Financial Literacy: How Do Women Fare?,' *American Economic Review P&P*, 98(2): 413–17.

————(2009). 'How Ordinary Consumers Make Complex Economic Decisions: Financial Literacy and Retirement Readiness,' NBER Working Paper No. 15350. Cambridge, MA: National Bureau of Economic Research.

————C. Curto (2010). 'Financial Literacy among the Young: Evidence and Implications for Consumer Policy,' *Journal of Consumer Affairs*, 44(2): 358–80.

Mandell, L. (2004). *Financial Literacy: Are We Improving?* Washington, DC: Jump$tart Coalition for Personal Financial Literacy.

Mastrobuoni, G. (2005). 'Do Better-Informed Workers Make Better Retirement Choice? A Test Based on the Social Security Statement,' Princeton University Working Paper. Princeton, NJ: Princeton University.

Miles, D. (2004). *The UK Mortgage Market: Taking a Longer-Term View*. London, UK: HM Treasury. http://news.bbc.co.uk/nol/shared/bsp/hi/pdfs/12_03_04_miles.pdf

Mitchell, O. S. (1988). 'Worker Knowledge of Pensions Provisions,' *Journal of Labor Economics*, 6: 28–9.

——J. Moore (1998). 'Can Americans Afford to Retire? New Evidence on Retirement Saving Adequacy,' *Journal of Risk and Insurance*, 65: 371–400.

Moore, D. (2003). 'Survey of Financial Literacy in Washington State: Knowledge, Behavior, Attitudes, and Experiences,' Social and Economic Sciences Research Center Technical Report 03-39. Pullman, WA: Washington State University.

Moore, J. and O. S. Mitchell (2000). 'Projected Retirement Wealth and Saving Adequacy,' in O. S. Mitchell, B. Hammond, and A. Rappaport, eds, *Forecasting*

Retirement Needs and Retirement Wealth. Philadelphia, PA: University of Pennsylvania Press, pp. 68–94.

National Council on Economic Education (NCEE) (2005). *What American Teens and Adults Know About Economics.* Washington, DC: NCEE.

Venti, S. and D. Wise (2001). 'Choice, Chance, and Wealth Dispersion at Retirement,' in S. Ogura, T. Tachibanaki, and D. Wise, eds, *Aging Issues in the United States and Japan.* Chicago, IL: University of Chicago Press, pp. 25–64.

Yakoboski, P. and J. Dickemper (1997). 'Increased Saving but Little Planning. Results of the 1997 Retirement Confidence Survey,' *EBRI Issue Brief* 191. Washington, DC: Employee Benefit Research Institute.

Chapter 3

Pension Plan Distributions: The Importance of Financial Literacy

Robert L. Clark, Melinda S. Morrill, and Steven G. Allen

The disposition of retirement assets is one of the most important and long-lasting decisions that retiring workers confront. If employees are covered by a traditional defined benefit (DB) plan, the default option is that they receive a life annuity that begins when they leave the firm or reach the plan's retirement age. However, many DB plans offer workers the option of receiving a lump sum distribution at retirement, roughly equal to the present value of the annuity.[1] Typically, this is a one-time option that the worker must make upon termination. If the lump sum is selected, retirees cannot subsequently decide that they want the annuity. Of course, they could subsequently purchase a private annuity, but this process would likely result in the individual bearing higher costs and administrative fees. Similarly, in cash balance plans, workers must be given a choice of a life annuity or a lump sum payment.[2]

Workers with defined contribution (DC) plans such as a 401(k), 403(b), or 457 face a similar choice in whether to accept a lump sum or purchase a life annuity, but the distributional choice is framed differently.[3] In these plans, retirees know the value of their accounts and must decide how to allocate these funds over the retirement period. The difference in how pension benefits are reported or framed may influence the distribution decision by retiring workers. This chapter considers what factors appear to shape worker preferences to elect the nondefault options and request alternative forms of distributions from their DB and DC plans.

Standard economic theory predicts that actuarially fair annuitization of assets would be welfare-enhancing for risk-averse individuals, as it provides a hedge against longevity risk and outliving one's assets. However, in the United States and elsewhere, relatively few people voluntarily purchase annuities in the open market.[4] A variety of authors have attempted to explain this tendency of retirees to opt for lump sum distributions from retirement saving accounts by expanding the economic model and by appealing to the concept that how the choice is framed determines whether retirees select annuities as opposed to lump sum distributions.[5] Nevertheless, few studies have examined the lump sum choice in DB plans as a component of retirement income planning.[6] In this chapter, we examine active workers' plans for pension distributions from both DB and DC plans. Thus, we are able to explore two different ways the pension distribution choice is framed. For DB plans, the default option is an annuity. We find that only 30 percent of individuals plan to take a lump sum distribution of their pension. On the other hand, the DC plans default to a lump sum, and we find that only 22 percent plan to annuitize. In addition to describing the individual choices, we are able to assess how individuals combine these two choices.

The choice of the form of distribution will necessarily be based on the individual's financial literacy and knowledge of retirement programs. This chapter examines pension plan distributions using survey data from two large employers. These data are a part of a new unique dataset that we have developed based on surveys of participants in retirement planning seminars provided by employers to retirement-eligible employees. Using these data, we estimate whether the older workers are currently planning to take a lump sum distribution from their DB plan and whether they plan to annuitize some or all of their account balances in their DC plans. The analysis focuses on the role of financial literacy in the choice of benefits and how this choice changes after the seminar.

Economics of choosing between an annuity and a lump sum

Researchers call the low demand for annuities the 'annuity puzzle' and have put forward a number of reasons why individuals might prefer lump sum distributions to annuities. One possible explanation for this seemingly suboptimal choice is the availability of other sources of annuity income, such as Social Security, that may represent a large percentage of total wealth for many retirees. Other reasons that individuals might prefer lump sum distributions include spouses and close relatives with whom risks can be shared, the bequest motive, and concern about large and lumpy future expenditures (especially those associated with health care expenses). Retirees may also worry about rising prices and a fixed retirement income associated with the annuity.

More recently, several studies have suggested that the framing of the annuity choice tends to influence whether individuals purchase annuities. Hu and Scott (2007) posit that the way individuals view annuities drives their decision to purchase an annuity. They refer to this as mental accounting and conclude that the 'most important potential reason for annuities being unpopular is mental accounting'; further, this mental accounting can lead retirees to believe that purchasing an annuity is a gamble that increases risk (Hu and Scott, 2007: 18). Brown et al. (2008) suggest that there are two possible ways of viewing annuities: the 'consumption frame', which focuses on consumption over time, and the 'investment frame', which allows individuals to consider that the total payout is dependent on survival years and thus makes annuities a risky investment. Small-scale experiments (Agnew and Szykman, 2011) indicate that if the choice is put in a consumption frame, individuals will select the annuity; however, if the choice is put in an investment frame, individuals will prefer a lump sum distribution of assets into saving accounts.

Most of the literature focuses on the utilization of funds in retirement saving accounts or other assets that individuals have as they enter retirement. In other words, the question is what decision retirees make in purchasing an annuity with these funds, versus retaining control of their assets and gradually drawing them down to finance consumption in retirement. However, a related decision confronts many individuals who have DB plans. By law, DB plans offer retirees a life annuity, but plan sponsors can also include other choices such as lump sum distributions. Accordingly, this choice should be considered as part of the demand for life annuities facing many retirees. Examining the distributions from both types of plans allows us to examine the importance of how the choice is framed compared to other potential determinants of how retirement funds are accessed and managed.

The data set we use for the analyses was developed to examine the effectiveness of employer-provided financial education and pre-retirement planning programs. The Participants Attending Retirement Seminars (PARS) dataset is based on approximately ninety seminars held in 2008 and 2009 across the country by six large employers. Over 1,000 participants completed a survey before and after the seminars. Participants completed a detailed survey before and after the seminar, including information on their own (and their spouses') economic and demographic information. Participants were also asked about their retirement plans, including whether they planned to take a lump sum distribution from their DB plan (i.e., decline the annuity and accept a lump sum payment), and whether they would annuitize some or all of their account balances in their DC accounts. Retirement-eligible employees were invited to participate in these programs, which ranged from a half-day to two days in duration.[7]

In this chapter, we focus on the two firms with the largest samples, seminar participants at Progress Energy and Becton, Dickinson and Company (BD). Sample means, shown in Table 3A.1, indicate that the average age was 58, the sample was 58 percent male, and 78 percent of respondents were married. These employees had an average of 27 years of service and almost half had college degrees. All were covered by a DB plan and all had access to a DC plan. Interestingly, 40 percent of the respondents planned on working after they retired from their current jobs. In general, this was a relatively high-income sample of older workers who were wealthier than average and who reported that they were in good health.

Employees were asked if their employer allowed them to take a lump sum distribution from their DB plan and if so, did they currently plan on opting for the lump sum. Prior to the seminar, just less than 30 percent reported intending to take a lump sum distribution of their pension, and this number dropped to 28 percent after attending. In addition, participants were asked whether they planned to annuitize some or all of the funds in their DC accounts. Prior to the seminar, approximately 22 percent reported planning to annuitize their DC plans; the fraction increased to 29 percent after the seminar. Next, we explore the determinants of these choices and characteristics of individuals that changed plans.

Company benefits and framing the distribution choice

As the two companies in this analysis offered a DB plan, a 401(k) plan, and retiree medical coverage, the workers clearly had more generous benefits than many American workers. Both firms allowed retirees the choice of a lump sum distribution from their DB plan; further, one firm, Progress Energy, regularly reported account balances equal to the available lump sum distribution. Annuity options were unavailable for the Progress Energy 401(k) plan but were offered by the BD plan. These differences allow us to consider the distribution choice in both DB and DC plans and also permit a comparison of the framing between a traditional DB plan and a cash balance plan.

Progress Energy froze a final average pay pension formula in 2003 and converted to a cash balance pension formula.[8] Annual statements sent to each employee indicate the annuity they could receive under the old formula and the account balance in the cash balance plan. At retirement, there is an annuity value and a lump sum value associated with the old formula and the new cash balance formula. The pension summary that individuals receive from Progress Energy at retirement includes the higher of the two annuity values from the two formulas and the higher of the two lump sum values of the two formulas. Given that the old formula was frozen in 2003 and the terms of the transition to the cash balance formula at the time of the conversion, most individuals who attended the seminars in 2008 and 2009 would have higher values from the cash balance formula. Payment options include a variety of life annuity options, phased withdrawals, and a total lump sum distribution. Account balances from the 401(k) plan could be withdrawn as a total lump sum, the retiree could specify monthly payouts, the funds could be rolled over to an Individual Retirement Account (IRA), or the funds could be left in the plan until a later date. The individual could not purchase an annuity through the plan, but of course, they could roll the funds over to an IRA and purchase an annuity through the IRA. Retirees were allowed to remain in the employer-provided health plan.

BD maintained a final average pay plan with a 1 percent multiplier for final covered compensation and a 1.5 percent multiplier for final excess compensation.[9] At retirement, individuals had the option of a single life annuity, several joint and survivor annuities, or a lump sum distribution. BD also offered a Saving Incentive Plan with a 75 percent match on the first 6 percent of salary contributed by employees. Retirees were also eligible to remain in the BD health plan.

Choosing a distribution option

To model respondents' planned distribution choices, we use responses to two questions in the survey, as described in Table 3A.2. Note that the wording differed slightly between the two employers for one of the questions. We consider whether workers report planning to make an active choice of the nondefault option versus responding 'No', 'Have not yet decided', or leaving the question blank.

Table 3.1 separates the distributional preferences reported before participants attended the seminar into several categories. The first category indicates the respondents planned to accept the pension payout in the form indicated by the default; in other words, to accept an annuity from the DB plan and take the account balance from the DC plan as a lump sum payment. Over half reported plans to take the default options, indicating that the defaults were an important predictor of planning. The next column indicates plans to take a lump sum distribution from both plans, that is, to not accept the default annuity from the DB plan and to accept the default lump sum from the DC plan. Twenty-two percent of all respondents reported planning to elect the lump sum of both.

The third column represents respondents planning to take annuities from both their DB and DC retirement plans. This group reported planning to accept the default annuity from the DB plan and also annuitize the account balance in the 401(k) plan. Fourteen percent of respondents reported having these plans. Finally, the fourth column indicates respondents indicating they would take the non-default option in both plans. This combination of pension distributions was planned by 8 percent of these older workers. This group indicated they would annuitize the account balance in the 401(k) plan and take a lump sum distribution from the DB plan. The proportion of workers planning to select a lump sum distribution of their pension assets is broadly consistent with the rates reported by Hurd and Panis (2006) for the respondents in the Health and Retirement Survey.

Next, we report the percentages of each group that elect each of the possible disposition combinations described above. The significance levels

TABLE 3.1 Disposition choices by respondent characteristics (%)

	Percent of sample	Default options	Lump sum (DB choice)	Annuitize (DC choice)	Nondefault choice
Full sample	100	56.1	21.8	14.4	7.7
Progress Energy	38	61.9**	13.1***	19.1***	5.9
BD	62	52.6**	27.1***	11.5***	8.9
Women	42	60.9**	22.1	12.0	5**
Men	58	52.8**	21.5	16.0	9.7**
Married	78	52.9***	22.6	15.4	9.1**
Not married	22	67.4***	18.8	10.9	2.9**
Some college	47	56.7	24.6	11.6*	7.2
High school	53	55.7	19.3	16.8*	8.3
Years of service <20	22	64.7**	19.9	8.8**	6.6
Years of service 20+	78	53.7**	22.3	15.9**	8.1

Notes: Statistical significance of differences are within the two categories, where * indicates significance at the 10 percent level,
** is 5 percent, and
*** is 1 percent. The sample consists of all respondents that completed surveys and answered at least five out of the nine knowledge questions in both surveys 1 and 2 (no more than four blanks allowed). The sample also excludes individuals with missing values for birth year, education, job tenure, marital status, and sex. The sample is restricted to individuals born between 1943 and 1959. The planned choices represented here are all reported by respondents prior to attending the seminar. Data are from surveys conducted by the authors in 2008 and 2009. The total number of observations is 620.

Source: Authors' calculations; see text.

reported indicate differences in means between the groups. Employees at Progress Energy were more likely to choose the default for both plans and more likely to choose annuitizing both (i.e., taking the default option for the DB and annuitizing the DC) than workers at BD. Interestingly, Progress Energy did not allow for the purchase of an annuity from within the 401(k) plan, while BD did, yet far more workers at Progress Energy chose to annuitize. Nevertheless, in the regression analysis reported below there is no statistical difference in the choice to annuitize some, or all, of one's retirement saving plan between workers at Progress Energy and BD once additional controls are added to the model.

The next row presents the planned distribution choices broken down by gender. Previous research has found that women are less likely to purchase annuities, even though they have longer life expectancies, perhaps due to lower level of financial literacy, or a lack of financial planning. We find that women are indeed significantly more likely to choose both default options. In our data, married individuals are significantly less likely to plan to take the default choices, perhaps due to strategic plans of couples in generating a diversified portfolio. Somewhat surprisingly, those without a college degree were slightly more likely to report planning to annuitize both their 401(k) and their pension. Individuals with fewer years of service are not more likely to take a lump sum from their pension but are significantly less likely to annuitize their 401(k).

Respondents were asked the same questions concerning plan distributions after their retirement planning seminar ended. It is interesting to observe the changes in retirement plans based on the information presented in the seminar. Figures 3.1 and 3.2 demonstrate how workers altered their reported plans. In Figure 3.1, we see that before attending the seminar 29.5 percent of workers reported planning to take a lump sum distribution of their DB pension, while 70.5 percent (437 observations) reported either not wanting to take the lump sum or that they were unsure. Of the 437 workers that did not plan to take a lump sum distribution from their DB plan prior to the seminar, 11 percent (forty-nine respondents) changed to planning to take a lump sum afterwards. Among the forty-nine respondents that switched plans in this way, forty-nine respondents had previously said they did not know this option was available. This shift clearly indicates how a gain in knowledge concerning the options available in a pension can affect retirement plans. Figure 3.2 presents a similar breakdown of transitions between plans for 401(k) disposition choices. Of the 438 individuals that were not initially reporting plans to purchase an annuity, 22 percent (106 individuals) changed to intending to purchase an annuity.

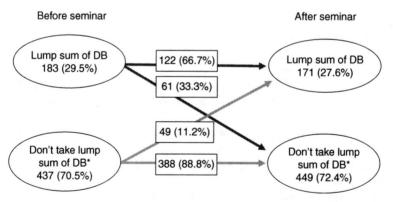

Figure 3.1 How learning affects plans for disposition of employer-provided pensions

Notes: Sample size 620. Data from surveys conducted by the authors in 2008 and 2009. *These cells include those that responded 'No', 'Don't know', or left the question blank.

Source: Authors' calculations; see text.

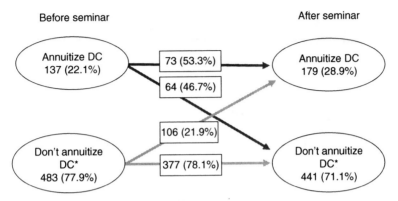

Figure 3.2 How learning affects plans for 401(k) disposition choice

Notes: Sample size 620. Data from surveys conducted by the authors in 2008 and 2009. *These cells include those that responded 'No', 'Don't know', or left the question blank.

Source: Authors' calculations; see text.

Factors associated with retirement plan disposition choice

We more formally explore how these factors interact to predict disposition choice by running a series of multivariate regressions of the choice to take the nondefault options. The first two columns of Table 3.2 report estimates of the factors predicting the following plans prior to attending the seminar: taking a lump sum distribution of one's pension (Column 1), and purchasing an annuity from one's retirement saving plan (Column 2). In both cases, the nondefault option was the choice modeled, so in Column 1, the individual is reporting a choice not to accept the default of an annuitized pension, and in Column 2, the individual reports a choice to purchase an annuity from 401(k) saving.

Interestingly, there is a slightly positive and significant correlation between the choice to take a lump sum of the DB pension and to annuitize the 401(k). If plans for distributional choices were based on careful investment planning, we might expect these choices to be negatively correlated; in other words, a person might desire to have all of his/her retirement income as a lump sum, or all as an annuity. If framing of the choice was the main driver of this decision, then the two choices should be positively related. The cost of annuities in the market and the unbundling of DB annuities make annuitizing the retirement saving account, while taking a lump sum distribution from the DB plan makes an unexpected choice. Perhaps, individuals chose both default options because of a lack of finan-

TABLE 3.2 Disposition choices for defined benefit and defined contribution plans

	DB: choice to take lump sum	DC: choice to annuitize	DB: choice to take lump sum if previously No or Don't know	DC: choice to annuitize if previously No or Don't know
	(1)	(2)	(3)	(4)
Plan to annuitize 401(k)	0.079			
	[0.045]			
Plan to take lump sum DB		0.069		
	[0.040]*			
Progress Energy	−0.233	0.034	−0.021	0.095
	[0.040]***	[0.043]	[0.036]	[0.046]**
Years of service	0.004	−0.001	0.000	0.002
	[0.002]**	[0.002]	[0.002]	[0.002]
Women	−0.062	−0.062	0.061	0.014
	[0.043]	[0.044]	[0.033]*	[0.045]
Married	0.065	0.057	0.026	0.020
	[0.047]	[0.043]	[0.035]	[0.047]
College degree	0.025	−0.090	−0.020	−0.055
	[0.038]	[0.036]**	[0.036]	[0.044]
Total wealth 25–100k	0.006	−0.032	−0.036	0.099
	[0.046]	[0.046]	[0.038]	[0.052]*
Total wealth 100k+	0.078	−0.053	−0.016	0.075
	[0.047]*	[0.044]	[0.039]	[0.047]
DC account 1–5 years' salary	0.009	0.055	−0.099	0.009
	[0.063]	[0.054]	[0.064]	[0.063]
DC account 5+ years' salary	0.036	0.069	−0.038	−0.088
	[0.075]	[0.065]	[0.074]	[0.073]
Medium health	0.107	−0.046	0.046	−0.044
	[0.057]*	[0.056]	[0.039]	[0.065]
High health	−0.003	−0.008	0.053	0.028
	[0.058]	[0.060]	[0.044]	[0.069]
25–75% survive 75^	−0.044	−0.051	−0.046	0.097
	[0.076]	[0.071]	[0.067]	[0.063]
75–100% survive 75^	−0.013	−0.033	−0.043	0.117
	[0.078]	[0.072]	[0.072]	[0.065]*
Medium knowledge score^	0.166	−0.002	0.030	0.052
	[0.042]***	[0.040]	[0.040]	[0.050]

High knowledge score^	0.107	–0.103	–0.009	–0.006
	[0.057]*	[0.050]**	[0.043]	[0.053]
Observations	620	620	437	438
R-squared	0.12	0.06	0.04	0.06

Notes: Coefficients are from linear probability models with standard errors in brackets, where * indicates significance at the 10 percent level,
** is 5 percent, and
*** is 1 percent. Note that all specifications also include the following covariates: age, a constant term, and indicators for no response for total wealth, DC account balance, own health, and own survival probability. The dependent variable in Column (1) is whether the individual planned to take a lump sum distribution of her pension at retirement reported before attending the seminar, and Column (2) is whether the individual planned to annuitize some or all of her 401(k) account at retirement before attending the seminar. Column (3) includes only individuals that did not originally report planning to take a lump sum distribution of their pension, with the dependent variable being a change to reporting after the seminar plans to take a lump sum of the pension. Column (4) includes only individuals that did not originally report planning to annuitize some or all of their 401(k) accounts, with the dependent variable being a change to reporting after the seminar plans to annuitize the 401(k).
^ Indicates variables that are measured before the seminar in Columns (1) and (2) and after the seminar in Columns (3) and (4). Data are from surveys conducted by the authors in 2008 and 2009.

Source: Authors' calculations; see text.

cial literacy and/or a lack of understanding of the two plans. This conclusion would suggest that more educational and retirement planning events would improve choices. It also emphasizes the importance of plan design and defaults on workers' choices.

In Column 1 of Table 3.2, we see that, contrary to expectations, individuals at Progress Energy were significantly less likely to choose a lump sum distribution from their pension, despite the differences between BD and Progress Energy in the framing of the choice (recall that Progress Energy had a cash balance plan). On the other hand, for the choice to annuitize the 401(k) there is no difference between workers at the two firms, even though BD allowed for annuitization within the plan. The importance of framing the choice seems to be rather limited, although here we only consider data from two employers, and the impact of framing may be less important than other unmeasured differences between these companies.

Next, in Column 1 of Table 3.2 we see that a worker's tenure at an employer is positively associated with his/her plans to take a lump sum distribution from his/her DB plan, although the effect is small in magnitude. Note that years of service is positively related to the size of the DB pension annual benefit, so that we can interpret this coefficient as indicating that larger pension amounts lead to higher probabilities of taking lump sum distributions. Economic theory predicts that it may be more sensible to take a lump sum distribution from a pension if the total amount is quite small. Surprisingly, having more years of service is positively related to the probability of taking a lump sum.

In the first two columns of Table 3.2, there is no statistical difference along gender or marital status once the additional controls are added. However, individuals with a college degree are significantly less likely to plan to annuitize their DC plan relative to their less educated coworkers. This is a surprising finding if we believe that the benefits of purchasing an annuity are felt later in life, indicating the plans to purchase an annuity should be positively associated with patience and risk aversion. However, it may be the case that those with more education feel that they can manage their assets more efficiently and therefore prefer not to purchase life annuities. There is a positive and significant association between having the highest level of wealth, relative to the lowest, and planning to take a lump sum of one's pension.

Annuities may be more valuable to those individuals having private information indicating a longer than average life expectancy. It may also be the case that individuals concerned about the potential costs of a sudden health shock might want to keep some or all assets liquid. Interestingly, with the exception of being in medium health in Column 1, there is no statistically significant relationship between a respondent's health or subjective survival probability and his/her plans to annuitize. These results indicate that distributional choices are based on something besides a simple present value calculation and an attempt to insure against longevity risks.

Finally, using a measure of financial knowledge described in the data appendix, we see that the most knowledgeable individuals are more likely to report planning to take a lump sum of their pension and less likely to be planning to annuitize their 401(k). Often lack of financial literacy is cited to explain why individuals do not purchase annuities or simply accept the default options. These results indicate that individuals with the most financial literacy prefer to retain control over their assets. One limitation of this study is that we do not ask how an individual plans to invest (or divest) saving in retirement. It may be the case that individuals are planning to take a lump sum from their pension and roll it over to an IRA or an alternative retirement account that provides an annuity option. It may be that the most financially savvy are best able to navigate the secondary market for annuities.

Column 3 of Table 3.2 presents results from a sample of individuals who had not intended to take the lump sum distribution of their pension preseminar. For these individuals, we then model those who change to reporting plans to take a lump sum from their DB plans after attending the seminar. Similarly, Column 4 of Table 3.2 reports estimates for the sample of individuals that did not report intentions to annuitize some or all of their DC plans prior to the seminar. In that column, we then model the change after the seminar to planning to annuitize one's DC plan. When interpreting the change in intentions, it is important to consider that these estimates apply only to the group that previously was planning to accept the default or had not developed a plan, rather than the entire population of attendees. Because the questions were asked at the end of the seminar, we can infer that (except for response error and measurement error inherent in surveys) respondents were changing their plans due to information they obtained during the seminar.

The estimates reported in Columns 3 and 4 of Table 3.2 indicate that among participants who initially planned on taking the default option (or who had not yet decided), the standard economic and demographic variables are not significantly related to the probability of changing plans after the seminar. Although in Column 1 we found that workers at Progress Energy were significantly less likely to report planning to take the lump sum option from their DB plan prior to the seminar, among those that were not planning initially we see no difference in the propensity to change plans between workers at the two companies. Similarly, in Column 2 of Table 3.2, we found no significant difference between workers at BD and Progress Energy in their choice to annuitize their DC plans, but we now find a large and statistically significant effect indicating that workers at Progress Energy were around 10 percentage points more likely to change their plans relative to workers at BD regarding the choice to annuitize some or all of one's DC plan. This is approximately 50 percent of the total probability of changing plans (22 percent).

In Column 3 of Table 3.2, we see that women were significantly more likely to change their plans to take a lump sum from their pension. Higher wealth was associated with changing plans to annuitize retirement saving, while higher levels of DC wealth were associated with a reduced probability of changing plans to annuitize. There is no significant effect of knowledge on changes in plans, but we do find that individuals with higher life expectancies were slightly more likely to change plans to annuitize some or all of their 401(k) account balance after the seminar.

Conclusion

This chapter examined data on retirement-eligible workers from two large employers, focusing on their preferences for retirement income before and after their participation in a retirement planning seminar. These two companies offered workers both DB plans and the opportunity to contribute to 401(k) plans. The employers also allowed workers to remain in the company health plans in retirement. We show that about three-quarters of all respondents planned to accept the default option in their retirement prior to participation in the seminar. Nevertheless, this means that one-quarter of the respondents rejected the default and planned to make an active choice to receive their benefit in another form. After the program, 18 percent of participants modified their plans concerning the DB plan and 28 percent changed their preferred distributional choice for the DC. Thus, the presentation of material fundamental to making retirement choices seemed to influence the distributional choices of approximately one-quarter of retirees. How many workers were influenced by the framing of the benefit choice is uncertain, as many retirees likely would have chosen this form of retirement benefit in any case.

The choice between annuitized retirement income or lump sum distributions and self-management is one of the most important decisions a person will make. Making the right decision requires workers to have sufficient financial literacy and knowledge of their retirement programs. Company-provided retirement planning programs can provide information that allows workers to re-evaluate their plans. Many retiring workers seek to maintain a portion of their retirement assets in accounts that they can continue to control and spend according to their preferences. While framing of the distributional choice with annuity defaults can increase the proportion of retirees selecting an annuity option, simply making an annuity the first choice is not sufficient to entice many workers to prefer this type of retirement income.

Acknowledgments

This research is funded, in part, by a grant from FINRA Investor Education Foundation. The authors thank Jennifer Maki, Mehtab Randhawa, and Evan Rogers for excellent research assistance, and Annamaria Lusardi and Olivia S. Mitchell for useful comments. The authors also gratefully acknowledge the cooperation of the partner companies on this research.

Data Appendix

The data are from a survey of workers attending employer-provided pre-retirement planning seminars during 2008 and 2009. Surveys were completed immediately before and after the seminar, which enables the comparison of knowledge and retirement plans before and after acquiring information at the seminar. We received 431 surveys from BD and 274 from Progress Energy, for a total of 705. Once we restricted the sample to those answering at least five out of nine knowledge questions (rather than leaving them blank) in both survey one and two the final sample was 620 observations. Table 3A.1 presents the means for the sample, while Table 3A.2 describes how the key dependent variables are defined. Table 3A.3 describes some covariates used. Table 3A.4 defines the knowledge score.

TABLE 3A.1 Respondents' descriptive statistics

Variable	Before seminar	After seminar
Age	58.2	
Male (%)	58.4	
Married (%)	77.7	
Years of service	27.1	
College degree (%)	47.3	
Plan to work after retirement (%)	39.2	
Annual earnings of $50,000–$100,000 (%)	47.7	
Annual earnings of $100,000 and over (%)	23.1	
Account balance in 401(k)/403(b) plans 1–5 years of earnings (%)	64.5	
Account balance in 401(k)/403(b) plans over 5 years of earnings (%)	20.5	
Home equity $50,000–$200,000 (%)	46.8	
Home equity over $200,000 (%)	32.6	
Financial assets $25,000–$100,000 (%)	27.1	
Financial assets over $100,000 (%)	35.6	
Fair or poor health (%)	12.3	
Very good or excellent health (%)	44.7	
Postretirement investment strategy: no change (%)	14.4	
Postretirement investment strategy: more aggressive (%)	3.5	
Planned to take lump sum of pension (%)	29.5	27.6
Planned to annuitize all or part of DC saving (%)	22.1	28.9
Mean knowledge score	5.2	6.3
Percent low knowledge (%)	53.1	26.6
Percent high knowledge (%)	13.4	30.3
Probability of living to 75: 0–24% (%)	8.1	8.3
Probability of living to 75: 75–100% (%)	56.6	51.1
Probability of living to 85: 0–24% (%)	23.1	20.5
Probability of living to 85: 75–100 (%)	28.0	25.4
Number of respondents that were married	482	
Spouse earned more than $50,000 in the past year (%)	24.9	
Number of observations of valid retirement age before and after	504	526
Mean retirement age	62.4	62.6

Notes: The total number of observations is 620.

Source: Authors' calculations; see text.

TABLE 3A.2 Dependent variable definitions

Dependent variable	Definition	Survey wording	Response options
Choice to take a lump sum of pension	1: if response is Yes 0: if response is No, Have not yet decided, or left blank	[BD:] Do you plan on taking your entire pension as a lump sum distribution so that you will not receive a monthly benefit from the pension plan?	1: Yes 2: No 3: Have not yet decided
		[Progress Energy:] If your pension plan allowed lump sum distributions of some or all of the pension benefit, would you take this option when you retire?	
Choice to annuitize some or all of 401(k)	1: if response is Yes 0: if response is No, Have not yet decided, or left blank	Are you planning on buying a life annuity with your retirement savings?	1: Yes 2: No 3: Have not decided

Notes: The survey included a lead-in question which asked the respondent if he/she could take a lump sum of his/her pension. The actual survey question is as follows: Can you take a lump sum distribution of some or all of your pension plan (do not include income from your [Savings Incentive Plan/401(k) Plan])? Answer options were: Yes; No (skip to question 14); Don't know (skip to question 14).

Source: Authors' calculations; see text.

TABLE 3A.3 Key covariate definitions

Covariate	Question	Responses
Total wealth	What is the total value of the stocks, bonds, and savings accounts that you own outside of the retirement plans offered by BD (include any 401(k), 403(b) or 457 plans or IRAs you have from previous employers (do not include retirement plans owned by your spouse or partner)?	1: Less than $25,000 2: $25,001–$50,000 3: $50,001–$75,000 4: $75,001–$100,000 5: $100,001–$250,000 6: Over $250,000
Earnings	Last year, what were your total earnings, including earnings from BD and any other payments you may have had from other employers (do not include income earned by other members of your household or income from interest, rents, or dividends)?	1: Less than $25,000 2: $25,001–$50,000 3: $50,001–$75,000 4: $75,001–$100,000 5: $100,001–$150,000 6: Over $150,000
DC Acct	[BD:] What is the total value of your Saving Incentive Plan (do not include the value of retirement plans held by your spouse or partner)?[Progress Energy:] What is the total value of the stocks,	1: Less than one year salary 2: One to two years salary 3: Three to five years salary 4: More than five years salary

	bonds, and savings accounts that you own outside of the retirement plans offered by your current employer (include any 401 (k), 403(b) or 457 plans or IRAs you have from previous employers; do not include retirement plans owned by your spouse or partner)?	
Health	How would you rate your health generally?	1: Poor 2: Fair 3: Good 4: Very good 5: Excellent
Survive 75	As you plan for retirement, what do you think the chances are that you will live to age 75?	1: 0–24% 2: 25–49% 3: 50–74% 4: 75–99% 5: 100%

Source: Authors' calculations; see text.

TABLE 3A.4 Knowledge score questions

Survey question	Responses
What is the earliest age you can start Social Security benefits?	62 (correct)
What is the age that you can receive a full or unreduced Social Security benefit (this is called the normal retirement age)?	66 (correct)
If you start Social Security benefits at the earliest possible age, you will receive a benefit that is _____ percent of the benefit that you would have received at the normal retirement age	60% 75% (correct) 80% 100% Don't know
Is the reduction in Social Security benefits for early retirement permanent or does the reduction end when you reach the normal retirement age?	*Benefit decrease is permanent* (correct) Benefit decrease ends when you reach the normal retirement age Don't know
After you start receiving Social Security benefits, these benefits are:	The same for the rest of my life Are increased annually by the rate of inflation (correct) *Are increased annually but by less than the rate of inflation* Are increased annually but by more than the rate of inflation Don't know 65 (Correct)

(*continued*)

TABLE 3A.4 Continued

Survey question	Responses
What is the earliest age that you will be eligible for Medicare?	
Do you think the following statement is true or false? 'Buying a single company stock usually provides a safer return than a diversified portfolio.'	True *False* (Correct)
Assume that your retirement income increases by 2 percent per year and that the annual rate of inflation is 4 percent per year. After one year, will you be able to:	Buy more goods and services with your increased income *Buy fewer goods and services with your increased income* (correct) Buy exactly the same amount of goods and services with your increased income Don't know
Does (your company) offer you the opportunity to stay in the company health plan after you retire?	*Yes* (correct) No Don't know

Source: Authors' calculations; see text.

Endnotes

[1] The US Bureau of Labor Statistics (BLS, 1990) reported that in 1989 only 2 percent of DB plans offered by medium and large firms gave workers the option of taking a lump sum distribution, but by 1997, the proportion of these firms with plans that included a lump sum distribution had risen to 23 percent (BLS, 1999; also see Moore and Muller, 2002). Data from the National Compensation Survey indicated that 48 percent of workers covered by a DB plan in 2003 and 52 percent in 2007 were in plans that provided employees with the option of selecting a lump sum distribution instead of accepting the life annuity (BLS, 2005, 2007; Purcell, 2009).

[2] Lump sum distributions from DB plans are calculated using an interest rate to determine the present value of the promised life annuity. The interest rate used by the plan to make this conversion may not be equal to an individual's discount rate. Thus, retiring workers can assess whether the lump sum equivalent is worth more or less than that of the life annuity in utility terms.

[3] Ameriks (2002) provides evidence of the desire for lump sum distributions among individuals in DC plans by examining the response of participants in TIAA-CREF to a change in its distributional policy. Prior to 1989, TIAA-CREF required participants to annuitize their account balances. After this restriction

was removed, the proportion of participants electing life annuities fell to 46 percent in 2001.

[4] An exception to this observation seems to be the behavior of retirees in Switzerland. Avanzi (2009) reports that almost two-thirds of the Swiss converted all of their retirement assets into annuities, while only one-fourth requested that all of the assets be paid as a lump sum.

[5] Mitchell et al. (1999), Johnson et al. (2004) and Brown (2008) provide in-depth reviews of these and other reasons why so few individuals purchase annuities to help smooth consumption in retirement. Individuals may also have better information concerning their life expectancy than the actuarial calculation. Thus, the value of an annuity to an individual might differ from the offer price. For individuals with poor health or lower life expectancies, the price of the annuity may be too high and it would be optimal to select a lump sum distribution. In fact, sellers facing unknown longevity of the population willing to purchase annuities may price the product too high for the average retiree (Friedman and Warshawsky, 1990). Davidoff et al. (2005) provide a formal model that explains the lack of demand for annuities in this way.

[6] Much of the research examining lump sum distributions from DB plans focuses on workers who terminate service prior to retirement. The major focus of these studies tends to be whether the funds are spent on current consumption or saved for retirement. In comparison, this study examines the planned distributional choices of workers who are retiring from career jobs.

[7] A more detailed description of this project, the employer partners, and the surveys can be found in Clark et al. (2010).

[8] Employees could accrue no new benefits in the old plan after 2003.

[9] In 2007, BD introduced a cash balance plan and gave workers a one-time option of switching to the cash balance plan. Virtually all older workers with significant tenure would have had higher values in the old plan, and thus would have chosen to stay in the old plan.

References

Agnew, J. and L. Szykman (2011). 'Annuities, Financial Literacy and Information Overload,' in O. S. Mitchell and A. Lusardi, eds, *Financial Literacy: Implications for Retirement Security and the Financial Marketplace*. Oxford, UK: Oxford University Press.

Ameriks, J. (2002). 'Recent Trends in the Selection of Retirement Income Streams Among TIAA-CREF Participants,' Research Dialogue No. 74. New York, NY: TIAA-CREF Institute.

Avanzi, B. (2009). 'What is It That Makes the Swiss Annuitize? A Description of the Swiss Retirement System,' UNSW Australian School of Business Research Paper No. 2009ACTL06. Sydney, Australia: UNSW.

Brown, J. (2008). 'Understanding the Role of Annuities in Retirement Planning,' in Annamaria Lusardi, ed., *Overcoming the Saving Slump: How to Increase the Effectiveness of Financial Education and Saving Programs.* Chicago, IL: University of Chicago Press, pp. 178–206.

——J. Kling, S. Mullainathan, and M. Wrobel (2008). 'Why Don't the People Insure Late Life Consumption? A Framing Explanation of the Under-Annuitization Puzzle,' NBER Working Paper No. 13748. Cambridge, MA: National Bureau of Economic Research.

Clark, R., M. Morrill, and S. Allen (2010). 'Employer-Provided Retirement Planning Programs,' in R. L. Clark and O. S. Mitchell, eds, *Reorienting Retirement Risk Management.* Oxford, UK: Oxford University Press, pp. 36–64.

Davidoff, T., J. Brown, and P. Diamond (2005). 'Annuities and Individual Welfare,' *American Economic Review,* 95(5): 1573–90.

Friedman, B. and M. Warshawsky (1990). 'The Cost of Annuities: Implications for Saving Behavior and Bequests,' *Quarterly Journal of Economics,* 105(1): 135–54.

Hu, W. and J. Scott. 2007. 'Behavioral Obstacles to the Annuity Market,' Pension Research Council Working Paper No. 2007-10. Philadelphia, PA: Pension Research Council.

Hurd, M. and C. Panis (2006). 'The Choice to Cash Out Pension Rights at Job Change or Retirement,' *Journal of Public Economics,* 90(12): 2213–27.

Johnson, R., L. Burman, and D. Kobes (2004). *Annuitized Wealth at Older Ages: Evidence from the Health and Retirement Study.* Washington, DC: Urban Institute. http://www.urban.org/UploadedPDF/411000_annuitized_wealth.pdf

Mitchell, O. S., J. Poterba, M. Warshawsky, and J. Brown (1999). 'New Evidence on the Money's Worth of Individual Annuities,' *American Economic Review,* 76(3): 297–313.

Moore, J. and L. Muller (2002). 'An Analysis of Lump-Sum Pension Distribution Recipients,' *Monthly Labor Review,* May: 29–46.

Purcell, P. (2009). *Pension Issues: Lump-Sum Distributions and Retirement Income Security.* CRS Report for Congress. Washington, DC: Congressional Research Service.

US Bureau of Labor Statistics (BLS) (1990). *Employee Benefits in Medium and Large Firms, 1989.* Bulletin 2363. Washington, DC: US Bureau of Labor Statistics.

——(1999). *Employee Benefits in Medium and Large Establishments, 1997.* Bulletin 2517. Washington, DC: US Bureau of Labor Statistics.

——(2005). *National Compensation Survey: Employee Benefits in Private Industry in the United States, 2003.* Bulletin 2577. Washington, DC: US Bureau of Labor Statistics.

——(2007). *National Compensation Survey: Employee Benefits in Private Industry in the United States, 2005.* Bulletin 2589. Washington, DC: US Bureau of Labor Statistics.

Chapter 4

Financial Literacy and 401(k) Loans

Stephen P. Utkus and Jean A. Young

Defined contribution plans (DC), more commonly known as 401(k) plans, are today the dominant form of private-sector pension provision in the United States, covering more than 60 million workers. One of the unique elements present in many 401(k) plans is a loan feature. Plan participants are able to borrow a portion of the assets in their retirement accounts and repay the loan with interest over time. The loan feature is subject to various legal and plans-specific limits, most notably the requirement that not more than half of the vested account balance can be borrowed (with the maximum loan amount not to exceed $50,000). Unique among sources of credit for US households, 401(k) loans impose no credit underwriting limits, as participants are in effect borrowing from their own accumulated retirement assets. As of year-end 2008, 18 percent of DC plan participants had a loan outstanding against their account, with a mean value borrowed of $7,191 or 16 percent of the average account balance (Holden et al., 2009).[1]

One of the perennial questions surrounding loans in 401(k) plans is whether they pose an undue risk to retirement security (USGAO, 2009). When a participant terminates employment, any outstanding loan balance is due and payable to the account; otherwise, the amount of the unpaid loan, which represents an asset held in the retirement account, is written off and reported as a 'deemed distribution' subject to taxes and penalties. Such deemed distributions amounted to some $600 million in 2007, representing 0.2 percent of $3.7 trillion in assets held in DC plans (USDOL, 2010). While such costs are small relative to the aggregate asset holdings, they may be high for particular groups of economically vulnerable or financially unsophisticated participants. Loans also pose a potential opportunity cost for plan participants, generating a fixed income rate of return rather than a possibly higher return based on a balanced portfolio with a higher equity allocation.[2] At the same time, there is evidence that loans may raise participation or contribution rates in DC plans, thereby at the margin enhancing old-age income security (USGAO, 1997; Munnell et al., 2002; Mottola and Utkus, 2005; Mitchell et al., 2007). These 401(k) loans;

also offer a low-cost source of borrowing to households that are liquidity-constrained, although it is not clear whether 401(k) participants fully take advantage of this benefit relative to other types of borrowing, such as credit card debt (Li and Smith, 2008).

This chapter considers a specific question about the nature of the risks posed by 401(k) loans; namely, to what extent is financial literacy related to loan-taking behavior in US 401(k) plans? Outside of these plans, there is much evidence that financial literacy and poor borrowing habits are intertwined, whether with respect to payday loans, credit cards, or mortgages (FINRA, 2009). Yet 401(k) loans are different from these other sources of borrowing in that no profit-seeking financial intermediary is involved, and borrowing takes place in a relatively noncommercial setting, the workplace, as an adjunct to a broader retirement saving program sponsored by the employer. A 401(k) loan also represents individuals' propensity to borrow from their own accumulated wealth, rather than from other savers in the economy intermediated by lending institutions.

Our research draws on a survey of nearly 900 plan participants conducted in August and September 2008 and augmented with relevant 401(k) administrative records. Our survey asked plan participants four questions relating to general financial knowledge, from which we construct a simple financial literacy index. We find, first, that job tenure has the strongest link to 401(k) borrowing. Less educated, lower-income, younger, and, somewhat paradoxically, higher-income households are more likely to borrow. Second, loan-taking is strongly related to financial literacy. A low literacy score raises the probability of having a 401(k) loan by 6 percentage points, an increase of 27 percent relative to the 22 percent of participants in our sample who have a loan outstanding. Finally, we find that 401(k) loan-taking is strongly correlated with other behaviors, such as low 401(k) employee contributions, low nonretirement wealth, and the failure to repay credit card debt each month. These results together suggest that 401(k) borrowing does not occur in isolation, but is related to a common unobserved variable relating to impatience in financial decision-making, namely high discount rates in time preferences (i.e., the tendency to 'spend now and save later'). Thus, efforts by policymakers or plan sponsors to educate participants about the benefits and risks of 401(k) loans may need to be broader in scope than previously imagined, and they must consider households' overall ability to manage income, expenses, and debt, not simply the 401(k) loan feature.

In what follows, we begin by describing our dataset, the characteristics of 401(k) borrowers, and our literacy index. We then consider a simple logistic model of loan-taking behavior incorporating financial literacy and other metrics of financial behavior. We conclude with a discussion of findings and implications for financial education efforts.

Data and descriptive statistics

Our survey sample is drawn from a dataset of 1.3 million participant accounts in 707 401(k) plans offering a loan feature; the dataset was extracted as of June 30, 2008, from Vanguard's 401(k) recordkeeping system. Our survey was administered by telephone in August and September 2008; a total of 895 complete participant responses (in 249 plans) were received. The survey sample was drawn from the recordkeeping dataset based on various loan behaviors; as a result, all responses from respondents are reweighted back to the original dataset.[3] Table 4.1 provides descriptive

TABLE 4.1 Descriptive statistics (%)

	All participants		Participants with loan outstanding	
	Survey sample	Recordkeeping sample	Survey sample	Recordkeeping sample
	(A)	(B)	(C)	(D)
Sex				
Male	66	33	67	36
Female	34	16	33	17
Missing	0	51	0	47
Age				
Under 35	26	25	17	17
35–50	43	43	53	52
Over 50	31	32	30	31
Income				
<$75,000	38	42	44	55
$75,000–$100,000	31	15	27	16
>$100,000	21	22	23	18
Refused/unknown	10	21	6	11
Job tenure				
<4 years	27	33	8	12
4–10 years	29	27	26	31
>10 years	44	39	66	56
Missing	0	1	0	1
Education				
High school or less	21	N/A	32	N/A
Some college	28	N/A	38	N/A
College graduate or higher	51	N/A	30	N/A

(continued)

Table 4.1 Continued

	All participants		Participants with loan outstanding	
	Survey sample	Recordkeeping sample	Survey sample	Recordkeeping sample
	(A)	(B)	(C)	(D)
401(k) employee contributions				
<$3,000	44	50	56	57
$3,000–$10,000	36	33	37	35
>$10,000	20	17	7	8
401(k) account balance				
<$10,000	24	33	8	16
$10,000–$50,000	31	30	37	42
>$50,000	45	37	55	42
Nonretirement wealth				
<$25,000	40	42	59	25
$25,000–$100,000	31	27	24	54
>$100,000	23	22	11	13
Refused/unknown	6	9	6	8
n (unweighted)	895	1,628,273	308	337,505
n (weighted)	857		190	

Notes: Survey responses are weighted to the recordkeeping population by age and loan status; see text. Recordkeeping sample was extracted as of June 30, 2008. Survey sample is as of August and September 2008. 401(k) contributions are for entire year 2008.

Source: Authors' calculations; see text.

statistics for the two samples. These variables include age, household income, job tenure, and levels of educational attainment, as well as employee contributions to their 401(k) account in 2008, 401(k) account balance, and nonretirement wealth (measuring the mean wealth of households in the same zipcode).[4] Columns A and B compare the survey sample with the recordkeeping dataset. The two are virtually identical, except for a tendency of the survey sample to be somewhat overweighted in participants with more than 10 years of job tenure (44 percent of the survey sample versus 39 percent for the recordkeeping sample), 401(k) account balances greater than $50,000 (45 percent of the survey sample versus 37 percent for the recordkeeping sample), and participant incomes under $75,000 (38 percent versus 42 percent).

Descriptive statistics for 401(k) participants with a current loan outstanding appear in Columns C and D. Current borrowers tend to have somewhat higher incomes and 401(k) account balances compared to all participants, but they are more likely to have low nonretirement wealth (below $25,000). They are also older and longer-tenured. In part, these effects due to age, tenure, and account balance may reflect the need for participants to accumulate sufficient saving before borrowing from their account. Most plans in our sample impose a $1,000 loan minimum, and thus participants under typical circumstances would need an account balance of at least $2,000 before being able to take a loan. Another reason for these effects may be that participants become more familiar with the features of their 401(k) plan over time.

Our survey also includes four literacy questions shown in Table 4.2 that address four topics: compounding, credit card debt, stock market risk, and investment returns. These questions are designed to test participants' general awareness of personal finance ideas, not their knowledge of 401(k) plans or 401(k) loan features. Table 4.3 summarizes responses of participants with a current 401(k) loan outstanding, and compares them with those of participants with no current loan. Participants with a 401(k) loan outstanding are less likely to answer the credit card question correctly than those with no loan outstanding (78 percent for borrowers versus 82 percent for nonborrowers, respectively); borrowers are also less likely to provide the correct response to the stock market risk question (60 percent for borrowers versus

TABLE 4.2 Financial literacy questions

Question category	Question text	Answer choices	Correct answer
Compounding	If you are saving for a future goal, it's better to start early so that your money earns more and builds up faster over time.	True or false	True
Credit card debt	Keeping a balance on your credit cards is okay as long as you can make the minimum payments each month.	True or false	False
Stock market risk	If you were to invest $1,000 in a stock mutual fund, it would be possible to have less than $1,000 when you withdraw the money.	True or false	True
Investment returns	In which ONE of the following products would you choose to invest your money for the highest expected long-term growth?	A savings account, a certificate of deposit, an insurance policy, a stock mutual fund	A stock mutual fund

Notes: Question category are for reference only and were not included in the question to respondents.

Source: Hilgert et al. (2003), John Hancock Financial Services (2002), and Jump$tart Coalition for Personal Financial Literacy (2004).

TABLE 4.3 Financial literacy scores (%)

	Respondents with loan outstanding	Respondents without loan outstanding	All respondents
Compounding			
Correct	99	99	99
Incorrect	1	1	1
Not sure/refused	0	0	0
Credit card debt			
Correct	78	82	81
Incorrect	20	16	17
Not sure/refused	2	2	2
Stock market risk			
Correct	60	78	74
Incorrect	22	14	16
Not sure/refused	18	8	10
Investment returns			
Correct	71	77	75
Incorrect	18	15	16
Not sure/refused	11	8	9
Summary of responses			
Zero correct	1	0	0
One correct	6	2	3
Two correct	19	15	16
Three correct	33	27	29
All four correct ('high literacy')	41	56	52
n (unweighted)	308	587	895
n (weighted)	190	667	857

Source: Authors' calculations; see text.

78 percent for nonborrowers) and the general question on investment returns (71 percent for borrowers versus 77 percent for nonborrowers). At least in terms of descriptive statistics, some aspects of general financial literacy appear linked to 401(k) borrowing behavior.

Just over half of the population, or 52 percent, can provide correct answers for all four literacy questions, and we classify this subset as the 'high' literacy group. Another 29 percent of respondents answered three questions accurately; 16 percent of respondents two questions; and 3 percent of respondents, only one question. This second subset (48 percent of the survey) we classify as 'low' literacy participants. Table 4.4 provides descriptive statistics

TABLE 4.4 Financial literacy score by various characteristics (%)

	Low financial literacy score	High financial literacy score	All respondents
Sex			
Male	57	74	66
Female	43	26	34
Age			
Under 35	30	23	26
35–50	40	45	43
Over 50	30	32	31
Income			
<$75,000	45	33	39
$75,000–$100,000	19	24	22
>$100,000	26	34	30
Refused/unknown	10	9	9
Job tenure			
<4 years	29	26	27
4–10 years	30	28	29
>10 years	41	46	44
Education			
High school or less	31	13	21
Some college	27	28	28
College graduate or higher	42	59	51
401(k) employee contributions			
<$3,000	58	32	44
$3,000–$10,000	30	42	36
>$10,000	12	26	20
401(k) account balance			
<$10,000	32	17	24
$10,000–$50,000	32	29	31
>$50,000	36	54	45
Nonretirement wealth			
<$25,000	44	37	40
$25,000–$100,000	26	36	31
>$100,000	22	23	23
Refused/unknown	8	4	6
n (unweighted)	454	441	895
n (weighted)	447	410	857
Percent of sample	52	48	100

Notes: Literacy score of 4 is defined as 'high'; otherwise 'low'. See Table 4.1 for more information on survey sample.

Source: Authors' calculations; see text.

for the 'high' and 'low' literacy groups. Low-literacy participants are disproportionately female (43 percent versus 57 percent), younger, and have lower
levels of income and educational attainment. They are also more likely to
have lower 401(k) contribution amounts and balances.

Factors related to 401(k) borrowing

We examine the relationship between 401(k) borrowing and demographic,
literacy, and behavioral variables, using a straightforward logistic regression
model of loan-taking behavior. In equation (1), $BORROWER_{i,j}$ refers to
the probability that the ith participant has a 401(k) loan outstanding in
the jth plan as of September 2008, the time of our administrative data
extraction:

$$BORROWER_{i,j} = \alpha DEMOGRAPHICS_i + \beta LITERACY_i + \gamma FIN_{BEHAVIOR_i} + v_i + c_{i,j,t}$$

where the dependent variable takes a value of 1 if the participant has a loan
outstanding in September 2008, and 0 otherwise. In our survey sample, the
mean (weighted) value of $BORROWER_{i,j}$ is 22.2 percent. The DEMO-
GRAPHICS vector includes measures of the demographic factors in
Table 4.1, including sex, age, income, job tenure, and education.[5] LITER-
ACY is an indicator variable indicating whether the participant has a low
literacy score. FIN_BEHAVIOR includes indicators for a variety of variables
relating to the non-401(k)-loan elements of participant financial profiles,
including 401(k) contributions, 401(k) account balance, nonretirement
plan wealth, and whether the household carries credit-card debt from
month to month.

Table 4.5 reports results for three logistic regression models: Model
A uses only standard demographic variables as explanatory variables,
while Model B adds the financial literacy measure. Model C uses additional
financial characteristics. In Model A, job tenure has the strongest relationship with 401(k) borrowing: participants with more than ten years of job
tenure are 21 percentage points more likely to have a loan outstanding, a
relative increase of nearly 100 percent on a mean borrowing rate of 22
percent. The least educated are also more likely to have a loan outstanding.
401(k) borrowers are also more likely to be under the age of 35 and have
incomes below $75,000. Paradoxically, borrowers are also more likely to
have incomes over $100,000. In Model B, low financial literacy is associated
with a 6 percentage point increase in the probability of having a loan
outstanding, a relative increase of 27 percent. It is also statistically significant at the 1 percent level. Introducing a literacy variable into the model

TABLE 4.5 Logistic estimation of the probability of a loan outstanding

	Demographic characteristics		With literacy score		With financial characteristics	
	Estimated coefficient	Marginal effects (%)	Estimated coefficient	Marginal effects (%)	Estimated coefficient	Marginal effects (%)
	Sex (reference: male)					
Female	−0.034	−1	−0.065	−1	−0.102	−2
Age (reference: over 50)						
Under 35	0.141	3	0.102	2	0.221	3
35–50	−0.379**	−9	−0.363	−8	−0.399***	−6
Income (reference: $75,000–$100,000)						
Less than $75,000	0.188	4	0.173	4	−0.087	−1
More than $100,000	0.104	2	0.102	2	0.146*	7
Job tenure (reference: 4–10 years)						
Under 4 years	−1.092***	−25	−1.103***	−23	−0.725***	−11
Over 10 years	0.921***	21	0.942***	20	0.641***	10
Education (reference: some college)						
High school graduate or less	0.400***	9	0.309**	7	0.227	4
College graduate or higher	−0.693***	16	−0.626	−13	−0.467***	−7
Financial literacy (reference: high)						
Low			0.275***	6	0.273***	4
401(k) employee contributions (reference: $3,000–$10,000)						
Less than $3,000					0.830***	13
More than $10,000					−1.046***	−16
401(k) account balance (reference: $10,000–$50,000)						

(continued)

TABLE 4.5 Continued

	Demographic characteristics		With literacy score		With financial characteristics	
	Estimated coefficient	Marginal effects (%)	Estimated coefficient	Marginal effects (%)	Estimated coefficient	Marginal effects (%)
Less than $10,000					-1.167***	-18
More than $50,000					0.784***	12
Nonretirement wealth (reference: $25,000–$100,000)						
Less than $25,000					0.543***	9
More than $100,000					-0.394*	-6
Credit card balance (reference: no)						
Yes					0.283**	4
n (unweighted)	895		895		895	
n (weighted)	857		857		857	
R-square	0.191		0.204		0.315	

Notes: The dependent variable was whether a 401(k) participant had a loan outstanding (1 = yes, 0 = no). The mean was 22.2 percent. Logistic regression with clustering for plan-level heteroskedasticity. * Indicates significance at the 10 percent level,
** is 5 percent, and
*** is 1 percent. Also includes controls for missing variables.

Source: Authors' calculations; see text.

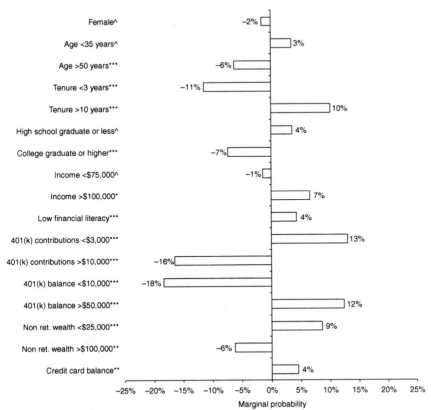

Figure 4.1 Full model marginal effects predicting an outstanding loan

Notes: Logistic regression with clustering for plan-level heteroskedasticity.
* Indicates significance at the 10 percent level, ** is 5 percent, and *** is 1 percent;
^ indicates no significance. Also includes controls for missing variables.

Source: Authors' calculations; see text.

has the effect of reducing the relative impact of tenure, education, age, and income on borrowing behavior. For example, in Model B the relative effect of having a high school education (or less) is only 7 percentage points, compared to 9 percentage points in the demographics-only model.

Table 4.5 and Figure 4.1 report on results for Model C, which incorporates a variety of other financial characteristics relating to the participant's wealth, saving, and borrowing behavior. Perhaps the most striking finding is the relationship between 401(k) plan contribution behavior and borrowing. Participants who contribute $3,000 a year to their 401(k) plans are 13 percentage points more likely to have a loan outstanding, compared to the reference group of those saving between $3,000 and $10,000 a year (after controlling on other differences, including income and education that might influence propensity to save). This is a relative increase in propensity to borrow of 59 percent (13 divided by 22) among low savers. All things being equal, 401(k) borrowers appear also to be 401(k) low savers. By contrast, high savers (those contributing $10,000 or more a year) are 16 percentage points less likely to have a 401(k) loan outstanding compared to the reference group—again, controlling on other differences that would influence the propensity to save.

Another important effect is the impact of the expanded model specification on the role of income. In prior models, having earned higher (above $100,000 per year) or lower (below $75,000 per year) income is associated with increased loan-taking. In this expanded model, lower-income is no longer significant, while the marginal effect of a higher income is now 7 percentage points—an increase of nearly one-third compared to a 22 percent loan-taking rate. Although the result is significant only at the 10 percent level, it is nonetheless suggestive that high-income households are the most likely to take advantage of a 401(k) loan feature, in a more robust model of loan-taking, including other financial assets and behaviors.

401(k) and nonretirement plan wealth are also linked to the propensity to have a 401(k) loan, although with opposite effects. The propensity to borrow rises with 401(k) account balances, with participants having balances below $10,000 being 18 percentage points less likely to borrow than the reference group (with balances between $10,000 and $50,000). Meanwhile, those with balances above $50,000 are 12 percentage points more likely to borrow than the reference group. The larger the 401(k) balance—the larger the resources available for borrowing—the more likely it is that a participant has a loan outstanding. In contrast, nonretirement wealth has just the opposite effect. Those with low retirement wealth are more likely liquidity-constrained outside the 401(k) plan and so more likely to rely on the plan's loan feature (by 9 percentage points); those with high retirement wealth are more likely less liquidity-constrained, and so they are less likely to borrow (by –6 percentage points) through the 401(k) plan. A final variable in Table 4.6 measures whether or not a participant had an outstanding balance on his or her credit cards in the prior month. Those answering 'Yes' were 4 percentage points more likely to have a loan outstanding—a relative increase of 18 percent (4/21). This is on par with the marginal effect of 4 percentage points associated with 'low' financial literacy.

We interpret these results broadly as suggesting that 401(k) loan behavior is reflective of participants' unobserved time preferences or discounting behavior—how patient or impatient people are when balancing present and future consumption. Participants with high-discount rates—impatient

TABLE 4.6 Reported use of loan proceeds (%)

	Low financial literacy score	High financial literacy score	All respondents
Home improvement or repairs (I)	35	58	32
Purchase or refinance home (I)	17	22	19
Purchase automobile (I)	12	16	14
College/education expenses (I)	10	13	11
Bill consolidation/pay off debt (C)	41	37	39
Medical expenses (C)	12	10	11
Vacation expenses (C)	7	4	6
Wedding costs (C)	5	1	3
Other (C or I)	16	12	15
Summary			
Investment (I)	36	43	40
Consumption (C)	37	33	35
Both investment and consumption	26	22	24
Not sure or refused	1	2	1
n (unweighted)	316	263	579
n (weighted)	137	108	245
Percent of sample (weighted)	56	44	100

Notes: Multiple responses allowed. Consumption expenditures are classified as 'C'; investments are classified as 'I'.

Source: Authors' calculations; see text.

decision-makers who place high value on current consumption and a low value on current saving—are less likely to contribute to their 401(k) plans, more likely to take 401(k) loans, and more likely to carry balances on their credit card from month to month. For such participants, higher 401(k) balances appear to pose a greater temptation for borrowing. Low nonretirement plan wealth is also indicative that 401(k) borrowers may have lower saving rates outside the plan as well, all other things being equal. All of these factors are correlated with lower financial literacy levels. Conversely, patient investors, with low discount rates, are likely to be associated with a set of exactly the opposite behaviors: they have larger 401(k) contributions and fewer 401(k) loans, pay off their credit cards monthly, have high nonretirement plan wealth, and display higher financial literacy.

Use of loan proceeds

One question in our survey asks 401(k) borrowers with a loan outstanding in September 2008 as well as those who had previously borrowed from their 401(k) plans and repaid the loans, about their use of the loan proceeds.[6] While 401(k) loans can be used for essentially any purpose, under federal law loans are classified as either general purpose (having a term of five years or less) or for home purchase (having a term of up to thirty years). Ninety-five percent of loans in our broad recordkeeping sample are of the general purpose type, although even such loans can be used at the time of home purchase for either home downpayments and closing costs or new home expenses.

Table 4.6 reports on use of loan proceeds. Survey respondents can indicate multiple responses: four in ten respondents indicate that the 401(k) loan was used for bill or debt consolidation, while 32 percent report that proceeds were used for home improvement or repair. A total of 19 percent of respondents indicate the loan was used for home purchase, 14 percent for the purchase of an automobile, and 11 percent for college expenses.

We separately classified these uses of funds as to whether they are predominantly 'consumption' related, 'investment' related, or both. A total of 40 percent of respondents report uses that are principally investment-related; 35 percent report uses that are consumption-related; and for 24 percent, uses fell into both categories. Table 4.6 also tabulates use of proceeds by our financial literacy score. There is a tendency for low-literacy respondents to use proceeds for consumption, rather than investment purposes, but the differences are small and none are statistically significant. Our tentative conclusion is that, conditional on loan-taking, financial literacy seems unrelated to whether a loan is ultimately used for consumption or investment purposes (or both). Additional research with a larger sample could yield a different result, however.

Conclusion

One of the unique features of many 401(k) plans is the presence of a loan feature, whereby participants may borrow a portion of their account balance and repay it, with interest, over time. Just under one-fifth of 401(k) participants typically have a loan outstanding at any point in time. Although a small fraction of the average participant's account balance is borrowed, 401(k) loans may still pose a risk to retirement wealth accumulation in that they are typically due and payable upon job change, job loss, or retirement. If the loan goes unpaid at the time of employment termination, the loan is treated as a taxable distribution of funds from the participant's account and gives rise to both a tax liability and a penalty. In effect, the loan amount borrowed from the account is no longer able to be replenished. At the same time, loans are thought to encourage contributions into 401(k) plans, inasmuch as they reduce the illiquidity associated with a tax-deferred retirement plan account.

We examine the role that financial literacy plays in the decision to borrow from a 401(k) plan using a survey of nearly 900 plan participants. Our measure of literacy uses a simple four-question index assessing participant knowledge of compounding, stock market risk, investment returns, and credit card debt. We find that low financial literacy is associated with an increase in the probability of having a loan outstanding of 4–6 percentage points. Thus, in our sample, where 22 percent of participants had an outstanding loan, low levels of general financial literacy on a relative basis mean an 18–27 percentage point increase in the chances of borrowing from a 401(k) plan, depending on the model specification.

Equally important, however, is that 401(k) borrowing is correlated with a wide range of other financial decisions and behaviors. In particular, borrowing from one's 401(k) is inversely related to 401(k) plan contributions: low savers are more likely to borrow from their 401(k) plan, while high savers are less likely to do so (this after controlling on other factors that influence the propensity to save). The tendency to carry a credit card balance from month to month is also correlated with 401(k) borrowing. As well, low levels of nonretirement financial wealth are linked to 401(k) borrowing, suggesting that non-401(k) saving rates are also low. We interpret these findings as indicative of impatience in financial decision-making, namely high discount rates in time preferences.

One way for plan sponsors and policymakers to mitigate the potential risks of 401(k) borrowing is to offer greater financial education. Yet our results suggest that 401(k) borrowing does not exist in isolation, but rather it appears linked to behaviors associated with having high discount rates or impatience in financial decision-making. Efforts to educate participants would therefore need to be comprehensive in scope, addressing not only the merits and risks of the 401(k) loan feature itself, but also participants' attitudes and behaviors regarding saving and borrowing, both within and outside retirement plans. This latter type of education, of course, would likely be more complex and costly compared to the former. Moreover, it remains to be seen whether and how financial education can fundamentally alter a constellation of behaviors—401(k) loans, credit card loans, low 401(k) saving, low nonplan saving—that are so inextricably related.

Acknowledgments

The authors acknowledge support from Vanguard for the participant survey instrument and the provision of recordkeeping data under restricted access conditions. Opinions and conclusions are solely those of the authors, and do not reflect views of the institutions supporting the research, with whom the authors are affiliated.

Endnotes

[1] The lifetime incidence of loan usage is no doubt higher than this point-in-time estimate.

[2] Based on historic asset class returns over the 1926–2009 period, for a participant with a 70 percent allocation to stocks and a 30 percent allocation to bonds (the average allocation of all participants in our population), a shift to 60 percent stocks and 40 percent bonds would reduce the participant's real average annual rate of return from 5.85 to 5.48 percent, a reduction of thirty-seven basis points. A shift in allocation of twenty points would roughly double this amount.

[3] The sample was drawn from four categories of loan behavior: participants with a current loan; participants who had previously taken out and paid off a loan, but had none outstanding at the time of the data extraction; participants who had never taken a loan from their current employer's 401(k) plan; and a fourth group of participants who had terminated employment with a loan outstanding in the twelve months ending June 30, 2008. Given our initial interest in the relationship of literacy factors and loan-taking behavior, the fourth group was excluded from the analysis, and a final survey sample resulted in 895 participants, weighted back to the original recordkeeping sample of 1.3 million by age and loan-taking behavior.

[4] The IXI company provides a measure of average wealth held outside retirement plans within a ZIP+4 area.

[5] The econometric model also corrects for plan-level heteroskedasticity (v_i).

[6] Some 401(k) borrowers responded that they did not currently or previously have a plan loan. The question about the use of loan proceeds was asked only of those indicating that they currently or previously had a plan loan.

References

FINRA (2009). *2009 National Financial Capability Study*. Washington, DC: FINRA Investor Education Foundation. http://www.finrafoundation.org/resources/research/p120478

Hilgert, M. A., J. M. Hogarth, and S. G. Beverly (2003). 'Household Financial Management: The Connection between Knowledge and Behavior,' *Federal Reserve Bulletin*, July: 309–22.

Holden, Sarah, J. VanDerhei, and L. Alonso (2009). *401(k) Plan Asset Allocation, Account Balances and Loan Activity in 2008*. Washington, DC: Investment Company Institute. http://www.ici.org/pdf/per15-02.pdf

John Hancock Financial Services (2002). *Insight into Participant Investment, Knowledge and Behavior: Eighth Defined Contribution Survey*. Boston, MA: John Hancock Financial Services. http://www.mfcglobal.com/gsfp/survey2002.pdf

Jump$tart Coalition for Personal Financial Literacy (2004). *Jump$tart Survey of Personal Financial Literacy among High School Students*. Washington, DC: Jump-$tart Coalition for Personal Financial Literacy. http://www.jumpstart.org/survey.html

Li, Geng and P. A. Smith (2008). 'Borrowing from Yourself: 401(k) Loans and Household Balance Sheets,' Federal Reserve Working Paper 2008-42. Washington, DC: Federal Reserve.

Mottola, Gary R. and S. P. Utkus (2005). *Life-Cycle Funds Mature: Plan and Participant Adoption*. Malvern, PA: Vanguard Center for Retirement Research. https://institutional.vanguard.com/iip/pdf/LifeCycleStudy.pdf

Mitchell, Olivia S., S. P. Utkus, and T. Yang (2007). 'Turning Workers into Savers: Incentives, Liquidity and Choice in 401(k) Plans,' *National Tax Journal*, 60: 468–89.

Munnell, Alicia, A. Sunden, and C. Taylor (2002). 'What Determines 401(k) Participation and Contributions?,' *Social Security Bulletin*, 64(3): 64–75.

United States Department of Labor (USDOL) (2010). *Private Pension Plan Bulletin: Abstract of 2007 Form 5500 Annual Reports*. Washington, DC: US Department of Labor, Employee Benefits Security Administration. http://www.dol.gov/ebsa/pdf/2007pensionplanbulletin.pdf

United States Government Accountability Office (USGAO) (1997). *401(k) Pension Plans: Loan Provisions Enhance Participation But May Affect Income Security for Some*. Washington, DC: US Government Accounting Office. http://www.gao.gov/archive/1998/he98005.pdf

—— (2009). *401(k) Plans: Policy Changes Could Reduce the Long-Term Effects of Leakage on Workers' Retirement Savings*. Washington, DC: US Government Accounting Office. http://www.gao.gov/products/GAO-09-715.

Chapter 5

Financial Illiteracy and Stock Market Participation: Evidence from the RAND American Life Panel

Joanne Yoong

Financially illiterate households who consistently make suboptimal decisions may suffer lasting consequences for long-term wealth accumulation. This is particularly true for the US population given institutional changes shifting the burden of postretirement planning to the individual via the spread of defined contribution (DC) pension plans, leaving those who do not plan for retirement with lower net wealth (Lusardi and Mitchell, 2006, 2007). This population is also increasingly diversified, with a growing number of foreign-born households that face further language, educational, and cultural barriers to entry into formal financial systems (Braunstein and Welch, 2002). Many public and private stakeholders—including the federal government, nonprofit groups, and employers—have responded by supplying more education and tools for planning, under the implicit assumption that increases in financial literacy will lead to changes in behavior.

Evidence regarding the impact of financial illiteracy on financial behavior, however, has been both scarce and mixed (e.g., Martin, 2007; Agarwal et al., 2011). One reason for these limitations is that a substantial fraction of existing studies that address this question are based on the evaluation of specific financial education programs and policies. Bayer et al. (1996) and Bernheim et al. (2001) showed that employer-based financial education increases participation in saving plans, while financial education mandates in high school significantly increase adult propensity to save. Recently, however, other researchers (e.g., Duflo and Saez, 2003; Cole and Shastry, 2009) have found surprisingly small impacts of financial education programs on financial decision-making, particularly in comparison to other factors, such as peer effects and psychological biases. Yet detecting effects of financial literacy in such analyses is problematic: in addition to questions about external validity and program heterogenity, the observed efficacy of such programs depends on not one but two relationships: the ability of the program to affect literacy, and the effect of literacy on behavior. Further, financial education programs may fail to affect literacy for many reasons. Nevertheless, research that links survey measures of knowledge to observed behavior more consistently finds that financial literacy is correlated with financial behavior, even if causality is difficult to establish. Hilgert et al. (2003) find that individuals with more financial knowledge are more likely to engage in recommended financial practices. Lusardi and Mitchell (2006, 2007) demonstrate that consumers with better financial knowledge are more likely to plan, to try to succeed in planning, and to invest in complex assets, a relationship which the authors show to be causal.

This chapter contributes to the evidence linking financial illiteracy and behavior by focusing attention on one aspect of household investment behavior critical to long-term wealth accumulation: stock market participation. Using a novel instrumental variables (IV) strategy, we establish a negative causal relationship between financial illiteracy and participation.

Standard portfolio theory results imply that all households, regardless of risk preferences, should hold some portion of their portfolio in stock, but 60–70 percent of US households hold no stocks at all (Haliassos and Bertaut, 1995; Campbell, 2006). The 'stockholding puzzle' has been related to features of the environment such as fixed costs (Vissing-Jorgenson and Attanasio, 2003), credit-constraints (Constantinides et al., 2002), and the wedge between borrowing and lending rates (Davis et al., 2006). Other work has examined cognitive, behavioral, and social explanations such as inertia and departures from expected utility maximization (Haliassos and Bertaut, 1995), trust and culture (Guiso et al., 2005), and the effect of social interactions (Hong et al., 2004; Christelis et al., 2005). Christelis et al. (2006) detect a positive relationship between cognitive ability and the decision to invest in stocks using the recent Survey of Health, Ageing, and Retirement in Europe (SHARE), as measured by mathematics, verbal fluency, and recall skills.

Several recent studies specifically address financial illiteracy and stock market participation; Guiso and Jappelli (2005) study the lack of awareness of stocks among Italian households, while Lusardi and Mitchell (2007) find a positive relationship between financial literacy measures and stock market participation in the 2004 US Health and Retirement Study (HRS). Endogenity bias, however, is a concern; for example, unobservable preferences can systematically lead individuals to purposively learn about stocks to participate in the market (Martin, 2007). One study that goes further is that of van Rooij et al. (2007), who use the Dutch DNB Household Survey (DHS) to develop a sophisticated measure of financial literacy. The authors find a significant positive relationship between advanced financial literacy and participation, establishing causality using economics education as an instrument. Nevertheless, their identification approach depends heavily on institutional features particular to the Netherlands that guarantee the exogenity of economics education, where the authors note that there is virtually no access to financial education outside formal schooling. In the United States, however, this is clearly not the case: Bayer et al. (1996) report that by 1994, the majority of large employers offered some sort of financial education.

In what follows, we build on the work of van Rooij et al. (2007) and Lusardi and Mitchell (2007). We construct a stock-related investment illiteracy score based only on knowledge relevant to stock market participation, and we implement a novel IV strategy for establishing causation between stock-related investment illiteracy and stock market participation.[1]

Data and measurement in the RAND American Family Life Panel

The American Life Panel (ALP) is an ongoing Internet panel modeled after the CentERpanel in the Netherlands. At present, there are approximately 2,500 ALP respondents, representative of the general US population, and as of December 2007 the sample consisted of about 1,000 individuals aged 40 and older. ALP respondents are recruited through the monthly survey of the University of Michigan's Survey Research Center (SRC). This is the leading US consumer sentiment survey, incorporating the long-standing Survey of Consumer Attitudes (SCA), and yields the widely used Index of Consumer Expectations. Respondents in the panel either use their own computer to log on to the Internet or are supplied with a Web TV. This improves representativeness by allowing respondents lacking Internet access to participate in the panel.

About once a month, ALP respondents receive an email with a request to visit the ALP website and fill out questionnaires on the Internet. Typically an interview takes less than 30 minutes. Respondents are paid an incentive of about $20 per thirty minutes of interviewing (and proportionately less if an interview is shorter). Questions cover a wide range of topics, including health status, preferences over retirement, social preferences, and investment games, to study how people make financial decisions. The environment facilitates extensive survey experimentation, aiming for optimal presentation of information to respondents, gauged through the use of visual displays and requests for feedback to and from respondents.

Sample construction and summary statistics

For this analysis, we merged data collected from the same individuals over multiple waves of the ALP Monthly Surveys (MS). Information about income and asset portfolios is collected in wave 1 (MS1), risk aversion

TABLE 5.1 American Life Panel sample summary statistics

Statistic	Value
Sex (%)	
Female	56.3
Age (years)	
Mean	54.7
Median	54.0
Annual 2002 Income*	
Mean ($)	206,523
Median ($)	61,000
Education (%)	
Grade school only	0.2
Some high school	1.9
HS grad	13.0
Some college	34.3
College grad	26.6
Higher degree	24.0
Percent owning stocks (including mutual funds)	68.0

Notes: Sample is based on 533 observations. *: Only available for 462 observations.

Source: Authors' calculations; see text.

measures in waves 2 and 3 (MS2 and MS3), and a detailed assessment of financial knowledge in wave 5 (MS5).

As the ALP is ongoing, the design is such that new respondents are recruited to the panel monthly. For this reason, the composition of the sample changes over time.[2] The sample for most of the analysis in this chapter consists of 533 observations, for which we have complete information on financial literacy, asset ownership, and at least one experimental measure of risk aversion (described later in the text). Table 5.1 provides summary statistics, which illustrate that the unweighted sample is clearly not typical of the US population. Mean age is approximately 55 in each sample, with a slight female majority. Respondents are better off and better educated than average, with median incomes of above $60,000 and over 80 percent having some education above high school level. Most strikingly, almost 70 percent own stocks.

A key variable needed to model demand is risk aversion, which we model here as a categorical variable based on the Barsky et al. (1997). This was elicited in MS2 of the ALP using hypothetical lotteries over lifetime income. Others, including van Rooij et al. (2007), have also adopted this measure when respondents are asked to imagine that they are the only income earner in their household but they have to change jobs due to allergies that require that they move. The first job guarantees total family income for life, while the second has uncertain income. Respondents are not given any information about nonmonetary attributes of each job. Respondents then choose between guaranteed lifetime income 'c' at current levels, and a 50/50 gamble that would double income or cut it by different proportions $(1 - \lambda)$. An individual maximizing the expected value of utility '$U(\cdot)$' will select the safe option if $(1/2)\,U(2c) + (1/2)\,U(\lambda c) < U(c)$.

In the survey, the respondent was first asked to choose between the safe option and a 50/50 chance of doubling income or cutting income by 1/3. If the safe option was chosen, the respondent was presented with a choice of the safe option and a 50/50 chance of doubling income or cutting income by 1/5. If the safe option was again chosen, the respondent was asked to choose between the safe option and a 50/50 chance of doubling income or cutting income by 1/10, and then the set of questions was complete. If the risky option was chosen in the first question, the respondent was presented with a choice of the safe option and a 50/50 chance of doubling income or cutting income by 1/2. If the risky option was again chosen, the respondent was asked to choose between the safe option and a 50/50 chance of doubling income or cutting income by 3/4 and then the set of questions was complete. To measure risk aversion, we categorize individuals into groups based on the threshold value of λ, at which the respondent is willing to switch from the safe to the risky option: the more risk averse he/she is, the less he/she is willing to gamble with lifetime income.[3]

Measuring financial illiteracy: basic and advanced questions

The battery of questions for the evaluation of financial knowledge fielded in MS5 allow the respondent to refuse to answer, which means that he or she chooses to skip the question and move ahead in the survey.[4] In MS5, this occurs at a very low frequency, at most once for any of the questions listed later. In the first *basic* module, respondents are asked five questions listed in Table 5.2, each of which addresses a particular financial concept. These questions cover respondents' ability to perform simple calculations, understand how compound interest works, and understand inflation. Respondents are also asked to answer an *advanced* module, including specific questions that address higher-order knowledge about investing (e.g., van Rooij et al., 2007). These questions assess knowledge of assets, risk diversification, the working of market institutions, and the relationship between bond prices and interest rates. These questions, and the responses, are also listed in Table 5.2.

As one might expect, this sample is very financially knowledgeable, relative to the population. We benchmark this result using the nationally

TABLE 5.2 Financial literacy assessment questions (%)

	American Life Panel	Health and Retirement Study
Basic questions		

A. Compound interest

1. Suppose you had $100 in a savings account and the interest rate was 2% per year. After 5 years, how much do you think you would have in the account if you left the money to grow?

	American Life Panel	Health and Retirement Study
(i) More than $102	92.3	67.1
(ii) Exactly $102	2.3	22.2*
(iii) Less than $102	3.2	
(iv) Do not know	2.3	9.4

2. Suppose you had $100 in a savings account and the interest rate is 20% per year, and you never withdraw money or interest payments. After 5 years, how much would you have in this account in total?

	American Life Panel
(i) More than $200	77.7
(ii) Exactly $200	15.6
(iii) Less than $200	4.1
(iv) Do not know	2.6

B. Inflation

3. Imagine that the interest rate on your savings account was 1% per year and inflation was 2% per year. After 1 year, how much would you be able to buy with the money in this account?

	American Life Panel	Health and Retirement Study
(i) More or exactly the same as today	0.9	13.4
(ii) Exactly the same	3.0	**
(iii) Less than today	94.2	75.2
(iv) Do not know	1.9	9.4

4. Suppose that in the year 2010, your income has doubled and prices of all goods have doubled too. In 2010, how much will you be able to buy with your income?

	American Life Panel
(i) More than today	3.2
(ii) The same	78.8
(iii) Less than today	16.7
(iv) Do not know	1.3

C. Time value of money

5. Assume a friend inherits $10,000 today and his sibling inherits $10,000 3 years from now. Who is richer because of the inheritance?

	American Life Panel
(i) My friend	77.6
(ii) His sibling	4.7
(iii) They are equally rich	10.2
(iv) Do not know	7.5

Advanced questions

Institutions 1

1. Which of the following statements describes the main function of the stock market?

	American Life Panel
(i) The stock market helps to predict stock earnings	10.0
(ii) The stock market results in an increase in the price of stocks	1.3
(iii) The stock market brings people who want to buy stocks together with those who want to sell stocks	75.9
(iv) None of the above	7.5
(v) Do not know	5.3

(*continued*)

Table 5.2 Continued

	American Life Panel	Health and Retirement Study
Institutions 2		
2. Which of the following statements is correct?		
(i) Once one invests in a mutual fund, one cannot withdraw the money in the first year	1.5	
(ii) Mutual funds can invest in several assets, for example invest in both stocks and bonds	72.9	
(iii) Mutual funds pay a guaranteed rate of return which depends on their past performance	6.8	
(iv) None of the above	4.0	
(v) Do not know	14.9	
Returns 1		
3. Considering a long time period (e.g., 10 or 20 years), which asset normally gives the highest return?		
(i) Savings accounts	1.3	
(ii) Bonds	18.1	
(iii) Stocks	70.9	
(iv) Do not know	9.8	
Volatility 1		
4. Normally, which asset displays the highest fluctuations over time?		
(i) Savings accounts	1.5	
(ii) Bonds	1.7	
(iii) Stocks	90.0	
(iv) Do not know	6.8	
Volatility 2		
5. Stocks are normally riskier than bonds.		
(i) True	82.6	
(ii) False	4.1	
(iii) Do not know	13.1	
Bond prices 1		
6. If the interest rate falls, what should happen to bond prices?		
(i) Rise	37.9	
(ii) Fall	27.6	
(iii) Stay the same	13.2	
(iv) Do not know	21.2	
Diversification 1		
7. Buying a company stock usually provides a safer return than a stock mutual fund.		
(i) True	4.5	13.2
(ii) False	78.8	52.3
(iii) Do not know	16.5	33.7
Diversification 2		
8. When an investor spreads his money among different assets, does the risk of losing money.		
(i) Increase	4.9	
(ii) Decrease	81.9	
(iii) Stay the same	7.0	
(iv) Do not know	6.2	

Notes: Numbers may not add up to exactly 100% due to refusals. *: The HRS study gave as an answer option 'Exactly or less than $102' which is the statistic reported here.
** The HRS study did not give 'Exactly the same' as an answer option for this question.

Source: Authors' calculations; see text.

representative 2004 HRS described by Lusardi and Mitchell (2007), focusing on adults over the age of 50. Table 5.2 displays the answers to a subset of the MS5 questions that are the same as three questions administered by Lusardi and Mitchell in the HRS module; the second column shows the comparable results from the (unweighted) HRS sample. There are two principal explanations for the observed difference: mode effects and sample selection. Mode effects refer to the fact that presentations on a computer screen may affect respondents' ability to answer compared to the HRS, which is conducted on the phone. In addition, ALP respondents may also be able to receive help in answering the survey, which is unobservable. Dominitz and Hung (2006) analyze the gap in financial literacy between the MS and the HRS-derived sample in detail. They find that HRS respondents with Internet access display higher levels of financial literacy than respondents without Internet access. While difference in responses across the two surveys may result from sample selection, this issue remains to be further examined. To construct our financial literacy score, we follow van Rooij et al. (2007),[5] but depart from it in some key respects.

First, we construct an index for basic financial knowledge by performing principal components analysis (PCA) on binary indicators for the correct answers to the five questions in the basic module. We retain the first principal component and treat the score for this component as our index for basic knowledge. Next, instead of performing the same exercise for advanced financial literacy, we reclassify the 'advanced' questions about investment into two mutually exclusive groups, based on their relevance to stock market participation. We group knowledge of the relative risk/return of stocks, the stock market, stock mutual funds, and diversification (Questions 1–5, 7, and 8 in Table 5.3) together as being directly related to the decision to participate in the stock market. The remaining question, knowledge of the inverse relation between bond prices and interest rates, is not directly related (Question 6 in Table 5.2).

It is important to note that financial illiteracy (which we define as not having any knowledge of financial matters) is distinct from having mistaken subjective beliefs, and has different implications for behavior. If individuals are ambiguity-averse, they prefer known risks over unknown risks. In this case, a financially illiterate individual with no financial knowledge will be less likely to participate than someone with some knowledge about stocks and their relative risks/returns (Gollier, 2006). On the other hand, consider someone who erroneously believes that stocks are not risky and have high returns. Such an individual is expected to be more likely to participate in the stock market, compared to the correctly informed person.

We therefore explicitly emphasize the difference between 'Don't know' responses to knowledge questions (which measure illiteracy or lack of knowledge, and therefore should reduce stock market participation, all

TABLE 5.3 Multivariate OLS estimates: individual financial literacy questions and stock market participation

	(1)	(2)	(3)	(4)	(5)	(6)	(7)
	Own any stock	Own any stock	Own any stock	Own any stock	Own any stock	Own any stock	Own any stock
Don't know: Institutions 1	−0.25** (0.09)						
Don't know: Institutions 2		−0.29*** (0.05)					
Don't know: Returns			−0.29*** (0.07)				
Don't know: Volatility 1				−0.20* (0.08)			
Don't know: Volatility 2					−0.19*** (0.06)		
Don't know: Diversification 1						−0.35*** (0.05)	
Don't know: Diversification 2							−0.26** (0.08)
N	533	533	533	533	533	533	533
R-squared	0.12	0.15	0.14	0.12	0.13	0.18	0.13

Notes: Mean of dependent variable 'owning any stock' = 0.68. All specifications include constant term and controls for gender, age, marital status, education, retirement status, and risk aversion. Upper threshold for p-values: *** 0.01, ** 0.05, and * 0.10.

Source: Authors' calculations; see text.

else equal) and incorrect responses (which may or may not reduce participation, depending on the question). We focus on the former, and control for the latter. To measure illiteracy, we construct an index for ignorance of stock market investment by performing PCA on seven binary indicators for 'Don't know' answers to the seven questions in the advanced module related to stock market investment, retaining one principal component and treating the score for this component as our index for stock market investment illiteracy.

Empirical analysis

In the multivariate analysis, we estimate equations of the following form, with stock ownership as the dependent variable Y:

$$Y_i = \beta X_i + \delta Z_i + \epsilon_i$$

where X_i is a vector of measures of interest and Z_i is a vector of individual-level control variables. With a binary dependent variable, when estimated by ordinary least squares (OLS), this specification is directly interpretable as a linear probability model. The vector of controls includes controls for age and education, with the lowest category in both cases omitted; gender; and, importantly, risk aversion. Our main hypothesis of interest is that $\beta < 0$ for our measures of stock-related investment ignorance.

Ordinary least squares/probit estimation

Tables 5.3 and 5.4 present results from estimating the impact of binary indicators for answering 'Don't know' to the individual questions about stock market investments. Individually, each of the regressors has the expected negative and strongly significant sign. We note also that the effects of most demographic controls also have the anticipated signs (not shown). Participation is strongly increasing with general education, and married

TABLE 5.4 Probit estimates: individual financial literacy questions and stock market participation

	(1)	(2)	(3)	(4)	(5)	(6)	(7)
	Own any stock	Own any stock	Own any stock	Own any stock	Own any stock	Own any stock	Own any stock
Don't know: Institutions 1	−0.27** (0.10)						
Don't know: Institutions 2		−0.31*** (0.06)					
Don't know: Returns			−0.30*** (0.08)				
Don't know: Volatility 1				−0.21* (0.09)			
Don't know: Volatility 2					−0.21** (0.07)		
Don't know: Diversification 1						−0.37*** (0.06)	
Don't know: Diversification 2							−0.28** (0.09)
N	533	533	533	533	533	533	533

Notes: Mean of dependent variable 'owning any stock' = 0.68. All specifications include controls for gender, age, marital status, education, retirement status, and risk aversion. Upper threshold for p-values: *** 0.01, ** 0.05, and * 0.10.

Source: Authors' calculations; see text.

TABLE 5.5 OLS/probit estimates: stock market illiteracy and participation

	(1)	(2)	(3)	(4)
	Own any stock	Own any stock	Own any stock	Own any stock
	OLS	Probit	OLS	Probit
Stock market illiteracy index			–0.13*** (0.02)	–0.14*** (0.02)
Don't know: Institutions 1	–0.00 (0.09)	–0.01 (0.11)		
Don't know: Institutions 2	–0.15* (0.06)	–0.17* (0.08)		
Don't know: Returns	–0.18* (0.08)	–0.20* (0.09)		
Don't know 4: Volatility 1	0.04 (0.09)	0.04 (0.09)		
Don't know 5: Volatility 2	–0.05 (0.06)	–0.07 (0.07)		
Don't know: Diversification 1	–0.24*** (0.06)	–0.25*** (0.07)		
Don't know: Diversification 2	0.00 (0.09)	–0.01 (0.10)		
N	533	533	533	533
R-squared	0.20		0.17	
F-stat: all DK variables = 0	8.75			
p-value	0.00			

Notes: All specifications include constant term (for OLS) and controls for gender, age, marital status, education, retirement status, and risk aversion. Upper threshold for *p*-values: *** 0.01, ** 0.05, and * 0.10.

Source: Authors' calculations; see text.

couples are also more likely to hold stocks. It appears at first that participation is increasing in our age dummies, but the overall effect is counterbalanced by the large negative and significant coefficient on retired status. With the presence of controls, risk aversion is not independently significant.

Table 5.5 presents the results of including all the binary indicators together in the OLS and probit regressions. The results show effects that are either negative and significant, or not significantly different from zero, which is consistent, but the high degree of correlation between the literacy variables makes these results hard to interpret meaningfully. We do, however, strongly reject the null hypothesis that all the coefficients on the literacy variables are jointly zero (see Column 1). Finally, Columns 3 and 4 present the results using the stock market illiteracy index alone, which is normalized to a mean of 0 and a standard deviation of 1. The estimates suggest that stock-related

TABLE 5.6 OLS estimates: stock market illiteracy, beliefs, and participation

	(1)	(2)	(3)	(4)
	Own any stock	Own any stock	Own any stock	Own any stock
Stock market illiteracy index	−0.13*** (0.02)	−0.12*** (0.02)	−0.10*** (0.02)	−0.10*** (0.02)
Basic financial knowledge index		0.05** (0.02)	0.06** (0.02)	0.06** (0.02)
Overestimate risk relative to returns		−0.13** (0.05)	−0.10 (0.06)	
Underestimate risk relative to returns		−0.04 (0.13)	0.06 (0.14)	
Don't know: Bond pricing		−0.02 (0.05)	0.00 (0.06)	
Log of 2002 income			0.05** (0.02)	0.06** (0.02)
Constant	0.25 (0.15)	0.27 (0.15)	−0.14 (0.23)	−0.18 (0.23)
N	533	533	462	462
R-squared	0.17	0.20	0.19	0.18

Notes: All specifications include constant term and controls for gender, age, marital status, education, retirement status, and risk aversion. Upper threshold for p-values: *** 0.01, ** 0.05, and * 0.10.

Source: Authors' calculations; see text.

investment illiteracy is significantly negatively related to stock market participation, with an effect of 12–13 percent. The OLS and probit analyses deliver qualitatively similar results in all these specifications, so for ease of exposition, we refer exclusively to OLS from here on.

Table 5.6 introduces additional controls to the initial estimates, which are reproduced in Column 1. In Column 2, we introduce controls for other types of knowledge, primarily the basic financial knowledge index of van Rooij et al. (2007). Adding controls reduces the estimated impact of illiteracy, but the result is generally robust. The impact of basic knowledge is positive and significant, although relatively small. In Columns 2 and 3, we also control for unrelated investment knowledge (bond pricing) and incorrect beliefs. First, we include an indicator for not knowing the relationship between bond prices and interest rates, along with two proxies for having mistaken beliefs about the relative risk/returns of stocks. If an investor believes that stocks are safer than bonds/saving and have a higher return, we regard this as having underestimated risk relative to returns. On the flip side, we treat the belief that stocks are riskier than bonds or saving and have a lower return as having overestimated risk relative to returns. In line with our earlier arguments, knowledge of the mechanics of bond pricing or the lack thereof has no economically or statistically significant relation to stock market participation. Finally, the model suggests that wealth is excludable, but this arises solely as a consequence of our choice of utility function. For completeness, therefore, we also wish to introduce wealth as a control. Unfortunately, the ALP does not contain a comprehensive measure of wealth. In Columns 3 and 4, we include reported log 2002 income instead. The coefficients on our proxies for mistaken beliefs show that investors who overestimate the risk/return tradeoff are less likely to participate (although this effect is not robust to controlling for wealth), while there is no consistent or significant effect for investors who underestimate the risk/return tradeoff. Our wealth proxy positively affects participation. However, we note that the estimated coefficient on the illiteracy index is robust to this inclusion. Our preferred specification is thus Column 4, which suggests that an increase of one standard deviation above the mean level of illiteracy results in a 10 percent fall in stock market participation.

Instrumental variables analysis

Because linear regression may not lead us to correct inferences about the causal link between financial literacy and stock market participation, in this section, we turn to an instrumental-variables strategy as a check on our results. We test the validity of a set of candidate instruments, by checking for relevance and exogeneity of the instrument set, and select our preferred instruments. We then test for the endogeneity of our stock market illiteracy index.

It should be noted that endogenity can lead to biased coefficients, but the presence as well as direction of overall bias is not clear *a priori*. Endogeneity could lead to bias in two directions. First, intrinsic unobservable characteristics may cause some people to seek information because they want to improve their financial results. The relationship between literacy and stock market participation will be underestimated if individuals who are strongly ambiguity-averse may respond more strongly to ignorance about the stock market by not participating. Also, if people are automatically enrolled in stock-holding retirement funds, we would expect that people with little or no knowledge of the stock market may be made to invest in stocks. On the other hand, learning-by-doing would instead lead to overestimation (van Rooij et al., 2007). Selection may also play a role: financially literate investors may be better at investing, and unsuccessful, less literate investors may be more likely to leave the market. There is also room for measurement error, as measures of illiteracy may have a significant amount of noise.

TABLE 5.7 Testing for valid instrumental variables (IV)

	(1)	(2)	(3)	(4)
	Own any stock	Own any stock	Own any stock	Own any stock
	2SLS	2SLS	2SLS	GMM
	IV(2)	IV(3)	IV(4)	IV(4)
Stock-related investment illiteracy index	−0.80* (0.39)	−0.75 (0.60)	−0.11 (0.07)	−0.11 (0.07)
Basic financial knowledge index	−0.07 (0.08)	−0.06 (0.12)	0.06* (0.03)	0.06* (0.03)
Anderson LR stat (under-identification)	4.87	1.81	56.89	56.89
Anderson LR stat: p-value	0.09	0.40	0.00	0.00
Cragg-Douglas F-statistic (weak instruments)	2.37	0.88	29.29	29.29
Sargan test statistic (over-identification)	0.00	0.00	0.22	
Sargan test statistic: p-value	1.00	0.99	0.64	
Pagan-Hall test statistic (homoskedasticity)	2.53	1.64	18.07	18.15
Pagan-Hall test statistic: p-value	1.00	1.00	0.20	0.20
N	462	462	462	462

Notes: All specifications include constant term and controls for gender, age, marital status, education, retirement status, and risk aversion. Upper threshold for p-values: *** 0.01, ** 0.05, and * 0.10. Also included are: IV(1), availability of financial education in high school; IV(2), availability of financial education in workplace; IV(3), self-assessed degree of economics education; IV(4), no knowledge of bond pricing.

Source: Authors' calculations; see text.

As the degree and sign on the bias are theoretically ambiguous, we take an empirical approach to accounting for this potential issue, using IV. In the ALP, there are four potential candidate instruments. We have two supply-related education variables: the availability of financial education in high school and in the workplace. Drawing on Bernheim et al. (2001), high school education may be determined largely by curricular mandates and so may be considered exogenous. Workplace education is more salient to the individual, but less plausibly exogenous. In particular, Bayer et al. (1996) suggest that employers tend to offer training on a remedial basis; that is, when participation by lower-wage employees in the 401(k) plan is low enough to fail discrimination testing.

We have also available a measure of self-reported economics education constructed by asking respondents how much of their education was devoted to economics. Responses are categorized on a scale of 0 (none) to 3 (all). van Rooij et al. (2007) argue that self-reported economics education is a valid instrument in the Netherlands because economics education is available in high school and confined to formal schooling. There are no retirement seminars, as the vast majority of Dutch employees participate in mandatory, collective defined benefit (DB) pensions.

Novel to the analysis is our additional instrument, namely bond pricing knowledge. Here, the identification assumption is based on the notion that bond pricing knowledge, in theory, should not determine the stock market participation decision, but knowledge of bond pricing is likely to be highly correlated with aspects of financial literacy that are. The exclusion restriction is supported by estimates shown previously which demonstrated that the lack of knowledge of bond pricing has no direct impact on stock market participation. This is our preferred IV candidate.

Table 5.7 offers estimates of the specification using two-stage least squares, with the availability of high school financial education in combination with each of our three remaining candidates as instruments included in the first-stage regression. Basic financial knowledge and log annual income are also regressors, in addition to the demographic controls. In each specification, we check for exogenity by reporting the Sargan–Hansen test of overidentifying restrictions. The joint null hypothesis is that the additional instrument is uncorrelated with the error term, and that the excluded instruments are correctly excluded from the estimated equation. Under the null, the test statistic is distributed as chi-squared in the number of overidentifying restrictions. To check for relevance, we also report the Anderson (1984) canonical correlations test, a likelihood-ratio test of whether the equation is identified (i.e., that the excluded instruments are correlated with the endogenous regressors).[6]

The results in Table 5.7 are striking. Column 1 shows that using financial education in the workplace marginally passes the test for relevance and fails the weak-instrument criterion. In Column 2, we also find that the instrument suggested by van Rooij et al. (2007) is not useful, as it does not pass the test of relevancy, nor does it satisfy the weak instruments criterion.[7] By contrast, in Column 3, our preferred candidate performs well with respect to all three tests. The bias introduced by the other two candidate instruments is clearly reflected in the relative size of the estimates.[8]

Specification testing using valid instruments

We note that in the two-stage least squares (2SLS) specification of our choice, the coefficient on stock market illiteracy is negative, but that it is now significant only at a 10 percent level ($p = 0.07$). Given that we have now established a set of valid IV, it is possible to address our previous concern about the potential endogeneity of literacy, which otherwise cannot be verified. We therefore test for endogeneity using both the Wu-Hausman and Durbin–Wu-Hausman tests. The results show that we do not reject the hypothesis of exogenity under either test.[9] This suggests that the difference between the OLS and IV estimates is, in practice, small enough to allow us to treat literacy as exogenous. That is, endogeneity is not sufficiently serious as to warrant the less efficient method of IV estimation (which in our small sample, again, may represent a significant compromise). We can therefore legitimately treat the more precise OLS results as our preferred estimates.[10]

Further analysis

Planners

One major shortcoming of the analysis is our inability to account for respondents' use of investment professionals and planners. The use of planners complicates the analysis, as planners generally suggest investment in stocks and may themselves impart literacy. In the ALP, we have information on the reported incidence of consultation with financial planners for retirement planning, but the question was asked only to people who indicated they had started thinking about retirement and only about retirement planners, rather than to people who used financial planners for all investment decisions. Moreover, the questions were not asked of the self- or otherwise employed. Nevertheless, one-third of our sample did report using a planner. For this group, we find that individuals who had consulted a planner were much more likely to invest in stocks. But conditional on having a planner, the effect of financial illiteracy was not significant. Individuals who have not consulted a planner, conversely, were less likely to invest. More importantly, the impact of own illiteracy was twice as large and strongly significant. In other words, the evidence is consistent with the use of planners offsetting the effects of poor financial literacy, and for those without planners, the basic results are strengthened (Table 5.8).

Varying risk aversion measures

As an alternative to the Barsky et al. (1997) measure of risk aversion used thus far, a separate measure of risk aversion is available for a subset of respondents using the multiple price list method proposed by Holt and Laury (2002). Comparing the effects of using the two different experimentally based risk aversion measures, we find our basic results qualitatively unchanged.[11]

TABLE 5.8 Split-sample analysis with and without a planner

	(1)	(2)
	Own any stock	Own any stock
	With planner	Without planner
Stock market illiteracy index	−0.05 (0.06)	−0.08** (0.03)
Basic financial knowledge index	0.02 (0.04)	0.06* (0.03)
N	157	305
R-squared	0.16	0.18

Notes: All specifications include constant term and controls for log 2002 income, gender, age, marital status, education, retirement status, and risk aversion. Upper threshold for *p*-values: *** 0.01, ** 0.05, and * 0.10.

Source: Authors' calculations; see text.

Other social/behavioral factors: trust and social interaction

Another reason people may not invest in the stock market may be that they lack trust in financial institutions. Guiso et al. (2005) report that 'trusting' individuals were significantly more likely to buy stocks and risky assets and, conditional on investing in stock, they invested a larger share of their wealth. Their proxy for trust was a binary indicator for the level of generalized trust, based on a question asked in the World Values Survey: 'Generally speaking, would you say that most people can be trusted or that you have to be very careful in dealing with people?' The effect of this indicator was sizable: trusting others increased the probability of buying stock by 50 percent of the average and raised the share invested.

The ALP lacks questions that address 'generalized trust', but we can construct an alternative measure of trust based on a module designed to gather subjective expectations of particular events. Guiso et al. (2005) argue that trust increases investment, based on investor perceptions of the risk of expropriation. By the same logic, we include as the relevant measure the subjective probability of having property stolen in the next year.

In related literature, Hong et al. (2004) found that social interaction positively influences stock market participation, with those who reported interaction with neighbors or church attendance participating more in the stock market. Again, we lack a perfect proxy for these variables in the ALP. Instead, we use two other subjective measures, including whether or not the person felt alone often, and whether the person participated in a team or individual sport.

In other results not reported in detail here, we find our results are robust to the inclusion of these factors. Notably, we find no effect from subjective property expropriation risk, or from the subjective assessment of being alone. We do, however, find that individuals who participated in sports (including team sports) were more likely to hold stocks, consistent with the findings of Hong et al. (2004).

Conclusion

This study has suggested that ignorance of financial matters, or financial illiteracy, negatively affects stock market participation, even for people whose wealth, education, and financial literacy are high relative to the general population. This finding is robust to the use of different risk metrics and background controls including income, social factors, and behavioral proxies for other explanations suggested in the literature. The external validity of the survey findings must, of course, be regarded with an eye to the selection inherent in the sample.[12] However, the findings do suggest that lack of familiarity with finance can be a meaningful impediment to financial participation, and for individuals who are highly averse to the unknown, building a basic awareness of investing may affect the long-term ability to accumulate wealth.

Several potential avenues are available for future research. First, the model does not account for how time-discounting and compounding enter the asset allocation problem, nor do we model life-cycle-related considerations, which may be relevant given the older age profile of our sample. Second, the empirical analysis is restricted to the binary stock participation decision; a natural next step is to move in the direction of structural estimation of the model's parameters. Third, the construction of literacy indexes is in itself a topic for extensive further research. Work currently underway with the ALP explores other, more sophisticated approaches, including a literacy assessment that directly addresses more functionally diverse areas. Fourth, other types of behavior (financial and otherwise) and their relationship to financial literacy remain to be explored. Finally, one interesting future topic for complementary research is the experimental elicitation of ambiguity preferences, allowing us to further explore the link between illiteracy and behavior.

These results shed additional light on the debates over financial literacy, and provide policymakers and practitioners with new evidence linking financial literacy to financial behavior.

Acknowledgments

The author thanks Arie Kapteyn, Angela Hung, Annamaria Lusardi, and Jeff Dominitz for guidance, Sandy Chien for direction regarding the American Life Panel data, Prakash Kannan for helpful discussions, Erik Meijer for specific remarks on information aggregation, and especially Daniel Kopf for outstanding research assistance. This work was conducted while the author was a Summer Associate at the RAND Corporation.

Endnotes

[1] For a more theoretical treatment of this relationship based on an extension of the standard portfolio choice model, the reader is referred to Yoong (2007), which explores in more depth the rationale for why only some types of financial literacy affect participation.

[2] For a description of the panel, its methodology, and to access the data subject to registration, see http://www.rand.org/labor/roybalfd/american_life.html

[3] As discussed by Barsky et al. (1997), under the assumption of relative risk aversion (CRRA), increasing values of this categorical measure can be used to compute (increasing) numerical bounds for the coefficient of risk aversion.

[4] The questions designed by Annamaria Lusardi and Olivia Mitchell correspond to the two modules in the DNB Household Survey designed by van Rooij et al. (2007). Almost all the same questions are asked, with identical wording.

[5] In very brief, the authors first conduct a factor analysis which indicates that there are two main factors with different loadings on the two separate groups of questions. Based on this initial finding, the authors generate two indices by performing separate factor analyses using all the questions in each of the two modules separately, retaining one latent factor in each case which is interpreted as 'basic' and 'advanced literacy'. In the case of basic literacy, they use a binary indicator for the correct answer to each question, as the proportion of respondents indicating ignorance is low. In the case of advanced literacy, the authors account for ignorance versus mistakes by including both binary indicators for correct answers as well as 'Don't know' answers. For a more detailed technical description that does better justice to the methodology underlying the advanced literacy index, please see Appendix A of van Rooij et al. (2007).

[6] The null hypothesis of the test is that the matrix of reduced form coefficients has rank $= K - 1$, where K is number of regressors, that is, the equation is under-identified. We also test for weakness by reporting the Cragg–Donald F-statistic from the first stage regression, which must be sufficiently large relative to the Stock–Yogo critical values (which we will take to be the rule-of-thumb value of 10).

To pass both the exogenity and relevance criteria, we must not fail to reject the null under the Sargan–Hansen test for exogenity, but reject the Anderson canonical correlations test for relevance. We also look for an F-statistic larger than 10 to avoid weak-instruments bias.

[7] In a separate analysis, available from the author, we replicate the analysis of van Rooij et al. (2007) using the ALP sample, and obtain qualitatively similar results for basic literacy. We find, however, that even under their specification, the instrument is not valid for the ALP.

[8] We also report the Pagan-Hall test for heteroskedasticity in an IV regression. If heteroskedasticity is in fact present, the generalized-methods-of-moments (GMM) estimator is more efficient. However, the GMM estimator has poor small-sample properties, and in particular tends to over-reject the null. Given the small sample size in this analysis, this is a significant issue and it is not desirable to use GMM unless necessary. In Column 3, we would very marginally accept the null of no heteroskedasticity at an 80 percent level of significance. In Column 4, we therefore replicate the analysis using a GMM estimator. Comparison of Columns 3 and 4 reveals that the results are not significantly altered. Given also that we do not strongly reject the null, we choose to proceed without implementing GMM.

[9] The test statistics are Wu-Hausman F test [0.044]; $F(1,447)$ p-value [0.84]; Durbin–Wu-Hausman chi-squared test [0.045]; and Chi-sq(1) p-value [0.82].

[10] An important caveat to the straightforward application of PCA in the construction of the indices is that this technique, strictly speaking, is developed for continuous variables, rather than discrete data. Most of the theoretical results, including the implicitly used consistency of the estimates of the factor loadings, are derived under the normality assumption. More sophisticated techniques based on polychoric correlations may be adapted to further refine the index.

Alternative methods of data aggregation were also attempted, including the latent factor analysis in van Rooij et al. (2007). It should be noted that this analysis is also subject to the critique earlier, and that the factor analysis model should instead be estimated from the tetrachoric correlation matrix. When a latent factor model was estimated using maximum-likelihood methods, however, we arrived at a Heywood solution for the basic knowledge index, meaning that the variance estimates are negative. The source of this problem may lie in the current small sample size. As the ALP sample becomes larger, this analysis will be revisited.

[11] The Holt and Laury (2002) method requires respondents to participate in a series of lotteries with small hypothetical cash prizes. Respondents are asked to choose between two lotteries, A or B. If the person indicates that he/she is indifferent, the choice of A or B will be made randomly. After each decision, the chosen lottery is played and payoffs realized. The respondent faces ten such decisions. The payoffs are specified such that a risk/neutral individual will pick option A, the safer lotteries, four times before switching to option B. Note that in the last lottery, all respondents should pick B, the higher payoff, as this is now a certainty. We use the number of times the safe lottery is chosen as a measure of increasing risk aversion.

As the Holt and Laury (2002) questions are fielded in a relatively recent wave of the survey for which data is currently being gathered, we have a significantly smaller number of observations where both measures have been elicited. Column 1 of Table 5.7 shows our original preferred estimates using the Barsky et al. measure

(1997) and the larger sample size. Retaining only the smaller sample of 228, we compare the results using the Barsky et al. measure (1997) (Column 2) and Holt and Laury (2002) (Column 3). The results are (surprisingly) robust to the use of both measures, and to the sharp decline in sample size.

[12] We might speculate that, in a population that is less wealthy and less educated, literacy might be more of a barrier to investment, but this remains to be investigated, potentially in future waves of the Health and Retirement Survey.

References

Anderson, T. W. (1984). *An Introduction to Multivariate Statistical Analysis.* New York, NY: John Wiley and Sons.

Agarwal, S., G. Amromin, I. Ben-David, S. Chomsisengphet, and D. D. Evanoff (2011). 'Financial Counseling, Financial Literacy, and Household Decision-Making,' in O. S. Mitchell and A. Lusardi, eds, *Financial Literacy: Implications for Retirement Security and the Financial Marketplace.* Oxford, UK: Oxford University Press.

Barsky, R. B., F. T. Juster, M. S. Kimball, and M. D. Shapiro (1997). 'Preference Parameters and Behavioral Heterogeneity: An Experimental Approach in the Health and Retirement Study,' *The Quarterly Journal of Economics,* 112: 729–58.

Bayer, P. J., B. D. Bernheim, and J. K. Scholz (1996). 'The Effects of Financial Education in the Workplace: Evidence from a Survey of Employers,' NBER Working Paper No. 5655. Cambridge, MA: National Bureau of Economic Research.

Bernheim, B. D., D. M. Garrett, and D. M. Maki (2001). 'Education and Saving: The Long-Term Effects of High School Financial Curriculum Mandates,' *Journal of Public Economics,* 80(3): 435–65.

Braunstein, S. and C. Welch (2002). 'Financial Literacy: An Overview of Practice, Research and Policy,' *Federal Reserve Bulletin,* November: 445–57.

Campbell, J. Y. (2006). 'Household Finance,' *Journal of Finance,* 61: 1553–604.

Christelis, D., T. Jappelli, and M. Padula (2005). *Health Risk, Financial Information and Social Interactions: The Portfolio Choice of European Elderly Households.* Salerno, Italy: University of Salerno. http://www.csef.it/1st_C6/cjp_June16.pdf

——————(2006). 'Cognitive Abilities and Portfolio Choice,' Working Paper No. 157. Salerno, Italy: University of Salerno.

Cole, S. and G. K. Shastry (2009). 'Smart Money: The Effect of Education, Cognitive Ability, and Financial Literacy on Financial Market Participation,' Harvard Business School Working Paper 09-071. Cambridge, MA: Harvard University.

Constantinides, G. M., J. B. Donaldson, and R. Mehra (2002). 'Junior Can't Borrow: A New Perspective on the Equity Premium Puzzle,' *The Quarterly Journal of Economics,* 117: 269–96.

Davis, S. J., F. Kubler, and P. Willen (2006). 'Borrowing Costs and the Demand for Equity over the Life Cycle,' *The Review of Economics and Statistics,* 88: 348–62.

Dominitz, J. and A. Hung (2006). 'Financial Literacy in HRS and ALP,' Seminar Presentation, University of Michigan, September 2nd.

Duflo, E. and E. Saez (2003). 'The Role Of Information And Social Interactions In Retirement Plan Decisions: Evidence From A Randomized Experiment,' *The Quarterly Journal of Economics*, 118: 815–42.

Gollier, C. (2006). *Does Ambiguity Aversion Reinforce Risk Aversion? Applications to Portfolio Choices and Asset Pricing*. Toulouse, France: Institut d'Economie Industrielle (IDEI). http://old.nhh.no/sam/stabssem/2006/gollier-ambiguity5.pdf

Guiso, L. and T. Jappelli (2005). 'Awareness and Stock Market Participation,' *Review of Finance*, 9: 537–67.

——P. Sapienza, and L. Zingales (2005). 'Trusting the Stock Market,' NBER Working Paper No. 11648. Cambridge, MA: National Bureau of Economic Research.

Haliassos, M. and C. C. Bertaut (1995). 'Why Do So Few Hold Stocks?,' *The Economic Journal*, 105: 1110–29.

Hilgert, M. A., J. M. Hogarth, and S. G. Beverly (2003). 'Household Financial Management: The Connection between Knowledge and Behavior,' *Federal Reserve Bulletin*, July: 309–22.

Holt, C. A. and S. K. Laury (2002). 'Risk Aversion and Incentive Effects,' *American Economic Review*, 92: 1644–55.

Hong, H., J. D. Kubik, and J. C. Stein (2004). 'Social Interaction and Stock-Market Participation,' *Journal of Finance*, 59: 137–63.

Lusardi, A. and O. S. Mitchell (2006). 'Financial Literacy and Planning: Implications for Retirement Wellbeing,' PRC Working Paper 2006-01. Philadelphia, PA: Pension Research Council.

——————(2007). 'Financial Literacy and Retirement Planning: New Evidence from the RAND American Life Panel,' MRRC Working Paper 2007-157. Ann Arbor, MI: Michigan Retirement Research Center.

Martin, M. (2007). 'A Literature Review on the Effectiveness of Financial Education,' Working Paper 07-03. Richmond, VA: Federal Reserve Bank of Richmond.

van Rooij, M., A. Lusardi, and R. Alessie (2007). 'Financial Literacy and Stock Market Participation,' NBER Working Paper No. 13565. Cambridge, MA: National Bureau of Economic Research.

Vissing-Jorgensen, A. and O. P. Attanasio (2003). 'Stock-Market Participation, Intertemporal Substitution, and Risk-Aversion,' *American Economic Review*, 93: 383–91.

Yoong, J. (2007). *Essays in Development and Finance*. PhD Dissertation. Stanford, CA: Stanford University Department of Economics.

Part II

Evaluating Financial Literacy Interventions

Chapter 6

Fees, Framing, and Financial Literacy in the Choice of Pension Manager

Justine Hastings, Olivia S. Mitchell, and Eric Chyn

> 'If households make investment mistakes, it may be possible for financial economists to offer remedies that reduce the incidence and welfare costs of these mistakes.'
>
> —John Campbell, Presidential Address to the American Finance Association (2006)

Recent research and policy analysis has begun to explore the nexus between financial literacy and household saving for several reasons. First, financial literacy levels in the general population are remarkably low, both in the United States and elsewhere (Bernheim et al., 2001; Lusardi and Mitchell, 2007*a*, 2007*b*, 2007*c*, 2009; Hastings and Tejeda-Ashton, 2008) which poses grave concern about whether consumers are capable of making sensible saving and investment decisions (Hilgert et al., 2003; Lusardi and Mitchell, 2010). Second, financial products are growing increasingly complex (e.g., 'teaser rates' in credit cards and 'no-income-no-down-payment mortgages'), which would seem to undermine the long-term trend toward asking individuals to assume greater control over their retirement accounts and other investments (Campbell, 2006). Indeed, prior research finds that many people tend to be overly sensitive to framing of saving and investment decisions, chase past returns even in passively managed index funds, and take out too much debt (Ausubel, 1991; Benartzi and Thaler, 2001; Choi et al., 2007; Cronqvist and Thaler, 2004; Lusardi and Tufano, 2008; Ponce-Rodriguez, 2008). Furthermore, those who prove to be least financially literate also tend to be among the most economically vulnerable, such as minorities, the least-educated, women, and low earners (Lusardi and Mitchell, 2006, 2008, 2010). Consequently, those who most need financial skills and tools with which to make optimal financial decisions also prove to be the least well-equipped, rendering the already-disadvantaged even more vulnerable, and potentially impairing the efficient functioning of financial markets.

The present study offers a unique opportunity to evaluate the relationship between financial literacy and economic outcomes, exploring how the presentation of fees and charges for financial services can help people make the most cost-effective saving decisions. Specifically, we evaluate the role of framing in shaping peoples' awareness of fees and commissions associated with retirement saving. We ask whether people are more or less sensitive to pension fee information presented as gains versus losses, and we also evaluate whether less financially literate individuals are more or less sensitive to the way in which fees and commissions are presented.

The question of how people select pension fund managers and integrate fees into this decision process is particularly important in Chile, a nation that mandated private defined contribution (DC) pensions in 1981.[1] Yet even after almost thirty years of the AFP system (Asociación de Fondos de Pensiones), many participants appear to have only a rudimentary understanding of how these costs affect their pension accumulations (Arenas et al., 2008). In the present chapter, we draw on a new study that we conducted in cooperation with the Chilean Social Protection Survey (EPS, or Encuesta de Protección Social) to examine the factors that influence worker selection of pension fund managers and to assess how framing of pension costs might further influence this retirement choice. Our particular focus is to assess the degree to which financial illiteracy can be overcome via different ways of presenting pension fund fees and charges. We find that individuals with lower levels of education, income, and financial literacy depend more on employers, friends, and coworkers than on cost fundamentals when selecting a pension fund from a menu of possible offerings. We also find that these same types of individuals are more responsive to information framing when interpreting the relative benefits of different investment choices.

The discussion proceeds in three parts. First, we offer a brief background on the Chilean pension system and our experimental design. Next, we provide a descriptive analysis of selected characteristics of our sample population and the experimental results. A final section reviews the results, and concludes with some thoughts on the implications these results have on addressing issues of financial literacy and retirement planning.

Setting, experimental methodology, and data

Chile's national retirement system was privatized in 1981, and today pension accruals are substantial, since contributions total 10 percent of wages for workers in the formal sector. Fund managers charge a front-end load fee on contributions and invest the assets following a DC approach; these fees have a small but economically significant impact on investment returns. Workers must select which pension manager they wish to hire to manage their retirement accumulations, and only one manager can be selected at a time. Statistics on each fund manager's load and past return experience appear on the Chilean Government's Pension Superintendency website and are provided to participants in annual statements mailed to their residence. At present, the official government website reports monthly fees in pesos for each AFP relative to the cheapest AFP, while participant statements received annually present fees in annual percentage terms. Both of these approaches depict the data in terms of one-year results.

Despite the fact that the DC pension system has been in place in Chile for several decades, there is evidence that many people still do not understand the system's contribution and benefit structures. For instance, Arenas et al. (2008) report that many people do not know what contribution requirements are under the system, how much they pay in commissions, and how they have their funds invested. Mitchell et al. (2008) find that very few Chileans are aware of what commissions or fees are charged on their pension accruals. Moreover, this lack of understanding is concentrated among women, the lowest paid, and the least educated, the very groups most at risk of falling short of retirement saving.

For this reason, there is substantial interest in determining how to enhance participants' understanding and awareness of how fees and charges influence pension accumulations. One way to accomplish this is to determine whether people become more price-sensitive to fees when they are depicted in alternative formats. Specifically, a pilot study in Mexico (Hastings and Tejada-Ashton, 2008) suggested that giving workers information in pesos rather than annual percentage fees can alter how workers rank their pension fund options. That study did not, however, explore whether behavior is influenced more strongly when the *long-term* impact of gains or losses is illustrated.

In what follows, we report on a special experiment that we designed and implemented in the Chilean EPS to determine whether showing workers different information on pension fund fees alters respondents' responses regarding their ranking of pension funds on a menu of possible choices. Specifically, in the 2009 EPS survey, we randomly presented two choices to interviewees, showing them hypothetical pension outcomes in terms of gains and losses in pesos over a ten-year period. For each of the five AFPs in the system at the time of the survey, we calculated the expected balance for each surveyed individual using the past returns and commissions of the AFPs and each individual's wage, balance, age, and gender responses in the demographic section of the survey.[2] We hypothesize that individuals will be better able to understand the impact of higher AFP fees when these fees are reported as influencing the gains from contributing to a pension versus losses. To test this hypothesis, one set of respondents received a document showing how hypothetical AFP account balances would be anticipated to grow depending on each AFP's actual fees, where the results were projected over a ten-year period. The second group received a document showing the difference between the largest accounts that one might anticipate from selecting the lowest-cost AFP versus the likely accumulation in the more expensive AFPs over the same period. After receiving a randomly assigned fee information sheet, each respondent was then asked to rank three AFPs to recommend to a hypothetical close friend who wished to figure out where to invest his pension money. This recommendation was recorded by the interviewer, and the sheets were left with the respondents post-interview. Comparing these two groups will indicate whether the presentation of fund fees as gains or losses in peso terms is associated with the respondent selecting the lowest-cost pension fund manager.[3]

The nationally representative sample of individuals surveyed in the EPS also includes a rich set of information on individual-level characteristics, which we use to determine which individuals are most influenced by how pension fund fees are presented. Beginning in 2002, and following up in 2004, 2006, and 2009, the University of Chile's Microdata Center has included in the EPS a wide range of questions similar to those used in the US Health and Retirement Study (HRS) (NIA/NIH, n.d.); this includes extensive information on schooling, labor market history, health, pension system participation, and investment behavior, as well as wealth.[4] The EPS also asks respondents to answer several questions measuring financial literacy and risk preferences (devised by Lusardi and Mitchell [2007a, 2007b] and used by Hastings and Tejeda-Ashton [2008]). Here, we focus on two sets of questions, with the first set being the 'basic' financial literacy questions and the second the more 'sophisticated' set:[5]

1. *Basic financial literacy questions*:
   - *Chance of disease*: If the chance of catching an illness is 10 percent, how many people out of 1000 would get the illness?
   - *Lottery*: If five people share winning lottery tickets and the total prize is 2 million Chilean pesos, how much would each receive?
   - *Numeracy in investment context*: Assume that you have $100 in a savings account and the interest rate you earn on this money is 2 percent a year. If you keep this money in the account for five years, how much would you have after five years? Choose one: more than $102, exactly $102, or less than $102.

A second set of questions measures more sophisticated financial literacy concepts, such as compound interest, inflation, and risk diversification; it has also been fielded in an HRS module (Lusardi and Mitchell, 2009).

2. *Sophisticated financial literacy questions*:
- *Compound interest*: Assume that you have $200 in a savings account, and the interest rate that you earn on these savings is 10 percent a year. How much would you have in the account after two years?
- *Inflation*: Assume that you have $100 in a savings account and the interest rate that you earn on these savings is 1 percent a year. Inflation is 2 percent a year. After one year, if you withdraw the money from the savings account, you could buy more/less/the same?
- *Risk diversification*: Buying shares in one company is less risky than buying shares from many different companies with the same money. True/False?

Using these questions, we first evaluate individual differences in financial literacy, and, second, assess whether people with different attributes respond to the distinct formats for pension fees in terms of selecting the lowest-cost pension fund manager.

Findings

Table 6.1 reports summary statistics for the total number of financial literacy questions answered correctly arrayed by respondent characteristics including their age, sex, education, income, and whether the respondent had any form of saving. On average, younger individuals and men were more likely to give correct answers to more of the financial literacy questions. Similarly, financial literacy rises strongly with education levels, with those getting over half of the questions correct being more likely to have completed at least their secondary schooling. Average monthly income levels were also strongly positively correlated with financial literacy, as was the propensity to have some form of saving, and to be a member of an AFP plan.

Next, we focus on AFP participants (as self-identified) and examine how respondents performed on specific financial literacy questions. Table 6.2 shows that those who answered each question correctly were more likely than those who did not know the correct answers to have higher monthly income, to have secondary education, and to have some form of saving. Of particular interest is the *Compound interest* question, which asked respondents to calculate the exact amount they would have in a saving account after two years if they started with $200 and the account paid 10 percent interest annually. Very few—only 154 respondents out of more than 8,000 asked the question—answered it correctly, giving a response of $242. This handful of respondents was substantially wealthier and more educated than the sample as a whole.

TABLE 6.1 Financial literacy and other characteristics of 2009 EPS interviewees

Number of correct financial literacy questions (out of 6)	Age (years)	Male (%)	Secondary education (%)	Average monthly income (CP$)*	Any savings (%)**	AFP member (%)	N
0	57	42	11	177,730	15	47	3,551
1	51	44	18	212,408	20	65	2,788
2	48	49	27	264,283	26	72	2,781
3	46	52	40	349,340	28	79	2,588
4	45	58	52	398,306	30	83	1,792
5	45	62	64	557,379	36	85	675
6	45	75	85	932,039	31	87	68
Average	50	49	29	287,731	24	68	–

Notes: The total number of observations is 14,243. * Average monthly income calculation excludes those with zero income.
** This statistic is built from Question D27 in the EPS. Interviewees have savings if they respond that they have any of the following: (*a*) Savings for a home (at a bank); (*b*) AVF savings (Housing Fund admin.); (*c*) Voluntary pension savings; (*d*) Account 2 AFP savings; (*e*) Bank savings account; (*f*) Term deposits; (*g*) Mutual fund investments; (*h*) Company shares or bonds; (*i*) Third-party loans; (*j*) Other savings (cash, dollars, 'polla', etc.).

Source: Authors' calculations; see text.

TABLE 6.2 Financial literacy responses and respondent characteristics of AFP participants

Financial literacy question	Age (years)	Male (%)	Secondary education (%)	Average monthly income (CP$)	Any savings (%)*
Chance of disease	43	58	48	397,895	31
Lottery	44	58	48	403,792	30
Simple interest	44	56	46	386,233	32
Compound interest	43	79	84	750,137	39
Inflation	45	59	50	427,395	32
Risk diversification	44	56	43	377,870	31

Notes: * This statistic is built from Question D27 in the EPS. Interviewees have savings if they respond that they have any of the following: (*a*) Savings for a home (at a bank); (*b*) AVF savings (Housing Fund admin.); (*c*) Voluntary pension savings; (*d*) Account 2 AFP savings; (*e*) Bank savings account; (*f*) Term deposits; (*g*) Mutual Fund investments; (*h*) Company shares or bonds; (*i*) Third-party loans; (*j*) Other savings (cash, dollars, 'polla', etc.).

Source: Authors' calculations; see text.

Financial literacy and reasons for AFP choice

Prior literature has found that few Chileans are particularly aware of how the national retirement saving system works (Arenas et al., 2008). To explore this further, we added questions to the EPS that elicited the major factors influencing their fund choice, following Hastings and Tejeda-Ashton (2008). Table 6.3 provides odds ratios from Logit analysis of respondents' top reasons given for selecting their current AFP, relating these to control variables, as well as respondent financial literacy scores (0–6).[6] The first row gives the mean of the dependent variable; that is, the fraction of people who listed each factor as their top reason for selecting their current AFP. Overall, the most popular rationales for selecting their current AFPs include a friend's recommendation, the AFP's net returns (profitability), and an employer's suggestion or recommendation. The rows provide insight into how the factors included influence fund manager selection. For instance, older respondents were significantly less likely to say that they depended on friends' or employers' recommendations when choosing an AFP, but they were more likely to select an AFP to 'help a salesman' or because of the institution's perceived 'financial stability'. Respondents having above median income were substantially more likely to select an AFP based on the fund's higher past returns; in fact, those with above median income have 63 percent higher odds of offering this reason. The higher income group was also much less likely to rely on employer advice when making an AFP selection, and was more likely to seek perceived financial stability.

Next, we examine the links between financial literacy and education as influences on reasons given for AFP choice. Participants who had more than secondary-level education (technical training or university attendance) were more likely to say they elected their AFPs based on past returns, and less likely to say they depended on employer recommendations. The same holds for financial literacy: the odds of listing returns as important rose with the number of correct financial literacy answers, while the odds of relying on one's employer fell for the more financially literate. To illustrate the relative magnitudes of the coefficients, we find that correctly answering four financial literacy questions has the same positive impact on the probability of choosing an AFP as having above median income.

Financial literacy and sensitivity to information framing

The fact that financially illiterate, less-educated, and lower-paid participants rely more on their employers when choosing an AFP, and less on fund return characteristics, suggests that such individuals may also be more sensitive to information and framing when making a pension choice decision.

TABLE 6.3 Logit analysis of reasons for AFP choice and other controls (odds ratios reported)

	Friend recommended	Profitability	To help salesman	Good service	Advertising	Gift offered	Low fixed commission	Low variable commission	Employer
Mean of dependent variable	0.17	0.18	0.06	0.04	0.05	0.01	0.03	0.00	0.32
Age	0.96**	1.03	1.11**	1.03	1.04	1.00	1.03	0.96	0.96**
	(0.02)	(0.02)	(0.04)	(0.03)	(0.03)	(0.07)	(0.05)	(0.10)	(0.01)
Age-squared	1.00*	1.00	1.00**	1.00	1.00	1.00	1.00	1.00	1.00**
	(0.00)	(0.00)	(0.00)	(0.00)	(0.00)	(0.00)	(0.00)	(0.00)	(0.00)
Above median income (1/0)	1.08	1.62**	1.32*	1.04	0.88	1.33	1.02	2.55	0.58**
	(0.08)	(0.12)	(0.16)	(0.14)	(0.11)	(0.34)	(0.17)	(1.34)	(0.03)
Male (1/0)	0.88	1.21**	0.81	1.21	0.94	1.04	0.78	1.89	1.03
	(0.06)	(0.08)	(0.09)	(0.16)	(0.11)	(0.24)	(0.12)	(0.91)	(0.06)
Married (1/0)	0.89	1.02	0.93	1.22	1.04	1.18	1.04	2.09	0.92
	(0.06)	(0.07)	(0.10)	(0.15)	(0.12)	(0.27)	(0.17)	(0.93)	(0.05)
Secondary education (1/0)	1.04	1.37**	1.49**	1.08	1.24	1.46	0.94	1.35	0.61**
	(0.08)	(0.10)	(0.18)	(0.15)	(0.16)	(0.35)	(0.16)	(0.56)	(0.04)
No. financial literacy questions (0–6)	0.98	1.12**	1.01	0.97	1.04	1.04	0.97	1.07	0.91**
	(0.02)	(0.03)	(0.04)	(0.04)	(0.04)	(0.08)	(0.05)	(0.14)	(0.02)
Any savings (1/0) [+]	1.04	0.95	1.19	1.19	0.78	0.91	1.34	1.06	0.93
	(0.08)	(0.07)	(0.13)	(0.15)	(0.10)	(0.21)	(0.21)	(0.43)	(0.06)
Observations [++]	6,884	6,884	6,884	6,884	6,884	6,884	6,884	6,884	6,884

Notes: Standard errors in parentheses. * Indicates significance at 5%;
** indicates significance at 1%.

[+] Defined as previously described in Tables 6.1 and 6.2.

[++] Observations are only for individuals who have all nonmissing demographic responses and are AFP members. Thus, the sample is fewer than the 9,671 self-identified AFP holders.

Source: Authors' calculations; see text.

TABLE 6.4 Factors associated with respondent ranking the lowest-cost AFP the best (AFP participants)

Ranked lowest-cost AFP best	Saw gains sheet (%)	Age (years)	Male (%)	Secondary education (%)	Average monthly income (CP$)*	Any savings (%)**	N
No	48	45	54	32	297,491	28	4,923
Yes	53	46	54	41	371,975	29	3,691
Average	50	45	54	36	329,873	28	–

Notes: There are 8,614 observations in total, which is less than 9,671 self-identified AFP holders because some interviewees do not receive the experiment. * Average monthly income calculation excludes those with zero income.
** This statistic is built from question D27 in the EPS. Interviewees have savings if they respond that they have any of the following: (*a*) Savings for a home (at a bank); (*b*) AVF savings (Housing Fund admin.); (*c*) Voluntary pension savings; (*d*) Account 2 AFP savings; (*e*) Bank savings account; (*f*) Term deposits; (*g*) Mutual Fund investments; (*h*) Company shares or bonds; (*i*) Third-party loans; (*j*) Other savings (cash, dollars, 'polla', etc.).

Source: Authors' calculations; see text.

To examine this further, our experimental framework offers a unique setting. We combine respondent reported income levels from the 2006 EPS with historical returns and fees data for each fund manager, in order to estimate an anticipated ten-year fund balance net of fees for each EPS respondent under all AFPs in the marketplace. These hypothetical account balance figures are then reported to respondents receiving the 'gains' version of the fee information worksheet used in the experiment. To construct the 'losses' version of worksheets, we compute the difference between the largest ten-year account balance for each individual and each of the other four AFPs in the menu. After fielding these experimental worksheets, we matched each respondent's 'top three AFPs they would recommend to a friend' to our own ranking of the AFPs for that individual.[7]

Results appear in Table 6.4. Of the total of 8,614 participants who received this information, 10 percent more of the respondents who saw the gains sheet (53 percentage points) elected the lowest-cost AFP, versus 48 percentage points of those receiving the loss sheet. Evidently, people seem more responsive to behavioral change when offered rewards, compared to losses. Table 6.4 also indicates that men, the better educated, and the higher paid were more likely to elect the lowest-cost AFP, particularly when shown the 'gains' sheet.

We further examine how information framing and other factors affect fund choice by testing for interaction effects of framing and literacy. This permits us to evaluate which population subgroups may be most sensitive to information framing. Table 6.5 reports Logit odds ratio results from analyses of whether respondents selected their lowest-cost AFPs, as a function of whether respondents received the gains or losses worksheet, and other factors. The first column presents odds ratio results, pooling the experimental choices across respondents who were given AFP information as gains or losses. Receiving a gains sheet was very powerful, as this boosted the odds of choosing the most profitable AFP and increased the odds of selection by 26 percentage points. Quantitatively, showing participants the gains worksheet has a measured impact as large as the impact of having a post-secondary education, and twice as large as the impact of having above-median income. The measured effect is slightly larger than the impact of a one-unit increase in the financial literacy index.

Next, we add an interaction between financial literacy and information framing in the second column, to assess whether financially literate respondents are more affected by information framing. Now the odds ratio is significant and less than 1, implying that a one-unit increase in the financial literacy index reduces the impact of information framing by approximately 10 percentage points. It is also of interest to ask how framing interacts with both education and income. When we add an interaction for having received a gains sheet and having post-secondary education, the odds ratio is significantly less than 1 for the interaction, and the indicator with financial literacy becomes insignificant. Interestingly, the coefficient on the interaction between information framing and financial literacy is stable across the two specifications—only the significance changes—suggesting that financial literacy scores and educational attainment are sufficiently uncorrelated to effectively test their separate contributions to AFP choice. The results suggest that education, rather than financial literacy, is a stronger determinant of how sensitive respondents are to viewing information in gains rather than losses. Lastly, we add yet another interaction term testing for a joint effect of higher income and receiving a gains sheet; here, the new interaction term is not statistically significant and the reported odds ratio is near 1.

Conclusion

We measure financial literacy as a person's ability to understand basic concepts like inflation, compounding, and investment returns. Using a new microeconomic dataset linked to experimental evidence, we have generated responses to framing of pension fund fees and we show that, when choosing pension funds, people with lower levels of education, income, and financial literacy rely far more heavily on employers, coworkers, and friends than they do on cost fundamentals. These same types of individuals are also more responsive to fund fee framing when identifying the

TABLE 6.5 Logit analysis of factors associated with respondent ranking the lowest-cost AFP the best (odds ratios reported)

Dependent variable: respondent ranked lowest-cost AFP best				
Saw gains sheet (1/0)	1.26**	1.57**	1.65**	1.66**
	(0.07)	(0.15)	(0.16)	(0.18)
Age	1.06**	1.06**	1.06**	1.06**
	(0.01)	(0.01)	(0.01)	(0.01)
Age-squared	1.00**	1.00**	1.00**	1.00**
	(0.00)	(0.00)	(0.00)	(0.00)
Above median income (1/0)	1.13**	1.13**	1.13**	1.15
	(0.07)	(0.07)	(0.07)	(0.10)
Male (1/0)	0.92	0.92	0.92	0.92
	(0.05)	(0.05)	(0.05)	(0.05)
Married (1/0)	0.98	0.98	0.98	0.98
	(0.06)	(0.06)	(0.06)	(0.06)
Secondary education (1/0)	1.26**	1.26**	1.47**	1.47**
	(0.08)	(0.08)	(0.12)	(0.13)
Number of correct financial literacy questions × saw gains sheet	1.22**	1.28**	1.26**	1.26**
	(0.02)	(0.03)	(0.03)	(0.03)
Any savings (1/0)[†]	0.92	0.92	0.92	0.92
	(0.05)	(0.05)	(0.05)	(0.05)
Number of correct financial literacy questions × saw gains sheet		0.91**	0.94	0.94
		(0.03)	(0.03)	(0.04)
Secondary education × saw gains sheet			0.73**	0.74**
			(0.08)	(0.09)
Having above-median income × saw gains sheet				0.98
				(0.11)
Observations[††]	6,132	6,132	6,132	6,132

Notes: Standard errors in parentheses. * Significant at 5%;
** significant at 1%.
† This indicator is built from Question D27 in the EPS. Interviewees have savings if they respond that they have any of the following: (*a*) Savings for a home (at a bank); (*b*) AVF savings (Housing Fund admin.); (*c*) Voluntary pension savings; (*d*) Account 2 AFP savings; (*e*) Bank savings account; (*f*) Term deposits; (*g*) Mutual Fund investments; (*h*) Company shares or bonds; (*i*) Third-party loans; (*j*) Other savings (cash, dollars, 'polla', etc.).
†† Observations are only for individuals who have all nonmissing demographic responses and are AFP members that received the experiment. Thus, the sample is fewer than the 9,671 self-identified AFP holders.

Source: Authors' calculations; see text.

relative attractiveness of pension fund managers. Moreover, the impact of viewing information as gains is sizable, relative to the impact of various economic and demographic factors. Specifically, seeing investment choices as gains rather than losses is as important as the impact of having a post-secondary education, and twice as large as the impact of having above-median income. Those who do not understand these concepts make poor fund choices that can seriously prejudice their retirement security.

The policy implications of our findings are profound. Specifically, participant awareness of higher net-return funds can be greatly enhanced when information on fees is simplified in terms of likely gains from selecting higher net return funds. The impact of fund fee framing is largest for the least financially literate and the lowest-educated groups. By contrast, choices made by the financially well-informed tend to be less responsive to the information presentation, since those individuals tend to better understand the financial concepts necessary to translate annual percentage rates into costs and benefits.

Our results should interest policymakers in Chile, as well as in other nations, including the United States, who seek to determine how to better shape the environment in which workers make retirement saving choices. Our research is also relevant to the broader issue of whether consumers benefit from having more choice when it comes to products offered in financial markets. Recent research suggests that significant cognitive costs shape consumer decisions in a wide range of such markets from education (Hastings and Weinstein, 2008) to credit cards (Ausubel, 1991) to Medicare Part D (McFadden, 2006; Kling et al., 2008; Abaluck and Gruber, 2009) to saving and retirement investment choices (Madrian and Shea, 2001; Ashraf et al., 2006; Choi et al., 2006, 2007; Hastings and Tajeda-Ashton, 2008; Duarte and Hastings, 2009), implying that market outcomes may be inefficient when greater choice and consumer autonomy is introduced. For example, decision-making costs might induce consumers to place more weight on brand names versus price in a world where product prices are not easy to understand. If such decision-making costs were negatively correlated with education, income, and wealth, such information could arouse adequacy and equity concerns.[8] As a consequence, increased choice could actually increase socioeconomic disparities, compared to the traditional public provision model.

Acknowledgments

This research is part of the NBER programs on Aging and Labor Economics, and it was supported by grants from the US Social Security Administration (SSA) to the Michigan Retirement Research Center (MRRC) and the Financial Literacy Center, as well as the TIAA-CREF Institute, the Boettner Center/Pension Research Council at The Wharton School, Yale Institution for Social and Policy Studies, the Centro de Microdatos at the University of Chile, and the Inter-American Development Bank. The authors also acknowledge support from NIH/NIA grant AG023774-01, NIH/NIA Grant # P30 AG12836, and NIH/NICHC Population Research Infrastructure Program R24 HD-044964, all at the University of Pennsylvania. We thank David

Bravo, Jere Behrman, Fabian Duarte, Raissa Fabregas, Peter Frerichs, Daniela Fuentes, Carolina Orellana, Sandra Quijada, José Luis Ruiz, Sergio Urzua, and Javiera Vasquez for helpful suggestions and comments. Opinions and errors are solely those of the authors, and not of the institutions providing funding for or with which the authors are affiliated.

Endnotes

[1] More than two dozen other Latin American countries have followed Chile's lead in adopting funded individual-account pensions; that nation's pension system has also drawn substantial attention in the United States and elsewhere.

[2] We presented projected balances based on AFP-specific returns for two reasons. First, this calculation is very close to the official calculation the government uses. Second, we tested for persistence in AFP performance and found some evidence that some AFPs persistently outperform others, and that this persistent outperformance was present in all funds within the outperforming AFP.

[3] In the future, using administrative linkages, it should be possible to determine whether participants provided with different formats for the fee tables differentially and systematically changed their own AFP portfolios.

[4] The EPS also has linked respondent records to a wide range of historical administrative files on contribution patterns, benefit payments, and other program features (Bravo et al., 2004, 2006), but we do not use these here.

[5] In work currently underway (Behrman et al., 2010), we also evaluate questions on key aspects of the Chilean retirement system, including the mandatory contribution rate, the legal retirement age for women (60) and men (65), how pension benefits are computed in the DC system, whether people are aware of the welfare benefit available under the law, and whether people know they may contribute additional funds to the Voluntary Pension system.

[6] Note that the sample here is restricted to only those members of the EPS who state that they participate in an AFP and have responses for all selected demographic variables.

[7] Because some fund fees vary with contribution amounts, these valuations must be tailored to each respondent's own particulars.

[8] Hastings and Tejeda-Ashton (2008) and Duarte and Hastings (2009) analyze this possibility in the context of Mexican pensions. Arenas et al. (2008) evaluate these arguments in the Chilean context.

References

Abaluck, J. and J. Gruber (2009). 'Choice Inconsistencies Among the Elderly: Evidence from Plan Choice in the Medicare Part D Program,' NBER Working Paper No. 14759. Cambridge, MA: National Bureau of Economic Research.

Arenas de Mesa, A., D. Bravo, J. R. Behrman, O. S. Mitchell, and P. E. Todd (2008). 'The Chilean Pension Reform Turns 25: Lessons from the Social Protection Survey,' in S. J. Kay and T. Sinha, eds, *Lessons from Pension Reform in the Americas.* Oxford, UK: Oxford University Press, pp. 23–58.

Ashraf, N., D. Karlan, and W. Yin (2006). 'Tying Odysseus to the Mast; Evidence from a Commitment Savings Product in the Philippines,' *The Quarterly Journal of Economics,* 121(2): 635–72.

Ausubel, L. M. (1991). 'The Failure of Competition in the Credit Card Market,' *American Economic Review,* 81(1): 50–81.

Behrman, J., O. S. Mitchell, C. Soo, and D. Bravo (2010). 'Financial Literacy, Schooling, and Wealth Accumulation,' Pension Research Council Working Paper No. 2010-24. Philadelphia, PA: Pension Research Council.

Benartzi, S., and R. H. Thaler (2001). 'Naïve Diversification Strategies in Defined Contribution Saving Plans,' *American Economic Review,* 91(1): 79–98.

Bernheim, D., D. Garrett, and D. Maki (2001). 'Education and Saving: The Long-term Effects of High School Financial Curriculum Mandates,' *Journal of Public Economics,* 80(3): 435–65.

Bravo, D., J. Behrman, O. S. Mitchell, and P. Todd (2004). *Análisis y Principales Resultados: Primera Encuesta de Protección Social (Historia Laboral y Seguridad Social, 2002).* Santiago, Chile: Universidad de Chile. http://www.proteccionsocial.cl/docs/AnalisisPrincipalesResultadosPrimeraEncuestaProteccionSocial.pdf

————————(2006). *Encuesta de Protección Social 2004: Presentación General y Principales Resultados.* Santiago, Chile: Universidad de Chile. http://www.proteccionsocial.cl/docs/Encuesta_Protecci%C3%B3n_Social%2020041.pdf

Campbell, J. (2006). 'Household Finance,' *Journal of Finance,* 61(4): 1553–604.

Choi, J. J., D. Laibson, and B. C. Madrian (2006). 'Why Does the Law of One Price Fail? An Experiment on Index Mutual Funds,' NBER Working Paper No. 12261. Cambridge, MA: National Bureau of Economic Research.

—————(2007). '$100 Bills on the Sidewalk: Suboptimal Investment in 401(k) Plans,' NBER Working Paper No. 11554. Cambridge, MA: National Bureau of Economic Research.

————A. Metrick (2007). *Reinforcement Learning and Investor Behavior.* Cambridge, MA: Harvard University. http://www.economics.harvard.edu/files/faculty/37_reinforcementlearning.pdf

Cronqvist, H. and R. H. Thaler (2004). 'Design Choices in Privatized Social-Security Systems: Learning from the Swedish Experience,' *American Economic Review (Papers and Proceedings),* 94(2): 424–8.

Duarte, F. and J. Hastings (2009). *Fettered Consumers and Sophisticated Firms: Evidence from Mexico's Privatized Social Security System.* Durham, NC: Duke University. http://aida.econ.yale.edu/~jh529/papers/Duarte&Hastings-20091030.pdf

Hastings, J. and L. Tejeda-Ashton (2008). 'Financial Literacy, Information and Demand Elasticity: Survey and Experimental Evidence from Mexico,' NBER Working Paper No. 14538. Cambridge, MA: National Bureau of Economic Research.

——J. M. Weinstein (2008). 'Information, School Choice and Academic Achievement: Evidence from Two Experiments,' *Quarterly Journal of Economics*, 123(4): 915–37.

Hilgert, M. A., J. M. Hogarth, and S. G. Beverly (2003). 'Household Financial Management: The Connection between Knowledge and Behavior,' *Federal Reserve Bulletin*, 89: 309–22.

Kling, J. R., S. Mullainathan, E. Shafir, L. Vermeulen, and M. V. Wrobel (2008). 'Confusion and Choice in Medicare Drug Plan Selection.' Unpublished manuscript.

Lusardi, A. and O. S. Mitchell (2006). 'Financial Literacy and Planning: Implications for Retirement Wellbeing,' Pension Research Council Working Paper No. 2006-01. Philadelphia, PA: Pension Research Council.

————(2007*a*). 'Baby Boomer Retirement Security: The Roles of Planning, Financial Literacy, and Housing Wealth,' *Journal of Monetary Economics*, 54: 205–24.

————(2007*b*). 'Financial Literacy and Retirement Planning: New Evidence from the RAND American Life Panel,' Pension Research Council Working Paper No. 2007-33. Philadelphia, PA: Pension Research Council.

————(2007*c*). 'Financial Literacy and Retirement Preparedness: Evidence and Implications for Financial Education,' *Business Economics*, 42: 35–44.

————(2008). 'Planning and Financial Literacy: How Do Women Fare?,' *American Economic Review (Papers and Proceedings)*, 98(2): 413–17.

————(2009). *Financial Literacy: Evidence and Implications for Financial Education.* New York, NY: TIAA-CREF Institute. http://www.tiaa-crefinstitute.org/pdf/research/trends_issues/ti_financialliteracy0509a.pdf

————(2010). 'How Ordinary Consumers Make Complex Economic Decisions: Financial Literacy and Retirement Readiness,' NBER Working Paper No. 15350. Cambridge, MA: National Bureau of Economic Research.

——P. Tufano (2008). 'Debt Literacy, Financial Experience, and Overindebtedness,' NBER Working Paper No. 14808. Cambridge, MA: National Bureau of Economic Research.

Madrian, B. and D. F. Shea (2001). 'The Power of Suggestion: Inertia in 401(k) Participation and Savings Behavior,' *The Quarterly Journal of Economics*, 116: 1149–87.

McFadden, D. (2006). 'Free Markets and Fettered Consumers (Presidential Address to the American Economic Association),' *American Economic Review*, 96(1): 5–29.

Mitchell, O. S., P. Todd, and D. Bravo (2008). 'Learning from the Chilean Experience: The Determinants of Pension Switching,' in A. Lusardi, ed., *Overcoming the Saving Slump: Making Financial Education and Saving Programs More Effective.* Chicago, IL: University of Chicago Press, pp. 301–23.

National Institute on Aging/National Institute of Health (NIA/NIH) (n.d.). *Growing Older in America: The Health and Retirement Study.* US Department of Health and Human Services. Washington, DC: GPO.

Ponce-Rodriguez, A. (2008). *Teaser Rate Offers in the Credit Card Market: Evidence from Mexico.* Palo Alto, CA: Stanford University.

Chapter 7

Investor Knowledge and Experience with Investment Advisers and Broker-Dealers

Angela A. Hung, Noreen Clancy, and Jeff Dominitz[1]

During the tenure of Chairman Arthur Levitt, the Securities and Exchange Commission (SEC) commissioned the 1995 Report of the Committee on Compensation Practices (the 'Tully Report') responding to a concern about conflicts of interest in the retail brokerage industry. This report (Tully and Levitt, 1995) identified 'best practices' as those that attempted to more closely align the interests of the investor, the registered representative, and the firm. Fee-based accounts, as opposed to commissioned transactions, were highlighted as a best practice because these reduce the likelihood of abusive sales practices such as churning, high-pressure sales tactics, and recommending unsuitable transactions. Fee-based accounts allow for registered representatives to be compensated based on the amount of assets in an account regardless of transaction activity.

The release of the Tully report coincided with an increase in competition in the US retail brokerage industry, as well as falling transaction-based commissions, the traditional source of income for registered representatives. As a result, more brokerage firms began to offer fee-based programs. As such fee-based accounts were similar to advisory programs offered by investment advisers, there was some concern that broker-dealers that offered such accounts would be providing advice that was more than 'solely incidental' to the transaction and trigger application of the Investment Advisers Act of 1940 (US Statutes, 1940).

The 1940 Act regulates activities of investment advisers, whereas the Securities Exchange Act of 1934 (US Statutes, 1934) regulates the activities of broker-dealers, who are also subject to oversight by self-regulating organizations (SROs). The 1940 Act defines 'investment adviser' as 'any person who, for compensation, engages in the business of advising others, either directly or through publications or writings, as to the value of securities or as to the advisability of investing in, purchasing, or selling securities, or who, for compensation and as part of a regular business, issues or promulgates analyses or reports concerning securities' (US Statutes, 1940). In order to avoid duplicate regulation of broker-dealer activities, the 1940

Act makes an exception for 'any broker or dealer whose performance of [advisory] services is solely incidental to the conduct of his business as a broker or dealer and who receives no special compensation therefor' (US Statutes, 1940).

The SEC studied these new fee-based brokerage programs and concluded that they were traditional brokerage offerings that had been re-priced, rather than new advisory programs. Therefore, in 1999 the SEC proposed a rule (202(a)(11)-1) that, among other things, exempted broker-dealers offering fee-based brokerage accounts from being subject to the Advisers Act. The SEC thought that if the 1940 Act applied to broker-dealers providing such fee-based programs, it would discourage the offering of such programs and that these fee-based programs would be beneficial to brokerage customers (SEC, 2005).

Many commentators on the 1999 proposed rule felt that such an exclusion would blur the lines between broker-dealers and investment advisers, and it might also confuse investors about their rights and the obligations owed to them under each type of financial relationship. In response to these and other comments, the SEC modified and reproposed the rule in 2005. The reproposed rule, 'Certain Broker-Dealers Deemed Not To Be Investment Advisers', expanded the disclosure requirements of broker-dealers offering investment advice by ensuring that any advertisements or literature identifies the account as a brokerage account (SEC, 2005).

Although the 2005 rule has since been vacated, the rulemaking process did raise concerns by the SEC as to what investors understand regarding brokerage and advisory accounts, the legal obligations of each type of account, and the effect of titles and marketing used by investment professionals on investors' expectations. As a result, the SEC commissioned the RAND Corporation to study the issue of what investors understand about the differences between investment advisers and broker-dealers. As part of that study, RAND conducted a household survey and a series of focus groups, to be described later. The policy question of how to address or harmonize the regulatory differences has recently been resurrected as part of financial regulatory reform legislation following the 2008 financial market collapse.[2]

This chapter asks what investors understand about a range of issues, including whether investors understand distinctions between broker-dealers and investment advisers. We also seek to learn about their experiences interacting with the financial service industry and their expectations of service provided by individual professionals and firms in the financial service industry. To address these points, we administered a large-scale national household survey, and also conducted six intensive focus-group discussions. The focus groups complement the national survey by providing a deeper understanding of how investors interact with the financial service industry and what they do and do not understand about the nature of that relationship. Participants in both the survey and the focus groups represent a range of ages, income levels, and racial and ethnic groups.

Our results show that most people lack a clear understanding of the boundaries between investment advisers and broker-dealers. Even those who have employed financial professionals for years are often confused about job titles, types of firms with which they are associated, and payments made for their services. Participants also understand relatively little about the legal distinctions between investment advisers and broker-dealers. Despite this confusion, people report that they are largely satisfied with the services they receive from financial professionals.

In what follows, we first review literature on investor perceptions and expectations of financial service providers. We then discuss results from our own research, results from a household survey, and focus-group discussions. The household survey addresses several major topics, including beliefs about the differences between investment advisers and broker-dealers and experience with different types of financial service providers. The focus-group results amplify the results from the household survey.

Prior literature: investor perceptions and expectations of financial service providers

A handful of studies examine investors' understanding of the differences between financial service providers, and particularly between investment advisers and broker-dealers.

The Zero Alpha Group (ZAG, 2004) and the Consumer Federation of America commissioned a survey of 1,044 investors regarding regulation of brokers and investment advisers, who were asked, 'Based on your knowledge of stockbrokers, such as Merrill Lynch, Morgan Stanley, and Edward D. Jones, which ONE of the following statements do you believe BEST describes the services they provide to their customers?' About the same fraction (28 percent) of respondents believed that brokers' primary service was to provide financial advice, as those who believed that brokers' primary service was to conduct stock market transactions (26 percent). When asked the following question, 86 percent of respondents answered 'Yes': 'Stockbrokers receive financial incentives from investment product sponsors to recommend particular investments to their customers. If, for example, a stockbroker receives cash payments, vacation trips or other forms of compensation from a mutual fund company as an inducement to sell a particular mutual fund to his or her clients, should the stockbroker be required to disclose that fact to a customer buying the mutual fund?'

Almost all of the respondents (91 percent) reported that they thought that, if stockbrokers and financial planners offered the same type of investment advice services, the same investor protection rules should apply. Further, 65 percent of respondents reported that they would be much or somewhat less likely to use a stockbroker for investment advice, if brokers were subject to weaker investor protection rules than financial planners (Opinion Research Corporation, 2004).

In 2005, the SEC commissioned a study by Siegel and Gale, LLC and Gelb Consulting Group (2005). Four focus groups of investors in Tennessee and Maryland proved not to know the difference between brokers, financial advisors/financial consultants, investment advisers, and financial planners.

TD Ameritrade (2006) surveyed 1,000 investors and found that, even with the new 2005 disclosure rules, investors were still unclear about the distinction between brokers and investment advisers. When asked, 'Are you aware that stockbrokers and investment advisors offer fee-based financial advice but provide different levels of investor protection?', 43 percent of respondents reported they were unaware, and 47 percent of respondents reported that they did not know that brokers need not disclose all conflicts of interest. Over 60 percent of respondents believed that brokers had a fiduciary duty, and 90 percent of respondents believed that investment advisers had a fiduciary duty. Further, most respondents said they would not seek services from a broker if they knew that brokerage services provided fewer investor protections, that brokers lacked a fiduciary duty, or that brokers were not required to disclose all conflicts of interest. When shown the 2005 disclosure statement, 79 percent of respondents reported they would be less likely to seek financial advice from a brokerage firm. Moreover, 64 percent reported that they did not expect an unbiased response if they were to ask a broker about the differences between brokerage and advisory accounts.

A few studies focus on dimensions of service that help determine investors' satisfaction with their brokers. Fusilier and Schaub (2003) examine brokerage clients' perceptions and points of satisfaction, drawing on two surveys of investors: one in 1998 (bull market) of 760 respondents, and another in 2002 (bear market) of 388 respondents. Survey questions asked about perceptions of broker practices and satisfaction. They found that satisfaction was influenced by investor perception of broker honesty, expertise, knowledge, and service. Furthermore, they found that investor perceptions and level of satisfaction did not change significantly from the bull to the bear market. In a content analysis of 740 customer reviews of online brokerage services, Yang and Fang (2004) identified several quality dimensions related to satisfaction: responsiveness (e.g., prompt service, order execution, and order confirmation), service reliability (e.g., accurate quotes, order fulfillment, and calculation of commissions), competence (e.g., research capacity), and security (e.g., privacy). Chao et al. (2002) surveyed 139 investors with assets ranging from $1,000 to $1,300,000 to investigate features that matter to online traders. The most highly ranked features were lower trading costs, trading security, customer service, and technical support. The dimensions that mattered the least were reputation of the firm, ease of use of the website, reliability of trades, and ease of account opening and access. Service dimensions such as execution speed, real-time quotes, and access to IPOs were ranked as only moderately important.

Perceptions of provider performance

We collected data from US households via an Internet survey of investment behavior and preferences, experience with financial service providers, and perceptions of the different types of financial service providers. The survey was administered to members of the American Life Panel (ALP), a probability sample of over 1,000 individuals age 18+, who either used their own computers or a WebTV provided by RAND to participate in the panel. About once a month, respondents received an email with a request to visit the website and fill out questionnaires. Typically, an interview took less than 30 minutes. Respondents were paid an incentive of about $20 per 30 minutes of interviewing (and proportionately less if an interview was shorter).

The household survey was administered for six weeks, from September 26 through November 6, 2007, and, because it was conducted online, we had quick access to the results. During this time, 654 households completed the survey. Respondent age varied from 19 to 89, with average age of 52. Eleven percent of the sample had a household income of less than $25,000; 22 percent of the sample had a household income between $25,000 and $50,000; 23 percent of the sample had a household income between $50,000 and $75,000; and 45 percent of the sample had a household income over $75,000. More than 98 percent of respondents had a high school degree or GED, and over half had a bachelor's degree. ALP respondents had more education and income than the broader US population,[3] so our results will likely overstate the levels of financial knowledge, experience, and literacy of the US population at large.

The survey began with an assessment of investment experience. We then asked several questions on the differences between investment advisers and broker-dealers. Next, respondents who used a financial service provider were asked detailed questions about their interactions with their providers. Respondents who did not use a financial service provider were asked why they did not. Finally, we presented respondents with definitions of a broker and an investment adviser, including a description of common job titles, legal duties, and typical compensation. Respondents were then asked to report the likelihood of their seeking services (in general) from a broker or investment adviser, the likelihood of seeking investment advice (in particular) from a broker or investment adviser, and the degree to which they would trust investment advice from a broker or an investment adviser.

We labeled respondents as 'experienced' investors if they held investments outside of retirement accounts, had formal training in finance or investing, or held investments only in retirement accounts but answered positively to questions gauging their financial understanding, such as the nature and causes of increases in their investments, seeking out information about their investments when necessary, and knowing the different investment options available to them. If respondents did not meet these requirements, then we labeled them as 'inexperienced' investors. We used an identical classification method to determine participation in the focus groups. In our sample, about two-thirds of survey respondents were categorized as experienced investors and one-third were categorized as inexperienced investors.

Beliefs about the differences between investment advisers and brokers

We first presented respondents with a series of specific financial services and obligations and asked them to indicate which items applied to any of the following financial service professionals: (*a*) investment advisers; (*b*) brokers; (*c*) financial advisors or financial consultants; (*d*) financial planners; or (*e*) none of the above.[4] Table 7.1 summarizes the survey results, and shows that respondents perceived differences between investment advisers and brokers in terms of services provided, as well as duties and obligations.

Respondents were more likely to report that investment advisers, rather than brokers, provided advice about securities, recommended specific investments, and provided planning services. On the other hand, respondents were more likely to say that brokers, rather than investment advisers, executed stock transactions and earned commissions. Respondents were slightly more likely to report that investment advisers rather than brokers were required to act in the client's best interest and disclose any conflicts of interest. These differences are small in magnitude, but they are statistically significant.

Respondents also tended to report that financial advisors and consultants were more similar to investment advisers than to brokers in terms of

TABLE 7.1 Respondent beliefs about financial service professionals (%)

Does the professional:	Investment advisers	Brokers	Financial advisors or financial consultants	Financial planners	None of these
Provide advice about securities (e.g., shares of stocks or mutual funds) as part of their regular business	80	63	78	63	3
Execute stock or mutual fund transactions on the client's behalf	29	89	28	23	3
Recommend specific investments	83	51	72	50	2
Provide retirement planning	51	12	80	91	2
Provide general financial planning	42	13	80	88	1
Receive commissions on purchases or trades that the client makes	43	96	34	22	1
Typically get paid based on the amount of assets that the client holds	49	40	50	34	12
Act in the client's best interest as required by law	49	42	59	55	19
Disclose any conflicts of interest as required by law	62	58	57	51	18

Notes: Based on 651 respondents.

Source: Authors' calculations based on the ALP survey; see text.

the services provided, compensation methods, and duties. However, as noted in Hung et al. (2008), *financial advisor* and *financial consultant* are titles commonly used by investment advisory-firm employees as well as brokerage-firm employees. Furthermore, we present evidence later that the most common titles of financial service providers that these respondents employ are generic terms, such as *advisor* or *financial advisor*.

Respondents who used financial service providers

In our sample, 47 percent of respondents reported that they used a financial service provider for 'conducting stock market and/or mutual fund transactions' and/or 'advising, management, and/or planning'.[5] These

TABLE 7.2 Respondents who use financial professionals by respondent characteristics (%)

Characteristic	Responding yes
All respondents	47.3
40 and older	50.3
Under 40	33.9
College degree or more	55.4
No college degree	38.8
Household income of at least $75,000	55.0
Household income less than $75,000	40.7
Experienced	59.4
Inexperienced	23.4

Notes: Based on 647 respondents' answers to the question: 'Do you currently use any professional service providers for (*a*) conducting stock market or mutual fund transactions or (*b*) advising, management, or planning?'

Source: Authors' calculations based on the ALP survey; see text.

respondents were more likely than other respondents to be over age 40, have at least a college degree, have household income of at least $75,000, and be an experienced investor (see Table 7.2). Of the 306 respondents who reported using a financial service provider, 73 percent reported receiving professional assistance for advising, management, or planning, and 75 percent reported receiving professional assistance for conducting stock market or mutual fund transactions. Initially, almost half reported using professional assistance for both types of services. In discussing the services they received, respondents were given another opportunity to report whether their financial service professional provided both types of services. In response to that follow-up question, we found that more than 70 percent of the reported financial service professionals provided both types of services.

We also asked respondents who reported they used a financial service provider whether there was a specific person, rather than a firm, that provided these financial services. Almost 81 percent of respondents personally interacted with an individual professional, and of those respondents, 31 percent personally interacted with more than one individual professional. Just over one-third (35 percent) reported employing at least one firm where they did not interact regularly with a specific person. To better assess whether respondent experiences differed depending on whether they interacted with a specific individual rather than a firm, we distinguish between these experiences when presenting results.

Job titles and firm types of financial service providers

Respondents who reported that they used a specific person, or an individual professional, were then asked for that person's title (or brief job description). Respondents gave 449 titles for 323 individual professionals.[6] The vast majority (248) of these individual professionals reportedly provided both advisory and brokerage services, whereas forty-five of these individual professionals reportedly provided brokerage services but not advisory services, and thirty-four reportedly provided advisory services but not brokerage services. Respondents reported a wide variety of titles that their financial service providers used. Summarized in Table 7.3, the most commonly reported title is *financial adviser* or *financial advisor*, regardless of the type of service provided by the individual professional. In fact, if these titles are combined with *financial consultant* and *advisor*, they account for almost one-quarter of all listed titles. *Financial planners* were listed forty-four times and Certified Financial Planners (CFPs) were listed twenty-one times. *Broker, stockbroker,* or *registered representative* was used thirty-eight times, and *investment adviser* or *investment advisor* was used twenty-two times.

For any given title, the individual professional was most likely to be reported as offering both types of services. Reported titles for individual professionals who provided only advisory services or only brokerage services suggest some confusion on respondents' parts, although these num-

TABLE 7.3 Professional titles most commonly reported by respondents

Title	All individual professionals	Provide advisory services only	Provide brokerage services only	Provide both types of services
Advisor	11	1	1	9
Banker	21	2	8	11
Broker, stockbroker, or registered representative	38	0	8	30
CFP	21	3	3	15
Financial adviser or financial advisor	78	7	11	60
Financial consultant	25	2	0	23
Financial planner	44	6	1	37
Investment adviser or investment advisor	22	3	3	16
President or vice president	20	0	2	18

Notes: 449 titles were reported. Entries indicate the number of times that the title was reported.

Source: Authors' calculations based on the ALP survey; see text.

bers were small. For example, of the twenty-two individual professionals with a reported title of *investment adviser* or *investment advisor*, respondents reported that three provided brokerage services only. Furthermore, recall that responses to the questions on beliefs about financial service providers indicated that respondents viewed financial advisors or financial consultants as being more similar to investment advisers than to brokers. But when asked about job titles and service provided, responses indicated that financial advisors were more likely to provide brokerage services only than to provide advisory services only. Lastly, we note that twenty-six responses were left blank or explicitly stated that the respondent did not know the individual professional's job title or job description.

Respondents who worked with at least one individual professional were asked about the kinds of firms that employed the individual professional who provided financial services. Respondents were then asked to check all that applied: investment advisory firm, brokerage firm, bank, or other. The order of the first two categories was randomized between subjects. For firms that are associated with an individual professional, the most common response to the type-of-firm question was for the first two categories to be checked—that is, both investment advisory firm and brokerage firm (see Figure 7.1). We refer to these firms as *dual investment advisory-brokerage firms.*

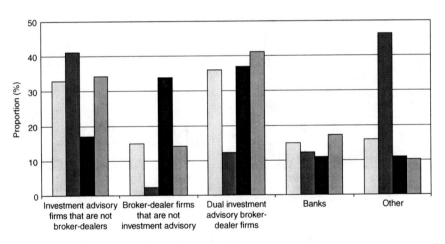

□ All firms associated with individual professionals (326)
■ Individual professional at the firm provides respondent with advisory services only (52)
■ Individual professional at the firm provides respondent with brokerage services only (46)
▨ Individual professional at the firm provides respondent with both types of services (228)

Figure 7.1 Types of firms that employ individual professionals
Source: Authors' calculations; see text.

The second most common response is for the category of investment adviser to be checked but not the brokerage category to be checked. We refer to these firms as *investment advisory firms that are not broker-dealers*. There were fifty-two other firm categories checked, and respondents specified thirty-seven of them. The most commonly mentioned other type of firm was insurance firm (ten), and the second most commonly mentioned type of firm was accounting firm (seven).

Respondents who did not interact with a specific person were asked to report what kinds of firms they used for financial services. As before, respondents were asked to check all that applied: investment advisory firm, brokerage firm, bank, or other, where the order of the first two categories was randomized between subjects. For firms not associated with an individual professional, the most common response to the type-of-firm question was for the brokerage category to be checked, but not the category for investment advisers to be checked. We refer to these firms as *brokerage firms that are not investment advisers*. The second most common is investment advisory firms that are not broker-dealers (see Figure 7.2).

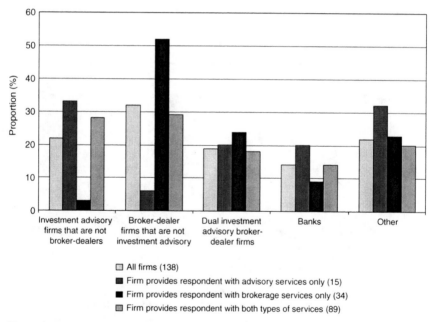

Figure 7.2 Types of firms used that are not associated with individual professionals
Source: Authors' calculations; see text.

Experiences with financial service providers

We also asked respondents detailed follow-up questions on the first individual professional or the first reported firm not associated with an individual professional.[7] We received detailed responses on 246 individual professionals and eighty-five firms. Comparing these professionals and firms about which respondents gave us detailed information, we found that the firms were less likely to provide both advisory and brokerage services, according to our respondents. Of the 246 individual professionals about whom respondents gave us detailed information, 12 percent provided advisory services only, 11 percent provided brokerage services only, and 76 percent provided both types of services. Of the eighty-five firms about which respondents gave us detailed information, 18 percent provided advisory services only, 29 percent provided brokerage services only, and 53 percent provided both types of services.

Methods of payment for financial services

Figure 7.3 shows what methods of payment respondents used for advisory or brokerage services: commission, rate (hourly, monthly, or annual), flat fee, a fee determined by a percentage of assets, or other. The most com-

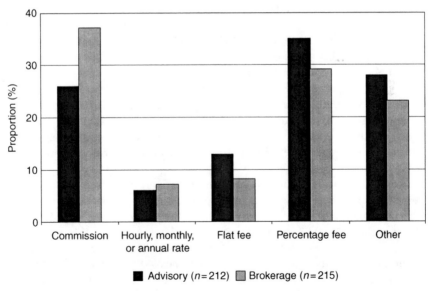

Figure 7.3 Methods of payment to individual professionals for financial services
Source: Authors' calculations; see text.

monly reported compensation method to individual professionals for brokerage services was commission (37 percent), and the most commonly reported compensation method for advisory services was a fee determined by percentage of assets (35 percent). When asked to estimate their annual expenditure for the different types of services, respondents whose individual professional provided advisory services ranged from $0 to $30,000, with an average of $1,374. Answers from respondents whose individual professional provided brokerage services ranged from $0 to $21,500, with an average of $1,131. Yet the median annual expenditure on advisory services from individual professionals was $125, and the median annual expenditure on brokerage services from individual professionals was $200. The large difference between average and median expenditure indicates that a small proportion of respondents reported paying a large amount for these services. Indeed, 10 percent of the responses on annual expenditure for advisory services from an individual professional were at least $3,000. Likewise, 10 percent of the responses on annual expenditure for brokerage services were at least $2,400.

Many respondents were confused about the methods of payment or the type of firm with which their individual professional was associated. For example, eighty-four respondents indicated that they received advisory services (either alone or in conjunction with brokerage services) from an investment advisory firm that was not also a brokerage firm. Of these respondents, 19 percent reported that they paid for these advisory services based on a percentage fee, and 22 percent indicated that they paid commission for advisory services. However, Hung et al. (2008) found that 97 percent of SEC-registered investment advisers that were not registered broker-dealers reported that they were compensated by asset-based fees, and only 10 percent reported that they received commissions.[8] Finally, fourteen respondents did not answer the estimated annual expenditure question for advisory services, and forty-one reported that they paid $0. For brokerage services, eighteen respondents did not answer the estimated annual expenditure question, and thirty-four reported that they paid nothing.

Respondents also reported that the most common form of compensation for brokerage services for firms, as opposed to individual professions, was commission and, for advisory services, was 'Other' (see Figure 7.4). The most common explanations for other responses were that the respondent did not pay for the service (six responses) or did not know what he or she paid for the service (four responses). When asked to estimate their annual expenditures for the services provided by firms, rather than directly from individual professionals, the respondents' answers ranged from $0 to $5,700, with an average of $278. The answers from respondents with firms providing brokerage services ranged from $0 to $8,000, with an

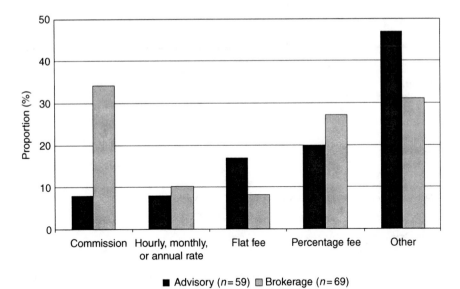

Figure 7.4 Methods of payment to firms for professional services
Source: Authors' calculations; see text.

average of $476. For advisory services, eight respondents did not answer the estimated annual expenditure question, and twenty-one reported that they paid $0. For brokerage services, five respondents did not answer the estimated annual expenditure question, and fourteen reported that they paid nothing.

How respondents located their financial service provider

Regardless of the types of services received, the most common way in which respondents found their current individual professional was by referral from a friend or family. The second most common way was by professional referral (see Table 7.4). When asked about how respondents found the current firm that they employed for financial services, the most common response was 'Other'. Of the thirty-two other responses, there were nineteen explanations. The most frequently mentioned explanation (six responses) was that the respondent found the firm through their place of work. The second most common method was by referral from a friend or family (see Table 7.5).

TABLE 7.4 Methods of locating individual professionals (%)

Method	All responses	Advisory service only	Brokerage service only	Both types of services
Professional referral	30.5	23.3	13.8	34.4
Referral from friend or family	45.6	43.3	34.5	47.8
Mailing	3.3	6.7	0.0	3.3
Print ad	3.8	0.0	6.9	3.9
Television ad	0.8	0.0	3.4	0.6
Internet	1.3	0.0	6.9	0.6
N	239	30	29	180

Source. Authors' calculations based on the ALP survey; see text.

TABLE 7.5 Methods of locating financial service firms (%)

Method	All responses	Advisory service only	Brokerage service only	Both types of services
Professional referral	18.1	14.3	12.0	22.7
Referral from friend or family	28.9	28.6	28.0	29.5
Mailing	2.4	0.0	0.0	4.5
Print ad	10.8	7.1	8.0	13.6
Television ad	6.0	0.0	4.0	9.1
Internet	8.4	0.0	12.0	9.1
Other	36.1	50.0	44.0	27.3
N	89	14	25	44

Source. Authors' calculations based on the ALP survey; see text.

Length of relationship and satisfaction with financial service provider

In general, respondents reported that they had been working with the current individual professional for several years. When respondents were asked how long they had been working with their current individual professional, 34 percent reported at least ten years, 26 percent reported five to ten years, 32 percent reported one to five years, and 8 percent reported less than one year. For respondents who received only advisory services and for respondents who received both types of services from their individual professionals, the most common length of relationship was more than ten years. For respondents who received brokerage services only, ten respondents reported that the length of the relationship was between one

TABLE 7.6 Length of time with same individual professional and customer satisfaction (%)

	All responses	Advisory service only	Brokerage service only	Both types of services
About how long have you been doing business with this individual?				
Less than 1 year	7.5	20.0	6.9	5.6
1–5 years	31.8	23.3	34.5	32.8
5–10 years	26.4	20.0	27.6	27.2
More than 10 years	34.3	36.7	31.0	34.4
I am very satisfied with the service that I receive from this individual.				
Strongly disagree	7.1	0.0	6.9	8.3
Disagree	2.1	3.3	3.4	1.7
Neither agree nor disagree	15.9	26.7	10.3	15.0
Agree	41.4	43.3	62.1	37.8
Strongly agree	33.5	26.7	17.2	37.2
I trust that this individual acts in my best interest.				
Strongly disagree	7.1	0.0	3.4	8.9
Disagree	2.5	6.7	6.9	1.1
Neither agree nor disagree	15.1	26.7	17.2	12.8
Agree	35.1	33.3	51.7	32.8
Strongly agree	40.2	33.3	20.7	44.4
I believe that this individual provides me with a valuable service.				
Strongly disagree	7.5	0.0	6.9	8.9
Disagree	1.7	0.0	6.9	1.1
Neither agree nor disagree	11.7	20.0	17.2	9.4
Agree	41.0	53.3	51.7	37.2
Strongly agree	38.1	26.7	17.2	43.3
N	239	30	29	180

Source: Authors' calculations based on the ALP survey; see text.

and five years, and nine respondents reported that the length of the relationship was more than ten years (see Table 7.6).

Most respondents were satisfied with their individual professionals: at least 70 percent reported that they agreed or strongly agreed with the statements: 'I am very satisfied with the service that I receive from this individual; I trust that this individual acts in my best interest; I believe that this individual provides me with a valuable service.' Respondents who had worked with their individual professional for at least ten years expressed even greater satisfaction: 78 percent agreed or strongly agreed that they were very satisfied with the service that they received, 83 percent agreed or strongly agreed that their individual professional acted in their best inter-

TABLE 7.7 Length of time with same firm and customer satisfaction (%)

	All responses	Advisory service only	Brokerage service only	Both types of services
About how long have you been doing business with this firm?				
Less than 1 year	7.2	7.1	12.0	4.5
1–5 years	25.3	21.4	28.0	25.0
5–10 years	25.3	7.1	32.0	27.3
More than 10 years	42.2	64.3	28.0	43.2
I am very satisfied with the service that I receive from this firm.				
Strongly disagree	7.2	7.1	4.0	9.1
Disagree	1.2	0.0	4.0	0.0
Neither agree nor disagree	19.3	21.4	24.0	15.9
Agree	38.6	35.7	32.0	43.2
Strongly agree	33.7	35.7	36.0	31.8
I trust that this firm acts in my best interest.				
Strongly disagree	6.0	7.1	4.0	6.8
Disagree	2.4	0.0	8.0	0.0
Neither agree nor disagree	31.3	28.6	40.0	27.3
Agree	31.3	35.7	20.0	36.4
Strongly agree	28.9	28.6	28.0	29.5
I believe that this firm provides me with a valuable service.				
Strongly disagree	7.2	7.1	4.0	9.1
Disagree	1.2	0.0	0.0	2.3
Neither agree nor disagree	19.3	21.4	20.0	18.2
Agree	34.9	28.6	36.0	36.4
Strongly agree	37.3	42.9	40.0	34.1
N	83	14	25	44

Source: Authors' calculations based on the ALP survey; see text.

est, and 82 percent agreed or strongly agreed that they were being provided with a valuable service (see Table 7.7).

As we found with the results on individual professionals, respondents tended to be satisfied with their firms. At least 70 percent of respondents reported that they agreed or strongly agreed with these statements: 'I am very satisfied with the service that I receive from this firm; I trust that this firm acts in my best interest; I believe that this firm provides me with a valuable service.' When we condition on the type of service provided, one category in which respondents indicate a lower level of satisfaction is the degree to which they trust that the firm that provides brokerage services acts in their best interest. In this case, only 48 percent of respondents agreed or strongly agreed with the statement. Longer-term relationships were also rated more positively.

TABLE 7.8 Reasons given for not using a financial professional (%)

Reason	Brokerage and advisory services	Brokerage services	Advisory services
No money for investments	47.1	35.5	17.6
Too expensive	13.2	9.7	20.6
Too hard to choose one	6.2	0.0	2.9
Do not need assistance with financial decisions	21.5	12.9	52.9
Had one and did not like him, her, or the firm	8.2	0.0	11.8
N	340	31	34

Source: Authors' calculations based on the ALP survey; see text.

Reasons not to use a financial service provider

We asked respondents who reported that they did not use a financial service provider for the reasons that they did not employ one. Respondents who used a financial service provider only for advisory services were asked why they did not use a financial service provider for brokerage services. Likewise, to respondents who used a financial service provider only for brokerage services, we asked why they did not use a financial service provider for advisory services. The results are summarized in Table 7.8.

Respondents were given five choices for why they might not employ a financial service provider, in addition to an 'Other' category, and they were asked to choose all that applied: no money for investments; too expensive; too hard to choose one; did not need assistance with financial decisions; or had one and did not like him, her, or the firm. For respondents who did not use a financial service provider at all, the most common answer (47 percent) was 'No money for investments'. For respondents who did not use a financial service provider for brokerage services, the most common specified reason (36 percent) was 'No money for investments'. Among respondents who do not use a financial service provider for advisory services, the most common reason (18 percent) is that the respondent does not 'need assistance with [his or her] financial decisions'.

Relative inclination to seek services from brokers or investment advisers

Respondents were then presented with definitions of broker and investment adviser, including a description of common job titles, legal duties, and typical compensation. We first asked them: 'On a scale from 0 to 100, what do you

TABLE 7.9 Inclination to seek future services from investment advisers and brokers (%)

	Investment adviser			Broker		
	Mean	Median	N	Mean (%)	Median	N
Percent chance of seeking *services* from [investment adviser/broker] in the next five years	37.1	25	634	36.6	20	637
Percent chance of seeking *investment advice* from [investment adviser/ broker] in the next five years	51.9	50	454	47.7	50	458
I would trust investment advice from [investment adviser/broker] (1 = strongly disagree, 5 = strongly agree)	3.4	3	635	3.1	3	637

Source: Authors' calculations based on the ALP survey; see text.

think is the percent chance that you will seek (or continue to seek) services from a [broker/investment adviser] in the next five years?' For respondents who reported a positive probability, we followed up with a question on investment advice: 'On a scale from 0 to 100, what do you think is the percent chance that you will seek (or continue to seek) investment advice from a [broker/investment adviser] in the next five years?' Last, we asked respondents to rate the degree to which they agreed with the following statement: 'I would trust investment advice from a [broker/investment adviser].'

As shown in Table 7.9, respondents were roughly equally likely to seek services in general, and investment advice in particular, from investment advisers and broker-dealers. On average, respondents were equally likely to seek services, in general, from investment advisers and brokers, but the median response was slightly higher for services from an investment adviser (25 percent versus 20 percent). Almost 29 percent of respondents reported no chance that they would seek services from a broker, and 28 percent of respondents reported no chance that they would seek services from an investment adviser. Among respondents who reported a positive probability that they would seek services from a broker or an investment adviser, the median response indicated an equal willingness to seek investment advice from either.

Assistance respondents seek for financial matters

We asked all respondents, 'What kind of professional assistance with financial matters would you find most helpful at this point in your life?', with the following options: asset management, college-saving planning, debt consolidation or management, developing a budget and saving plan, estate planning, executing stock or mutual fund transactions, general financial planning, investment advising, retirement planning, or other. A majority of respondents (62 percent) indicated they would like assistance with retirement planning. Many respondents would also like assistance with investment advising (41 percent), financial planning (38 percent), and estate planning (35 percent). We replicated the analysis conditioning on age, education, income, investment experience, and whether the respondent reported using a financial service provider.[9] Across all groups, the most commonly selected option was 'retirement planning'. Across all groups, the second most common was 'investment advising', except for respondents who did not have a college degree, respondents who did not report using a financial service provider, or respondents who were classified as inexperienced. For the first three of those groups, the second most commonly selected option was 'general financial planning'. For the last group, respondents classified as inexperienced, the second most commonly selected option was 'developing a budget and savings plan'.

Focus groups

Focus groups allow for in-depth and interactive discussion of the topics, and they also allow moderators to follow up on beliefs and understanding behind responses. Although focus-group participants are not nationally representative and data collected during focus groups are only qualitative, this method often provides researchers with important evidence on the more nuanced issues surrounding topics. To illustrate the understanding learned from this approach, we first discuss our methodology, followed by impressions from the focus groups regarding the financial service industry. We then describe participants' financial decision-making and experience with financial service providers. Last, we examine some of the perceived differences between investment advisers and broker-dealers.

Methods

We conducted six focus groups of ten to twelve participants each, representing both experienced and inexperienced investors. As with survey respondents, focus-group participants were deemed to be experienced investors if they held investments outside of retirement accounts, had formal training in finance or investing, or held investments only with retirement accounts but answered positively to questions eliciting their self-assessed financial understanding (such as the nature and causes of increases in their investments, seeking out information about their investments when necessary, and knowing the different investment options available to them). Participants who did not meet these requirements were deemed inexperienced investors.

The sixty-seven participants ranged from 22 to 77 years of age, with two-thirds of participants older than 40. The mix of racial and ethnic background included forty-four white but not Hispanic, eighteen black, two Hispanic, and three Asian participants. The focus groups were held in Alexandria, Virginia and Fort Wayne, Indiana in September and October 2007. We employed the services of outside firms to recruit our participants. For the Virginia focus groups, we used a recruiting firm that maintained a database of approximately 17,000 individuals from the Washington, DC, metropolitan area, including northern Virginia and parts of Maryland. For the Indiana focus groups, we used a local recruiting firm that maintained a database of approximately 35,000 individuals, mainly from Allen County, Indiana, with a small percentage (9–10 percent) of individuals who reside in counties immediately adjacent to Allen County. Each location included two groups of experienced investors and one group of inexperienced investors. The approximate ratio of two-thirds experienced investors and one-third inexperienced investors is similar to the ratio among the ALP respondents. We asked them a range of questions about their level of understanding and experience with the financial services industry. We also presented them with sample advertisements from both broker-dealers and investment advisers, and asked what types of products and services and levels of interaction they expected from each.

Investment experience

Almost all participants held investments in retirement accounts, primarily through their employers. Many had investments outside of retirement accounts, primarily in mutual funds, and some held individual stocks and annuities. A few individuals who were particularly uncertain about what to do with their money had put their saving into money-market accounts (MMA) and certificates of deposit (CDs). These participants felt that they had received poor financial advice in the past and were unsure how to invest it, so they went with the perceived security of MMAs and CDs. Participant age ranged from 22 to 77 years, and investment experience ranged from 2 to 40 years. Most participants described their level of financial knowledge as low, including many who had been investing for several years. About 10 percent of participants considered their level of financial knowledge to be good or advanced. Participants attributed their lack of knowledge to having little interest in finances, lack of time to learn and keep up, and the fact that financial literature is complicated and confusing. Some mentioned that conflicting information left them unsure about which sources to trust.

General impressions of the financial service industry

When asked about their general views of the financial service industry, participants tended to characterize the industry as complicated. As with any industry, people felt that there were both honest and dishonest individuals within the financial service industry. Some noted that recent corporate scandals (e.g., WorldCom and Enron) led the public to view the financial services industry with more skepticism. As it is an industry based on trust, many participants noted that they did not trust the industry. Many of those with investments acknowledged that they were unsure what they were being charged for the investments they currently held. They believed that there were hidden fees and that investment professionals would not provide them with certain information unless they specifically asked for it. They believed that one must know the right questions to ask or end up at a disadvantage. When asked about financial service advertisements they might have seen, participants believed that advertisements of investment professionals tried to make people think it was easy to get started and that the company would work for its clients to help them attain a certain lifestyle.

Participants cited several reasons they saw as to why people failed to invest. These included the fact that they thought it was necessary to have a large amount of disposable income to invest; they had no money to invest; they feared losing their money in investments; they lacked knowledge about investing; and they believed that the financial service industry was too complex to navigate.

Investor decision-making and experience with financial service professionals

Participants reported obtaining information about financial products and services from a variety of sources, including the Internet, friends and family, financial magazines, television, prospectuses, presentations at work, and financial service professionals (including advisers, accountants, insurance agents, and their bank). Roughly half of participants reported that they used a financial service provider. Those who had investments but did not use a financial service provider explained that they trusted themselves as much as a professional with their money.

In fact, trust of the individual financial service professional was the most-cited feature of what investors sought, cited as more important than trust of the firm for which that individual worked. Many participants had a preference for older, established firms, because they showed staying power and the ability to ride out hard times. Most participants currently working with a financial service provider located that provider through personal or professional referral. When we asked participants who did not currently use a financial service provider how they would find one if they chose to employ one in the future, referral was the most common response. Although the majority of those who used a financial service provider were happy with the relationship and the service, several participants did note that they were unsatisfied, because of lack of personal interaction (these comments were similar to those reported by ALP respondents). Many respondents had gone years without hearing from their financial service providers, although some recognized that they were partly responsible for this lack of communication. Others noted that their financial service provider did not seem to do much.

Participants were also asked what they liked about their relationship with their financial service provider, if they currently used one; otherwise, they were asked what they would seek in a relationship with a financial service provider if they were to employ one. Some participants preferred a very 'hands-off' relationship, stating that they had neither the inclination nor the time to follow the markets and were happy to turn that job over to a professional. Other participants thought that they would like to be a partner in their financial decisions and to have a say in what was done with their money. However, these participants tended to realize that there was much about the financial service industry that they did not know or understand, so it would be important to have a financial service provider who would take the time to educate them about the market and the various products available. Many participants felt that, because their assets were too modest, they would not be of interest to the majority of financial service providers to spend the necessary amount of time to work with and educate them.

Contact with investment professionals

Some participants said that they would prefer to communicate with an individual professional via the phone, while others preferred face-to-face meetings or email. In an ideal relationship, participants felt that they would want to meet with their representatives more frequently at first (monthly), and then on a quarterly or semi-annual basis after they felt comfortable in the relationship. Participants who felt fairly knowledgeable about their investments sought less contact with their investment professional.

Desired services

Of those who sought professional help, all cited retirement that would involve not only saving for retirement but also determining how the funds should be spent and invested during retirement. The other desired services that participants mentioned most were education planning, insurance planning, and estate planning. A few participants noted needing help with budget planning and saving to buy a house. Participants were divided over whether it was better to have all their investments handled by one firm, or to have several firms helping them. Convenience was an advantage to having one firm: the individual professional could see the whole financial picture and better advise the client and reduce the amount of paperwork to track. Other participants wanted to spread their investments across a couple of firms, believing that this would reduce their risks. They also noted that some firms specialized in certain types of investments and that it might be better to play to the strengths of certain firms. Still others preferred the idea of entrusting some of their money to financial service providers but also investing a portion of their money on their own.

Perceived differences between investment advisers and brokers

Focus-group participants displayed some confusion regarding the role of investment advisers and brokers, as observed with ALP respondents; focus-group discussion helped illuminate the sources of confusion. To assess participant levels of understanding regarding the roles of various financial service professionals, we administered a short questionnaire prior to the detailed discussion on the distinction between investment advisers and brokers, to capture their understanding on coming into the focus-group session and not reflect anything they might learn during the focus-group session. Participants were presented with a series of specific services and obligations and were asked to indicate which items applied to the following financial service professionals: investment advisers, brokers, financial advisors, financial consultants, financial planners, or none of the above. Table 7.10 provides the results of that questionnaire,[10] and it indicates that focus-group responses were quite similar to those of the household survey.

The main differences between focus-group participants and survey respondents were that a much smaller share of focus-group participants (5 percent) believed that investment advisers received commissions than did survey respondents (43 percent). Focus-group participants were more likely to report that both investment advisers and brokers were required to act in the client's best interest (64 and 63 percent, respectively) than did

TABLE 7.10 Participants' beliefs about financial service professionals (%)

Does this professional:	Investment advisers	Brokers	Financial advisors or consultants	Financial planners	None of these
Provide advice about securities (e.g., shares of stocks or mutual funds) as part of their regular business	85	61	76	63	0
Execute stock or mutual fund transactions on the client's behalf	27	84	22	18	0
Recommend specific investments	93	46	67	46	0
Provide retirement planning	39	12	81	91	0
Provide general financial planning	33	16	79	91	0
Typically receive commissions on purchases or trades that the client makes	5	96	43	33	0
Get paid based on the amount of assets that the client holds	51	57	45	19	6
Act in the client's best interest, as required by law	64	63	58	57	18
Disclose any conflicts of interest, as required by law	60	70	61	72	18

Notes: Based on sixty-seven participants.

Source: Authors' calculations based on focus-group survey; see text.

ALP respondents (49 and 42 percent, respectively). Furthermore, focus-group participants were more likely than survey respondents to report that brokers were required to disclose any conflicts of interest. In fact, focus-group participants were more likely to report that brokers, rather than investment advisers, must disclose conflicts, whereas ALP respondents were more likely to report that investment advisers must disclose conflicts.

Reactions to investment advisers' and broker-dealers' advertisements

The first set of advertisements presented to focus-group participants was general advertisements from actual firms taken from magazines, with identifying information or marks stripped. Firm A's brokerage services advertisement stressed the importance of building a relationship with one's financial consultant based on trust. The advertisement further described financial consultants' expertise and research tools (with fine print detailing that the research tools provide general, not personal, advice). The advertisement specifically mentioned mutual funds and stocks. Firm B's advertisement, taken from an investment advisory firm, stressed the importance of careful planning so that the reader's estate would be left to his or her beneficiaries, rather than to the Internal Revenue Service (IRS). This advertisement also highlighted the firm's experience and expertise. The advertisement specifically mentioned philanthropy, asset management, and sophisticated wealth-transfer strategies.

In discussing what appealed to them about Firm A, many participants mentioned that they liked the trust message and that the advertisement implied that all of its employees were well trained. A commonly mentioned dislike of the firm was the fine print detailing that the research tools were not personal advice. Regarding Firm B, many participants mentioned that they believed that they thought that they could benefit from its services, such as asset management. However, given the tone of the advertisement, many participants also thought that they did not have enough money to be a client at Firm B.

Inclination to seek services from investment advisers or brokers

Participants were presented with fact sheets on investment advisers and brokers, which included the same information as the descriptions given to ALP survey respondents: definitions of *broker* and *investment adviser*, including a description of common job titles, legal duties, and typical compensation. Even after being presented with fact sheets, participants were still confused by the titles. They noted that the common job titles for investment advisers and broker-dealers were so similar that people were easily confused about which type of professional they were consulting. Some participants said they knew which type of investment professional they had, but most did not. Participants expressed interest in the fact that brokers have to be certified and investment advisers do not. Several interpreted this to mean that advisers were less qualified than the brokers.

Many respondents did not understand the term *fiduciary* and whether fiduciary was a higher standard than suitability. Some participants did not think that the legal requirements for either investment advisers or brokers were stringent enough. Several participants mentioned that, if an investment adviser made a costly mistake with a client's money, they thought that it would be difficult to prove that the adviser was not acting in the client's best interest. Other participants did not like that brokers had to recommend products that were suitable for them. They thought that *suitable* was too vague a term and that it was not clear how the broker would determine suitability. Many participants also noted that investment advisers had to disclose conflicts of interest, while brokers did not.

Conclusion

Our review of the literature and our survey evidence shows that many people do not understand key distinctions between investment advisers and broker-dealers—their duties, the titles they use, the firms for which they work, or the services they offer. Nevertheless, people tend to have relatively long-term relationships with their financial service professionals, expressing high levels of satisfaction with their services. This satisfaction was often reported to arise from the personal attention the investor received. Unfortunately, we lack evidence on how levels of satisfaction varied with financial returns, but we know from focus-group participants with investments that many were unsure about the fees they paid for their investments. Additionally, people are unclear regarding the roles of broker-dealers and investment advisers, commenting that 'We do it all' advertisements make it difficult to discern broker-dealers from investment advisers. Furthermore, even though we sought to explain fiduciary duty and suitability in plain language, respondents struggled to understand the differences between the standards of care. Even after explaining that a fiduciary duty is generally a higher standard of care, focus-group participants expressed doubt that the standards are different in practice.

Despite this confusion, however, most respondents and participants expressed satisfaction with their financial service providers. The most commonly cited reasons for the satisfaction of survey respondents were their professional's attentiveness and accessibility, mentioned even more often than expertise. Although focus-group members also mentioned these qualities, they more often mentioned trust. Finally, respondents and participants often indicated that they recognized the value of investment advice. Those who currently received investment advice often reported that they found the service to be valuable. Many of those who did not currently receive investment advice expressed a desire to receive these services, but they were concerned that their relatively low amount of investable assets made it difficult to obtain these valuable services.

Endnotes

[1] This chapter is drawn from Hung et al. (2008).

[2] As of this writing, a consolidated House and Senate financial regulatory reform bill had not passed. The House of Representatives version of a financial regulatory reform bill passed in December 2009. This legislation directs the SEC to adopt rules that apply a standard of conduct to broker-dealers and investment advisers who provide personalized investment advice to retail customers to act in the best interest of their customers (a fiduciary duty). The Act goes on to say that broker-dealers are not subject to a continuing duty of care or loyalty to the customer, after providing personalized investment advice about securities. Broker-dealers are required to disclose any material conflicts of interest (such as the sale of only proprietary products) and obtain consent from the customer. In general, the SEC is directed to require simple, clear disclosures to investors regarding their relationship with their financial professionals, including any material conflicts of interest. The SEC is also directed to adopt rules, where appropriate, to restrict or prohibit sales practices, conflicts of interest, and compensation schemes by broker-dealers and investment advisers that are contrary to investors' interests. The Senate Banking Committee proposed the 2010 Restoring American Financial Stability Act. This legislation calls for a study by the SEC on whether brokers should be subject to the same fiduciary standard that applies to registered investment advisers. Under the bill, the SEC would have one year to report to Congress on what it finds and another year to implement any necessary changes.

[3] According to the March 2007 Current Population Survey, 85 percent of Americans aged 18 and older had at least a high school diploma or GED, and 26 percent had at least a bachelor's degree. The distribution for US household income is 22 percent with less than $25,000; 27 percent greater than $25,000 but less than $50,000; 20 percent between $50,000 and $75,000; and 31 percent greater than $75,000. See US Census Bureau (2007).

[4] Between subjects, we randomly varied the order of *broker* and *investment adviser* as they appeared on the computer screen.

[5] When we posed the question, 'Do you currently use any professional service providers for (*a*) conducting stock market or mutual fund transactions or (*b*) advising, management, or planning?' we randomly varied the order of the services between subjects as the question appeared on the computer screen.

[6] Some respondents provided more than one title for an individual professional (e.g., financial planner, stockbroker, and insurance agent).

[7] The frequency distributions for these first individual professionals are similar to those for all individual professionals in the previous section. Likewise, for the first firm reported, the frequency distribution of firm types is similar to those for all firms reported. For further details, see Hung et al. (2008).

[8] An alternative explanation for this inconsistency could be that the firms that our respondents used were state-registered rather than SEC-registered firms, and state-registered firms are less likely than SEC-registered firms to charge asset-based fees.

[9] Complete results are available from the authors by request.

[10] A data appendix (available on request) provides a breakdown of questionnaire responses by age, education, location, investment experience, and whether the participant has a financial service provider.

References

Chao, C. N., R. J. Mockler, and D. Dologite (2002). 'Online Trading: The Competitive Landscape,' *Review of Business*, 23(3): 44–8.

Fusilier, M. and M. Schaub (2003). 'Broker-Client Contact and Client Satisfaction: Are Client Attitudes Towards Brokers Bullish and Bearish with the Stock Market?,' *Journal of Financial Services Marketing*, 8(1): 63.

Hung, A. A., N. Clancy, J. Dominitz, E. Talley, C. Berrebi, and F. Suvankulov (2008). *Investor and Industry Perspectives on Investment Advisers and Broker-Dealers*. Santa Monica, CA: RAND Corporation, TR-556-USSEC. http://www.sec.gov/news/press/2008/2008-1_randiabdreport.pdf

Opinion Research Corporation (2004). *Regulation of Stockbrokers and Financial Advisors: What American Investors Understand, Think Is Right: Summary of Survey Findings*. Princeton, NJ: Briefing for Zero Alpha Group and Consumer Federation of America.

Siegel and Gale, LLC and Gelb Consulting Group (2005). *Results of Investor Focus Group Interviews About Proposed Brokerage Account Disclosures: Report to the Securities and Exchange Commission*. San Francisco, CA: Siegel and Gale, LLC and Gelb Consulting Group. http://www.sec.gov/rules/proposed/s72599/focusgrp031005.pdf

TD Ameritrade (2006). 'TD AMERITRADE Survey Reveals Need for Clarity,' Omaha, NE: TD Ameritrade, May 10.

Tully, D. P. and A. Levitt (1995). *Report of the Committee on Compensation Practices*. Washington, DC: US Securities and Exchange Commission.

US Census Bureau (2007). *March 2007 Current Population Survey*. Washington, DC: United States Census Bureau.

US Securities and Exchange Commission (SEC) (2005). *Certain Broker-Dealers Deemed Not to Be Investment Advisers*. Releases 34-51523 and IA-2376, file S7-25-99. Washington, DC: US Securities and Exchange Commission.

US Statutes (1934). Title 48, Section 881, Securities and Exchange Act, June 6, 1934.
—— (1940). Title 54, Section 847, Investment Advisers Act, November 1, 1940.

Yang, Z. and X. Fang (2004). 'Online Service Quality Dimensions and Their Relationships with Satisfaction: A Content Analysis of Customer Reviews of Securities Brokerage Services,' *International Journal of Service Industry Management*, 15(3): 302–26.

Zero Alpha Group (ZAG) (2004). 'Survey: In Blow to SEC Rule Proposal, 9 Out of 10 U.S. Investors Back Equally Tough Broker, Investment Adviser Regulation,' Washington, DC: ZAG, October 27.

Chapter 8

Pecuniary Mistakes? Payday Borrowing by Credit Union Members

Susan P. Carter, Paige M. Skiba, and Jeremy Tobacman

This chapter examines how households choose between financial products. We build from three main contexts. First, the realm of options most households face is large and complicated, especially for households with low levels of financial sophistication (Lusardi and Mitchell, 2007, 2009). Lusardi and Tufano (2009) show in particular that people with lower levels of 'debt literacy' are more likely to use expensive sources of financing, such as payday loans. This past work invites a search for situations where it appears consumers could make better financial decisions.

Second, we study the context of a category of financial institutions that, as specified in their charters, have the purpose of benefiting their customer-members. Credit unions are not-for-profit financial cooperatives that are governed by their members, who historically had to be united by a 'common bond of occupation or association, or belong to groups within a well-defined neighborhood, community, or rural district' according to the Federal Credit Union Act of 1934. In 1935, only about 1 percent of the population belonged to a credit union, but by the end of 2008 there were 7,806 state and federal credit unions in operation with 88.5 million members and $811 billion of assets. In 2007, total household saving and loans outstanding in credit unions reached $632 billion and $527 billion, respectively. The credit union share of outstanding loans is about 4 percent.

Although credit unions have become increasingly important in the past several decades, economists have studied them infrequently. Most of the existing scholarship has focused on competition between credit unions and commercial banks and the effects on the deposit rates of both institutions (Emmons and Schmid, 1999, 2000; Feinberg, 2001, 2002). The other area of focus for research on credit unions has been the effects of credit union governance rules (Davis, 2001) and consolidation of credit unions through mergers and acquisitions (Goddard et al., 2009). The two studies closest to ours study consumer financial decision-making and credit unions. Rauterkus and Ramamonjiarivelo (2010) analyze the determinants of credit union deposits, and Bubb and Kaufman (2009) explain theoretically and empirically why consumers may often receive better terms on financial products from credit unions than from for-profit financial institutions.

Third, with this chapter we seek to interface with the literature on the 'liquid debt puzzle'. This term refers to the observation that many debtor households in fact have low-interest paying liquid assets which they could use, at least in part, to pay off higher-interest debt. Gross and Souleles (2002) found, 'over 90 percent of people with credit card debt have some very liquid assets in checking and saving accounts, which yield at most 1 to 2 percent'. Not all authors consider this fact pattern puzzling, and Zinman (2007) provides a particularly careful treatment of explanations for 'borrowing high and lending low' that are consistent with rational choice models. Our view is that the probability is a liquid debt puzzle is really present and is increasing with the size of the interest losses. In this chapter, we describe borrowing high and lending low as a 'pecuniary mistake' and we try to measure its size, while reserving judgment about whether 'rationality' can generate the behavior.

A variety of alternative decision-making perspectives are consistent with the presence of 'pecuniary mistakes'. Lusardi (2007) points out that mistakes in financial planning are not rare, and that without proper financial guidance, individuals may routinely fail to save enough for retirement, invest in assets that are too risky or too conservative, and not take advantage of what the employer matches. These points emphasize that an individual's level of financial literacy is associated with the types of sources he/she relies on for advice, and more broadly with how efficiently he/she manages his/her financial resources.

Other sources of information about 'liquid debt puzzles' and payday loans include the following. First, the 2008 Survey of Consumer Finances found that one-third of payday borrowers had been denied some type of loan within the past five years, compared to one-tenth of non-payday borrowers (Logan and Weller, 2009). Second, Agarwal et al. (2009) perform a similar study to ours using matched administrative datasets of credit cards and payday loans. They find that people took out payday loans when liquidity on their credit card was still available at a lower interest rate. Specifically, average interest losses in their study were $200 over a three-year period. Quantitatively, those results resemble our finding here of an average of $88 in interest losses during an observation period of six-and-a-half months. In this chapter, we include checking account balances, in addition to alternative sources of loans, which likely is causing our results to be even higher.

In this chapter, we introduce a new administrative credit union dataset, provide some new evidence from it on basic transaction patterns, report our findings on 'pecuniary mistakes', and briefly discuss our results and conclusions.

Credit union dataset

We conduct our analysis using a proprietary transaction-level dataset from a credit union with more than half a million members. In the case of this particular credit union, access is restricted to people living in the region where the credit union operates and to people working for a particular company that sponsors the credit union. Historically, credit unions—which are not-for-profit—have accepted restrictions on membership in exchange for tax-exempt status.

The dataset includes a population of 3,845 members who had an electronic debit to a payday lender during our observation period (January 1, 2006 to June 14, 2006), plus a representative random sample of 12,467 other credit union members who do not borrow from the payday lender. Of this sample, we restrict the data to the 15,478 members who were in the dataset for the whole time period.

For all credit union members in the sample, we have information on the dates and amounts of credits and debits in their checking, saving, and line of credit accounts during the period of observation. A total of 2.75 million transactions are included, representing an average of about one per member per day. The dataset also includes information on members' initial balances, allowing computation of balances and available liquidity at any point in time. In addition, we observe members' Fair Isaac Corporation (FICO) scores on January 11, 2006 and March 26, 2006, and internal customer scores assigned to them by the credit union at the time of the most recent application for credit. Finally, the dataset flags electronic debits to the local market-leading payday lender.

Transaction patterns and credit scores
of payday borrowers

Table 8.1 shows summary statistics for both the representative random sample and for the payday borrowers in our dataset. The FICO scores (pulled on January 11, 2006 and March 26, 2006) are lower for payday borrowers. Additionally, payday borrowers tend to have a decrease in their FICO scores from January 11 to March 26, while the change in credit score of nonpayday borrowers is quite small. This result could suggest that payday borrowers are having financial troubles that cause them to not pay their debts (lowering their score), or that payday borrowers, in general, make poor choices that lead to lower scores.

Table 8.1 also reports a high frequency of transactions made by payday borrowers. Over the whole sample period, payday borrowers made an average of 364 total transactions, relative to 123 made by the random

TABLE 8.1 Summary statistics

	Credit union representative sample	Credit union payday borrowers
FICO 1/11/2006	720 (83.3)	584 (84.7)
FICO 3/26/2006	720 (68.0)	581 (69.5)
Percent above low CU score threshold	96	76
Provide above high CU score threshold	82	31
Total number of transactions	123 (167)	364 (199)
Number of checking transactions	105 (159)	338 (192)
Mean absolute checking transactions ($)	295 (627)	145 (86.7)
Average number of payday loans	0	3.28 (2.69)
Average payday loan amount ($)	0	449 (220)
Average payday loan interest paid ($)	0	175 (171)
Total liquidity on 1/1/2006 ($)	6,529 (22,469)	832 (2,434)
N	11,824	3,654

Notes: Summary statistics for a representative sample of members of the credit union and for the population of members who had an electronic payment to a payday lender during the observation period (1/1/2006–6/14/2006). Standard deviations are in parentheses. The CU score thresholds affected access to credit from the credit union and affected the interest rate. All differences between columns are significant at the 1 percent level.

Source: Authors' calculations based on administrative data from a credit union; see text.

sample. The cause of this previously undocumented fact remains unclear. One hypothesis is that payday borrowers have fewer accounts outside this credit union, and hence use these accounts more. Alleviating financial stress may be more challenging to the extent stressed households create costs for financial institutions by making more transactions of small dollar amounts.

Pecuniary mistakes?

Previous papers have shown that people often make pecuniary mistakes by taking out more expensive loans when cheaper substitutes are available. With access to information on the amounts available in customers' lines of credit, checking accounts, and saving accounts, we can determine whether they could have reduced their interest rates by borrowing elsewhere, or whether they could have avoided borrowing altogether. Our estimates are a lower bound because we lack information on other loan options available to the payday borrower (such as liquidity on a credit card).

To find the amount available to customers in their Line of Credit (LOC) on any given day, we first took the LOC limit given on January 1 and April 1. Then, by calculating the running balance of LOC (determined by the initial balance on January 1 minus any credits to the LOC and plus any debits), we found the LOC available on any day to be the LOC limit minus the LOC balance. Some people in the dataset have a zero LOC limit on January 1 but a positive LOC balance. These people had their account closed and were just paying off their balance. Based on the January 1 and April 1 LOC limits, 70.1 percent of payday borrowers have a zero LOC limit. In a similar fashion to the line of credit, to find checking and saving account levels, we used the initial balance on January 1 and added or subtracted debits or credits made to the account over time.

We inferred the amount of a customer's payday loan from the repayment amount (which is known from the electronic debit) and the interest rate (which is fixed here by state law). We then estimated interest losses using a maximally conservative method.

We computed minimum levels of liquidity from LOCs, checking accounts, and saving amounts between payday loan repayments. We then compared the estimated payday loan amount to the amount available in each of the consumer's accounts, and total liquidity combined across accounts. Assuming that consumers take out payday loans when their accounts were at a minimum gives a lower bound for the percent of 'mistakes' made.

Figure 8.1 illustrates the dynamics of an individual's checking, line of credit, and saving accounts from fifty-six days before to fifty-six days after the first payday loan repayment was made (for the sample of payday loan borrowers who took out their first payday loan between February 23 and April 18, 2006). Checking account balances start to rise five days before the payday loan repayment. The checking account balance then begins to fall, starting on the day the payday loan repayment was made and continues to fall until about ten days afterward. The typical payday borrower makes deposits several days in advance in order to cover payday loan repayments, but then checking account balances continues to fall for days after the payment, before leveling off again. Their LOC available balance and saving balance remain steady but are continuously rising throughout the time period.

To estimate the interest losses from not using a line of credit, we first need to estimate the alternative interest rate from using money from a member's checking account or line of credit. We restrict the length of loan to be forty-five days, which is the maximum length a person can take out a payday loan in this state, and estimate what the interest payment would be if the borrower used line of credit instead of a payday loan; in other words, if a payday borrower took out a payday loan during this time period, we make his/her alternative option (taking out a line of credit or using a checking account balance) to be as expensive as possible. We add up all available balances in the borrower's account on the day of his/her minimum balance and compare it to the estimated payday loan. If a borrower had $100 in his/her accounts while taking out a $200 payday loan, then his/her

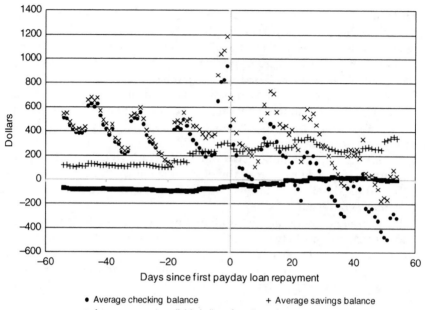

Figure 8.1 Liquidity over time

Notes: This figure reports the evolution of several forms of household liquidity around the time of credit union members' first observed payday loan repayments. We restrict the sample to individuals who are observed for fifty-four days before and fifty-four days after the repayment (i.e., to individuals whose first repayments occurred between 2/23/2006 and 4/18/2006).

Source: Authors' calculations based on administrative data from a credit union; see text.

loss would be the 100 dollars times the interest payment on a line of credit for forty-five days. Using this method, we find the average loss per payday loan borrower to be $87.91 over the six-and-a-half month period. The spread of losses is depicted in Figure 8.2.

We next consider what characteristics predict these pecuniary 'mistakes'. In Table 8.2 we regress the losses for credit union members on characteristics of the borrower that were known at the beginning of the period (FICO scores, checking, savings, line of credit, and VISA balances and availability) using OLS. In Columns 1 and 2, we run regressions restricting the sample to people who take out at least one payday loan. Not surprisingly, people with lower FICO scores are more likely to make losses. Interestingly, borrowers with higher checking account balances on January 1 are more likely to make more losses, while people with greater LOC balances on

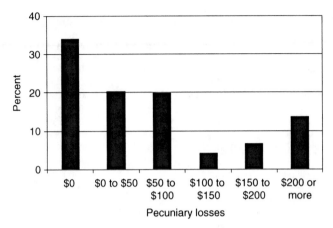

Figure 8.2 Histogram of pecuniary losses

Notes: Losses incurred from use of payday loans instead of other liquidity from 1/1/2006 to 6/14/2006.

Source: Authors' calculations based on administrative data from a credit union; see text.

January 1 also make more losses. In Columns 3 and 4 we include the random sample of credit union members and weight the sample to represent all members at the credit union at this time. Nonpayday loan borrowers have zero losses from payday borrowing. As before, we find that members with lower FICO scores and higher line of credit balances on January 1 are more likely to have greater losses. Checking account balance is no longer significant. Line of credit and VISA account limits (as well as availability) in January are significant predictors of losses; however, the line of credit limit is significantly negative, while the VISA limit is positive. The magnitude of the effects are, however, close to zero.

Finally, we study the impact that access to credit outside payday lending has on an individual's decision to take out a payday loan. In Figure 8.3, we plot the number of payday loans taken out over this time period on the credit scores (represented on the graph as the standard deviation of the credit score and centered around the credit score mean). As one can see in the graph, the number of payday loans is approximately level at lower credit scores, but starts to fall as credit scores get even higher. We use a regression discontinuity approach to estimate whether a cut-off for line of credit interest rates significantly impact the number of payday loans used. If there is a significant change at the credit score cut-off, it would indicate that the mere access to the credit is causing a jump in the number of payday loans. Our results indicate some evidence that at the first cut-off for a change in interest rates there is a significant change in the slope and

TABLE 8.2 Predictors of pecuniary losses from payday borrowing

	Column 1	Column 2	Column 3	Column 4
FICO 1/11/2006	−0.17***	−0.17***	−0.016***	−0.016***
	0.038	0.038	0.00072	0.00072
Check balance 1/1/2006	0.0039***	0.0039***	0.0000019	0.0000019
	0.0011	0.0011	0.0000015	0.0000015
Savings balance 1/1/2006	0.00098	0.0010	0.0000028***	0.0000028***
	0.0025	0.0025	0.00000064	0.00000064
LOC balance 1/1/2006	0.0078***	0.0079***	0.00024***	0.00020***
	0.0025	0.0010	0.000033	0.000030
LOC limit 1/1/2006	0.000062		−0.000038***	
	0.0026		0.0000058	
VISA balance 1/1/2006	−0.0015	0.0015	−0.000024	−0.0000040
	0.0032	0.0014	0.000015	0.000013
VISA limit 1/1/2006	0.0031		0.000020***	
	0.0028		0.0000029	
LOC available 1/1/2006		0.0001		−0.000038***
		0.0026		0.0000058
VISA available 1/1/2006		0.0031		0.000020***
		0.0028		0.0000029
Constant	176.15***	176.15***	12.38***	12.38***
	22.20	22.20	0.54	0.54
N	3,238	3,238	12,894	12,894
Adjusted R^2	0.027	0.027	0.0075	0.0075

Notes: By regressing losses from using payday loans on initial characteristics, Table 8.2 identifies predictors of pecuniary mistakes. Columns 1 and 2 include only people who took out payday loans between 1/1/2006 and 6/14/2006, while Columns 3 and 4 include payday loan borrowers and the random sample of credit union members, weighted to represent the entire population of members at the credit union. Standard errors are reported below the coefficients. *** Indicates significance at the 1 percent level.

Source: Authors' calculations based on administrative data from a credit union; see text.

level of payday loans. These results are expanded more in the Appendix to the chapter, and they begin to explore the impact that access to liquidity elsewhere has on the use of payday loans.

Conclusion

This chapter highlights several characteristics about payday borrowers associated with making pecuniary mistakes. First, payday borrowers had lower credit scores and their scores were falling over the time. Second, payday borrowers made almost three times as many transactions as nonpayday borrowers, and payday borrowers' typical transaction sizes are half as large as nonpayday borrowers' transaction sizes. Third, payday borrowers accumulated checking account liquidity in order to repay their payday loans.

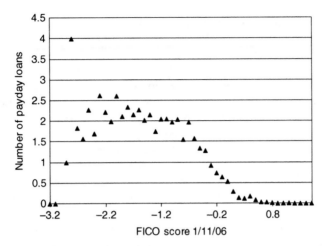

Figure 8.3 Payday borrowing as a function of credit scores

Notes: Displays the relationship between FICO scores on 1/11/2006 and the number of payday loans taken out between that date and 6/14/2006. The FICO scores are centered around the credit score mean and are represented in standard deviations of the score. Each point represents the average number of payday loans in a bin, where the bins have width equal to one-tenth of a standard deviation.

Source: Authors' calculations based on administrative data from a credit union; see text.

Comparing estimated payday loan amounts to liquidity available in the borrowers' checking accounts, saving accounts, and lines of credit, we estimated losses incurred by using a payday loan rather than money available in the other accounts. These losses amounted to around $88 during the six-and-a-half month period.

This chapter has focused on a group of borrowers—payday loan borrowers with credit union accounts—that would significantly benefit by making better financial decisions. Further work will investigate how credit scores influence access to liquidity, the impact of such access on payday borrowing and interest losses, and strategies that credit unions and others can use to help consumers make good financial decisions.

Appendix

The credit union uses external and internal credit scores, as well as other information, to determine who receives a line of credit and at what interest rate. We know the basic external credit score cut-offs for interest rates on a line of credit used at this credit union. Given a member's FICO score, we can therefore estimate what level of interest payments the individual would have to pay. Referring back to Figure 8.3, we can see that there is a continual decline in the number of payday loans taken out as credit scores reach a certain level. Using a regression discontinuity approach, we study whether access to a line of credit at a lower interest rate causes a decrease in the number of payday loans used. In simple terms, a regression discontinuity examines people who have similar credit scores, but some are below the cut-off and some are above the cut-off. Through the regression, we can determine whether the credit score or the access to lower interest rates is causing a difference in the use of payday loans.

We must first check whether there is a clustering of credit scores above or below the cut-off; we, therefore, look at the density of credit scores in Appendix Figure 8A.1. If there are jumps around the credit score cut-off, it may indicate that something else, not the interest rate access, is causing

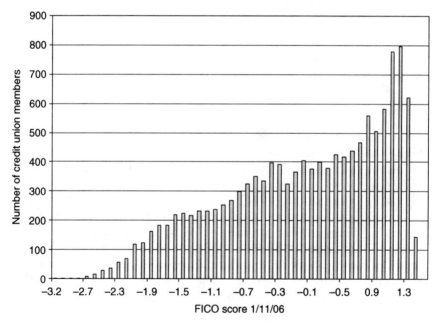

Figure 8A.1 Distribution of credit union members' credit score

Notes: Displays the distribution of credit union members' 1/11/2006 normalized FICO scores. The scores are centered around the FICO 1/11/2006 mean and divided by the 1/11/2006 standard deviation.

Source: Authors' calculations based on administrative data from a credit union; see text.

TABLE 8A.1 Regression discontinuity

	Column 1	Column 2	Column 3	Column 4
AboveThr	0.069***	0.052***	0.017***	0.0060
	0.0037	0.0038	0.0050	0.0066
BelowThr	0.36***	−1.44*	−9.50**	22.38
	0.089	0.74	4.71	37.94
FICO_Above	0.00000470***	0.00016***	0.0030***	0.017***
	0.00000031	0.000010	0.00031	0.0038
FICO_Below	−0.00037**	0.0065**	0.054*	−0.21
	0.00016	0.0028	0.028	0.31
FICO_Above^2		−	−0.0000077***	−0.000068***
		0.00000020***		
		0.000000013	0.00000081	0.000015
FICO_Below^2		−0.0000066**	−0.00010*	0.00069
		0.0000027	0.000057	0.00096
FICO_Above^3			0.0000000050***	0.000000088***
			0.00000000054	0.000000020
FICO_Below^3			0.000000061	−0.0000010
			0.000000038	0.0000013
FICO_Above^4				−
				0.000000000038***
				0.0000000000091
FICO_Below^4				0.00000000052
				0.00000000066
N	12,894	12,894	12,894	12,894
Adjusted R^2	0.021	0.022	0.022	0.022

Notes: Regression of the number of payday loans taken out after 1/11/2006 and before 6/14/2006. AboveThr (BelowThr) is a dummy indicating that the credit score is above (below) the cut-off. FICO_Above (FICO_Below) is the FICO score for an individual above (below) the cut-off point. We use a linear, squared, cubed, and quartic function of the credit score. The regressions are weighted to represent all the members at the credit union. ***, **, and * represent significance at the 1 percent, 5 percent, and 10 percent level, respectively.

Source: Authors' calculations based on administrative data from a credit union; see text.

more payday loans. There do not, however, appear to be any significant jumps.

We use the following regression specification to test whether there are significant changes around the cut-off point:

$$\text{NumberPDLs}_i = \beta_1 \text{AboveThr}_i + \beta_2 \text{BelowThr}_i + f(\text{FICO\_Above}_i) + f(\text{FICO\_Below}_i) + \epsilon_i$$

where $f(\cdot)$ is a function of the credit score. NumberPDLs is the number of payday loans during our sample, but after the FICO score reported on January 11. AboveThr (BelowThr) is a dummy indicating that the credit score is above (below) the cut-off. FICO_Above (FICO_Below) is the FICO score for an individual above (below) the cut-off point. We use a linear, squared, cubed, and quartic function of the credit score. The regressions are weighted to represent all the members at the credit union at this time.

The results from these regressions are shown in Appendix Table 8A.1. The dummies for before and after the threshold are both significant in the first three columns; however, surprisingly, the dummy for below the threshold is negative in Columns 2 and 3, indicating that people below the threshold are less likely to take out payday loans. Additional tests (not shown) find that the levels and slopes for above and below the threshold are significantly different in all specification, except when quartic FICO scores are used. Similar results are found when using the number of payday loans repaid after the FICO score reported on March 26.

References

Agarwal, S., P. M. Skiba, and J. Tobacman (2009). 'Payday Loans and Credit Cards: New Liquidity and Credit Scoring Puzzles?,' *American Economic Review Papers and Proceedings*, 99(2): 412–17.

Bubb, R. and A. Kaufmann (2009). *Consumer Biases and Firm Ownership*. Boston, MA: Harvard University. https://files.nyu.edu/rb165/public/papers/BubbKaufman_ConsumerBiasesandFirmOwnership.pdf

Davis, K. (2001). 'Credit Union Governance and Survival of the Cooperative Form,' *Journal of Financial Services Research*, 19(2–3): 197–210.

Emmons, W. R. and F. A. Schmid (1999). 'Credit Unions and the Common Bond,' *Review of the Federal Reserve Bank of St. Louis*, 81(5): 41–63.

——— (2000). 'Banks vs. Credit Unions: Dynamic Competition in Local Markets,' Federal Reserve Bank of St Louis Working Paper 2000-006A. St Louis, MO: Federal Reserve Bank of St Louis.

Feinberg, R. M. (2001). 'The Competitive Role of Credit Unions in Small Local Financial Services Markets,' *Review of Economics and Statistics*, 83(3): 560–3.

—— (2002). 'Credit Unions: Fringe Competitors or Cournot Competitors?' *Review of Industrial Organization*, 20(2): 105–13.

Goddard, J., D. G. McKillop, and J. O. S. Wilson (2009). 'Which Credit Unions are Acquired?' *Journal of Financial Services Research*, 36: 231–52.

Gross, D. and N. Souleles (2002). 'An Empirical Analysis of Personal Bankruptcy and Delinquency,' *Review of Financial Studies*, 15(1): 319–47.

Logan, A. and C. E. Weller (2009). *Who Borrows from Payday Lenders? An Analysis of Newly Available Data*. Washington, DC: Center for American Progress. http://www.americanprogress.org/issues/2009/03/payday_lending.html

Lusardi, A. (2007). 'Houshold Saving Behavior: The Role of Literacy, Information and Financial Education Programs,' NBER Working Paper No. 13824. Cambridge, MA: National Bureau of Economic Research.

——O. S. Mitchell (2007). 'Financial Literacy and Retirement Planning: New Evidence from the RAND American Life Panel.' Pension Research Council Working Paper No. 2007-33. Philadelphia, PA: Pension Research Council.

——— (2009). 'How Ordinary Consumers Make Complex Economic Decisions: Financial Literacy and Retirement Readiness,' NBER Working Paper No. 15350. Cambridge, MA: National Bureau of Economic Research.

——P. Tufano (2009). 'Debt Literacy, Financial Experiences, and Overindebtedness,' NBER Working Paper No. 14808. Cambridge, MA: National Bureau of Economic Research.

Rauterkus, A. and Z. H. Ramamonjiarivelo (2010). *Why Choose a Credit Union? Determinants of Credit Union Deposits.* Birmingham, AL: University of Alabama. http://ssrn.com/abstract=1571335

Zinman, J. (2007). *Household Borrowing High and Lending Low Under No-Arbitrage.* Hanover, NH: Dartmouth College. http://www.dartmouth.edu/~jzinman/Papers/Zinman_BHLL_apr07.pdf

Chapter 9

Annuities, Financial Literacy, and Information Overload

Julie Agnew and Lisa Szykman

Financial literacy plays an important role in many investment decisions and on saving behavior. Research shows that individuals who are less financially sophisticated avoid the stock market (Christelis et al., 2006; Kimball and Shumway, 2006; van Rooij et al., 2007, 2008), are less likely to save for retirement (Lusardi and Mitchell, 2006, 2007, 2008, 2009), and may be more likely to succumb to the default bias (Agnew and Szykman, 2005). In addition, individuals with less knowledge tend to make poor debt decisions related to mortgage refinancing (Campbell, 2006) and often transact in more costly manners than others (Lusardi and Tufano, 2009). Literature in this area continues to grow rapidly as researchers find an increasing number of investment behaviors that are influenced by financial knowledge.

This chapter contributes to this literature by examining a financial decision that is relatively understudied from the financial literacy perspective. With the shift from defined benefit (DB) plans to defined contribution (DC) plans, it is a decision that a growing number of retirees will face: specifically, whether they should annuitize their retirement savings.[1] This complicated decision requires that individuals consider not only their future consumption needs and portfolio allocation options but also their longevity risk. For many retirees, this can be a daunting task, especially for the least financially literate. In this chapter, we use data collected from a large-scale laboratory experiment to study how financial literacy relates to this decision, as well as how it influences the information overload that participants may experience. We also study whether these variables have an influence on participants' confidence and satisfaction levels once they have made their choices. Although the investment decision in our experiment is much less complicated than the one that people might encounter in the real world, the controlled setting of our experiment provides a good opportunity to study how financial literacy may influence this important retirement decision. Moreover, this chapter provides additional insight into why the annuity market may be smaller than theoretically expected. Researchers often refer to this finding as the 'annuity puzzle'.

We begin with a brief review of the existing literature. We then describe our laboratory experiment and the choice that participants were asked to make. Next, we discuss several of the quantitative measures that we include in the experiment. Finally, we present our results, provide our conclusions, and discuss their implications.

Prior studies related to annuities, financial literacy, and overload

The literature exploring the influence of financial literacy on important financial decisions related to retirement investing is growing rapidly. Several studies have shown that individuals with greater financial knowledge are more likely to plan for retirement, accumulate greater wealth, and participate in the stock market. For example, van Rooij et al. (2008) show that financial sophistication fosters stock market participation. They find that a one standard deviation increase in the level of financial sophistication increases the probability of owning stocks by 8 percentage points. They explain that 'a high level of financial skills lowers economic and psychological barriers to invest'. Furthermore, Lusardi and Mitchell (2009) show that, even after controlling for a range of socioeconomic factors, advanced financial knowledge is still significantly related to retirement planning. In addition, Agnew et al. (2009) find that individuals who do not understand several financial concepts are less likely to participate in both automatic enrollment and voluntary enrollment 401(k) plans. Agnew and Szykman (2005) also demonstrate that individuals with lower financial literacy are more likely to choose the default investment option in an experiment examining retirement investment choices.

Most of the focus on financial literacy in the retirement literature has centered on the asset accumulation phase of saving. To date, there has been relatively less focus on the decumulation phase and, specifically, the decision whether or not to buy annuities, which is the subject of this chapter. While annuities are an attractive choice for many retirees because they insure against longevity risk, the size of the actual lifetime annuity market is far smaller than theoreticians would expect, and it is unclear why. As a result, academics have worked to uncover 'rational' and, more recently, behavioral reasons for this finding. It is clear that the rational supply-side and demand-side explanations summarized by Brown (2008a, 2008b) do not completely explain the small market. That said, newer research focusing on behavioral factors appears promising and is providing new insight into the 'annuity puzzle' (e.g., Brown et al., 2008). As Brown (2008a) argues, the fact that behavioral biases may influence the decision to choose annuities suggests that financial knowledge may also play a role. He points out that those who are less financially literate may be more susceptible to framing and other biases. Brown (2008a) provides a helpful review of the limited research in this area and summarizes the often conflicting results.

One reason there has been relatively little work in this area is that it is difficult to find data that directly measure financial literacy. Until recently, education was often used as a proxy for financial literacy. The early studies using only this variable find mixed results relating educational attainment to annuity purchases. For example, Johnson et al. (2004) find, using Health and Retirement Study data, that annuity payments outside of Social Security payments increase with education. Given that higher educated individuals are more likely to have private pensions, this might be expected. Yet Brown (2001) examines stated intentions to annuitize DC balances and finds no significant relationship between education and this decision, after controlling for 'annuity equivalent wealth'. One issue with interpreting these findings is that education and financial literacy are not perfectly correlated, so schooling is an imperfect proxy (Lusardi and Mitchell, 2007). As a result, it has not been until recently that researchers have attempted to control for literacy in addition to education in their analyses.

In a new study, Previtero (2010) controls for both general education and financial education levels using a unique dataset of 18,000 participants enrolled in IBM's DB plan from 2000 to 2008. The main focus of that paper is to determine whether past stock performance influences the decision to annuitize. The author finds evidence that it does, but no evidence that having prior financial education on its own matters. Interestingly, he argues that those with past financial education may weigh recent stock returns more heavily in their decisions. This evidence of excessive extrapolation is another example of a behavioral bias influencing the decision to annuitize. It is important to note that he finds that those with financial education are also susceptible to excessive extrapolation behavior. Agnew et al. (2010) also find evidence of excessive extrapolation in their experimental work concerning annuities.

In another empirical study, Mottola and Utkus (2007) examine individuals in two DB plans and conclude that individuals who are more affluent, married, and male are more likely to choose a lump sum over an annuity. They remark that individuals that choose the lump sum have demographic characteristics often characterizing individuals with higher levels of financial experience and financial literacy. Similarly, we find evidence that financial literacy is negatively related to choosing an annuity in an early analysis of the same experimental data we use in this study (Agnew et al., 2008). As we mention in that article, the preference for the investment option may be driven by familiarity with investment vehicles, proxied for by high financial literacy scores or by participants' overconfidence in their ability to invest. It could also be because the added complexity of the investment decision made the annuity option relatively more attractive for those with less financial literacy. Our current study expands this earlier analysis to control for additional factors that may affect the overall significance of our financial literacy measure.

One of the new factors we add to our study is the analysis of information overload (both cognitive and emotional). When people experience information overload, they can become overwhelmed by the task at hand and may experience anxiety and stress. In some cases, they may simply avoid the decision or use a simple heuristic to make a choice. This strategy can have a negative consequence on financial outcomes, depending on the heuristic used.[2] Eppler and Mengis (2004) argue that specific personal characteristics (such as existing knowledge) can influence how much overload a person experiences, suggesting that financial literacy may have an influence on overload. We also find evidence of this in our past research, suggesting that people with less financial knowledge do report greater levels of information overload (Agnew and Szykman, 2005). Furthermore, in a preliminary analysis of the data to be described later, we find additional support for the inverse relationship between overload and financial literacy (Agnew and Szykman, 2010). We also show that those who experience more overload are more likely to choose annuities. This current chapter advances this analysis by examining in more detail the important relationship between overload and financial literacy, as well as overload and the annuity decision, by using more sophisticated statistical techniques that control for important variables. We also expand the analysis to include confidence and satisfaction measures. To our knowledge, this is the first time that these measures have been analyzed in the context of the annuity decision.

The annuity experiment

Our data were collected in a large experiment first described in Agnew et al. (2008), where we reported that message framing influences choice. The present study focuses specifically on new findings that relate to the annuity decision and to financial literacy and information overload.[3]

Our basic experimental design is a three (annuity bias, investment bias, no bias) by three (annuity default, investment default, no default) between-subjects design. In the experiment, participants start with a ten-question financial literacy quiz designed to measure their financial sophistication. Once all participants complete the quiz, we measure their risk preferences by using a lottery choice experiment (Holt and Laury, 2002). Next, participants are shown a five-minute slide show that contains the framing manipulation (annuity bias, investment bias, no bias). At the conclusion of the slide show, participants are led through detailed instructions and examples on how to play our 'retirement game'. Next, we tell participants they have $60 in an 'account' to begin the game. Participants then decide whether to 'purchase an annuity', which would give them a fixed payment every round, or allocate their money between a simulated 'market' and a risk-free 'holding account'. Unfair annuity pricing and adverse selection are avoided by making the annuity price actuarially fair and making subjects aware upfront of their identical survival probabilities over the six-period game. If participants choose the annuity, they receive $16.77 for every period they 'survive' in the game, which is determined by a die roll. If the investment choice is selected, the participant faces a series of decisions each round. During each round, he/she must decide how much to withdraw (to simulate living expenses), and then how much to allocate between the 'market' and the 'holding account'. Once these decisions are made, dice are rolled to determine the market gains or losses. After incorporating the new returns into each participant's account balance, another die roll is completed to determine whether the participant survives to continue playing another round of the game. Regardless of whether they choose the investment or the annuity choice, participants can live up to a maximum of six rounds.

The design of our specific experiment makes the annuity the less complicated choice because, with the annuity, participants must only make a single decision in the beginning of the game. With the investment option, participants must decide how much money to invest and withdraw in each round. Therefore, if someone is overwhelmed, confused, or overloaded, we would expect them to choose the annuity, because it requires less thought and fewer decisions. Of course, our findings are closely tied to the specific experimental design, and one might envision scenarios where the annuity choice would not be so easy. For example, the many different types of fixed and variable annuities offered in the current market might overwhelm a consumer unfamiliar with these products. The more annuity features and vendors the individual must consider, the more difficult is the decision. In our experiment, the participants only had to consider a simple life annuity that was fairly priced. In addition, the investment option in our experiment required that our consumers make periodic decisions about their portfolios. While participants should ideally be monitoring their portfolio choices and rebalancing as needed, research shows that individuals change their retirement allocations only infrequently over time (Ameriks and Zeldes, 2001; Agnew et al., 2003). This is commonly called inertia. Therefore, in a different scenario with multiple annuity options, and when individuals are prone to inertia, selecting the investment option may, in fact, be the path of least resistance. In addition, although we find no evidence of a default bias in our experiment, the potential influence of plan architecture on retirement decision-making cannot be denied, given prior research.[4] Therefore, it is possible that a particular plan design might influence one choice over another, based on how the information is presented or how the choice must be made. These caveats should be kept in mind when considering our results.

Measuring financial literacy

As mentioned earlier, before individuals participate in our retirement game, we measure their financial literacy with a ten-question exam. We also attempt to measure their perceived knowledge versus their actual knowledge by asking them how many questions they are very confident they got right on the exam, after they finished it. In previous work (Agnew and Szykman, 2005; Lusardi and Tufano, 2009), individuals' perceptions of their own knowledge has been found to be inconsistent with their actual knowledge. While it is not uncommon to use self-assessed measures in the marketing literature as proxies for actual knowledge, our earlier finding prompts us to gather both types of measure and carry out further analysis of the relationship between perceptions and actual scores.

Table 9.1 reports the actual questions in our exam. By design, these questions vary in difficulty from very simple to more advanced. For example, the first question asks whether it is true that it is best to start early when saving for a future goal. We anticipate that most people should know the answer to this. By contrast, we expect fewer people to be familiar with the answer to the more advanced question asking for the definition of beta (Question 9). Our goal for the quiz is to be able to separate the financially sophisticated participants from the less sophisticated, inasmuch as prior research relates more advanced knowledge to retirement readiness (van Rooij et al., 2007, 2008; Lusardi and Mitchell, 2009).[5]

Table 9.2 reports the accuracy of responses to each question, where most participants could correctly answer the first question (95 percent) but fewer could define beta correctly (25 percent). Two other questions also appear to be more difficult than the others, with accuracy rates below 75 percent: many participants do not know what securities are invested in a money market fund (Question 6, with 33 percent correct) and how interest rates and bond prices move relative to one another (Question 10, with 53 percent correct). In addition, the money market composition question and the beta question elicited more 'Not sure' responses (28 and 62 percent, respectively) compared to the others.[6]

Table 9.3 reports the overall distribution of raw scores. Approximately 56 percent of the sample answer seven or fewer questions correctly, while only 13 percent of the sample answer all of the questions correctly. We use

TABLE 9.1 Financial literacy questions

---

(1) *Saving for a future goal.* If you are saving for a future goal, it's better to start early. That way your money earns more and builds up faster over time.
(a) True   (b) False   (c) Not sure

(2) *Credit card balance.* Keeping a balance on your credit card is okay as long as you can make the minimum payment each month.
(a) True   **(b) False**   (c) Not sure

(3) *ARM.* If you take out an adjustable rate mortgage to buy a house, and interest rates go up, your monthly payments will also go up.
(a) True   (b) False   (c) Not sure

(4) *Lose money stock fund.* If you were to invest $1,000 in a stock mutual fund, it is possible to have less than $1,000 if you withdraw the money.
(a) True   (b) False   (c) Not sure

(5) *Highest long-term growth.* Historically, which option provides the highest long-term growth?
(a) Savings account   (b) Certificate of deposit (c) Insurance policy
(d) Stock mutual fund   (e) Not sure

(6) *Money market composition.* Which of the following types of investments are typically found in a money market fund?
(a) Stocks   (b) Bonds   **(c) Short-term debt securities**
(d) Not sure

(7) *Diversification.* When an investor diversifies his investments, does the risk of losing money increase or decrease?
(a) Decrease   (b) Increase   (c) Not sure

(8) *Relative risk money market.* A money market fund is riskier than a stock fund.
(a) True   **(b) False**   (c) Not sure

(9) *Beta.* A stock funds' beta rating can best be described as:
(a) A measure of relative   (b) A measure of relative (c) A measure of relative capital
volatility of the fund vs the   growth vs the S&P 500   outflow of the fund vs the S&P
S&P 500 index   index   500 index
(d) Not sure

(10) *Interest rates and bond prices.* If interest rates go up, then bond prices generally:
(a) Increase   **(b) Decrease**   (c) Not sure

Notes: Financial literacy subject categories are italicized; correct answers are in bold.

Source: Authors' calculations; see text.

the median to split the sample based on the score of seven and below for a low literacy group, and eight and above for a high literacy group. This division captures, in the high literacy category, those who are more likely to give a correct answer to the more difficult questions we previously identified.

Using these two literacy groups, Table 9.4 examines the influence of demographics. We find that more males fall in the high-literacy category than do females and the percentage of subjects with high literacy increases with education, income, and age. These results are broadly consistent with

TABLE 9.2 Accuracy of responses to financial literacy questions

Financial literacy question	Correct (%)	Not correct (%)	Not sure (%)
Question 1: Saving future goal	95	3	2
Question 2: Credit card balance	88	10	2
Question 3: ARM	86	7	7
Question 4: Lose money stock mutual fund	89	4	7
Question 5: Highest long-term growth	75	14	11
Question 6: Money market composition	33	39	28
Question 7: Diversification	82	11	8
Question 8: Relative risk money market	80	6	15
Question 9: Beta	25	14	62
Question 10: Interest rates and bond prices	53	28	19

Source: Authors' calculations; see text.

TABLE 9.3 Financial literacy raw scores

Actual score	Percent	Cumulative
1	0	0
2	2	2
3	4	6
4	6	12
5	10	22
6	14	36
7	20	56
8	19	75
9	12	87
10	13	100

Notes: There were 828 total observations.

Source: Authors' calculations; see text.

previous literature (e.g., Agnew and Szykman, 2005). In addition, using the participants' estimates of their quiz score relative to their actual financial score, we divide our participants into three groups: those who overestimate, those who correctly estimate, and those who underestimate their score on the exam. Those who underestimate may not have been confident with all of their answers and were forced to guess on some. Those who correctly predict their score most likely have a strong grasp of what they know and what they do not know in finance. Finally, those who overestimate their score are indicating that they feel very confident about the accuracy of some questions that they actually answered incorrectly.

In Table 9.5, Panel 1, the percentages of participants that underestimate, overestimate, and accurately predict their actual financial literacy scores are displayed. As those with a score of one cannot underestimate their scores and those with perfect scores cannot overestimate them, we do not

TABLE 9.4 Demographics and financial literacy (%)

	Low literacy	High literacy	Proportion of total sample	Number of observations
All	56	44	100	828
Sex				
Male	42	58	47	392
Female	68	32	53	435
Education				
High school or less	82	25	8	68
Some college	73	28	19	160
College	55	45	35	286
Graduate school	43	57	38	311
Income				
<$20,000	84	16	4	37
$20,000–$40,000	79	21	12	100
$40,001–$60,000	63	37	16	131
$60,001–$80,000	44	56	16	132
$80,001–$100,000	51	49	16	130
$100,001–$150,000	50	50	17	140
>$150,000	45	55	11	91
Age (years)				
<30	83	17	11	90
30–40	71	29	11	92
41–50	76	24	14	115
51–65	54	46	29	242
>65	36	64	35	286

Notes: The percentage of individuals in each demographic category may not add to one because of missing values.

Source: Authors' calculations; see text.

discuss the two extreme scores, and focus instead on those with scores between two and nine. It is interesting how the percentage of participants that overestimate (underestimate) their performance declines (increases) with increases in their scores. This result may be driven by the fact that there is less opportunity for individuals to overestimate (underestimate) as the score increases (decreases), but it might also be because as individuals become more financially literate, they are more likely to know what they know. The percentage that correctly estimates their performance does appear (in most cases) to generally increase with actual scores. An accurate

TABLE 9.5 Accuracy of self-assessed financial literacy score

Panel 1: Responses based on raw financial literacy score, whole sample (%)

Actual correct score	Underestimate	Correct	Overestimate	N
1	0	0	100	2
2	13	19	69	16
3	29	24	47	34
4	39	26	35	46
5	35	28	36	85
6	52	19	29	113
7	56	25	19	167
8	58	33	9	158
9	66	28	6	96
10	59	41	0	110

Panel 2: Responses by characteristics excluding individuals with scores of 1 or 10 (%)

Group	Underestimate	Correct	Overestimate	N
All	51	26	23	714
Sex				
Male	44	31	25	306
Female	57	23	20	408
Education				
High school or Less	42	19	39	64
Some college	55	19	26	152
College	54	26	19	242
Graduate school	48	33	19	255
Income				
⟨$20,000	46	29	26	35
$20,000–$40,000	44	24	32	95
$40,001–$60,000	52	25	24	122
$60,001–$80,000	57	17	26	107
$80,001–$100,000	47	36	17	116
$100,001–$150,000	61	22	17	118
>$150,000	40	43	18	68
Age (years)				
<30	51	27	22	85
30–40	48	26	26	88
41–50	51	26	22	107
51–65	49	24	27	211
>65	55	29	16	222

Source: Authors' calculations; see text.

understanding of one's own financial literacy is important because those who do not understand how much they do not know may be less likely to seek assistance.

Panel 2 of Table 9.5 allows us to look at literacy relative to demographics, having eliminated from the sample participants earning the two extreme scores. Interestingly, a larger percentage of men (25 percent) overestimate their scores compared to women (20 percent), consistent with overconfi-dence observed in men related to other financial behaviors such as trading (Barber and Odean, 2001). Education also seems to matter: the percentage of participants overestimating their performance declines with more edu-cation, from 26 percent with some college education to 19 percent with graduate training. Similarly, the percent of participants overestimating falls with income, from 32 percent for those making between $20,000 and $40,000 to 17–18 percent for those making more than $80,000. According-ly, it appears that some populations (the lowest income and least educated) identified in previous literature as vulnerable are more likely to overesti-mate how many questions they answered correctly in this study. Given the inaccuracy in many of the self-reported scores, we will use the actual tested financial literacy score for our literacy measure going forward.

Next, we use a multivariate probit analysis to examine how demographics relate to tested financial knowledge. Table 9.6 reports marginal effects for the regression relative to a 40- to 50-year-old, college-educated woman, who

TABLE 9.6 Marginal effects from multivariate probit analysis of tested financial literacy

Dependent variable	High financial literacy (1 = yes, 0 = no)
Sex	
Male	0.221*** (0.044)
Education	
High school or less	−0.137*** (0.050)
Some college	−0.066 (0.041)
Graduate school	0.048 (0.038)
Income	
<$40,000	−0.065 (0.053)
$60,001–$80,000	0.120* (0.062)
$80,001–$100,000	0.054 (0.057)
$100,001–$150,000	0.041 (0.056)
>$150,000	0.052 (0.062)
Age (years)	
<30	−0.086 (0.062)
30–40	0.005 (0.062)
50–60	0.166*** (0.055)
>65	0.267*** (0.055)
Marital status	
Married	−0.043 (0.041)
Pseudo R²	0.1799
Number of observations	753

Notes: Standard errors are in parentheses. Race/ethnicity is also con-trolled for. ***Significant at 1 percent level; **significant at 5 percent level; *significant at 10 percent level.

Source: Authors' calculations; see text.

is unmarried and earning between $40,000 and $60,000. The first column shows the results for the tested financial knowledge. We find older individuals are significantly more likely to be in the high literacy category. In addition, high-school educated individuals are 14 percent less likely to be in the high-literacy category, while men are more likely to fall in the high-literacy category by 22 percent. The findings are broadly consistent with others (e.g., Agnew and Szykman, 2005).

Information overload measures

To capture both the cognitive and emotional aspects of information overload, we use two different measures. The multi-item measures are based on the responses to questions found in Table 9.7, and responses for all questions in the scale are averaged to construct a composite score. We then use a median split for both measures to place individuals in two categories (high and low). As reported in Table 9.8, we estimate two multivariate probit regressions using our binary overload measures as dependent variables to test for a relationship between information overload and literacy. Results show that individuals in the high-literacy category are 10 percent

TABLE 9.7 Overload measures

Cognitive overload (Chronbach's α = 0.827)

Each question below answered based on the following scale:
Strongly disagree 1 2 3 4 5 Strongly agree
(1) There was too much information to consider before I had to choose between the investment option and the annuity option.
(2) This decision required a great deal of thought.
(3) This was a difficult decision.
(4) I found this decision to be overwhelming.
(5) It was difficult to comprehend all the information available to me.
(6) This task was stressful.
(7) It was a relief to make decision.

Emotional overload (Chronbach's α = 0.876)

Think about the information that was presented to you about the differences between the investment option and the annuity option. Using EACH pair of words listed below, indicate how the information made you feel.

Unafraid	1	2	3	4	5	6	7	Very afraid
Relaxed	1	2	3	4	5	6	7	Tense
Calm	1	2	3	4	5	6	7	Agitated
Restful	1	2	3	4	5	6	7	Excited

Source: Authors' calculations; see text.

TABLE 9.8 Marginal effects from multivariate probit analysis of cognitive and emotional overload

Dependent variable	High cognitive overload (1 = yes, 0 = no)	High emotional overload (1 = yes, 0 = no)
Sex		
Male	−0.086** (0.043)	−0.143*** (0.043)
Education		
High school or less	0.064 (0.101)	−0.039 (0.104)
Some college	−0.047 (0.062)	−0.030 (0.063)
Graduate school	−0.002 (0.048)	0.007 (0.050)
Income		
<$40,000	0.009 (0.079)	−0.100 (0.077)
$60,001–$80,000	0.052 (0.071)	0.049 (0.071)
$80,001–$100,000	−0.093 (0.071)	−0.044 (0.074)
$100,001–$150,000	0.033 (0.070)	0.045 (0.072)
>$150,000	−0.111 (0.078)	−0.041 (0.082)
Age (years)		
<30	0.162* (0.089)	0.286*** (0.083)
30–40	0.098 (0.082)	0.220*** (0.080)
50–60	0.052 (0.069)	0.045 (0.069)
>65	0.015 (0.071)	−0.128* (0.070)
Marital status		
Married	0.033 (0.057)	0.021 (0.057)
Financial literacy		
High literacy	−0.104** (0.045)	−0.099** (0.046)
Pseudo R²	0.051	0.0907
Number of observations	613	613

Notes: Standard errors are in parentheses. Analysis controls for race, biases, defaults, and risk included in regression but not reported. Race/ethnicity is also controlled for. ***Significant at 1 percent level; **significant at 5 percent level; *significant at 10 percent level.

Source: Authors' calculations; see text.

less likely to be in the high-cognitive-overload category. We find a similar result for emotional overload. Interestingly, we also find that certain demographics matter. Men are less likely to report information overload, regardless of the measure. In addition, those under age 30 are more likely to report cognitive overload (16 percent) and emotional overload (29 percent). One possible explanation for this may be that the young may not have been exposed to annuity products and may be less familiar with them.

Analysis of the annuity choice

Table 9.9 examines participants' actual decisions between annuities and investments in the experiment, where we build on Agnew et al. (2008) by including two additional measures of information overload as

TABLE 9.9 Marginal effects from multivariate probit analysis of decision to pick the annuity

	Dependent variable	
	Pick annuity (1 = yes, 0 = no)	Pick annuity (1 = yes, 0 = no)
Income		
$100,000–$150,000	–0.163** (0.065)	–0.153** (0.062)
Financial literacy		
High literacy	–0.142*** (0.045)	–0.123*** (0.043)
Overload		
Cognitive overload	0.040 (0.044)	
Emotional overload		0.085* (0.045)
Pseudo R^2	0.1129	0.1172
Number of observations	612	612

Notes: Standard errors are in parentheses. Variables of interest (overload and financial literacy) reported. Only statistically significant demographic coefficients reported. Other controls included but not reported include race, biases, defaults, additional demographics (age, income, education, marital status), and risk. ***Significant at 1 percent level; **significant at 5 percent level; *significant at 10 percent level.

Source: Authors' calculations; see text.

well as controls for demographics, risk aversion, and the framing conditions. Here, we report only the marginal effects for the demographic variables that are significant and our variables of interest—financial literacy and overload.[7]

Financial literacy might play a role in this decision in four possible ways. First, as mentioned earlier, the experimental annuity choice requires the least effort, so those with less financial literacy may prefer the less complicated annuity choice. Second, highly literate individuals may be overconfident in their investment abilities and, therefore, more likely to choose the investment option. This would be interesting, given that skill cannot influence the reported investment performance (it is based on dice rolls). Third, a familiarity bias might exist. More financially literate individuals may be more familiar with equities and, as a result, more likely to choose them. Conversely, individuals with low literacy may choose to avoid these types of securities. Finally, the more financially literate may be more likely to invest in the annuity because they appreciate the insurance against longevity risk.

The findings suggest that more financially literate individuals find our investment option more appealing. Thus, the first three theories presented cannot be ruled out. We also find that those with higher income are significantly less likely to choose the annuity, consistent with Mottola and Utkus (2007). A familiarity bias might be driving this result. Although only significant at the 10 percent level, we also find a positive relationship between emotional overload and the selection of annuities. Thus, those that felt overwhelmed were more likely to choose the simpler option.

Confidence and satisfaction

We are also interested in whether financial literacy relates to individuals' feelings about their choice immediately after they make it, and then again after the game is over and they know the final outcomes. While most research has focused on how literacy influences actual decisions and intended actions, we believe it is also important to understand how people feel after making their decisions. For example, are more financially literate individuals more content and confident with their choices because they understand their risks? If participants experience more overload, are they less likely to feel satisfied with their choices regardless of outcomes? If we can show that higher literacy and less overload are related to greater feelings of confidence and satisfaction, then this suggests there are additional benefits to financial training and simplifying investment information beyond encouraging sound investment decisions.

We examine how confident individuals are with their decision considering both their literacy and feelings of cognitive and emotional overload in Table 9.10. To measure confidence, we ask participants the following question immediately after making their choice: 'Thinking of the choice you just made between the investment option and the annuity option, circle a number from 1 to 10 to indicate how confident you are that you made a good decision' (1 = not confident; 10 = extremely confident). They answer this question prior to playing the game and before knowing the final financial outcome.

Once the game is over and participants know how much they earn, we ask them a series of three more questions to assess their overall satisfaction.[8] Using a scale from 1 (strongly disagree) to 5 (strongly agree), participants respond to the following three questions: (*a*) I am happy with my choice; (*b*) I am pleased with my choice; (*c*) I feel satisfied with my choice ($\alpha = 0.94$). We once again average the responses to get a summary score and then use a median split to divide the individuals into high-and low-confidence and satisfaction categories. As before, we estimate a multivariate probit regression, with the binary dependent variable equal to 1 for the high category and 0 for the low category. Likewise, we report only the statistically significant demographic variables. Looking first at pre-game confidence, financial literacy does not matter for confidence, but both types of overload have a significantly negative relationship with participant confidence levels. Those who are in the higher cognitive overload category are 30 percent less likely to be highly confident. Similarly, those who are

TABLE 9.10 Marginal effect for multivariate probit analysis of confidence and satisfaction

	Pre-game		Post-game	
	High confidence (1 = yes, 0 = no)	High confidence (1 = yes, 0 = no)	High satisfaction (1 = yes, 0 = no)	High satisfaction (1 = yes, 0 = no)
Sex				
Male	0.154*** (0.085)	0.148*** (0.042)	–0.051 (0.043)	–0.077* (0.044)
Age				
Over 65 years old	–0.129* (0.070)	–0.151** (0.072)	0.052 (0.073)	0.001 (0.074)
Financial literacy				
High literacy	0.060 (0.047)	0.068 (0.046)	0.064 (0.050)	0.092* (0.052)
Overload				
Cognitive overload	–0.304*** (0.043)		–0.169*** (0.050)	
Emotional overload		–0.237*** (0.045)		–0.221*** (0.058)
New controls				
Chose annuity	0.010 (0.050)	0.018 (0.051)	0.056 (0.060)	0.085 (0.063)
Total payout			0.008*** (0.002)	0.009*** (0.002)
High confidence			0.270*** (0.047)	0.274*** (0.046)
Round die			0.011 (0.023)	0.012 (0.023)
Pseudo R^2	0.105	0.078	0.190	0.204
Number of observations	571	572	563	564

Notes: Standard errors are in parentheses. Variables of interest (overload and financial literacy) reported. Only statistically significant demographic coefficients reported. Other controls included but not reported include race, biases, defaults, additional demographics (age, income, education, marital status), and risk. ***Significant at 1 percent level; **significant at 5 percent level; *significant at 10 percent level.

Source: Authors' calculations; see text.

emotionally overloaded are 24 percent less likely to be in the higher confidence category. We find no relationship between the actual option chosen (annuity or investment) and initial confidence levels following the decision.

Our post-game regressions examine overall satisfaction once the individuals know how much they earned. Additional control variables account for overall winnings and the number of periods each person 'lives'. We expect that individuals will be more satisfied if they 'live' through more periods and earn more money. We also control for their initial confidence in their decisions because attitude theory predicts that when people have strong attitudes toward something, they will create or change other attitudes that are inconsistent with the pre-existing attitudes (Eagly and Chaiken, 1993).[9] Once again, overload plays a large role. Individuals are less likely to be satisfied if they experience cognitive or emotional overload when making their decisions. This is an important finding because it suggests that financial planners may be able to improve their clients' satisfaction by reducing the likelihood that they will experience information overload during the decision-making process. So, while they cannot guarantee financial gains and cannot control for the individual characteristics of each client, they can control how the information is presented, which can improve satisfaction levels. Literacy is also important but not very significant (10 percent level) to post-game satisfaction.

Conclusion

The analysis presented in this chapter explores how financial literacy and feelings of emotional and cognitive overload relate to a financial decision of growing importance to the soon-to-be-retired: specifically, the decision of whether to annuitize retirement savings. Using data from a large-scale laboratory experiment, the analysis from this chapter not only sheds new light on how literacy and overload relate to each other but also reveals how these factors may influence financial choices in general, as well as relate to subsequent levels of satisfaction and confidence. Later, we summarize our main results from this chapter and their implications, as well as provide our recommendations for improving plan participants' decision satisfaction.

In our analysis, we outline several new financial literacy and information overload results with potentially negative implications for some retirement savers. For instance, we identify population subgroups that may be either systematically overestimating or underestimating their financial knowledge. For those who overestimate their knowledge, potential concerns can arise because they may not seek out financial advice due to overconfidence about what they know. As a result, financial educators must realize that they may not be reaching certain segments of the population because those consumers may not be seeking assistance.

In our analysis, we also demonstrate that lower financial literacy relates to more cognitive and emotional overload. Avoiding overloading consumers is a worthwhile priority for those who develop plan communications because overload may hamper individuals' decision-making and can even cause some people to avoid making decisions altogether. The results from this chapter suggest that plan communicators must keep in mind that low-literacy participants may be more susceptible to information overload and develop their materials accordingly.

We also find new evidence suggesting that there are additional benefits gained from reducing information overload beyond encouraging more thoughtful decision-making. Our findings suggest that while framing the choice in the simplest fashion may reduce overload, it may also increase individual feelings of confidence and satisfaction. Thus, efforts to make investment products and decisions easier to understand could improve how people feel about their decisions, as well as increase customer satisfaction levels reported to plan sponsors. Of course, financial markets will always be uncertain and even when individuals make informed and intelligent financial decisions, they will still suffer financial losses. Yet based on this evidence, we believe that overloaded individuals will be less confident and less satisfied than others experiencing similar financial performance because the overloaded individuals may not have made thoughtful choices. Simplifying the information presented so that it is more easily understood may help people better understand the associated risks and benefits of their options, enabling them to make more informed decisions. If consumers are less overwhelmed when deciding whether to annuitize, they may actually be more satisfied and confident with their decisions. Industry professionals could do well to focus on making the decision-making process less arduous and consider how important simplicity is in plan design.

Finally, as Choi et al. (2002) have shown in their research, the 'path of least resistance' has a powerful effect on decision-making. We add to this literature by finding additional evidence that this path might hold the most attraction to those who are the least financially literate. In our experiment, the least financially literate were more likely to choose the annuity. We theorize that as the required decisions related to the annuity in our experiment were fewer and less complicated than those required for the investment choice, choosing the annuity was the 'path of least resistance' because it minimized decision-making efforts in this context. As a result, plan architects should carefully consider the choices they present to participants and keep in mind that the choice option that requires the least effort may attract the least financially literate. In conclusion, we believe empowering investors through financial education, simplified plan design, and effective communication is not only good for the investor, as it should encourage more thoughtful and confident decision-making, but also of benefit to plan sponsors and the entire industry by producing more satisfied consumers.

Acknowledgment

This publication was made possible by a generous grant from the FINRA Investor Education Foundation.

Endnotes

1. We are referring to single-premium fixed lifetime annuities throughout the text.

2. One example of an ineffective investment heuristic is using past returns to choose investments. For example, when Sweden introduced their pension scheme, investors making an active investment choice were most likely to choose a technology and health-care fund that recorded the best five-year fund performance out of all 456 funds presented in their investment menu (Cronqvist and Thaler, 2004). Very likely, these individuals were overwhelmed with the number of options, so they relied on past performance to make their fund selection. Unfortunately for those who selected this fund, by 2003 the Internet bubble had burst and this fund had lost 69.5 percent of its value. One worthwhile exercise for the finance community would be to devise heuristics that lead to better outcomes. Regardless of how plans are designed or communication is simplified, there will always be somebody that is overwhelmed with the information. These individuals could benefit if they had at their disposal several basic heuristics that would lead to sound investment decisions.

3. Detailed explanations regarding the experimental procedure followed can be found in Agnew et al. (2008).

4. Existing studies examining the annuity decision and defaults provide mixed evidence of their influence. See Brown (2008a) for more details.

5. Our measure is not designed to measure cognitive ability, and we do not believe that it could serve as a proxy for this because most of the questions require some understanding of economics and finance. Lusardi et al. (2010) and van Rooij et al. (2007) control for IQ and cognitive ability in their study, and find the financial literacy variables remain statistically significant. Although previous research demonstrates that basic financial knowledge can also be important, we note that Lusardi and Mitchell (2009) find that when they include a sophisticated measure of financial literacy with a basic measure in their analysis, the basic measure is no longer significant.

6. We do not analyze our 'Not sure' responses here but Lusardi and Mitchell (2006, 2008) find that 'Do not know' responses can provide valuable insights. Therefore, we plan to examine our 'Not sure' responses further in future analysis.

7. Although not reported here but consistent with our previous research, we once again find a significant relationship between the framing condition and choice. In addition, those who are more risk averse are more likely to choose the annuities.

8. See Agnew et al. (2008) for detail about how this was calculated.

9. According to attitude theory, when formulating an attitude towards how satisfied one is with one's choice, a person will seek to be consistent with related attitudes that the person currently has (i.e., confidence). According to this, we would not expect a person reporting low satisfaction levels to have reported high confidence in their initial choice.

References

Agnew, J. and L. Szykman (2005). 'Asset Allocation and Information Overload: The Influence of Information Display, Asset Choice and Investor Experience,' *Journal of Behavioral Finance*, 6(2): 57–70.

——— (2010). 'Information Overload and Information Presentation in Financial Decision Making,' in Brian Bruce, ed., *Handbook of Behavioral Finance*. Cheltenham, UK: Edward Elgar Publishing, pp. 25–44.

——— P. Balduzzi, and A. Sundén (2003). 'Portfolio Choice and Trading in a Large 401(k) Plan,' *American Economic Review*, 93(1): 193–215.

——— L. Anderson, J. Gerlach, and L. Szykman (2008). 'Who Chooses Annuities: An Experimental Investigation of Gender, Framing and Defaults,' *American Economic Review: Papers & Proceedings*, 98(2): 418–22.

——— L. Szykman, S. P. Utkus, and J. A. Young (2009). 'Literacy, Trust and 401(k) Savings Behavior,' CRR WP 2007–10. Chestnut Hill, MA: Center for Retirement Research at Boston College.

——— L. Anderson, and L. Szykman (2010). *An Experimental Study of the Effect of Prior Market Experience on Annuitization and Equity Allocations*. Williamsburg, VA: College of William and Mary. http://financeseminars.darden.virginia.edu/Lists/Calendar/Attachments/64/Agnew.pdf

Ameriks, J. and S. P. Zeldes (2001). *How Do Household Portfolio Shares Vary with Age?* New York, NY: Columbia University. http://www1.gsb.columbia.edu/mygsb/faculty/research/pubfiles/16/Ameriks_Zeldes_age_Sept_2004d.pdf

Barber, B. and T. Odean (2001). 'Boys will be Boys: Gender, Overconfidence, and Common Stock Investment,' *Quarterly Journal of Economics*, 116: 261–92.

Brown, J. R. (2001). 'Private Pensions, Mortality Risk, and the Decision to Annuitize,' *Journal of Public Economics*, 82(1): 29–62.

——— (2008a). *Financial Education and Annuities*. Urbana-Champaign, IL: University of Illinois. http://www.oecd.org/dataoecd/38/0/44509379.pdf

——— (2008b). 'Understanding the Role of Annuities in Retirement Planning,' in A. Lusardi, ed., *Overcoming the Saving Slump: How to Increase the Effectiveness of Financial Education and Savings Programs*. Chicago, IL: University of Chicago Press, pp. 178–208.

——— J. R. Kling, S. Mullainathan, and M. V. Wrobel (2008). 'Why Don't People Insure Late Life Consumption? A Framing Explanation of the Under-Annuitization Puzzle,' *American Economic Review*, 98(2): 304–9.

Campbell, J. (2006). 'Household Finance,' *Journal of Finance*, 61(4): 1553–604.

Choi, J. J., D. Laibson, B. C. Madrian, and A. Metrick (2002). 'Defined Contribution Pensions: Plan Rules, Participant Decisions and the Path of Least Resistance,' in J. M. Poterba, ed., *Tax Policy and the Economy*, Vol. 16. Cambridge, MA: The MIT Press, pp. 67–113.

Christelis, D., T. Jappelli, and M. Padula (2006). 'Cognitive Abilities and Portfolio Choice,' CSEF Working Paper No. 157. Salerno, Italy: University of Salerno.

Cronqvist, H. and R. H. Thaler (2004). 'Design Choices in Privatized Social-Security Systems: Learning from the Swedish Experience,' *American Economic Review*, 94(2): 424–8.

Eagly, A. H. and S. Chaiken (1993). *The Psychology of Attitudes*. New York, NY: Harcourt Brace Jovanovich College Publishers.

Eppler, M. and J. Mengis (2004). 'The Concept of Information Overload: A Review of Literature from Organizational Science, Accounting, Marketing, MIS, and Related Disciplines,' *The Information Society*, 20: 325–44.

Holt, C. A. and S. K. Laury (2002). 'Risk Aversion and Incentive Effects,' *American Economic Review*, 92: 1644–55.

Johnson, R. W., L. E. Burman, and D. I. Kobes (2004). *Annuitized Wealth at Older Ages: Evidence from Health and Retirement Study*. Washington, DC: The Urban Institute. http://www.urban.org/UploadedPDF/411000_annuitized_wealth.pdf

Kimball, M. S. and T. Shumway (2006). *Investor Sophistication, and the Home Bias, Diversification, and Employer Stock Puzzles*. Ann Arbor, MI: University of Michigan. http://isites.harvard.edu/fs/docs/icb.topic446361.files/02_03_09_Kimball_1.pdf

Lusardi, A. and O. S. Mitchell (2006). 'Financial Literacy and Planning: Implications for Retirement Wellbeing,' Pension Research Council Working Paper No. 2006-01. Philadelphia, PA: The Wharton School.

————(2007). 'Baby Boomer Retirement Security: The Roles of Planning, Financial Literacy, and Housing Wealth,' *Journal of Monetary Economics*, 54(1): 205–24.

————(2008). 'Planning and Financial Literacy: How Do Women Fare?,' *American Economic Review*, 97(2): 413–17.

————(2009). 'How Ordinary Consumers Make Complex Economic Decisions: Financial Literacy and Retirement Readiness,' NBER Working Paper No. 15350. Cambridge, MA: National Bureau of Economic Research.

——P. Tufano (2009). 'Debt Literacy, Financial Experiences and Overindebtedness,' NBER Working Paper No. 14808. Cambridge, MA: National Bureau of Economic Research.

——O. S. Mitchell, and V. Curto (2010). 'Financial Literacy Among the Young,' *Journal of Consumer Affairs*, 44(2): 358–80.

Mottola, G. R. and S. P. Utkus (2007). *Lump Sum or Annuity? An Analysis of Choice in DB Pension Payouts*. Malvern, PA: Vanguard Center for Retirement Research. https://institutional.vanguard.com/iam/pdf/CRRLSA.pdf

Previtero, A. (2010). 'Stock Market Returns and Annuitization,' Anderson School of Management Working Paper. Los Angeles, CA: UCLA.

Van Rooij, M., A. Lusardi, and R. Alessie (2007). 'Financial Literacy and Stock Market Participation,' NBER Working Paper No. 13565. Cambridge, MA: National Bureau of Economic Research.

————(2008). *Financial Literacy, Retirement Planning, and Household Wealth*. Amsterdam, Netherlands: De Nederlandsche Bank. http://www.ech.wur.nl/NR/rdonlyres/78C9E59D-A152-465B-9216-348F21E97C3A/73915/AbstractRooij.pdf

Part III

Shaping the Financial Literacy Environment

Chapter 10

Financial Counseling, Financial Literacy, and Household Decision-Making

Sumit Agarwal, Gene Amromin, Itzhak Ben-David, Souphala Chomsisengphet, and Douglas D. Evanoff

Research suggests that consumers often make what appear to be welfare-reducing decisions. Many individuals do not hold a checking account (Hilgert et al., 2003); maintain large outstanding balances on credit cards when cheaper forms of credit are available (Gartner and Todd, 2005); take out payday loans at astronomical interest rates when cheaper forms of credit are available (Agarwal et al., 2009c); choose suboptimal credit contracts (Agarwal et al., 2006); fail to refinance mortgages when it would be optimal to do so (Agarwal et al., 2008a); and fail to plan for retirement, reaching it with little or no savings (Lusardi and Mitchell, 2006). A leading explanation for this behavior is that consumers are not financially literate—they lack sufficient information about financial concepts and instruments to make informed financial decisions.[1]

Surveys find that a large proportion of consumers, in the United States and in other countries, fail basic financial literacy tests. Many adults do not understand the difference between compound and simple interest; the characteristics of financial assets such as stocks and bonds; the benefits of portfolio diversification; or the important features of their own mortgages, Social Security, and pension plans (Lusardi and Mitchell, 2006, 2007a, 2007b).

If financial illiteracy drives suboptimal (or welfare-reducing) financial behavior, then improving literacy could increase consumer welfare. A growing literature investigates whether education programs are effective in improving financial literacy and behavior. Although the evidence is mixed, it appears that some financial education programs do improve the behavior and outcomes of their graduates. The effects appear to be strongest for the most financially vulnerable, especially those with low incomes and levels of education. However, the relationships among financial education, financial literacy, and financial behavior and outcomes are not straightforward. Some financial education programs improve financial literacy, but not financial behavior; others lead to improved behavior and outcomes without improving financial literacy; and still others do not appear to be effective at all.

In what follows, we review the existing literature and offer a critique of studies evaluating the extent of consumer financial literacy. We then evaluate the evidence on the effectiveness of financial education programs in improving participants' financial behavior and outcomes. We do not attempt a comprehensive survey of the literature in these areas; instead, we look for the most convincing evidence, paying particular attention to study design, data limitations, and potential sources of bias. We also devote particular attention to whether the perceived impact of educational programs can be attributed to increases in financial literacy. Overall, we find some evidence of beneficial effects of education programs on outcomes, and this is partially due to improvements in financial literacy. Yet, it is difficult to differentiate the factors contributing to the improvement. Some is due to the educational programs, some to the selection of participants, and some to auxiliary influences resulting from the educational program. We also discuss how the gains from financial literacy programs may wane over time, as financial decision-making becomes more difficult with age. We conclude with a discussion of the need for future research in this area.

Review of the literature on financial literacy and financial education programs

There is considerable evidence that a large segment of the US population is not financially literate. This means that many people do not understand basic financial concepts and products well enough to make sound short- and long-term financial decisions for themselves and their families. The evidence comes from surveys administered to various groups of consumers over the past two decades to ascertain their knowledge of financial products and understanding of basic concepts. While the surveys vary significantly in content and sample populations, they generally agree on several findings:

1. A large proportion of consumers are not financially literate, even among the wealthiest and most educated.
2. Financial literacy rates vary consistently by demographic groups, tending to be higher for those with more wealth and education, for men (although results vary), and for whites (in the United States).
3. Financial illiteracy leads to welfare-reducing financial behavior and outcomes.

While there is a fairly broad consensus that financial illiteracy leads to suboptimal decisions by consumers, there is significant disagreement as to how best to combat these ill effects, as well as on the effectiveness of the approaches that have been tried to date. Research efforts to evaluate the impact of such programs encounter an array of econometric issues that could bias the findings. Similarly, changes in behavior may not result from the educational benefits of these programs, but rather from auxiliary influences associated with the program. In the discussion that follows, we first evaluate the evidence on financial literacy and the adverse effects of suboptimal financial decisions; then, we discuss the impact of educational programs aimed at improving literacy, all the while emphasizing potential problems that arise when quantifying these effects.

Financial literacy

Most research on financial literacy has been conducted in the United States and accordingly we concentrate on that literature.[2] Early studies to measure adult financial literacy were conducted during the 1990s by private firms utilizing surveys that consisted of a small number of questions covering material specific to corporate interests (Volpe et al., 2006). Similarly, early studies of high school and college students asked relatively few questions and often sampled few institutions.[3] Perhaps, the most useful early studies assessing overall financial literacy were those conducted on high school and college students. The Jump$tart Financial Literacy Survey administered the same exam to randomly selected high school seniors every two years from 1997 to 2006. The exam included thirty-one questions on income, money management, saving and investment, and spending and credit and was intended to capture financial competence in a broad set of areas. Jump$tart's findings were not encouraging: students scored an average of 57 percent in 1997 (with 60 percent being a passing score), and scores declined by several percentage points in subsequent years (2000–6).[4]

Chen and Volpe (1998) find similarly low rates of financial literacy among college students. In a sample of thirteen public and private universities, the average respondent scored only 53 percent on a thirty-six-question exam covering general financial knowledge. The sample included a high proportion of business majors, who scored higher than their peers in other fields, who barely averaged 50 percent on the exam. Importantly, students scored highest on questions covering areas in which young people are likely to have some experience (e.g., auto insurance and apartment leases) and lowest where they are likely to have the least experience (e.g., taxes, life-insurance, and investment). This suggests that financial experience could increase financial literacy, and studies that find an effect of financial literacy on financial behavior should test for reverse causality.

Although these low financial literacy scores are worrisome, these results must be interpreted with caution, as they may be biases. Both studies have low response rates—51 percent for the survey of Chen and Volpe and much lower for the Jump$tart exams—and hence could suffer from nonresponse bias.[5] Chen and Volpe had also a disproportionally high share of responses from business majors. While business majors may have been oversampled to begin with, it is plausible that they were also more likely to respond to the survey as it was less costly for them to complete in terms of time and effort. The authors did not address this concern, nor did they weight results to reflect the demographic distribution of college students. Jump$tart suffered from a different sampling problem: the study randomly selected US public high schools and asked each to administer the survey to one class of seniors. Yet only 44 percent of high schools agreed to conduct the survey in 1997, and this rate dropped below 20 percent thereafter. High schools that declined to participate most often cited the need to prepare for state and federally mandated standardized tests, suggesting that the most disadvantaged schools were the least likely to participate. It is important to note that these nonresponse biases, if they exist, would bias the results of both studies upward, leading the studies to *understate* the pervasiveness of financial illiteracy.

It is also questionable whether the exams given by Jump$tart and by Chen and Volpe accurately evaluate respondent financial competence. Both exams consisted entirely of multiple choice questions, which means some correct responses were likely guesses, which would lead to an overstatement of financial literacy. On the other hand, inaccurate responses might not reflect ability to save, plan for retirement, manage debt, and make important financial decisions. For example, some questions sought factual data (e.g., how much would a college degree affect earning power), but respondents may have answered in terms of their own personal prospects. Additionally, certain questions concerned concepts with which high school students might not be familiar (e.g., down-payments and liquidity), and a current misunderstanding of such concepts could be a poor indicator of a student's future ability to make financial decisions. The Chen and Volpe (1998) survey questions were even more difficult, and often required specific financial knowledge that a competent individual might not have (e.g., the maximum amount of money that is FDIC-insured at a member commercial bank). Some questions were less difficult but more ambiguous.

Other research evaluates financial literacy among adults in more specific contexts. For instance, there is an extensive literature on the relationship between financial literacy and planning/saving for retirement. This literature yields two broad, but important findings. First, after controlling for a broad range of economic and demographic characteristics, more financially literate individuals are more likely to plan for retirement, and those who plan have greater net worth upon reaching retirement. Second, causation goes from literacy to planning to wealth.

Individuals accrue retirement assets both individually as well as through Social Security and employer-sponsored pensions. To figure out how much to save for retirement, individuals must know their expected dates of retirement, expected lifespan, and Social Security and/or pension entitlements. They must then calculate how much to save to maintain a certain standard of living in retirement, given the expected rate of return on saving. This planning process requires knowledge of Social Security and pension plan characteristics, as well as the ability to perform calculations involving compound interest and monthly accumulation. In practice, this is a difficult process, as illustrated by Bernheim (1988), Mitchell (1988), and Gustman and Steinmeier (2005). Many adults do not know important features of their Social Security entitlements and pensions, as found by Bernheim (1988). Using the Social Security Retirement History Survey (RHS), he showed that adults nearing retirement did not report accurate estimates of expected Social Security benefits. He compared expected benefits to realized benefits, finding that predictions were unbiased but 'noisy': indeed, expected benefits accounted for only 60 percent of the variation in realized benefits. In addition, over half of respondents provided no estimate.

Mitchell (1988) examined employee knowledge of company pensions and found that many workers were unaware of important features of the plan. She compared pension characteristics reported by individuals from the Survey of Consumer Finances (SCF) to accurate administrative data. Only half of employees who were required to contribute to their pensions reported doing so, and only half of those whose employers contributed said they did. Over one-third of respondents did not know about early retirement provisions and, among those who did, two-thirds described them inaccurately. Those who gave correct information were more likely to be white, have a higher income and level of education, and have greater firm seniority.

Gustman and Steinmeier (2005) confirm these findings using the 1992 Health and Retirement Survey (HRS), showing that a majority of those surveyed could not accurately report their Social Security or pension entitlements. Only 27 percent of respondents gave estimates within 25 percent of their true Social Security entitlements, and only 16 percent of respondents with pensions gave estimates within 25 percent of their true pension entitlements. Perhaps most surprising, over 40 percent of respondents were unable to provide any estimate. Being educated, having higher income, and being white and male predicted more accurate responses.

Even if consumers do have information about their Social Security and pension entitlements, they still have trouble performing the calculations necessary to plan for retirement. Significantly, many adults cannot correctly answer questions requiring a basic financial understanding. For instance, Lusardi and Mitchell (2006, 2007*a*) find that only 18 percent of 2004 HRS respondents thought that an account initially holding $100 and earning 20 percent compound annual interest would hold more than $200 after five years. In particular, many respondents thought the account would hold exactly $200, suggesting they did not understand compounding. An easier interest rate question from a three-question financial literacy module in the 2004 HRS yielded more correct responses, but it did not require respondents to understand the difference between compound and simple interest. Consistent with other research in this area, the probability of answering correctly was higher for those with more wealth and education, for whites, and for men. Nevertheless, mistakes persisted, even among the groups most likely to answer correctly. Lusardi and Mitchell (2007*b*) find that even in the RAND American Life Panel (ALP), a sample of educated and high-earning middle-aged adults, over a quarter of respondents could not accurately answer the more difficult HRS compound interest question.

Further research showed that facility with interest rates is only weakly related to age. Lusardi et al. (2009) found that respondents in their 20s do about as well as respondents in their 50s, with the same demographic characteristics predicting correct responses as in other studies.

These studies also revealed other forms of financial illiteracy. Many consumers answered a 'money illusion' question incorrectly, suggesting they did not understand the consequences of inflation (Lusardi and Mitchell, 2006, 2007*b*). Nearly half of HRS respondents missed a 'lottery division' question, which amounted to a simple division problem (Lusardi and Mitchell, 2007*a*). In the HRS financial literacy module, only 52 percent of respondents said investing in a mutual fund was less risky than investing in a single company's stock, indicating a misunderstanding of risk and portfolio diversification (Lusardi and Mitchell, 2006).

Additional examples of financial illiteracy are also found in mortgage markets. For example, many individuals who hold adjustable rate mortgages (ARMs) exhibit shocking ignorance of their mortgage terms. Bucks and Pence (2006) document this by comparing the distribution of household-reported mortgage characteristics in the SCF to distributions in three lender-reported datasets. They found that ARM borrowers often could not provide basic information about their own loans.[6] When ARM borrowers did report their loan characteristics, they regularly got them wrong, often underestimating their risks and potential liabilities. Agarwal et al. (2009*b*) corroborate this evidence with data from a mandatory loan counseling program for high-risk mortgage applicants in select Chicago zip codes.

Most of the applications were for ARMs. According to a summary of counselor assessments from the program, the 'overwhelming majority' of ARM applicants were unaware that their interest rate was not fixed for the life of the mortgage.[7] In addition, 9 percent of counseled borrowers gave a verbal description of the loan that was significantly different from loan documents.

These studies suggest that many consumers lack the financial knowledge and computational ability to make informed financial decisions. However, survey-based studies could still overstate the illiteracy in the population, as respondents often have little incentive to answer questions correctly. Respondents may ignore or give the wrong answer to a question they might answer accurately with more time and analysis. In contrast, if they realized there is a monetary impact resulting from a financial decision, there would be a stronger incentive to make the correct choice. Nevertheless, if higher financial literacy scores lead to positive financial behavior and outcomes, these tests will capture variables that seem to be important.

Some of the strongest evidence that the causal chain proceeds from literacy to outcomes comes from three papers by Lusardi and Mitchell (2006, 2007a, 2007b), who seek to link retirement planning, household wealth on entering retirement, and financial literacy. Using data from the 1992 and 2004 HRS and the RAND ALP they document that literacy, planning, and wealth are strongly and positively correlated, even after controlling for economic, demographic, and other characteristics. Furthermore, the authors established that causation proceeds from literacy and planning to wealth, and not from wealth to planning and literacy. They do so by testing for reverse causality using instrumental variable techniques. In particular, they regress a dummy variable for having planned for retirement on economic and demographic characteristics and on the previous year's regional change in housing prices. The last variable is thought to be a valid instrument for household wealth. The effect of the wealth instrument on planning is not significant, which suggests that individuals are not more likely to plan for retirement because they are wealthier.

Further analysis of the RAND ALP confirms the findings in the HRS. Lusardi and Mitchell (2007b) find that scores on a more detailed financial literacy test predict planning behavior. To eliminate endogeneity, they use answers to the following question as an instrument for financial literacy: *How much of your school's education (high school, college or higher degrees) was devoted to economics? A lot, some, little, or hardly at all?* Interestingly, the instrument produces an even larger estimate of the relationship between literacy and planning than the original test scores. The ALP asked a larger set of financial literacy questions than the HRS, many of which require more detailed knowledge of financial instruments. The authors find that after instrumenting for retirement planning, planning behavior still predicts financial literacy. Accordingly, while it is possible that planning affects literacy but not vice versa, it is unlikely that reverse causality fully explains the relationship.[8] In the realm of retirement planning and saving, the evidence suggests that financial literacy affects financial behavior and outcomes.

The correlation between financial literacy and behavior is also corroborated by studies of the loan market. In a survey of Washington State residents, Moore (2003) found that less financially literate consumers tended to make inferior mortgage product choices. Furthermore, consumers borrowing from lenders involved in a predatory lending lawsuit tended to do worse on questions about investing and compound interest, suggesting that financial illiteracy leaves consumers open to exploitation. In related studies, Stango and Zinman (2010) documented that consumers who were unable to calculate the interest rate on a loan—given the principal and a stream of payments—borrowed more, accumulated less wealth, and paid more for credit. Campbell (2006) found that less financially sophisticated households tend to make significant financial mistakes. In particular, they are less likely to refinance their mortgages under advantageous circumstances.

In summary, there is overwhelming evidence that many consumers are not financially literate and, further, that these consumers tend to make poor financial decisions.

Financial education, financial literacy, and financial behavior

If financial illiteracy causes undesirable financial behaviors, then increasing financial literacy could enhance consumer welfare. An array of financial education programs have been introduced in the United States for this purpose over the past few decades. These programs range from employer-provided seminars on retirement planning, to state-mandated personal finance classes in public schools, to one-on-one mortgage counseling. Are these programs effective? If so, which types of programs are more effective?

To answer these questions, we draw on several reviews of the financial education literature, not all of which agree on the strength of the available evidence. The most comprehensive of these reviews is a recent article by Collins and O'Rourke (2010), who are cautiously optimistic that financial education can be effective. Martin (2007) shared this optimism for programs targeting saving and retirement, credit, and homeownership, and Hogarth (2006) gives an even more sanguine assessment. Yet, some reviews have less positive outlooks: Hathaway and Khatiwada (2008) and Willis (2008, 2009) find no conclusive evidence that financial education programs are effective. In a review of five studies evaluating personal financial management courses, Caskey (2006) concludes that nonexperimental program evaluations—even ones that use instrumental variables and other modeling techniques to eliminate endogeneity—often fail to approximate results obtained under experimental conditions. This critique casts doubt on studies where treatment is not randomly assigned and, hence, on the vast majority of papers in the financial education literature.

While we concur with some of these critiques, we believe there is strong evidence that some financial education programs improve financial behavior and outcomes, with weaker evidence that these programs increase financial literacy. Yet, the link between education, literacy, and outcomes is still not clearly established. No study definitively demonstrates that a financial education program improved participant outcomes *through* financial literacy, and many studies find that the financial education programs evaluated were ineffective. We also find that the strength of evidence for financial education's effectiveness depends on the type of financial education program studied. In the next two sections, we discuss the effectiveness of financial education in the workplace and in schools, respectively, as this literature provides the strongest evidence that financial education can be effective. Then, we examine how evaluations of mortgage, bankruptcy, credit-repair, and other financial education programs augment these results. Finally, we document initial research into optimal programs and innovative study designs that could serve as models for future research.

Behavior and outcome: evidence from workplace programs

Evaluations of financial education programs may not produce credible impact estimates if the program suffers from potential selection bias: that is, when participation is voluntary, then exposure to treatment may be correlated with unobserved traits that affect outcomes. As a result, the impact may actually be attributable to these traits instead of to the treatment. To deal with this problem, studies of school and workplace financial education have looked for valid instruments for exposure to treatment. Workplace studies have used *availability* of workplace financial education programs rather than actual attendance, while school-based studies have used state financial education mandates. Overall, these studies find that financial education does affect outcomes, increasing saving rates, pension plan participation, and net worth later in life.

In a telephone survey of workers in the United States conducted by Merrill Lynch, Bernheim and Garrett (2003) show that the availability of workplace financial education predicted increases in saving rates, assets

held in 401(k) accounts and other retirement accounts, and 401(k) participation. However, the measured effect on total assets was not significant,
suggesting that differences could be due to asset substitution rather than
higher overall saving. The authors argued that availability of financial
education could be a valid instrument for treatment because workers did
not choose employers based on financial education offerings. In fact, it
appeared that workplace financial education was often remedial, which
could bias the estimated impact downward. In this case, a positive estimated impact could be interpreted as a lower bound on the true impact.

Offsetting these rather strong results, this study also potentially suffered
from a number of possible sources of bias. First, offering financial education seminars might be correlated with employer characteristics that attracted workers, even though the seminars were not a factor in the job
search process. This would lead to an overestimate of the seminar effect.
Second, the authors could not control for pension plan characteristics,
which could have driven differences in saving patterns. Although they cited
studies finding low correlations between plan features, participation, and
saving rates, other papers have found stronger relationships (Bayer et al.,
2009). Yet a third concern about this study is that it relied on self-reported
employee survey data. This is less reliable than employer-provided or
administrative data, particularly if respondents most influenced by workplace financial education were also more likely to recall that it was offered.
In this case, estimated impacts would be upwardly biased.[9]

A complementary paper by Bayer et al. (2009) corroborated Bernheim
and Garrett (2003) and also addressed some of these concerns. It used a
survey of employers taken over two consecutive years, providing more
accurate measures of employee 401(k) contributions and the availability
of workplace financial education. The study also controlled for pension
plan characteristics, and its longitudinal nature allowed them to control for
individual firm characteristics so as to eliminate a significant potential
source of selection bias. Cross-sectional results confirm that workplace
seminars have a significant and positive effect on 401(k) participation
and contributions, with a greater effect for low-income employees. In
addition, the authors confirmed that workplace seminars were often remedial, making cross-sectional estimates a lower bound of the true effect.
While the authors could not reject the possibility that increased participation and contribution rates are driven by asset substitution and individual
heterogeneity, the research helps confirm that workplace education programs can influence financial behavior.

In related analysis, Lusardi (2004) found that having attended a retirement seminar (most of which were employer-provided) predicted greater
overall saving, not just larger pension contributions. This finding fills an
important gap in earlier work. Drawing on the 1992 HRS, Lusardi could

control for individual heterogeneity to an extent that prior work could not. She concluded that having attended a retirement seminar increased several measures of total saving and wealth by economically significant amounts. She also found that differences were greatest (proportionally) for those who saved the least and were the least educated. Importantly, Lusardi noted that her estimates decreased but remained significant when a full set of individual controls was included.

These studies make a strong case that financial education can improve financial behavior. Further, they show that the effect is greatest for the most economically vulnerable populations. However, these studies do not show that the programs were effective because they increased financial literacy. For instance, workplace seminars may increase worker's awareness of these vulnerabilities, or alternatively, they may increase saving because they make peer effects more important (Duflo and Saez, 2003). They could also increase employees' exposure to plans offered by the firm, along with strong encouragement to contribute. These could shape behavior without improving employees' understanding of the benefits of saving or the specific financial products they are using. To get at these issues, several authors test explicitly whether workplace financial education increases financial literacy. Their results are somewhat mixed.[10] For instance, Hira and Loibl (2005) find in a survey of a large US insurance company that employees who attended a half-day retirement seminar reported increased knowledge in four areas: retirement needs, investing, planning for the future, and managing credit. However, these measures of financial knowledge were employee perceptions, not objective assessments. As people can perceive knowledge gains to be greater than actual gains, those who attended a seminar may claim to have derived some benefit whether or not they actually did (Willis, 2009).

Behavior and outcome: evidence from school-based programs

Studies of school-based financial education programs also provide mixed evidence of effectiveness. Some evaluate individual school-based programs and consistently find significant improvements in student financial knowledge and behavior.[11] Nevertheless, these studies were subsequently challenged on the basis of research design flaws or data limitations (e.g., small sample issues). Another set of papers that used state financial education mandates as an instrument for exposure to in-school financial education found some evidence that school programs affect saving and investment in adulthood. An oft-cited study by Bernheim et al. (2001) found that state financial education mandates lead to greater asset accumulation in adulthood. Bernheim et al. used the same Merrill Lynch survey as Bernheim and Garrett (2003), as many survey respondents were in school during the 1960s and 1970s, when the state mandates were introduced.

Several steps are required to argue that a link between state mandates and adult saving behavior is due to financial education. State mandates must be exogenous to population characteristics that might affect saving; they must lead to greater exposure to financial education; and they must be correlated with saving behavior. Bernheim et al. argued that state mandates are exogenous, usually driven by efforts from individual legislators and interest groups rather than broad public consensus. States with and without mandates do not differ significantly in income, proportion of high school graduates, or retail sales during the period studied. To demonstrate increased exposure, Bernheim et al. estimated a probit model and found that survey respondents who graduated high school after the introduction of a mandate in their state are more likely to report having been taught about household finance in school. The probability increases with the number of years in school after the mandate, suggesting mandates take time to implement. The authors checked whether a variable for 'years before mandate' affected the probability of exposure and found that the coefficient was small and statistically insignificant, suggesting that results did not reflect a general trend of increasing financial education independent of state mandates. Finally, Bernheim et al. found that more years in high school after a mandate predict higher reported saving rates and net worth.

Although the Bernheim et al.'s study is a contribution, it has been criticized in more recent studies. Cole and Shastry (2009) attempted to replicate Bernheim et al.'s results with US Census data and a more robust empirical specification, and the findings do not match. In particular, Cole and Shastry relaxed the assumption of a linear relationship between the number of years in school after imposition of a mandate and the outcome variables. They also controlled for statewide differences in economic conditions and augmented the Bernheim et al. specification to include a full set of birth-year cohort dummies and state fixed effects.[12] They find there is no clear break point at the time of mandate introduction, and perhaps most worryingly, coefficients for having graduated at least five years after a mandate are much smaller than the others; the relationship is not monotonic. One explanation for their finding is that mandates were introduced during times of high state GDP growth, which could explain why financial market participation and investment income went up both before and after the mandates. It is possible that these factors dominated any actual effects of state mandates.

Behavior and outcome: evidence from mortgage and other counseling programs

Studies of mortgage counseling programs build on the workplace- and school-based literature in three important ways. First, the studies evaluate specific financial education programs and so tell us more about the programs as well as the participants' financial circumstances before and after counseling. Second, mortgage counseling programs are very different in format from school and workplace programs, which are usually conducted in a classroom setting. Mortgage programs are usually offered in a one-on-one counseling format that addresses individual questions and needs. In addition, mortgage programs treat individuals who are at the point of making a critical financial decision. Finally, the mortgage programs discussed here are primarily targeted at low- to middle-income populations with characteristics that make them more likely to default on their mortgages. As this group has the lowest level of financial literacy, it may be most in need of counseling and is therefore an important group to study.

Once again, we find mixed evidence that mortgage counseling improves behavior and outcomes, with the same potential for sample selection bias. A program evaluation that sought to rigorously correct for the selection problem by Hirad and Zorn (2002) analyzed a large sample of high-risk borrowers whose mortgages were purchased by the Fannie Mae Affordable Gold program. Most borrowers were required to go through mortgage counseling before Fannie Mae would buy their loans from the original servicers, but some borrowers were exempt. Controlling for observable characteristics, counseled borrowers were less likely to become ninety days delinquent on their mortgages. The authors estimate a complex four-stage model for selection into treatment, type of organization providing treatment, and type of treatment received. Once selection was accounted for, certain types of treatment were still effective, but of unreasonably large magnitudes. In particular, one-on-one counseling was found to reduce delinquency rates by over 90 percent, while other forms of treatment had no effect. The authors noted that their selection model was a poor fit and included variables that were likely to be correlated with the error term in the original regression.

In follow-up studies by Hartarska and Gonzalez-Vega (2005, 2006) and Quercia and Spader (2008), pre-mortgage counseling was again related to loan outcomes, although the results are somewhat contradictory. Hartarska and Gonzalez-Vega found that counseled borrowers had lower default rates and exercised default more optimally, but prepayment behavior was not affected. In contrast, Quercia and Spader found better prepayment behavior, but no effect on default rates. These differences may reflect the period studied in each case; Hartarska and Gonzalez-Vega used the 1990s, whereas Quercia and Spader followed borrowers through 2006, a time of unusually low interest rates, which gave many borrowers the opportunity to refinance. There are also additional concerns with these studies. Quercia and Spader did not test whether there was selection into different types of counseling, nor did they control for selection into treatment—arguing instead that as treatment requirements were determined by lenders, riskier borrowers were more likely to have received treatment (they were unable to test this claim directly). In the Hartarska and Gonzalez-Vega analysis, counseled borrowers were not allowed to apply for a loan until they achieved nonnegative cash flow, defined as income net of expenses, mortgage, and other debt payments. Thus, counseling may have acted as a filter, preventing less financially able borrowers from taking out loans, which would upwardly bias their results. The authors did not discuss what happened to individuals who did not 'graduate' from counseling, leaving it unclear as to whether counseling led to better loan outcomes by improving financial management or by weeding out the less credit-worthy.

By contrast, Agarwal et al. (2009*b*) found little evidence that a state-mandated pre-mortgage counseling program for high-risk borrowers in select Chicago zip codes led to better mortgage choices. At the same time, their study shows how a financial education program can affect outcomes without necessarily improving literacy. The authors showed a significant drop in default rates of mortgages originated in the treated zip codes during the period of mandatory counseling, but it appeared to occur because the riskiest lenders and borrowers left the market, not because the remaining borrowers chose better mortgage products. The threat to lenders of increased oversight and potential fraud detection, as well as the perceived cost to borrowers of attending counseling sessions, dramatically reduced both the supply and demand for credit. Borrowers who were able to choose less risky products to avoid counseling did so, and lenders rejected far more loan applications and originated fewer low-documentation loans during the treatment period (activity resumed to normal levels when the program ended). While some borrowers followed the advice provided by counselors, many modified their loans in ways that were contrary to counselor recommendations, and others took out loans they had been told they could not afford.

Mortgage and credit counseling programs often include services apart from financial education, such as client advocacy and proactive intervention, which also can make it difficult to disentangle the effects of financial education. One such program is the Indianapolis Neighborhood Housing Partnership (INHP), a voluntary mortgage counseling program evaluated by Agarwal et al. (2010). The study found that, controlling for loan characteristics, borrowers who participated in INHP (some of whom had mortgages originated and serviced by INHP itself) had significantly lower default rates twelve and eighteen months after origination. This result was robust to several econometric specifications and to a matched propensity score model. Although it seemed that INHP's services improved outcomes, it was not clear how much of the effect was due to better loan terms, to INHP's proactive interventions when loans became delinquent, or to improved financial management on the part of borrowers.

The strongest evidence for the effectiveness of mortgage counseling comes from a study of a post-mortgage counseling program by Ding et al. (2008). That program treated over 25,000 borrowers with high-risk characteristics but low-risk mortgages. All loans were fixed-rate and 99 percent had thirty-year amortization periods, but borrowers had low credit scores, and loans had high loan-to-value ratios (three-quarters were over 95 percent). The authors found that telephone counseling delivered to forty-five-day delinquent mortgage borrowers led to a higher cure rate and a lower foreclosure frequency for those particular loans. The authors controlled for selection into treatment with a well-fitting model, noting that their estimates decreased in magnitude as a result, but remained positive and statistically significant. Apart from exemplifying the importance of controlling for unobserved borrower characteristics, this paper suggested that mortgage counseling can be effective if provided at a critical point in the decision process.

One non-mortgage counseling study produces further evidence that financial counseling can affect outcomes. Elliehausen et al. (2007) examine credit counseling programs that five agencies, approved by the National Foundation for Credit Counseling (NFCC), provided to 8,000 borrowers during the summer of 1997; a matched comparison group did not receive NFCC counseling. The study followed credit and payment histories until 2000 and revealed that credit scores, debt levels, and bank account usage improved for counseled individuals. Counseling was most effective for those with the worst initial credit scores and debt behaviors. Differences were much smaller but statistically significant after correcting for selection. This study benefited from uniformity in treatment; the NFCC had specific standards for its counseling providers, and treated borrowers did not receive other NFCC services in 1997. Unobserved financial services received by members of the comparison group would bias results downward, lending more credibility to the estimated effect of counseling.

Optimal program structure

A few papers have investigated whether different *types* of programs vary in effectiveness, and others have estimated the marginal impact of extra hours of treatment. Evidence on delivery methods is inconclusive, but it appears that extra hours of education or counseling have a positive impact on outcomes. For instance, Hirad and Zorn (2002), Quercia and Spader (2008), and Barron and Staten (2009) compare four types of treatment: home-study, telephone/Internet instruction, classroom education, and one-on-one counseling. Their findings do not consistently support one type of treatment over others. The first two studies evaluate mortgage counseling programs and find that classroom and one-on-one treatment— which tend to be more intensive than other forms—had larger impacts than telephone and home study, which had no significant effects. By contrast, Barron and Staten found that, in a credit counseling program, one-on-one counseling was not more effective than telephone or Internet counseling when clients were allowed to choose the type of treatment. The conflicting studies evaluate two different types of programs, which could explain their diverse findings. It is also possible that the limitations of the mortgage studies biased their results upward, or that Barron and Staten's results do not reflect true impacts due to selection bias.[13] In contrast to Hirad and Zorn (2002) and Quercia and Spader (2008), Ding et al. (2008) found that telephone counseling was effective for forty-five-day delinquent mortgage holders. Again, the different results may stem from program differences (or perhaps pre-mortgage counseling is simply less effective than post-mortgage counseling).

A program designer may also ask when diminishing returns may set in and cause additional counseling to be ineffective. There is evidence that more treatment leads to better outcomes in Clancy et al. (2001) and Collins (2007). The former study reports that for delinquent borrowers, extra hours of counseling (up to 5 hours) did reduce the probability of moving to a more serious stage of foreclosure, so the marginal effect of extra counseling was positive.[14] Clancy et al. (2001) study financial education classes for low-income participants in Individual Development Account (IDA) programs which involved matched savings accounts. Extra hours of class were positively correlated with saving behavior through 18 hours of treatment; someone receiving 12 hours of education saved over $100 more per year than someone receiving no education. The fourteen programs studied all had financial education requirements, but specific content varied. In general, education provided both financial information and strategies for effective saving, as well as instruction on more specific topics, such as home purchase. Although the authors used a two-stage selection model for leaving the program, they did not control for selection into hours of treatment. Thus, we do not know whether the results are due to endogeneity with characteristics of the borrowers or of the particular requirements of each IDA program.

To generate more robust information on treatment types and hours of treatment, it is necessary to correct for selection into treatment types and hours. At the very least, given that some financial education programs appear to be effective, this research agenda is worth pursuing.

Innovative research study designs

Several papers on financial education are notable for the design of their program evaluations. These papers provide instructive examples of randomization techniques that do not require denying treatment with a specific demographic focus, and using unconventional forms of treatment. This work is important, as many program evaluations suffer from endogeneity—that is, selection into a treatment, or into a type and intensity of treatment, is often not random. This problem is difficult to overcome when randomization requires denying treatment to some who want and need it. A few studies have delayed treatment for the control group (rather than denying it entirely), or offered an extra incentive to the treatment group to participate. These studies have had varying success in implementation, but their methods are instructive.

Two studies by Collins (2008) and Servon and Kaestner (2008) delay treatment. In the first, women in both treatment and control groups received the same financial education curriculum, but the control group received it a year after the treatment group. If similar changes in credit scores and saving behavior are observed for the two groups roughly a year apart, then the differences may be attributed to financial education. In the second paper, Servon and Kaestner used the same strategy to test whether access to what they called 'information and communications technologies' (including Internet and online banking services) could be a pathway to financial literacy. They studied a program that gave participants a computer, taught them how to use the Internet and online banking services, and provided financial literacy training. A treatment group was provided computers and instruction immediately, while a control group received the same services nine months later. The study is instructive for its experimental design and for its isolation of access to and facility with technology, although it suffered from implementation problems (imperfect randomization) and produced insignificant statistical results.

In Duflo and Saez (2003), the incentive strategy was illustrated by studying enrollment in a tax-deferred account program by employees at a large university. The authors offered a $20 incentive to attend a university-sponsored benefits information fair, randomly selecting departments within the university and then randomly selecting employees within the selected departments to receive the offer. This setup permitted the authors to compare behavior of treated employees to that of untreated employees in the same department and also to that of employees in untreated departments. The effect of financial education per se was not evaluated, but their design could be used to develop incentive-based financial literacy programs, thus providing exogenous difference in treatment take-up.

Since consumer educational needs vary widely, financial education programs are often targeted towards specific demographic and socioeconomic groups. As one example, Sanders et al. (2007) studied battered women at four emergency shelters. Two of the shelters had implemented a financial education curriculum tailored to the needs of these women, while the other two shelters had not yet implemented the program. The study suffered from having a small sample, and it only measured subjective measures of financial knowledge and 'self-efficacy'. Further, there was significant attrition before the follow-up exam. Nevertheless, such a research model is promising for situations with more observations, and objective knowledge and behavioral data if more effective follow-up could be done.

All these studies evaluated conventional forms of financial education, whereas more recently, innovative delivery methods have been adopted. Spader et al. (2009) analyzed one such case, a Spanish-language soap opera entitled 'Nuestro Barrio' (Our Neighborhood) that targeted low-income Hispanic immigrants. Information and instruction about financial products such as banking services and credit behavior were incorporated into the plot line to reach audiences that otherwise would not be exposed to financial education. The creators also hoped to overcome traditional barriers to participation in financial education programs, such as time and monetary costs, as well as mistrust of organizations providing the education. Quantifying the impact of this intervention will be difficult, although the cost of delivering the information is relatively low.

Conclusion

In this chapter, we review the literature on financial counseling, financial literacy, and consumer decision-making. Summarily, we found many consumers lack basic financial literacy and are ill prepared to meet their financial goals. In some cases, financial education appears to improve financial literacy and behavior, and is most effective for those who have the least financial knowledge, income, and savings. However, it is not clear that effective programs improve behavior through increased literacy, whether programs are cost-effective, or which types of programs are most effective. Answering these questions will require a great deal more research.

Fortunately, the recent proliferation of financial education programs provides ample opportunity to conduct such research. However, the designs of existing programs are rarely conducive to robust impact evaluations. In their review, Hathaway and Khatiwada (2008) call for the introduction of formal program evaluation methods into the design of financial education programs. This recommendation seems to us to be most appropriate.

Acknowledgments

The authors acknowledge constructive comments on earlier drafts from Annamaria Lusardi, Olivia S. Mitchell, Matt Rosen, and participants at the Pension Research Council's April 2010 Symposium: 'Financial Literacy: Implications for Retirement Security and the Financial Marketplace'. The authors also benefited from discussions with Michael Collins, and reviews of his past work. They want to thank Jacqui Barrett, Robert McMenamin, and Daniel Waldinger for superb research assistance, and Helen Koshy for similar editorial assistance. The views expressed are those of the authors and may not reflect the views of the Federal Reserve System, the Federal Reserve Bank of Chicago, or the Office of the Comptroller of the Currency.

Endnotes

[1] Others have linked financial literacy to cognitive ability. For example, Agarwal et al. (2008b, 2009a) find that some consumers are more likely to make suboptimal financial decisions by paying higher fees and interest rates, and they are less likely to learn from their mistakes. Agarwal and Mazumder (2010) explicitly link these mistakes to cognitive abilities.

[2] Several surveys conducted in other countries generally confirm the US findings (ANZ, 2003; Miles, 2004; OECD, 2005).

[3] Additional early studies by private firms include CFA/AMEX (1991), EBRI (1995), KPMG (1996), Oppenheimer Funds/Girls Inc. (1997), PSRA (1996, 1997), and Vanguard Group/Money Magazine (1997). Early studies of high-school programs include Bakken (1967), Langrehr (1979), Danes and Hira (1987), and Volpe et al. (1996).

[4] Mandell (2008) analyzes the results in detail and notes that income, parental education, and race are strong predictors of scores.

[5] It is not clear what the direction of this bias may be.

[6] Thirty-five percent did not know the per-period cap on interest rate changes; 41 percent did not know the maximum interest rate allowed; and 20 percent did not know the initial interest rate.

[7] Counseling information was provided by Housing Action Illinois (2007). For loans for which the counseling was aimed at protecting against predatory lending, they also found that 9 percent of loans had 'indications of fraud', 22 percent had interests rates over 300 basis points above the market rate, and half of all borrowers were deemed unable or nearly unable to afford the loan.

[8] The NLSY sample of young adults also performed just as well as the HRS cohort on the same measures of financial literacy, even though the HRS sample population was more likely to have thought about retirement (Lusardi and Mitchell, 2006; Lusardi et al., 2009).

[9] Though this bias could be potentially serious, if we assume that workplace financial education did not convince anyone to save less, then it would imply that financial education did have a positive effect, albeit a smaller one than estimated.

[10] See Kim et al. (1998), Garman et al. (1999), Clark and D'Ambrosio (2002), Kim (2007), and Holland et al. (2008).

[11] See Boyce and Danes (1998), Danes (2004), Peng et al. (2007), and Mandell (2008).

[12] One would expect to see no effect on outcomes for dummy variables indicating the number of years a respondent graduated before a mandate, and monotonically increasing (positive) estimates for each extra year in school after a mandate. Instead, the coefficients on all dummies are large and positive and most are statistically significant. This holds for both participation rates and investment income.

[13] As discussed previously, the selection model of Hirad and Zorn was a rather poor fit and included regressors that may have been positively correlated with the error term in the main specification. Quercia and Spader did not model selection into treatment at all, let alone selection into treatment types. Thus, the results in both papers may be upwardly biased. Barron and Staten do not model selection, but they do find evidence of selection that may have driven their results. In their credit counseling program, Internet clients had seen larger reductions in their credit scores during the year preceding counseling, which could indicate that these clients were particularly motivated to learn and change their behavior.

[14] Yet, the study suffers from a small sample, a short follow-up period of six months, and the possibility that borrowers were simultaneously exposed to other treatments. Furthermore, the instrument for hours of instruction—marketing efforts in the borrower's metropolitan area—leaves open the possibility that more motivated individuals received more counseling.

References

Agarwal, S. and B. Mazumder (2010). *Cognitive Ability and Financial Decision Making.* Chicago, IL: Federal Reserve Bank of Chicago. http://ushakrisna.com/cognitive.pdf.

——S. Chomsisengphet, C. Liu, and N. Souleles (2006). 'Do Consumers Choose the Right Credit Contracts?' FRB-Chicago Working Paper No. 2006-11. Chicago, IL: Federal Reserve Bank of Chicago.

——J. Driscoll, and D. Laibson (2008a). 'Optimal Mortgage Refinancing: A Closed Form Solution,' NBER Working Paper No. 13487. Cambridge, MA: National Bureau of Economic Research.

—— —— X. Gabaix, and D. Laibson (2008b). 'Learning in the Credit Card Market,' NBER Working Paper No. 13822. Cambridge, MA: National Bureau of Economic Research.

——J. Driscoll, X. Gabaix, and D. Laibson (2009a). 'The Age of Reason: Financial Decisions over the Life-Cycle and Implications for Regulation,' *Brookings Papers on Economic Activity*, 2: 51–117.

——G. Amromin, I. Ben-David, S. Chomsisengphet, and D. D. Evanoff (2009b). 'Do Financial Counseling Mandates Improve Mortgage Choice Performance? Evidence From a Legislative Experiment,' Federal Reserve Bank of Chicago Working Paper No. 2009-07. Chicago, IL: Federal Reserve Bank of Chicago.

——P. Skiba, and J. Tobacman (2009c). 'Payday Loans and Credit Cards: New Liquidity and Credit Scoring Puzzles?' *American Economic Review: Papers and Proceedings*, 99(2): 412–17.

——G. Amromin, I. Ben-David, S. Chomsisengphet, and D. D. Evanoff (2010). 'Learning to Cope: Voluntary Financial Education Programs and Loan Performance during a Housing Crisis,' *American Economic Review: Papers and Proceedings*, 100(2): 495–500.

Australia and New Zealand Banking Group (ANZ) (2003). *ANZ Survey of Adult Financial Literacy in Australia*. Melbourne, VIC: Roy Morgan Research. http://www.thesmithfamily.com.au/webdata/resources/files/ANZreportMay03.pdf

Bakken, R. (1967). 'Money Management Understandings of Tenth Grade Students,' *National Business Education Quarterly*, 36: 6.

Barron, J. M., and M. E. Staten (2009). *Is Technology-Enhanced Credit Counseling as Effective as In-Person Delivery?* Terre Haute, in: Networks Financial Institute at Indiana State University Conference: Improving Financial Literacy and Reshaping Financial Behavior May 14–15. http://www.networksfinancialinstitute.org/News/Documents/Staten.pdf

Bayer, P. J., B. D. Bernheim, and J. K. Scholz (2009). 'The Effects of Financial Education in the Workplace: Evidence From a Survey of Employers,' *Economic Inquiry*, 47(4): 605–24.

Bernheim, B. D. (1988). 'Social Security Benefits: An Empirical Study of Expectations and Realizations,' in R. Ricardo-Campbell and E. P. Lazear, eds, *Issues in Contemporary Retirement*. Stanford, CA: Hoover Institution Press, pp. 312–45.

——D. Garrett (2003). 'The Effects of Financial Education in the Workplace: Evidence From a Survey of Households,' *Journal of Public Economics*, 87: 1487–519.

—— —— D. Maki (2001). 'Education and Saving: The Long-Term Effects of High School Financial Curriculum Mandates,' *Journal of Public Economics*, 80: 435–65.

Boyce, L. and S. M. Danes (1998). *Evaluation of the NEFE High School Financial Planning Program, 1997–1998*. Englewood, CO: National Endowment for Financial Education. http://hsfpp.nefe.org/loadFile.cfm?contentid=646

Bucks, B. and K. Pence (2006). 'Do Homeowners Know Their House Value and Mortgage Terms?' FEDS Working Paper No. 2006–03. Washington, DC: Board of Governors of the Federal Reserve System.

Campbell, J. Y. (2006). 'Household Finance,' *Journal of Finance*, 61(4): 1553–604.

Caskey, John P. (2006). 'Can Personal Financial Management Education Promote Asset Accumulation by the Poor?' Networks Financial Institute Policy Brief No. 2006-PB-06, Indianapolis, IN: Networks Financial Institution.

Chen, Haiyang and Ronald P. Volpe (1998). 'An Analysis of Personal Financial Literacy Among College Students.' *Financial Services Review*, 7(2): 107–28.

Clancy, M., M. Grinstein-Weiss, and M. Schreiner (2001). 'Financial Education and Savings Outcomes in Individual Development Accounts,' Center for Social Development Working Paper No. 2001-02. St Louis, MO: Washington University.

Clark, R. L. and M. B. D'Ambrosio (2002). 'Financial Education and Retirement Savings,' TIAA-CREF Institute Working Paper No. 4-070102-A. New York, NY: TIAA-CREF Institute.

Cole, S. and G. K. Shastry (2009). 'Smart Money: The Effect of Education, Cognitive Ability, and Financial Literacy on Financial Market Participation,' Harvard Business School Working Paper 2009-071. Boston, MA: Harvard University.

Collins, J. M. (2007). 'Exploring the Design of Financial Counseling for Mortgage Borrowers in Default,' *Journal of Family and Economic Issues*, 28: 207–26.

—— (2008). *The Impacts of Mandatory Financial Education: Evidence From a Field Study.* Orange County, CA: AFCPE Annual Conference. http://content.hks.harvard. edu/journalistsresource/pa/economics/finance/impacts-of-mandatory-financial -education-evidence-from-a-randomized-field-study/

—— C. M. O'Rourke (2010). 'Financial Education and Counseling—Still Holding Promise Evaluating Financial Education and Counseling.' *Journal of Consumer Affairs*, 44(3): 483–98.

Consumer Federation of America and American Express Company (CFA/AMEX) (1991). 'Student Consumer Knowledge: Results of a National Test.' Washington, DC: Consumer Federation of America and American Express Company.

Danes, S. M. (2004). *Evaluation of the NEFE High School Financial Planning Program Curriculum: 2003–2004.* Minneapolis, MN: University of Minnesota. http://hsfpp. nefe.org/loadFile.cfm?contentid=273

—— T. K. Hira (1987). 'Money Management Knowledge of College Students,' *The Journal of Student Financial Aid*, 17(1): 4–16.

Ding, L., R. G. Quercia, and J. Ratcliffe (2008). 'Post-purchase Counseling and Default Resolutions among Low- and Moderate-Income Borrowers,' *Journal of Real Estate Research*, 30(3): 315–44.

Duflo, E., and E. Saez (2003). 'The Role of Information and Social Interactions in Retirement Plan Decisions: Evidence from a Randomized Experiment,' *Quarterly Journal of Economics*, 118(3): 815–42.

Elliehausen, G., E. C. Lundquist, and M. E. Staten (2007). 'The Impact of Credit Counseling on Subsequent Borrower Behavior,' *Journal of Consumer Affairs*, 41(1): 1–28.

Employee Benefit Research Institute (EBRI) (1995). 'Are Workers Kidding Themselves? Results of the 1995 Retirement Confidence Survey.' EBRI Issue Brief 168. Washington, DC: Employee Benefit Research Institute.

Garman, E. T., J. Kim, C. Y. Kratzer, B. H. Brunson, and S. Joo (1999). 'Workplace Financial Education Improves Personal Financial Wellness,' *Financial Counseling and Planning*, 10(1): 79–88.

Gartner, K. and R. M. Todd (2005). *Effectiveness of Online 'Early Intervention' Financial Education for Credit Cardholders*. Chicago, IL: Chicago Federal Reserve. http://www.chicagofed.net/digital_assets/others/events/2005/promises_and_pitfalls/paper_intervention.pdf.

Gustman, A. L. and T. L. Steinmeier (2005). 'Imperfect Knowledge of Social Security and Pensions,' *Industrial Relations*, 44(2): 373–97.

Hartarska, V. and C. Gonzalez-Vega (2005). 'Credit Counseling and Mortgage Termination by Low-Income Households,' *Journal of Real Estate Finance and Economics*, 30(3): 227–43.

——— (2006). 'Evidence on the Effect of Credit Counseling on Mortgage Loan Default by Low-Income Households,' *Journal of Housing Economics*, 15(1): 63–79.

Hathaway, I. and S. Khatiwada (2008). 'Do Financial Education Programs Work?' FRB-Cleveland Working Paper 2008-03. Cleveland, OH: Federal Reserve Bank of Cleveland.

Hilgert, M. A., J. M. Hogarth, and S. Beverly (2003). 'Household Financial Management: The Connection between Knowledge and Behavior,' *Federal Reserve Bulletin*, 89(7): 309–22.

Hira, T. K., and C. Loibl (2005). 'Understanding the Impact of Employer-Provided Financial Education on Workplace Satisfaction,' *Journal of Consumer Affairs*, 39(1): 173–94.

Hirad, A. and P. Zorn (2002). 'A Little Knowledge is a Good Thing: Empirical Evidence of the Effectiveness of Pre-Purchase Homeownership Counseling,' in N. Retsinas and E. Belsky, eds, *Low-Income Homeownership: Examining the Unexamined Goal*. Washington, DC: Brookings Institution Press, pp. 146–74.

Hogarth, J. M (2006). *Financial Education and Economic Development*. Moscow, Russia: Federal Reserve Board. http://www.oecd.org/dataoecd/20/50/37742200.pdf

Holland, J. H., D. Goodman, and B. Stich (2008). 'Defined Contribution Plans Emerging in the Public Sector: The Manifestation of Defined Contributions and the Effects of Workplace Financial Education,' *Review of Public Personnel Administration*, 28(4): 367–84.

Housing Action Illinois (2007). *Findings from the HB 4050 Predatory Lending Database Pilot Program*. Chicago, IL: National Low Income Housing Coalition. http://www.nlihc.org/doc/repository/IL-Findings.pdf

Kim, J. (2007). 'Workplace Financial Education Program: Does It Have an Impact on Employees' Personal Finances?' *Journal of Family and Consumer Sciences*, 99(1): 43–7.

——— D. C. Bagwell, and E. T. Garman (1998). 'Evaluation of Workplace Personal Financial Education,' *Personal Finances and Worker Productivity*, 2(1): 187–92.

KPMG Peat Marwick LLP (KPMG) (1996). *Retirement Benefits in the 1990s: 1995 Survey Data*. New York, NY: KPMG.

Langrehr, F. W. (1979). 'Consumer Education: Does it Change Students' Competencies and Attitudes?' *The Journal of Consumer Affairs*, 13: 41–53.

Lusardi, A. (2004). 'Saving and the Effectiveness of Financial Education,' in O. S. Mitchell and S. Utkus, eds, *Pension Design and Structure: New Lessons from Behavioral Finance.* Oxford, UK: Oxford University Press, pp. 157–84.

——O. S. Mitchell (2006). 'Financial Literacy and Planning: Implications for Retirement Wellbeing,' Pension Research Council Working Paper No. 2006-1. Philadelphia, PA: The Pension Research Council.

——— (2007*a*). 'Baby Boomer Retirement Security: The Roles of Planning, Financial Literacy, and Housing Wealth,' *Journal of Monetary Economics*, 54: 205–24.

——— (2007*b*). 'Financial Literacy and Retirement Planning: New Evidence From the RAND American Life Panel,' Michigan Retirement Research Center Working Paper No. 2007-157. Ann Arbor, MI: Michigan Retirement Research Center.

———V. Curto (2009). 'Financial Literacy Among the Young: Evidence and Implications for Consumer Policy,' Pension Research Council Working Paper No. 2009-09. Philadelphia, PA: The Pension Research Council.

Mandell, L. (2008). 'Financial Literacy of High School Students,' in A. Lusardi, ed., *Overcoming the Saving Slump: How to Increase the Effectiveness of Financial Education and Saving Programs.* Chicago, IL: University of Chicago Press, pp. 257–79.

Martin, M. (2007). 'A Literature Review of the Effectiveness of Financial Education,' FRB-Richmond Working Paper No. 07-03. Richmond, VA: Federal Reserve Bank of Richmond.

Miles, D. (2004). *The UK Mortgage Market: Taking a Longer-Term View.* London, UK: Controller of Her Majesty's Stationery Office.

Mitchell, O. S. (1988). 'Worker Knowledge of Pension Provisions,' *Journal of Labor Economics*, 6: 21–39.

Moore, D. (2003). 'Survey of Financial Literacy in Washington State: Knowledge, Behavior, Attitudes, and Experiences,' Washington State Technical Report 03-39. Olympia, WA: Washington State Department of Financial Institutions.

Oppenheimer Funds/Girls Inc. (1997). *Girls, Money, and Independence.* New York, NY: Oppenheimer Funds/Girls, Inc.

Organisation for Economic Co-Operation and Development (OECD) (2005). *Improving Financial Literacy: Analysis of Issues and Policies.* Paris, France: OECD.

Peng, T. M., S. Bartholomae, J. J. Fox, and G. Cravener (2007). 'The Impact of Personal Finance Education Delivered in High School and College Courses,' *Journal of Family and Economic Issues*, 28: 265–84.

Princeton Survey Research Associates (PSRA) (1996). *Investor Knowledge Survey,* Arlington, VA: Investor Protection Trust.

—— (1997). *Planning for the Future: Are Americans Prepared to Meet Their Financial Goals?* Princeton, NJ: Nations Bank/Consumer Federation of America.

Quercia, R. and J. Spader (2008). 'Does Homeownership Counseling Affect the Prepayment and Default Behavior of Affordable Mortgage Borrowers?' *Journal of Policy Analysis and Management*, 27(2): 304–25.

Sanders, C. K., T. L. Weaver, and M. Schnabel (2007). 'Economic Education for Battered Women: An Evaluation of Outcomes,' *Journal of Women and Social Work*, 22(3): 240–54.

Servon, L. J. and R. Kaestner (2008). 'Consumer Financial Literacy and the Impact of Online Banking on the Financial Behavior of Lower-Income Bank Customers,' *The Journal of Consumer Affairs*, 42(2): 271–305.

Spader, J., J. Ratcliffe, J. Montoya, and P. Skillern (2009). 'The Bold and the Bankable: How the Nuestro Barrio Telenova Reaches Latino Immigrants with Financial Education,' *The Journal of Consumer Affairs*, 43(1): 56–79.

Stango, V. and J. Zinman (2010). *Fuzzy Math, Disclosure Regulation, and Credit Market Outcomes: Evidence from Truth-in-Lending Reform*. Davis, CA: University of California. http://faculty.gsm.ucdavis.edu/~vstango/TILA_july_2010.pdf

Vanguard Group/Money Magazine (1997). 'Financial Literacy of Mutual Fund Investors,' *Money Magazine*. New York, NY, January.

Volpe, R. P., J. J. Pavlicko (1996). 'Personal Investment Literacy Among College Students: A Survey,' *Financial Practice and Education*, 6: 86–94.

——H. Chen, and S. Liu (2006). 'An Analysis of the Importance of Personal Finance Topics and the Level of Knowledge Possessed by Working Adults,' *Financial Services Review*, 15: 81–96.

Willis, L. E. (2008). 'Against Financial Literacy Education,' *Iowa Law Review*, 94: 197–285.

——(2009). 'Evidence and Ideology in Assessing the Effectiveness of Financial Literacy Education,' *San Diego Law Review*, 46: 415–58.

Chapter 11

Time Perception and Retirement Saving: Lessons from Behavioral Decision Research

Gal Zauberman and B. Kyu Kim

Individuals often make financial decisions that are not in their long-term best interest. One highly consequential example is undersaving for retirement: people often delay initiating or increasing saving programs that they themselves believe would be beneficial. Indeed, undersaving due to delay in initiating saving or low contribution rates might only further increase in its magnitude as a result of the recent financial crisis, which decreased the value of saving accounts as well as the availability of perceived and actual 'slack' in households' income.

Work in behavioral decision research and behavioral economics has aimed at identifying the reasons for often poor financial decision-making, including low retirement saving rates, and what can be done through policy and by individuals themselves, to facilitate better long-term decisions (based on individuals' own stated preferences, as well as commonly accepted levels of what will be required at retirement). In this chapter, we do not provide a broad review or replicate material covered in other chapters, but rather we focus on the findings and implications of behavioral research, examining the underlying psychological processes for retirement saving (see also Lynch and Zauberman, 2006). In particular, we focus on two key cognitive mechanisms relevant to this problem. The first relates to how people represent outcomes (costs and benefits) in the near and distant future, building on resource slack theory (Zauberman and Lynch, 2005) and related research on mental representation (Trope and Liberman, 2003; Malkoc and Zauberman, 2006). The second focuses on a perceived time-based discounting model (e.g., Kim and Zauberman, 2009; Zauberman et al., 2009) and examines how people perceive the time horizon itself (i.e., anticipated duration) between the present and a future target date. In the following sections, we discuss key implications of these behavioral tendencies for (*a*) why people delay setting up and raising retirement contributions; and (*b*) possible strategies that might be used to overcome the tendency for delay.

Intertemporal choice research and retirement saving

The study of *intertemporal choice*, decisions that involve a tradeoff between costs and benefits at different points in time, examines behavioral regularities in how people actually make such decisions compared to normative discounting models, drawing from psychology, behavioral decision research, and behavioral economics. This extensive literature is relevant to public policy issues where individuals seem to heavily discount future consequences, and thus highly relevant for the study of retirement saving decisions.

In studying intertemporal preferences, researchers often measure individuals' discount rates for delayed future outcomes. For instance, participants in laboratory and field experiments are presented with a choice between smaller but immediate rewards and larger but delayed rewards, and they report the dollar amount making them indifferent between the immediate and delayed rewards. If someone is indifferent between $100 today and $110 in one year, for this person, the value of $100 in one year is discounted only by 10 percent for the one-year delay. But if another person is indifferent between $100 and $1,000 in one year, the person discounts the value of the same delayed $100 by 900 percent. The higher the measured level of discounting is, the greater that person discounts outcomes in the future (e.g., benefits from retirement saving). Thus, this basic measure of delay discounting has been heavily used and validated as a measure of impatience and impulsivity (e.g., Green et al., 1994).

This simple notion of temporal discounting is relevant to the issue of low saving rates in two general ways. First, *individual differences* in measured discount rates might reflect stable differences across individuals in their propensity to save for retirement. Consistent with real-world observations, many studies of delay-discounting tasks have reported wide individual difference in observed discount rates (e.g., Green et al., 1994; Kirby, 1997; Kirby et al., 2002; Frederick, 2005; Shamosh et al., 2008). For example, in a study by Kim and Zauberman (2009), some participants revealed no discounting, while some others revealed almost 400 percent discount rate for the same $75 monetary reward delayed by three months. While discount rates in these studies are measured for relatively short-term delays compared to the prolonged periods involved for retirement saving (e.g., twenty years), the implication for such decisions is straightforward. Individuals with high discount rates are less likely to save for their retirement, because any delayed pleasures that they may derive from their saving will be heavily discounted. That is, the more than $100 one can spend in the future by saving $100 today looks much less attractive than $100 one can spend right now. Of course, for this perspective to be at all relevant, these individual discounting propensities need to be stable over time and across domain problems (e.g., retirement saving, healthy eating, etc.), and both of these aspects are controversial. Moreover, an individual difference approach, although it might point to a need for regulation, offers little in the way of behaviorally influencing individuals' decisions.

The second, and more central to our discussion, way in which intertemporal research might shed light on retirement saving decisions is that such decisions are *highly sensitive to changes in the decision context*. For example, the degree of discounting has been shown to vary depending on whether it is a gain or a loss, whether the amount is small or large, and whether the task is to delay a current amount or to expedite a future amount (for a review, see Frederick et al., 2002). But possibly most relevant for our discussion is the finding that peoples' tendency to discount delayed outcomes at different rates depends on when delay happens. Extensive empirical evidence shows that, in general, people discount delayed outcomes more heavily when the delay happens relatively soon (e.g., delaying consumption from today to tomorrow) than relatively far in the future (e.g., delaying consumption from 100 days later to 101 days later). That is, although the same outcome is delayed by the same time interval (e.g., one day), an outcome delayed one day from today is discounted at a higher discount rate than an outcome delayed one day from 100 days hence. This phenomenon, often labeled as *hyperbolic discounting*, is relevant to the undersaving problem by addressing why people plan to save in the future but do not do so when it comes to the time to save their income. Although, from today's perspective, saving a certain portion of your future income (or giving up a certain amount of future pleasure) seems reasonable, when that time approaches and individuals actually need to save, the cost of saving (or giving up a current pleasure) seems much larger than when it was originally envisioned because delaying immediate consumption is discounted more heavily than delaying consumptions in the future.

Behavioral determinants of temporal discounting

In order to be able to draw lessons from intertemporal choice research, one must isolate the relevant behavioral mechanism. Understanding the underlying processes that give rise to these behaviors can provide a more solid ground to build policy and interventions. Seeking to identify the psychological process, researchers initially focused on affective and visceral influences on myopic decisions. For instance, Loewenstein (1996) argued that some rewards are discounted more heavily than others, when those rewards satisfy visceral responses such as hunger, thirst, or sexual arousal. Once such states are activated, immediate consumption that satisfies one's immediate appetitive responses (or cravings) gets disproportionately higher weight compared to all other delayed consumptions that do not, thus resulting in a hyperbola-like discounting for delayed consumption (Loewenstein, 1996). Multiple examples documented in the literature illustrate these effects. In one study, participants who would not envision themselves engaged in morally questionable sexual behavior, reported intention to do so when they were sexually aroused (Ariely and Loewenstein, 2006). Similarly, in the context of food consumption, participants chose more vices (e.g., chocolate cake) than virtues (e.g., fruit salad) when they lacked cognitive resources and when rewarding stimuli were more vivid (e.g., when faced with the actual presence of dessert vs a picture of it; Shiv and Fedorikhin, 1999). These results are in line with 'hot/cool' systems of delay of gratification (e.g., Metcalfe and Mischel, 1999), as well as with empirical demonstrations that substance abusers show high discount rates for delayed addictive substances as well as money (Kirby et al., 1999; Baker et al., 2003). Collectively, these results all point to the idea that, when visceral states are activated, people tend to ignore delayed future consequences.

While these affective/visceral processes are no doubt relevant to many real-life decisions such as smoking, impulse buying, or overeating, they may be less directly applicable to more calculated decisions, such as saving for retirement or taking out loans. We present later a more cognitive 'cold' set of processes that have received relatively less attention but that we believe might be helpful in the context of such individual decisions. Specifically, we propose two distinct cognitive processes explaining myopic financial decision-making, one centering on the *perception of delayed outcomes* per se (e.g., perception of slack or different mental representation of outcomes), and the other centering on the *perception of temporal distance to the outcomes* (e.g., perception of duration until the receipt of delayed outcomes).

Accounts based on time-dependent perceptions of outcome

Next, we focus on how perceptions of outcomes and resource slack in the near and distant future impact observed discount rates.

Resource slack theory

Zauberman and Lynch (2005) proposed the concept of perceived 'resource slack' to explain why different resources might be discounted at different rates. They defined resource slack as 'the perceived surplus of a given resource available to complete a focal task', and tested slack theory in the domains of time and money. They found that, on average, people expect to have more time in the future, but this optimistic expectation was less pronounced for money, and as a result, people discount time investments more than money investments. Importantly, this greater discounting of time than money was observed only when people expected time (versus money) slack to grow more in the future. When people expected the opposite, however, they discounted future money more than future time. For example, when people expected a future raise, the perceived value of money was further discounted, resulting in a decrease in their saving. Note that this could be completely normative, but only when people's expectations are not biased, a condition that is often violated.

Beyond just different discount rates for time and money, resource slack theory also explains hyperbolic discounting and differential hyperbolic discounting for time versus money. Specifically, if individuals expect money at time t to be less than that at $t + n$, and the difference is greater when t is very near than when it is temporally more distant, they will discount delayed money at a different rate because of the differences in slack gain. This is especially true when people anticipate a raise in the future. Even though they plan to start saving a portion of their raise in the future, as the timing of the raise comes closer, any delayed consumption looks painful to them, and thus they will not be as likely to execute on their promise unless there is binding precommitment, which we will discuss further later.

Construal level theory

Construal level theory (Trope and Liberman, 2003; Liberman et al., 2007) provides a different cognitive account for how the representation of near and distant events can affect intertemporal preferences. Construal level theory argues that individuals represent events in the distant future at a relatively high level and events in the near future at a relatively low level. That is, for near events, people consider concretely the feasibility and the constraints of events, but for events in the distant future, they think more in terms of abstract thoughts and focus on the desirability of the same outcomes. For example, when asked to select assignments to be completed in the near-term, participants chose the less interesting assignment (a low desirability with high feasibility option), but when asked to choose for distant future, participants elect the more interesting but more difficult assignment (a high desirability with low feasibility option).

Construal level theory provides a cognitive reason for why people would discount hyperbolically. The pleasure in the future that one can receive by saving today is construed in a high level, but the duration over which one needs to forgo the pleasure by saving and the pleasure itself is construed in a lower level. Therefore, when deciding whether to spend now, or save and delay the spending, the delay gets more weight, leading the individual to seek immediate pleasure rather than save. However, when considering saving in the future, the amount of pleasure gets more weight than the pain from delaying it; thus the individual is willing to save his/her income occurring in the future. As a direct test of this explanation for hyperbolic discounting, in line with construal level theory, Malkoc and Zauberman (2006) manipulated participants' level of construal such that abstract construal of delayed consumption became more concrete, which attenuated the degree of hyperbolic discounting, supporting the role of construal in myopic decisions.

Implications for saving

Hyperbolic, or inconsistent, discounters experience intertemporal conflicts between when they plan to save in the future and when that day approaches, and they actually have to follow up on their decisions. When individuals plan to save, the delayed benefits from saving (vs the opportunity costs of not spending) are discounted relatively little, so future saving looks attractive. But when the future becomes the present, and people must decide to save now, the cost of saving (or the pain from giving up consumption) now seems much larger than it seemed from a distance. For this reason, many behavioral economists have suggested precommitment as a remedy to this conflict between the current and future selves. That is, by getting people today to precommit to a desirable action in the future, they then prevent themselves from yielding to the temptation of spending, even when the desirable action is no longer perceived as desirable, but instead perceived as a cost.

Several findings from behavioral decision research account for the effectiveness of such precommitment devices in increasing saving rate. Construal level theory predicts that when people make saving decisions in the present, short-term costs and constraints loom large, but when they are given an option to precommit to save their future raise for retirement saving, the consequence is temporally distant, and as a result, benefits of saving gets more weight than its costs. The perspective of resource slack theory also predicts the success of such precommitment device. People commonly expect that their expenses always just match or fall below their financial resources, and if they are too cash-constrained today, it is quite likely that they are just as cash-constrained in the future (as they adjust for their new income levels). But because people feel that they will have more financial slack after getting a raise, they are willing to precommit to save in the future. Resource slack theory further predicts that participants in a precommitment program would stick with the plan rather than opt out. The cost of opting out seems very small when one precommits several months before a raise is realized, but switching costs turn to be much more binding when the time arrives to incur them (Zauberman, 2003; Zauberman and Lynch, 2005). That is, when their raise arrives, people may wish to opt out, but they procrastinate doing so because they have to find the time.

Consistent with these predictions, the real-world application of a pre-commitment device, such as the trademarked plan 'Save More Tomorrow' by Thaler and Benartzi (2004), was shown to be very successful. In this plan, employees were provided with the option to precommit to save a portion of their future raises for retirement. This program resulted in a significant increase of employees' annual retirement saving rate from 3.5 percent to almost 14 percent in forty months (and they rarely opted out!).

Accounts based on perception of temporal distance

As discussed earlier, most studies of intertemporal decisions and related models have centered on changes in the perception of outcomes at different points in time. They tend to explain hyperbolic discounting by focusing on why individuals discount *the value of outcomes* per se at different rates. Recently, researchers have offered an alternative perspective, pointing to the importance of separating the effects of the perception of values from the effects of the *perception of delays* in temporal discounting (e.g., Read, 2001; Ebert and Prelec, 2007; Killeen, 2009; Kim and Zauberman, 2009; Zauberman et al., 2009). The argument is that when the two processes are separated, hyperbolic discounting can be simply explained by diminishing sensitivity to longer time horizons without making any assumption about the discounting of future outcomes per se. That is, if delays in the near future seem longer than delays in the far future, outcomes delayed in the near future will be discounted at a higher rate than outcomes delayed in the far future, resulting in hyperbolic discounting. To illustrate this point more concretely, Zauberman et al. (2009) present the following scenario: suppose an individual is indifferent among $100 today, $1,000 in one year, and $2,000 in three years. If his/her perception of time is unbiased (i.e., they perceive a three-year time horizon as three times longer than a one-year time horizon), the implied compound annual discount rate for this person is 230 percent for one year and 100 percent for three years, indicating present-biased preferences. This is the type of evidence most commonly reported for hyperbolic discounting (e.g., Thaler, 1981). Now, suppose that the above consumer has biased subjective time perceptions such that he/she perceives three years to be only 1.3 times longer than one year (as opposed to three times longer). Keeping the discount rate constant and adjusting the time from three to 1.3 before computing the discount rate, a discount rate of 230 percent for both the one-year and three-year time horizons is obtained. In other words, the same set of preferences ($100 today = $1,000 in one year = $2,000 in three years) can be modeled as accurately by using a constant discount rate with respect to *subjective* time as by using declining discount rates with respect to *objective* time.

An empirical demonstration of this hypothesis was obtained by measuring participants' perception of various anticipatory time horizons (Kim and Zauberman, 2009; Zauberman et al., 2009). The authors found that nonlinear functions fit participants' subjective time estimates better than a linear function, confirming diminishing sensitivity to time. Furthermore, they found that annual compound discount rates calculated without considering participants' subjective time estimates were decreasing as a function of time (i.e., hyperbolic discounting), as commonly reported in past research. But when the subjective time estimates were accounted for, discount rates were no longer decreasing for most time horizons (i.e., rates were consistent with exponential discounting). These results imply that individuals who show diminishing sensitivity to time may behave *as if* they have decreasing discount rates, even if they have constant (i.e., exponential) discount rates over perceived time.

This perceived time-based account of discounting has important implications for undersaving in retirement. Even when people have the intent to save for retirement, if they subjectively perceive the retirement very far away from the present, then they are unlikely to start saving today. As a result, any remedies to correct their subjective time perceptions would help them to increase saving. In the following section, we discuss various strategies to alleviate undersaving.

Changing perceived time to retirement

If temporal discounting can be driven by how people perceive time, then interventions designed to change subjective perception of future time can be used as a strategy to increase saving rates. To illustrate the situational dependence of time perception, we present different factors and discuss their implications. Previous research shows that sexually arousing stimuli have been shown to induce steeping discounting of monetary rewards (Wilson and Daly, 2003; Van den Bergh et al., 2008). To test whether even the effects of visceral factors might affect discounting as driven by subjective time perception, Kim and Zauberman (2010) asked heterosexual male participants to rate the attractiveness of the female models taken from the Victoria's Secret online catalogue (vs neutral objects) and measured their subjective time estimates for twelve anticipatory durations, ranging from one month to twenty-three months. They confirmed diminishing sensitivity to time horizons, regardless of whether participants rated models or neutral objects. Participants who were exposed to the sexually arousing images, however, perceived the same anticipatory durations to be longer compared to those who rated the neutral objects. They further showed that the impact of sexually arousing images on the changes in temporal discounting is due to the changes in time perception. That is, participants seeing the models revealed higher discount rates because they perceived the waiting time until the receipt of delayed rewards to be longer than those who rated neutral objects did.

While this finding that sexual cues influence temporal discounting by changing time perception is intriguing on its own and points to the important role of time perception in delay discounting, it is not directly applicable to the problem of undersaving for retirement. For financial decision-making for retirement, where spatial distance information often accompanies (i.e., people plan to move to a different place when they retire), more relevant context can be found in a recent study using space—time interdependence to influence discounting of monetary rewards. Specifically, Kim et al. (2010) investigated whether spatial distance to well-known retirement cities influences participants' subjective perception of time until their own retirement. They presented to participants a map of the United States where seven retirement cities were shown, and they were asked to memorize the locations of each city. About half of the participants were asked to imagine that they were going to live in Philadelphia until they retired and then would move to Gardnerville Ranchos (the long-distance condition), while the other half imagined moving to Cary (the short-distance condition) after they retired. When participants' subjective time estimates to their retirement were measured, those who imagined moving to Gardnerville Ranchos subjectively perceived the duration to retirement to be longer compared to those who imagined moving to Cary. These findings point to the important role of the context of the decisions, which can influence subjective perception of future time.

Research on how to shift decisions by changing time perception is only now emerging, and we can only speculate about its relevance for real money decisions. The potential implications, however, are intriguing. As the space manipulations earlier suggest, subtle changes in the message could alter how long or short a future event (retirement) might seem, thus changing the propensity to save. One possible extension is to draw on research on time perception of elapsed time that shows that manipulating 'markers' of time could shift how long or short a given duration seems (Zauberman et al., 2010). On the basis of this research, we would expect that when people think about many markers from now to retirement, they will think about it as further away, compared to just thinking about the time until retirement.

Conclusion

This chapter provides a selective review of issues in intertemporal choice research and possible implications for retirement saving. We focus on two cognitive mechanisms explaining why the future is discounted: (*a*) changes in the perception of delayed outcomes due to changes in mental representations and perceived slack; and (*b*) changes in the perception of temporal distance to delayed outcomes.

Regarding the changes in the perception of delayed outcomes, we reviewed two theories of the cognitive underpinnings of discounting: resource slack theory and temporal construal theory. In both, the key implication for practitioners and policymakers trying to increase saving for retirement is to manipulate people's temporal perspective. If an action involves some mixture of costs and benefits, construal level theory suggests that costs will loom larger in the near term than in the more distant future. In the near term, the costs may outweigh the benefits, but when viewed from a greater temporal distance, the costs seem to fade away and the benefits remain. To induce a pattern of long-term desirable behavior, one must induce people to precommit to a decision at some point in the more distant future. If undersaving problems come from underweighting future costs, then the policy prescription is the opposite: induce people to make decisions about the future as if the consequences were coming into effect immediately. From the perspective of resource slack theory, people imagine having more money slack in the future than they actually earn, so they mispredict how much of their income they will save in the future.

The other perspective on temporal discounting focuses on changes in the perceived temporal distance to delayed outcomes. According to this perspective, factors leading people to perceive their retirement is far away are less likely to save today because delayed benefits from saving are discounted to the extent of how long or short they perceive the delay to be. Although we reviewed two of the most recent demonstration of these factors (arousal and spatial distance), there are likely other factors that potentially influence how long they perceive the time to retire. These factors can be utilized to increase saving rates in various educational and commercial settings.

In sum, we conclude that better understanding of how people perceive *delayed outcomes* and *temporal distance to the outcomes* is critical to understanding and suggesting prescriptions for problems of retirement undersaving. Future interventions and public policy analysis will benefit from paying close attention to knowledge accumulated in this important area of behavioral research.

References

Ariely, D. and G. Loewenstein (2006). 'The Heat of The Moment: The Effect of Sexual Arousal on Sexual Decision Making,' *Journal of Behavioral Decision Making*, 19: 87–98.

Baker, F., M. W. Johnson, and W. K. Bickel (2003). 'Delay Discounting in Current and Never-Before Cigarette Smokers: Similarities and Differences across Commodity, Sign, and Magnitude,' *Journal of Abnormal Psychology*, 112: 382–92.

Ebert, J. and D. Prelec (2007). 'The Fragility of Time: Time-Insensitivity and Valuation of the Near and Far Future,' *Management Science*, 53: 1423–38.

Frederick, S. (2005). 'Cognitive Reflection and Decision Making,' *Journal of Economic Perspectives*, 19: 25–42.

——G. Loewenstein, and T. O'Donoghue (2002). 'Time Discounting and Time Preference: A Critical Review,' *Journal of Economic Literature*, 40: 351–401.

Green, L., A. F. Fry, and J. Myerson (1994). 'Discounting of Delayed Rewards: A Life-Span Comparison,' *Psychological Science*, 5: 33–6.

Killeen, P. R. (2009). 'An Additive-Utility Model of Delay Discounting,' *Psychological Review*, 116: 602–19.

Kim, B. K. and G. Zauberman (2009). 'Perception of Anticipatory Time in Temporal Discounting,' *Journal of Neuroscience, Psychology, and Economics*, 2: 91–101.

————(2010). 'Can Victoria's Secret Change the Future? Sexually-Arousing Images, Anticipatory Time Perception, and Impatience,' Working Paper. Philadelphia, PA: University of Pennsylvania.

————J. Bettman (2010). 'Feel More Distant to Your Retirement When You Retire to a Distant City? Space-Time Interdependence, Time Perception, and Impatience,' Working Paper. Philadelphia, PA: University of Pennsylvania.

Kirby, K. N. (1997). 'Bidding on the Future: Evidence Against Normative Discounting of Delayed Rewards,' *Journal of Experimental Psychology: General*, 126: 54–70.

——N. M. Petry, and W. K. Bickel (1999). 'Heroin Addicts have Higher Discount Rates for Delayed Rewards than Non-Drug-Using Controls,' *Journal of Experimental Psychology*, 128: 78–87.

——R. Godoy, V. Reyes-Garcia, E. Byron, L. Apaza, W. Leonard, E. Perez, V. Valdez, D. Wilkie (2002). 'Correlated of Delay-Discount Rates: Evidence from Tsimane' Amerindians of the Bolivian Rain Forest,' *Journal of Economic Psychology*, 23(3): 291–316.

Liberman, N., Y. Trope, and E. Stephan (2007). 'Psychological Distance,' in E. T. Higgins and A. W. Kruglanski, eds, *Social Psychology, Second Edition: Handbook of Basic Principles*. New York, NY: Guilford Press, pp. 353–84.

Loewenstein, G. F. (1996). 'Out of Control: Visceral Influences on Behavior,' *Organizational Behavior and Human Decision Processes*, 65: 272–92.

Lynch, J. G. and G. Zauberman (2006). 'When Do You Want It? Time, Decisions, and Public Policy,' *Journal of Public Policy and Marketing*, 25: 67–78.

Malkoc, S. A. and G. Zauberman (2006). 'Deferring Versus Expediting Consumption: The Effect of Outcome Concreteness on Sensitivity to Time Horizon,' *Journal of Marketing Research*, 43: 618–27.

Metcalfe, J. and W. Mischel (1999). 'A Hot/Cool-System Analysis of Delay of Gratification: Dynamics of Willpower,' *Psychological Review*, 106: 3–19.

Shiv, B. and A. Fedorikhin (1999). 'Heart and Mind in Conflict: The Interplay of Affect and Cognition in Consumer Decision Making,' *Journal of Consumer Research*, 26: 278–92.

Read, D. (2001). 'Is Time-discounting Hyperbolic or Subadditive?' *Journal of Risk and Uncertainty*, 23: 5–32.

Shamosh, N. A., C. G. Deyoung, A. E. Green, D. L. Reis, M. R. Johnson, A. R. Conway, R. W. Engle, T. S. Braver, and J. R. Gray (2008). 'Individual Differences in Delay Discounting,' *Psychological Science*, 19: 904–11.

Thaler, R. H. (1981). 'Some Empirical Evidence on Dynamic Inconsistency,' *Economic Letters*, 8: 201–7.

——S. Benartzi (2004). 'Save More Tomorrow: Using Behavioral Economics to Increase Employee Saving,' *Journal of Political Economy*, 112: 164–87.

Trope, Y. and N. Liberman (2003). 'Temporal Construal,' *Psychological Review*, 110: 403–21.

Van den Bergh, B., S. Dewitte, and L. Warlop (2008). 'Bikinis Instigate Generalized Impatience in Intertemporal Choice,' *Journal of Consumer Research*, 35: 85–97.

Wilson, M. and M. Daly (2003). 'Do Pretty Women Inspire Men to Discount the Future?' *Proceedings of the Royal Society of London, Series B: Biological Sciences*, 271: 177–9.

Zauberman, G. (2003). 'The Intertemporal Dynamics of Consumer Lock-In,' *Journal of Consumer Research*, 30: 405–19.

——J. G. Lynch (2005). 'Resource Slack and Propensity to Discount Delayed Investments of Time versus Money,' *Journal of Experiment Psychology: General*, 134: 23–37.

——B. K. Kim, S. Malkoc, and J. R. Bettman (2009). 'Time Discounting and Discounting Time,' *Journal of Marketing Research*, 47: 543–56.

——J. Levav, K. Diehl, and R. Bhargave (2010). '1995 Feels So Close Yet So Far: The Effect of Event Markets on Subjective Feelings of Elapsed Time,' *Psychological Science*, 21: 133–9.

Chapter 12

Making Savers Winners: An Overview of Prize-Linked Saving Products

Melissa S. Kearney, Peter Tufano, Jonathan Guryan, and Erik Hurst

Policy initiatives aimed at increasing household saving rates typically focus on things like mandating saving, changing the choice architecture of saving decisions, providing financial incentives, or embedding saving in a social network.[1] In this chapter, we review an alternative policy option: prize-linked saving (PLS) accounts. This mechanism adds a lottery-like feature to an otherwise standard saving account, creating an asset structure that might hold great appeal to the target low-saver segment of the population. While PLS accounts would be innovative in the United States, such accounts have already proven to be popular in other countries. In addition, such accounts are potentially a more cost-effective way of promoting saving compared to matching accounts or policies that use financial incentives to motivate saving behavior. The primary obstacle to the widespread adoption and offering of PLS accounts in the United States is the questionable legality of such products, which we discuss later.

PLS accounts differ from standard saving accounts in one specific way. Instead of, or perhaps in addition to, offering a fixed interest return, PLS accounts offer a stochastic return in that depositors periodically receive a chance to win a specified (and potentially large) amount that is a function of deposit amounts. In this sense, this chance is similar to a lottery ticket. The products are unlike a traditional lottery in that the principal is returned to the investor, either at the maturity of the instrument or on demand. The random component of the return on saving can take the form of in-kind prizes—as is commonly offered by commercial banks in Latin America—or as a cash prize awarded to account holders as a part of a regular drawing, as is the case with Britain's Premium Bonds.

There are two features of PLS accounts that would likely be attractive to potential savers. First, they offer a skewed distribution of returns. Many potential investors desire some exposure to upside risk (i.e., a chance to be rich). Second, to the extent that they offer a lottery-like component, PLS accounts potentially offer an element of entertainment or fun.

We present three pieces of existing indirect evidence in support of the view that PLS products would be popular among low- and moderate-income households in the United States. First, the propensity of many low- and middle-income US families to gamble on state lotteries indirectly suggests that a saving vehicle offering a low probability chance of a high payoff prize would be an attractive asset, particularly among low- and middle- income investors. Second, PLS assets are popular in several other countries and have been popular for over three centuries. Third, two recent PLS demonstration experiments in the United States show promising initial results in terms of consumer take-up. There is an important caveat to interpreting this evidence on the popularity of PLS products: to date, there is no evidence on the fundamental issue of whether these products increase total household saving. This remains an important question for future research.[2]

The appeal of PLS accounts

A consensus has emerged among academics and policymakers that traditional vehicles for increasing saving, including IRAs and 401(k)s, are not generally successful at raising saving by individuals at the lower end of the wealth distribution. Recent initiatives such as the Saver's Credit and Individual Development Accounts, which use matching funds as an additional enticement to save, are promising but require substantial government financial support (Tufano and Schneider, 2008).

The promotion of PLS products takes seriously the idea that potential savers place a high value on the chance to 'win big'. We speculate that there is unmet consumer demand in America for saving products that offer the (remote) prospect of changing current wealth status, rather than incrementally building wealth with certainty. If this speculation is correct, then an otherwise standard investment vehicle offering a financial return in the form of a chance to win a large prize, rather than a guaranteed modest return, would be an even more effective way to motivate individuals to contribute current income to investment accounts than schemes such as contribution matching. Furthermore, the lottery component of the PLS account might have direct appeal beyond the chance to win large prizes. For those who consider playing the lottery to be fun, a saving account with a lottery component may be more attractive than a standard saving account with stable returns.

The potential appeal of PLS accounts to US households

A fundamental policy question behind a PLS policy is whether observed preferences for uncertain payoffs could be leveraged to encourage saving. Our conjecture that it could is based on two sets of observations. The experience of lottery gambling in the United States demonstrates that there is widespread demand for low-probability, high-prize gambling products, in particular among low-income individuals and households. In the year 2008, forty-two states and the District of Columbia offered state lotteries, bringing in roughly $60 billion in sales or more than $540 per household nationwide (NASPL, 2010). In the same year, American households spent $430 per household on all dairy products, and $444 on alcohol (BLS, 2010). We buy more lottery tickets than milk or beer.

Lottery gambling is also popular among US low- and moderate-income households. The 1998 National Opinion Research Council (NORC) survey of gambling, the most recent nationally representative survey of gambling behavior in the United States, reveals three general facts (Kearney, 2005). First, lottery gambling extends across races, sexes, income, and education groups. Second, with regard to race, black respondents spend nearly twice as much on lottery tickets as do white and Hispanic respondents, and the highest rates of participation and expenditures are recorded among black male high school dropouts. Third, average annual lottery spending in dollar terms is roughly equal across the lowest, middle, and highest income groups. This implies that on average, low-income households spend a larger percentage of their wealth on lottery tickets than other US households.[3]

Much has been written about potential explanations for gambling among consumers. The case of state lottery gambling is particularly interesting to consider because state lottery tickets offer a negative expected return. On average, state lotteries offer a (negative) return of roughly 52 cents on the dollar (La Fleur and La Fleur, 2001). Given such a large negative return, why do more than half of American adults participate in lottery gambling? There are numerous possible explanations. Many casual observers associate lottery gambling with misinformation or confusion on the part of lottery gamblers. The choice to buy lottery tickets need not be a mistake, however. Traditional economic consumer choice theory would permit such gambles among risk-averse consumers, if these consumers received sufficient entertainment value from gambling or utility from giving in this way to a charity, since most states use the money for education or other public goods. Behavioral economists offer as a possible explanation that lottery gamblers overweight the small probabilities associated with winning.

Another possible explanation for lottery play, most relevant to this chapter, is that state lotteries provide some low-wealth would-be investors with a rare asset offering some chance at winning a life-altering amount of money. For those with few assets or who encounter other barriers—either real or psychological—to engaging in the world of traditional financial markets, a lottery ticket might fill the void of a 'missing market'. If a low- to moderate-wealth individual hopes to win a large payout—say, to purchase a car or make a downpayment on a house—this might be the only vehicle at his/her disposal capable of remotely reaching that goal.

The introduction of PLS products could provide an alternative to lottery tickets that offers a higher (and certainly less negative) return on one's 'investment'. Survey data corroborate this quasi-investment framing by some lottery players. A 2006 survey by the Consumer Federation of America and the Financial Planning Association on a representative sample of more than 1,000 US adults found that '21% of Americans, and 38% of those with incomes below $25,000, think that winning the lottery represents the most practical way for them to accumulate several hundred thousand dollars' (CFA, 2006).

The potential appeal of PLS products must also be understood in the context of alternative products. Emergency savers who demand liquidity and no principal loss are usually limited to some sort of low-yielding demand deposit. While theory might suggest that the power of compound interest would provide strong motivations to save, for an emergency saver whose uncertain horizon might be a few years or a few months, compounding does not offer compelling reasons to save. To be concrete, in March 2010, the average American Money Market Account (which has limitations on withdrawals) earned an Annual Percentage Rate (APR) of 0.82 percent (Bankrate.com, 2010). For an emergency saver with a balance of $1,500, the monthly interest earned would be $1.05, before the payment of income taxes. These sums—smaller than most lottery tickets—provide small savers with scant motivation to keep their money in the bank. A PLS structure allows one to forego these small sums, yet maintain liquidity and principal certainty, while offering a chance to win a large amount of money or a durable good.

In addition, in a series of experimental studies, Volpp et al. (2008*a*, 2008*b*) have shown that in specific settings, subjects can respond more strongly to stochastic incentives than to piece rates. The stochastic incentives they examine resemble the lottery portion of a PLS. In one experiment, subjects who were attempting to lose weight were eligible to be entered in a lottery, if at a monthly weigh-in their weight met personal weight-loss goals. Those in the lottery-incentive condition lost significantly more weight than subjects who had nonincentivized monthly weigh-ins, and slightly more weight than subjects who faced nonlottery incentives (although this latter difference was not statistically significant).

The potential appeal of PLS accounts to US issuers

Products come to market if they are attractive to both buyers and sellers. There are a number of reasons why a PLS structure would be popular to issuers. Here, we highlight four reasons why PLS accounts are relatively easy to design, operate, and market:

1. *Ease of marketing*: Unlike an indexed-linked structure, a PLS structure does not require the buyer to have knowledge of, or the seller to educate the buyer about, financial markets. To the contrary, the concept of lotteries is well understood.
2. *Ease of production*: A financial institution offering a PLS product can invest the proceeds from PLS instruments into relatively simple investments, rather than employ a complex investment management strategy.
3. *Apparent transparency*: One can create and maintain salient prizes (e.g., $100,000) by adjusting the odds over time as underlying investment returns or the size of the pool changes.
4. *Ease of providing liquidity*: A prize-linked program provider can provide easy liquidity merely by denying those making withdrawals eligibility to win prizes.

It may be worth pausing here to ask why PLS accounts are not widespread, given the appeal both to potential savers and to issuers. One issue is that, although one might think that all financial institutions would be eager to gather assets from all savers, real-world experience demonstrates this is not true. For example, minimum mutual fund investment amounts keep people with less than $2,500 to $3,000 from opening an account in many funds (Schneider and Tufano, 2007). In addition, as we discuss later, there are currently significant legal and regulatory obstacles to PLS accounts in the United States. Yet in places without such restrictions, PLS accounts have been both widespread and quite popular.

International evidence on the appeal of PLS accounts

In this section, we briefly review the historical evidence, broad international usage, and data from two modern versions of PLS in the United Kingdom and South Africa.

A brief history

PLS programs have existed since at least the 1694 'Million Adventure' in the United Kingdom (Murphy, 2005). Initially proposed to cope with debt from the Nine Years' War (1689–97), the Million Adventure offered 100,000 tickets at £10 each.[4] A small number (2,500 of the tickets or 2.5 percent) would win prizes from £10 per year to £1,000 per year for sixteen years. The Million Adventure was also a saving program, in that it paid ticket holders £1 per year until 1710, or a 6.15 percent annual return. While a single ticket in the Million Adventure was out of reach of most citizens, tickets were also made available through syndicates to those with small incomes. Thomas Neale, the 'Groom Porter to their Majesties' who oversaw the program, commented on the success of the Million Adventure to attract even small investors, 'many Thousands who only have small sums, and cannot now bring them into the Publick, [may now] engage themselves in this Fund' (Murphy, 2005: 231). The Million Adventure is reported to have attracted tens of thousands of investors (of the 5 to 6 million Britons at the time), making it an unprecedented large-scale financial saving tool.

Since 1694, many similar programs that combine gambling and saving have sprung up in many different countries all over the world. Levy-Ullmann, writing in 1896, surveyed PLS activity at that time. He found that PLS, in the form of lottery bonds, 'may be found in most of the financial markets of Europe, and of nationalities, German, Austrian, Spanish, Greek, Italian, Swedish and Swiss' (Levy-Ullman, 1896). Lottery bonds are still used in some countries, for example Sweden.[5]

Current examples

Table 12.1 lists examples of PLS products offered internationally by various commercial banks and governments around the world.[6] Guillen and Tschoegl (2002) survey the history and institutional details of numerous international offerings. As described in their survey piece, commercial banks have been offering prize-linked accounts throughout Latin America since the 1990s. Banco Bilboa Vizcaya, a private bank in Latin America, launched a lottery-linked product in Mexico (1996), Colombia (1997), Venezuela (1997), and Argentina (1997). Since 1990, Spanish private banks have offered accounts with periodic lottery prizes. Private financial institutions also market PLS products in Germany, Indonesia, and Japan. In Germany, since 1952, saving banks have offered accounts where depositors can allocate any new inflow into the account between saving in the bank (which offers a traditional return) and purchases of lottery tickets

TABLE 12.1 Prize-linked saving products

Country	Year start	Name and structure	Offering institution	Total balances (US$)	Maximum prize (US$)	Other prizes	Frequency prize drawings
Brazil	2003	HiperFundo account	Banco Bradesco	R$1.4 billion (48.4 million US$)	Car	Electric appliances, DVDs, travel, gold bars	Daily[b]
United Arab Emirates	1995	Mashreq Millionaire certificates	Mashreq Bank	n/a	AED 1 million ($272,000)[a]	Apartments	Monthly, special draws
Ireland	1956	Prize Bonds	The Prize Bond Company Ltd (joint venture between An Post & FEXCO)	€561.5 million ($701 million)	€150,000 monthly ($187,000)[a]	Weekly prize of €20,000; 5 prizes of €1,000; 10 prizes of €250	Weekly/monthly[b]
Great Britain	1956	Premium Savings Bonds	National Savings and Investments	£26.5 billion ($47 billion)	2 prizes of £1,000,000 ($1.79 million)[a]	£50–£100,000 prizes	Monthly[b]
Sweden	1918	Swedish Lottery Bonds	Swedish National Debt Office	SEK 40.9 billion ($5.7 billion)	SEK 1 million ($130,000)[a]	SEK 50	Annually
Pakistan	1972	Prize Bonds	State Bank of Pakistan, National Savings Organization	PKR 170 billion ($2.8 billion)	PKR 50,000,000 ($833,333)	PKR 1000 to PKR 20,000,000	Bi-monthly[b]
Pakistan	1998[c]	Crorepati (multi-millionaire) maala-maal accountCarAmad accountZarAmad account	Habib Bank, Muslim Commercial Bank, Bankers Equity, United Bank	PKR 47 billion (banks combined) ($780 million)	PKR 10 million (190,000 US$)	Cash, motorcycles, televisions, computers, and electronic gadgets	n/a

Country	Year	Account name	Bank				
Germany	1952	Gewinnsparen account	Gewinnsparverein e.V. (and local branches)	€6 million (approx.) ($7.5 million)	€100,000 ($125,000)	Cars and cash prizes from 4€ to 10,000€	Monthly[b]
Turkey	1950[d]	Lottery-linked accounts	Demirbank (now HSBC)	n/a	Cash prizes	Gold, apartments, and household items	n/a
Kenya	1978	Premium Bond	Kenya Post Office Savings Bank	$560,000 (1998) (approx.)	n/a	n/a	Monthly[b]
Indonesia	2002	BritAma account	Bank Rakyat Indonesia	Rp 14.46 trillion ($152.6 million)	Rp. 1 billion ($10,900)	5 prizes of Rp. 250 million; 10 prizes of Rp. 100 million; 30 prizes of Rp. 50 million; 300 prizes of Rp. 10 million	Semi-annually[b]
Spain	1996	'el libretón' account	Banco Bilbao Vizcaya Argentaria (BBVA)	n/a	100 cars	Cars, trips, encyclopedias, and cash	n/a
Mexico	1996	'el libretón' account	Bancomer BBVA	$178 million (1998)	Car (daily)	19,000 DVDs	Daily and monthly
Argentina	1997	'el libretón' account	BBVA Banco Frances	$233 million (1998)	Car	30 prizes of $1,000	Weekly
Argentina	1997	Prize-linked savings	Santander Rio	n/a	$220,000 (monthly)	$20,000 (daily)	Daily and monthly
Denmark	1972	Lottery bonds	Danmarks National Bank	DKK 200 million (approx.) ($34 million)	n/a	n/a	Semi-annually
Oman	1992	Mandoos Savings Account	Oman International Bank	RO 570 million (approx.) ($280 million)	RO 135,000 ($54,000)	20 prizes of RO 20,000; Mercedes cars	Monthly, special draws[b]

(continued)

TABLE 12.1 Continued

Country	Year start	Name and structure	Offering institution	Total balances (US$)	Maximum prize (US$)	Other prizes	Frequency prize drawings
New Zealand	1970	Bonus Bonds	ANZ Banking Group (Ministry of Finance and Post Office) Savings Bank until 1990)	n/a	$1,000,000 ($650,000)[a]	$100,000/$50,000/ $5,000/$500/$100/ $50/$20	Monthly[b]
Sri Lanka	1997	Ridee Rekha certificates	National Savings Bank	n/a	Rs. 2 million or a car ($20,000)	4000 prizes of Rs. 1,000; 5000 prizes of Rs. 500	Quarterly
India	1963	Premium Prize Bonds	Reserve Bank of India	n/a	n/a	n/a	Twice every 5 years[b]

[a] The following prize-linked savings schemes post prize money as tax-exempt: United Arab Emirates, Ireland, Great Britain, Sweden, New Zealand.

[b] Minimum holding periods vary between schemes: Brazil (7 days), Ireland (3 months), Great Britain (none), Pakistan (1 month), Germany (1 month), Kenya (3 months), Indonesia (none), Oman (1 month), New Zealand (1 month), Sri Lanka (1 year), India (5 years).

[c] Private prize-linked saving programs in Pakistan halted in 2001 after an adverse court ruling.

[d] Prize-linked saving programs at Turkey's Demirbank stopped in 1960.

Notes: Jan-Emmanuel de Neve and Emily Ekins assisted in the preparation of this table.

Source: Authors' calculations based on Cole et al. (2007), exhibit 8; see text.

from the regional association of saving banks. In 1986, BRI in Indonesia, a financial institution that specializes in microfinance lending to the poor, introduced accounts with stochastic interest rates between 0 and 1.25 percent per month (Morduch, 1999). In 1994, the Jonan Shinkin Bank in Japan introduced prize-linked one-year time deposits, despite Ministry of Finance disapproval. These accounts attracted deposits worth about US$ 305 million into the bank in a matter of days, attracting an additional thirteen banks to immediately offer similar products (Guillen and Tschoegl, 2002).

Many governments also offer some form of PLS products. Guillen and Tschoegl (2002) report that since 1918 the Swedish government has offered bonds with coupon payments determined by lottery; in recent years, such bonds have accounted for approximately 8 percent of the Swedish government's debt. Outside of Europe, government entities in Kenya and Pakistan, among others, have also offered such products. Later, we discuss one long-lived government program in the United Kingdom.

United Kingdom Premium Bonds

Prime Minister Harold Macmillan announced the invention of Premium Savings Bonds in April 1956, to encourage saving after World War II. Despite criticism from both parties in the House of Commons and religious groups, sales launched on November 1, 1956 in Trafalgar Square, with the byline 'Savings with a Thrill!' Macmillan reasoned that '[Premium Bonds] will appeal to those who are not attracted by the rewards of interest, but do respond to the incentives of fortune' (NSAI, 2006: 1, 4). Consumer response proved him quite right, with £5 million (near £84 million in 2005 pounds) purchased on the first day. In 1956, the top prize was £1,000 or about £16,729.30 in 2005 pounds (NSAI, 2010a). The bonds continue to be popular and have been immortalized in popular British culture, with one rocker's lyrics thanking the computer that picks the winners: 'Good old Ernie; he coughed up a tenner on a Premium Bond win' (Collecting-Tull.com, 2010).

The Premium Bond program is administered by National Savings and Investments (NSAI), an Executive Agency of the Chancellor of the Exchequer (NSAI is comparable to the US Department of Public Debt, which is part of the US Treasury). As described on the NSAI website, 'Instead of paying interest, bonds are entered into monthly prize drawings...When someone invests in Premium Bonds they are allocated a series of numbers, one for each £1 invested. The minimum purchase is £100 (or £50 when you buy by monthly standing order), which provides 100 Bond numbers and, therefore, 100 chances of winning a prize' (NSAI, 2010b). An individual investor can hold up to £30,000 in Premium Bonds. The monthly drawings include the chance at a £1 million jackpot prize as well as lower-tier prizes ranging from £25 to £100,000. Note that this structure of a jackpot prize plus lower-tier offerings is similar to the common structure of US state lottery jackpot games. Each month's prize fund is equal to one month's interest on the total value of all eligible bonds. The February 2010 annual prize fund interest rate was 1.50 percent. The interest rate used to calculate the prize fund, the number of jackpots, the share of prize fund allocated to each prize band, and the odds of winning are all variable. These bonds can be purchased by UK residents over the age of 16 for themselves or for their children or grandchildren. Premium Bond winnings are exempt from UK Income Tax and Capital Gains Tax.

Official figures report that there are 23 million bondholders holding £26 billion worth of Premium Bonds nationwide. The popularity of these bonds has soared in recent decades, with the amount invested rising from £4 billion in 1994 to £40 billion in 2008 (NSAI, 2010*b*). Tufano (2008) examines aggregate predictors of per capita Premium Bond sales considering the prize rate, top prize, and annual stock returns, among other aggregate series. The prize rate can be considered analogous to a bond yield, capturing information about the number and size of various prizes. Tufano notes that the prize rate has generally been lower than the rate paid on comparable government bonds, which (assuming that investors know this) suggests that Premium Bond investors are willing to forgo return to purchase this type of prize-linked instrument. His multivariate regression analysis finds that annual net sales are positively correlated with the size of the largest prize offered, the prize rate spread (prize rate less gilt rate), and annual stock returns. These correlated movements potentially suggest that Premium Bonds offer both an investment value (as demand moves positively with prize rate spread) and gambling consumption value (as demand increases with the size of the largest prize, conditional on prize rate).[7] The positive correlation with annual stock returns might suggest that these are not considered substitute products or that they are purchased by different sets of investors.

The United Kingdom's Family Resource Survey (FRS) provides information about who is investing in Premium Bonds: the FRS 2004–5 Annual Report tabulates information about the percent of households with different types of saving accounts (DWPUK, 2010). Among two-adult households without children (sample size of 9,178), 96 percent have any type of account; 30 percent have a Premium Bond account, 26 percent have stock holdings, and 5 percent have National Savings bonds. Among two-adult households with children (sample size of 5,714), 97 percent have any type of account; 19 percent have a Premium Bond account, 22 percent have stock holdings, and 1 percent have a National Savings bond. Among one-adult families with children (sample size of 2,050), 93 percent have any

TABLE 12.2 Families holding UK Premium Bonds by income quintiles (%)

Income quintiles	All families			Families with any type of account		
	All families	Married	Single	All families	Married	Single
1	8.8	21.1	6.6	10.4	22.8	8.0
2	13.2	24.3	10.6	14.4	25.1	11.9
3	18.1	24.4	10.6	19.0	25.1	11.5
4	23.4	26.9	13.0	24.0	27.4	13.9
5	31.1	36.3	19.4	31.7	37.0	20.0
Number of observations	33,182	16,005	17,177	30,992	15,464	15,528

Notes: Families with any type of account are defined as those who hold at least one type of account or investment. Income quintiles represent quintiles of total family income. The quintiles are calculated separately over samples of all families, married couples, and single adults. Tabulations are weighted to be representative of the UK population.

Source: Authors' calculations based on DWPUK (2010); see text.

type of account; 6 percent have a Premium Bond account, 5 percent have stock holdings, and 1 percent have National Savings Bonds.

Our tabulations of the 2004–5 FRS data show that Premium Bonds are held by households across the income distribution. Nineteen percent of families hold Premium Bonds; the figure is 27 percent among families headed by a married couple, and 12 percent among single-headed families. Tabulations by income quintiles, reported in Table 12.2, reveal that the likelihood of holding Premium Bonds increases with income, as is typical of investments more generally. These bonds might thus be considered 'normal' goods. Still, low-income households participate in this market, with nearly 9 percent of households in the lowest income quintile holding Premium Bonds and 13 percent in the second quintile. The general pattern of participation by income group is maintained if we consider only households with any type of account.

We can get a sense of the relative appeal of Premium Bonds by income group, by analyzing the fraction of that group that owns the product relative to the fraction owning the most popular product for that group. For example, among households making £200–£300 weekly, the most popular saving product is a society account, with 39 percent of households holding this account. In this same income group, 18 percent hold Premium Bonds, so that the fraction holding Premium Bonds scaled by the fraction holding the most common account type is 46 percent. Figure 12.1 shows this scaled holding measure: it indicates that Premium Bonds' relative appeal seems strongest among lower-income households, with some increase in relative appeal among higher-income households. The latter may reflect the fact that the bonds' winnings are exempt from taxation.

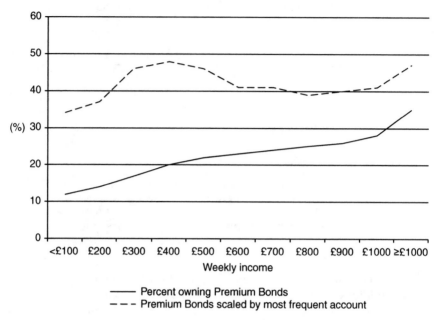

Figure 12.1 Breadth of Premium Bond ownership in the UK from 2005 to 2006

Notes: This figure shows the fraction of British households holding Premium Bonds as a function of weekly household income. It also shows this share scaled by the most widely held asset account (excluding transaction accounts) held by that income category. The survey covers a sample of 28,029 British households.

Source: Authors' calculations based on data taken from DWPUK (2010) Family Resources Survey 2005–6 (Table 5.8).

First National Bank of South Africa's
Million-a-Month Account

Next, we review another example of a PLS account: the South African bank First National Bank's Million-a-Month Account (MaMA). This provides a nice contrasting example to the UK program described earlier for two reasons: first, the MaMAs constitute a privately run PLS program. Second, whereas the government-run UK Premium Bond program is long-lived, the MaMAs were short-lived, owing to legal and regulatory barriers.[8]

First National Bank (FNB), one of the four largest retail banks in the South African market, introduced its MaMA in 2005. The MaMA was a no-fee saving account which paid a nominal interest rate (0.25 percent) and rewarded savers with one prize entry for every 100 rand invested.[9] Prize drawings were held monthly and at each drawing, 114 prizes were awarded, ranging in value from 1 million rand to 1,000 rand. The product was structured as a thirty-two-day notice account, a common South African account form akin to a certificate of deposit in that the account holder had to give thirty-two days' notice prior to withdrawing his/her funds from the program.

A bit of background on the South African financial services sector is useful in understanding this product. The majority (56 percent) of black South Africans are unbanked versus 7 percent of white South Africans. Nearly three-quarters (72 percent) of low-income South Africans were unbanked. In 2003, banks and the government entered into the Financial Sector Charter, in which banks committed to try to increase the fraction of low income banked South Africans from 28 to 80 percent. Banks expanded distribution outlets, designed low-fee small balance products, and created marketing campaigns to reach out to the unbanked.

FNB executives had studied the UK Premium Bond experience and visited other countries where PLS programs were in place. While there were no PLS programs in South Africa, they reasoned that a program of this sort would be successful in the country, based on the widespread popularity of gaming and the national lottery in the country:

In 2003, the national lottery had 99% consumer awareness and 72% of the population regularly entered to win the lottery's 20 to 30 million rand jackpot. In 2003, players purchased 3,772 million rand in tickets and the lottery board awarded 2,119 million rand in prizes to 31 million winners. Participation in the lottery was fairly evenly distributed across demographic groups, with little difference by education, race, income, gender, or education. Lower-income players spent less in absolute terms on the lottery than high-income players, though they spent a larger proportion of income. Among those with less than 800 rand in disposable monthly income, monthly lottery expenditures averaged 33.40 rand, about 8.5% of disposable income. Among those with more than 12,000 rand in monthly disposable income, lottery expenditures were much higher, at 126 rand, but as a percent of income much lower, at just 0.8% (Cole et al., 2007: 7).

The program ran from January 2005 through March 2008. During this time, the bank used print and television advertising and in-branch promotion to sell the product. By March 2008, FNB had opened over 1.1 million accounts and collected 1.4 billion rand in deposits (FDIC, 2009). Executives report that about 12 percent of the accounts were to KYC ('know your customer')-exempt accounts, a marker for the unbanked. They estimated that they opened accounts for 7.1 percent of all banked South Africans and brought 1.1 percent of the unbanked into the banking system.

The success of the system likely also brought about its ultimate closure, as the South African Lottery Board sued to have the program closed as an illegal lottery. Although the program no longer operates, the bank received ongoing benefits from the MaMA program. At the time the program was shut by the government, FNB offered to return monies to savers or they could elect to roll the funds into a more traditional thirty-two-day notice account. Fourteen months after the program was shuttered, the bank continued to maintain 53 percent of the accounts and 83 percent of the balances.

Recent PLS demonstration projects in the United States

Credit unions have been on the forefront of launching PLS products in the United States. Working with the nonprofit Doorways to Dreams (D2D) Fund and other partners, credit unions have implemented two demonstration projects designed to test the feasibility and popularity of PLS accounts among low- and moderate-income populations.[10]

Centra credit union project in Indiana

In October 2006, with funding support from the Filene Research Institute and Affinity Plus Federal Credit Union, D2D assisted the Indiana-based Centra Credit Union in a launch of 'Super Savings', a prize-based saving product. In order to comply with relevant law (reviewed later), this product was structured as a sweepstake with 'no purchase required'. In January 2009, assisted by the D2D Fund, the Filene Research Institute, the Center for Financial Services Innovation, and the Michigan Credit Union League, eight credit unions launched a PLS product called 'Save to Win'.

As part of the Centra Credit Union demonstration, a pre-pilot marketing survey was administered to gauge potential consumer interest in a PLS product. This survey was completed by 547 intercepted Wal-Mart customers in Clarksville, Indiana in November and December 2006. Clarksville is in Clark County, Indiana, which has a population of 103,569. According to US census figures, median household income in the county is $41,719 (compared to $48,451 nationally). The survey's principal question was 'Would you be interested in a savings account that awarded chances to win prizes based on the amount of money you save? The account would also have no fees, no minimum balance, and still earn interest.' The survey sought to gauge local interest in the product. While neither nationally representative nor random, the demographic correlates of expressed interest are potentially revealing about who might take up PLS products, should they be offered in the United States.

Among all respondents who completed the pre-pilot survey, 58 percent reported interest in the described PLS product, 26 percent reported not being interested, and 16 percent responded that they did not know. In multivariate analysis, including traditional demographic information, Tufano et al. (2008) find that expressed preference was stronger among people who claimed not to have regular saving plans, defined as those who either stated that they did not save or merely saved if they happened to have money that they had not spent that month. Compared to individuals or households with a saving plan, a nonsaver was 70 percent more likely to show interest in the PLS product. PLS demand was also strongest with people with almost no savings ($1–$2,000), relative to those with no savings whatsoever or those with more. They also found that optimism, measured by the belief that one's financial well-being will improve over the next five years, was a positive determinant of interest in PLS accounts. Finally, survey participants reporting spending of $100 or more in lottery games in the past six months were twice as interested as others.

In terms of consumer take-up, Centra opened over 1,300 Super Savings accounts and amassed over $500,000 in deposits within three months of launch, even with limited marketing. This represented 1.3 percent of its member base in early 2007. Additionally, most customers maintained their deposit balances in the product following the first three months of the launch. As a small pilot run by a single credit union, Centra's program prize offerings were quite small, which likely limited its ultimate success.[11] Additional experimental research is needed to ascertain how the design of PLS products, including the size of the top prize, affects consumer interest and take-up.[12]

Save to Win demonstration project in Michigan

Another PLS demonstration project was launched in 2009 in Michigan. The 'Save to Win' demonstration was run as a saving promotion in eight participating credit unions in the state of Michigan from late January 2009 to end December 2009. This demonstration was legally permissible under a unique provision in Michigan law that permits credit unions in the state to offer 'savings promotion raffles', with only those who save eligible to win prizes (in contrast to a sweepstake). The Save to Win project enabled several credit unions to join forces in order to offer a PLS product with a headline-grabbing $100,000 grand prize, in contrast to the small-scale issue faced by the Centra Credit Union experience described earlier.

At any time during 2009, members of participating credit unions could open a qualifying share certificate account to enter the saving raffle. This certificate was a twelve-month time deposit and required only $25 to open. Deposits were unlimited, but the number of entries in the raffle was capped at ten per month. The amount of interest paid on these certificates varied by credit union, but in 2009, ranged from one to 1.5 percent. Monthly prizes ranged in value from $15 to $400, and the number of prizes varied by month. The grand prize of $100,000 was awarded in early 2010. One withdrawal was allowed during the twelve-month period, and standard certificate early-withdrawal fees applied. However, unlike most CDs, savers could add money to their certificates over time.

In the eleven months in which *Save to Win* operated, the participating credit unions opened 11,600 accounts and generated over $8.6 million in deposits. To put this in context, the credit unions are located in some of the more economically depressed parts of the Mid-West. In locations such as Flint and Detroit, the demise of the auto industry has led to high unemployment and economic hardship. In terms of the rate of saving and the cost of delivery, this compares favorably to other efforts to foster new savers and new saving, such as Individual Development Account (IDA) matched saving programs.[13]

Each *Save to Win* certificate holder was also invited to complete a voluntary survey when he or she opened an account. By end December 2009, over half of certificate holders, some 6,027 credit union members, had completed this survey. Results show that certificates have been opened among credit union members of all ages, income levels, and past saving behavior. In particular, 56 percent of *Save to Win* certificate holders reported they had not saved money regularly before opening the *Save to Win* account; 39 percent reported financial assets (excluding home equity) of $5,000 or less; 59 percent reported spending money on the lottery in the last six months; 68 percent reported household income of less than $60,000; and 44 percent reported household income under $40,000.

The survey data from the *Save to Win* demonstration do not allow us to determine how effective the program was in generating new saving. Nonetheless, the apparent appeal of the PLS products offered in the Centra and *Save to Win* demonstrations, especially among people who claimed to have no other regular saving plans, suggest that a PLS product holds appeal for demographic groups that tend to have low levels of formal saving.

Legal barriers to PLS programs in the United States[14]

As defined by the National Bank Act, there are three essential components of a lottery: (*a*) the offering of a prize; (*b*) the awarding of the prize by chance; and (*c*) consideration (i.e., money or other thing of value advanced in exchange for the opportunity to win the prize). If PLS programs are deemed lotteries, they are shut down almost entirely. This legal prohibition arises from state anti-lottery laws, as well as state and federal banking regulations. The state anti-lottery laws prohibit private lotteries, in part to enable states to maintain a monopoly over these activities so as not to jeopardize the funds raised by lottery programs. The latter set of laws, for example, the National Bank Act, prohibit federally chartered banks and thrifts (regulated by the Office of the Comptroller of the Currency or Office of Thrift Supervision, respectively) from participating in lotteries to protect the safety and soundness of the banking system.[15]

The two US experiments cited earlier were able to exploit two legal loopholes. The Centra offering was structured as a sweepstake, not a lottery. People did not need to save to enter, but rather could mail in a card in lieu of saving. This explicit lack of 'consideration' supports a variety of bank promotions that use sweepstakes, such as JPMorgan Chase's 'Double your Deposit' promotion offered in early 2009, and the Maryland Saves' 'Roll in the Dough' saving campaign offered in early 2010 (FDIC, 2009). Sweepstake solutions permit nonsavers to win, add operational complexity to the program, and tend to be used primarily for ad hoc marketing campaigns. The *Save to Win* program rests on a different and unique state law. Section 411 of the Michigan Credit Union Act allows state-chartered credit unions to employ 'savings promotions raffles' defined as 'raffle(s) conducted by a domestic credit union where the sole consideration required for a chance of winning designated prizes is the deposit of at least a specified amount of money in a saving account or other saving program offered by the domestic credit union'.[16] Even if this carve-out were extended to other states, the ability to scale these programs would be limited. Credit union charters require that their membership be limited to a certain designated population, such as people affiliated with specific employers or organizations, or residing in defined geographic areas. These limits tend to preclude scale economics, making the prize structure less desirable to would-be participants. Running PLS through a consortium of credit unions, as is the case with *Save to Win*, helps to generate a larger deposit base. However, there would be inevitable coordination costs. In mid-2010, two additional states passed laws similar to Michigan's.

State-run PLS programs?

PLS products could be offered in the United States by the federal government (a federal Premium Bond) or by state governments. Given the lack of federal policy interest in the first option, we focus on state alternatives.

Shut down in the late nineteenth century as a result of fraud, and later revived by the State of New Hampshire in 1964, state lotteries have had a consistent mandate: to generate state revenue (Coughlin et al., 2006). But this lottery mandate may be at odds with the limited revenue stream a state lottery-based PLS product is likely to produce. Beyond this fact, in most cases lottery commissions are required to pay out in prizes a certain fraction of sales proceeds. In a PLS program, if deposits or bond purchases were to be counted as gross sales, it would be impossible to pay out in prizes the mandated portion of sales and still guarantee depositors that they will receive back their full principal investment. Only some of the *earnings* from a PLS pool could be paid out, with the remainder available for the payment of expenses and to deliver revenue to the state.

A real example highlights other legal constraints on a state-run program. The state of Maryland, in 1975, authorized a premium saving bond program modeled on the British Premium Bond, to be administered by the state lottery agency. Principal investments would be guaranteed and redeemable at any time, and bondholders would be eligible not for regular interest, but for what Maryland officials called a 'random interest award' (Phillips, 1975). The size of a person's investment would determine the number of entries in the drawing for a large monetary prize. Yet after the initial feasibility study, legal opinion warned that it was in essence a 'cloaked lottery' and 'would be subject to existing lottery laws'. These included limitations on marketing, accepting bond investments from anyone outside of Maryland, and using banks to sell the bonds. Furthermore, the product would need to be sold through lottery agents who were used to receiving a commission of roughly 5 percent on all lottery sales (Phillips, 1975). In short, even when defined as a lottery and run through the lottery agency, other structural considerations made the product not viable at that time.

Even if PLS is a sensible economic structure, existing US laws and regulations would likely need to be changed to permit issues, whether private or public. The South African MaMA provides reason to pause: when the product became popular, the South African Lottery Board brought suit against the bank to cease the offering of this 'illegal lottery', and the South African Supreme Court ruled in the Boards' favor. While the case has no direct precedent for US laws, the structure of the Court's arguments shows how laws similar to those in the United States could be applied to shut down a private PLS program.

Conclusion

Although no formal evaluation of US-based PLS exists, several lessons are evident. First, the product has been offered for more than three centuries, continuously in some jurisdictions for over five decades. From an operational point of view, this is a well-tested product. Second, the product's appeal is fairly widespread, and in particular it seems to be of interest to those who might otherwise not be able to use (or be interested in using) more standard products. Third, without a change in laws and regulations, adoption of this product will be fairly limited.

The good news–bad news of PLS underscores the importance of new and rigorous research on this saving structure. One consideration we have not discussed thus far is what effect, if any, the availability of PLS products might have on traditional lottery demand. More fundamentally, the key question yet to be answered is whether the availability of PLS would generate new savers and new saving, and if so by whom. Future research should address this question. In order to answer the question of what impact PLS products have on household saving behavior, researchers would need information on saving outcomes for individuals who were given access to a PLS product and a comparable set of individuals who were not. Ideally, this would be investigated through an experimental research design, allowing researchers to determine whether it is the prize-linked nature of the product that is driving take-up and saving, as opposed to, for example, associated marketing efforts. Moreover, crucially for policy analysts, such a design, coupled with detailed data about individuals in both groups, would allow investigators to determine whether new PLS accounts represent new saving at the individual or household level, and whether legal changes to allow wider adoption of PLS products are consistent with good public policy.

Acknowledgments

Tufano thanks the HBS Division of Research for financial support, and Andrea Ryan, Howell Jackson, Robert Keip and the staff of FNB Bank, the staff of Doorways to Dreams Fund, and his Consumer Finance students for many helpful discussions on this topic. We thank Seth Freedman and Kyung Park for their helpful research assistance.

Endnotes

[1] See Tufano and Schneider (2008) for an overview of existing policies aimed at promoting savings among low and moderate savers in the United States.

[2] This team of authors has attempted multiple projects designed to investigate whether prize-linked savings products generate new and increased levels of saving, as opposed to shifting assets from other vehicles. We have yet to implement a randomized design experiment, but we continue to seek research opportunities.

[3] Among those in the lowest income third of the NORC data—defined by having household income of less than $30,400 in 2005 dollars—reported annual lottery expenditures averaged $164. We can make an imperfect comparison of lottery gambling and savings by low-income individuals by comparing these numbers to the 1992, 1995, 1998, and 2001 waves of the Survey of Consumer Finances (SCF). Among individuals in the SCF with less than a high school degree, median assets in savings and checking accounts total $200 (in year 2005 dollars); likewise for median liquid assets. The SCF data suggest that this amount is comparable to median liquid assets and median savings and checking assets, both amounting to $200 for this income group.

[4] O'Donoghue et al. (2004) report a consistent inflation series from 1750 through 2003. Using this period (and assuming no inflation prior to 1750), the ticket would have cost over £1,400 in 2003 pounds.

[5] For an economic analysis of this program, see Green and Rydqvist (1997).

[6] This table, taken from Cole et al. (2007), was collected through literature reviews, web searches, and conversations with practitioners. It is unlikely to be complete, as some of these programs are not widely advertised.

[7] By way of comparison, Kearney's analysis (2005) of demand for US state lottery products, estimated at the level of game and week, similarly finds that lottery sales are positively driven by expected return—suggesting an investment motive and evaluation—as well as nonpecuniary characteristics, including the nominal top prize, numbers of digits chosen, and age of the game.

[8] Much of this section is drawn from Cole et al. (2007).

[9] The rand is the South African currency. At the time of writing, 1 rand was worth about 0.14 US dollars.

[10] Co-author of this chapter, Peter Tufano, is Chairman and Co-founder of the D2D fund. The mission of D2D is to expand access to financial services, especially asset-building opportunities, for low-income families by creating, testing, and deploying innovative financial products and services.

[11] Both Tufano (2008) and Lobe and Holzl (2007) demonstrate that large prizes are strongly related to sales of Premium Bonds.

[12] This is a feature that we have proposed testing in random design field experiments. As mentioned earlier, we have yet to successfully implement such an experimental design in the field. Guryan and Kearney are currently developing a laboratory experiment to be conducted at the Experimental Laboratory in the Department of Economics at the University of Maryland that would test this concept.

[13] For instance, over four years, 2,364 participants in the landmark American Dream Demonstration (ADD) IDA program accumulated $1.25 MM in savings (Schreiner et al., 2002).

[14] Andrea Ryan contributed to this section of this chapter. It draws upon work done by Angela Seensun Kang, Anooshree C. Sinha, and Howell Jackson of Harvard Law School, from the insights of Jackson and Tufano's students in their JD-MBA course on consumer finance, especially Daniel Preysman, and from work done by D2D Fund and its legal advisors. Readers should not rely on this document for legal advice, as the law in this area is quite complex.

[15] See 12 U.S.C. § 25a (2008).
[16] See Mich. Comp. Laws § 490.411 (2008).

References

Bankrate.com (2010). *Savings Overnight Averages*. North Palm Beach, FL: Bankrate. com. http://www.bankrate.com/checking.aspx

Bureau of Labor Statistics (BLS) (2010). *Average Annual Expenditures and Character- istics, Consumer Expenditure Survey*. Washington, DC: BLS. http://www.bls.gov/ cex/2008/Standard/age.pdf

Cole, S., D. Collins, D. Schneider, and P. Tufano (2007). *First National Bank's Golden Opportunity*. Cambridge, MA: Harvard Business School Case 208-072.

Collecting-Tull.com (2010). *Thick as a Brick*. London, UK: Collecting-Tull.com. http://www.collecting-tull.com/Albums/Lyrics/ThickAsABrick.html

Consumer Federation of America (CFA) (2006). *How Americans View Personal Wealth Versus How Planners View This Wealth*. Washington, DC: CFA.

Coughlin, C. C., T. A. Garrett, and R. Hernandez-Murillo (2006). 'The Geography, Economics, and Politics of Lottery Adoption,' *Federal Reserve Bank of St Louis Review*, 88(3): 165–80.

Department of Works and Pensions United Kingdom (DWPUK) (2010). *Family Resources Survey: United Kingdom, 2004–05*. London, UK: DWPUK. http://research. dwp.gov.uk/asd/frs/

Federal Deposit Insurance Corporation (FDIC) (2009). *Public Presentation by a Senior FNB Executive to the Prize-Linked Subcommittee of the FDIC Advisory Committee on Economic Inclusion*. Washington, DC: FDIC. http://www.vodium.com/MediapodLibrary/ index.asp?library=pn100472_fdic_advisorycommittee&SessionArgs= 0A1U0100000100000101

Green, R. and K. Rydqvist (1997). 'The Valuation of Non-Systematic Risks and the Pricing of Swedish Lottery Bonds,' *Review of Financial Studies*, 10: 447–79.

Guillen, M. and A. Tschoegl (2002). 'Banking on Gambling: Banks and Lottery- Linked Deposit Accounts.' *Journal of Financial Services Research*, 21(3): 219–31.

Kearney, M. (2005). 'State Lotteries and Consumer Behavior,' *Journal of Public Economics*, 89: 2269–99.

La Fleur, T. and B. La Fleur (2001). *La Fleur's 2001 World Lottery Almanac*. Boyds, MD: TLF Publications, Inc.

Levy-Ullman, H. (1896). 'Lottery-Bonds in France and in the Principal Countries of Europe,' *Harvard Law Review*, 9(6): 386–405.

Lobe, S. and A. Holzl (2007). *Why are British Premium Bonds So Successful? The Effect of Saving with a Thrill*. Regensburg, Germany: University of Regensburg. http:// 69.175.2.130/~finman/Reno/Papers/PremiumBond_i.pdf

Morduch, J. (1999). 'Between the State and the Market: Can Informal Insurance Patch the Safety Net?' *World Bank Research Observer*, 14(2): 187–207.

Murphy, A. L. (2005). 'Lotteries in the 1690s: Investment or Gamble?' *Financial History Review*, 12(2): 227–45.

National Savings and Investments (NSAI) (2006). *A Short History of Premium Bonds*. Glasgow, UK: NSAI. http://www.nsandi.com/files/asset/pdf/history_pb.pdf

—— (2010a). *History of Premium Bonds*. Glasgow, UK: NSAI. http://www.nsandi.com/products/pb/premiumbondstory

—— (2010b). *Premium Bonds*. Glasgow, UK: NSAI.

North American Association of State and Provincial Lotteries (NASPL) (2010). *Lottery Sales and Profits*. Geneva, OH: NASPL. http://www.naspl.org/index.cfm?fuseaction=content&PageID=3&PageCategory=3

O'Donoghue, J., L. Goulding, and G. Allen (2004). 'Consumer Price Inflation since 1750.' *UK Office for National Statistics, Economic Trends*, 604: 38–46.

Phillips, L. (1975). 'The Premium Savings Bond: Respectable Revenue through Legalized Gambling,' *Tulsa Law Review*, 11: 241–57.

Schneider, D. and P. Tufano (2007). 'New Savings from Old Innovations: Asset Building for the Less Affluent,' in J. S. Rubin, eds, *Financing Low-Income Communities*. New York, NY: Russell Sage, pp. 13–71.

Schreiner, M., M. Clancy, and M. Sherraden (2002). *Saving Performance in the American Dream Demonstration Project*. St Louis, MO: Center for Social Development, Washington University. http://csd.wustl.edu/Publications/Documents/ADDReport2002.pdf

Tufano, P. (2008). 'Savings Whilst Gambling: An Empirical Analysis of U.K. Premium Bonds,' *American Economic Review Papers and Proceedings*, 98(2): 321–6.

Tufano, P. and D. Schneider (2008). 'Using Financial Innovation to Support Savers: From Coercion to Excitement,' in R. Blank and M. Barr, eds, *Insufficient Funds*. New York, NY: Russell Sage, pp. 149–90.

—— N. Maynard, and J. De Neve (2008). 'Consumer Demand for Prize-Linked Savings: A Preliminary Analysis,' Harvard Business School Working Paper 08-061. Cambridge, MA: Harvard University.

Volpp, K. G., L. K. John, K., A. B. Troxel, L. Norton, J. Fassbender, and G. Loewenstein (2008a). 'Financial Incentive-Based Approaches for Weight Loss,' *Journal of the American Medical Association*, 300(22): 2631–7.

—— G. Loewenstein, A. B. Troxel, J. Doshi, M. Price, M. Laskin, and S. E. Kimmel (2008b). 'A Test of Financial Incentives to Improve Warfarin Adherence,' *BMC Health Services Research*, 8: 272.

Chapter 13

How to Improve Financial Literacy: Some Successful Strategies

Diana Crossan

Initiatives to improve New Zealanders' financial literacy have been gathering pace over the last decade. This chapter discusses five strategies which are delivering some successes. The first two—the development of a national strategy for financial literacy and the pursuit of public–private partnerships—underpin New Zealand's approach to financial education. The next two—the choice of a website supported by ongoing promotion as a fundamental tool for lifting financial literacy and the integration of financial education into schools and tertiary education—illustrate specific strategies. The fifth, reaching New Zealand's indigenous Māori population, is a strategy under development. However, a program developed with one Māori tribe offers some directions for a wider approach.

These and other developments in financial literacy are being tracked over time, with regular monitoring. The chapter finishes with a discussion of the importance of monitoring and evaluation, while noting the inherent difficulties in proving a causal link from financial education to greater financial literacy to improved financial well-being.

Where financial literacy fits

The connection between financial literacy and security in retirement is well accepted in New Zealand. There is an understanding that, to achieve security in retirement, people need to have the confidence and ability to make well-informed and lasting decisions about their personal finances throughout their lives. Nevertheless, financial literacy does not stand alone. As a developed nation, New Zealand also needs effective and stable government policy for retirement income and a trusted financial services sector with understandable and expert advice—which a financially educated population can then use with confidence.

New Zealand's Retirement Commission contributes to all three of these elements, which are vital to the country's retirement income framework.

Established in 1993, the Retirement Commission is a small, autonomous Crown entity. Its key activities are providing financial information, so people can prepare financially for retirement, and carrying out regular reviews of retirement income policy. The commission's role is not to increase saving directly, but to provide information so that New Zealanders can make informed decisions about their personal finances.

Most New Zealanders use some form of financial product or service, be it a bank account, mortgage, or lay-by agreement, therefore the commission's aim is to help all New Zealanders, from the age of 5 to 105, to be 'financially sorted'. New Zealand is unusual in having an independent government-funded agency with the main objective of promoting financial literacy. In other countries, financial education agencies often sit within larger organizations with wider market concerns, such as protection or regulation (O'Connell, 2009).

The New Zealand context

New Zealand is an island nation comparable in size to the United Kingdom or the Philippines. It has a population of just 4.3 million people. The population is diverse and multicultural, with the indigenous Māori making up around 15 percent (Statistics New Zealand, 2010).

A number of economic and social factors have shaped the approach to lifting New Zealanders' financial literacy. As in most developed countries, retirement income is a headline issue because of the aging of the baby boomer generation. One in five New Zealanders will be over 65 by 2031. At the last official count in 2009, there were 552,600 New Zealanders over the age of 65, making up 12 percent of the population. In twenty years, this will have almost doubled to 1,071,800, or 21 percent of the population. (Statistics New Zealand, 2009).

New Zealand moved very early to provide a state-funded old age pension and the public pension still underpins the country's retirement saving system. New Zealand Superannuation, or 'NZ Super' as it is known, is a basic, flat-rate, inflation-adjusted, taxable, universal state pension. It is abated for immigrants bringing state pensions from some countries. NZ Super provides a pension which is a proportion of the average wage and is paid to people eligible on the basis of residency and age—currently set at 65 years.

As a nation, New Zealanders have a high rate of home ownership—at the last census 75 percent of 65- to 79-year-olds owned their own home (Statistics New Zealand, 2007). Home ownership is an integral part of New Zealand's retirement income platform.

In the past two years, New Zealand has also introduced a voluntary, auto-enrolled workplace retirement saving plan. Called KiwiSaver, the plan includes government-funded incentives and compulsory employer contributions. Under certain circumstances, it also allows a one-off withdrawal for first-time home-buyers. Apart from KiwiSaver there are no other tax incentives attached to retirement saving. For 40 percent of New Zealanders aged over 65, NZ Super is virtually their only income, and for a further 20 percent it is their main source of income, along with other government transfers (Ministry of Social Development, 2009).

NZ Super has meant that New Zealanders are less at risk of hardship in later life than people in many other developed countries. This is important for groups that are more at risk of low or irregular earnings, such as many women (Retirement Commission, 2007).

However, managing on NZ Super alone is difficult. Most New Zealanders have some private savings. Financial Education through life will help New Zealanders prepare better financially for their retirement and help them to manage their money in retirement.

Interest in improving New Zealanders' financial literacy has increased over the last decade. This has intensified in the last three years, in part because of the collapse of several finance companies in New Zealand and the impact of the global financial crisis. Five strategies illustrate the range of approaches being taken and some of the successes to date.

National strategy for financial literacy

Two years ago, New Zealand became one of the first countries to develop a national strategy for financial literacy. Its aim is to ensure New Zealanders are financially literate and educated to make informed financial decisions throughout their lives. The strategy identifies financial literacy as one of eight factors that enable people to achieve personal financial well-being in an increasingly complex environment. These are shown in Figure 13.1.

The strategy sets a framework for New Zealand's financial literacy initiatives with three broad directions. These are:

- developing quality: providing relevant, impartial and accessible information and education, which people understand and can connect with;
- extending delivery: identifying and filling gaps, so that financial education reaches more New Zealanders; and
- monitoring and evaluation: understanding what works and sharing best practice.

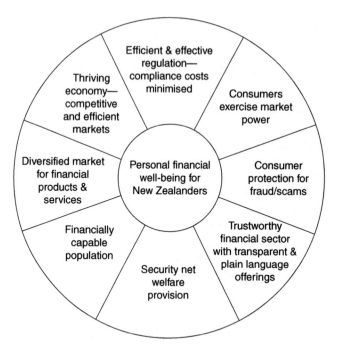

Figure 13.1 Components of personal financial well-being
Source: Retirement Commission (2008).

Led by the Retirement Commission, the strategy represents a successful collaboration across the public, private, and not-for-profit sectors, with all three contributing to its development and implementation. The strategy has wide support and is overseen by an advisory committee that brings together the heads of the Reserve Bank of New Zealand; the Securities Commission; the Retirement Commission; the private sector Investment, Savings, and Insurance Association; the Ministry of Education; and the Associate Dean for Māori and Pacific Development at the University of Auckland Business School. The committee reports annually to the New Zealand Parliament and updates the Minister of Finance every six months on the strategy's progress.

Developing public and private partnerships

The public–private collaboration of New Zealand's National Strategy for Financial Literacy makes it unusual internationally—national strategies in other countries tend to sit within a single government agency (O'Connell, 2009). The Retirement Commission decided to work directly with the private and not-for-profit sectors, so that the resulting strategy would deliver benefits for the wider New Zealand community. This approach required an understanding of the needs of different organizations within those sectors, and a full stakeholder management and communication strategy. The partnership approach extends beyond the national strategy and is reflected in many of the initiatives taking place under its umbrella. This means financial education is becoming the concern of many, with roots in different parts of the community, rather than remaining the responsibility of government.

There are a number of examples where this is producing benefits for the country. For instance, New Zealand is one of the few countries to have carried out a national survey of adult financial knowledge. With financial support from a major bank, this survey has been conducted twice since 2005. Furthermore, a national financial literacy summit, led every two years by the Retirement Commission, is partially funded by the country's banks and financial services companies, and several government agencies. Private-sector funding has also been secured to transform the website that hosts the national strategy into a focal point for sharing information on financial literacy. The main New Zealand banks also contributed funding to a pilot program in 2008, which led to personal financial education being integrated into the national school curriculum. This initiative is described below in more detail. In the not-for-profit sector, a bank has helped to introduce a personal financial management module to a nationwide parenting education program, giving families the tools they need to make informed decisions about their budgets and spending habits. This program combines the bank's financial expertise with the parenting education experience of the nongovernment organization (NGO).

At first, the Retirement Commission actively sought public–private partnerships for many of its activities, including individual programs, as well as national initiatives. As this approach has matured, the private sector is also now approaching the government and NGOs to develop partnerships.

Developing the 'sorted' approach

When the Retirement Commission was set up in 1993, its focus was on developing a public education program that would deliver independent and impartial information on financial planning for retirement. This program succeeded in reaching many New Zealanders. Yet, the 'Save for retirement' message did not resonate with the young or those with a discretionary income. Research showed the program was mainly attracting people who were already doing some saving for retirement.

Accordingly, in 2000 the commission decided to shift the program's focus from financial planning for retirement to financial skills for life and concentrate on the information needs of three broad target audiences—young people, families and households, and people at work. A new brand for the program was developed to take the emphasis off the 'R' word (retirement) and attract previously hard-to-reach audiences. The result was the Sorted brand and website, http://www.sorted.org.nz (New Zealanders use the term 'sorted' to mean 'prepared' or 'organized'). The new program not only broke from the past, but it marked a shift away from traditional print resources to web-based delivery at a time when the internet was still in its adolescence.

Today, one in three New Zealanders has used the Sorted website or its associated resources, and one in four has done so in the last twelve months (Retirement Commission, 2009). The majority of users say they will take some action with their personal finances as a result, with financial planning and budgeting the most common types of action planned (The Nielsen Company, 2009*a*). Since its launch, Sorted has grown from a site about saving and managing debt (with a limited set of calculators) to one focused on a wide range of financial topics, with more than forty interactive tools. The latest additions include an insurance calculator and a 'money tracker' tool, which links to an individual's personal online bank account to help him/her see where his/her money is going. In the past year, Sorted has also moved into social media, with a presence on Facebook and Twitter and a blog. The website's content and tools are syndicated through a range of New Zealand's most popular websites and portals, including TradeMe, the New Zealand equivalent of eBay.

Despite this growing digital presence, the program has recently returned to its roots with an increased emphasis on printed booklets. This move was prompted by research showing that booklets were preferred by people with low-to-medium financial literacy and delivered the most consistent learning results (Colmar Brunton, 2008). This shift has not been at the expense of the Sorted website. Pedagogy indicates that a mix of formats, catering to a range of adult learning styles, is needed to achieve the commission's financial education aims. The current mix includes the website, booklets, seminars, social media, and short online movies.

Producing high-quality resources is only one part of the strategy. The other is drawing people to them. Delivering the Sorted message, and in particular promoting Sorted's resources, makes up a significant part of the Retirement Commission's work and budget. In the year to June 2009, three-quarters of the commission's financial education and information budget was spent on promotion, with the remainder being spent on operations. This continual investment in the Sorted brand—raising awareness and building trust in it—has been a major part of the strategy over the past decade. More than 80 percent of New Zealanders are now aware of the brand, and while 'sorted' is a colloquial term in general use, 40 percent associate it with helping with money matters (The Nielsen Company, 2009*b*). A range of media is used to keep Sorted in the front of people's minds, including online, television and print advertising, search engine marketing, and public relations. Research has shown that usage falls without this active promotion.

Integrating financial education into schools and tertiary training

Promotion, albeit of a different sort, is a key plank in integrating financial education into New Zealand's national school curriculum and tertiary training qualifications. There are compelling reasons for ensuring every child receives financial education early in life—it is an essential literacy for the twenty-first century; children need good information early on so that they can build basic economic and financial concepts, and the financial system they deal with every day is increasingly complex.

Nevertheless, financial education tends not to be a central concern for teachers and Ministers of Education. In New Zealand, this meant providing them with evidence of the benefits of financial education over the course of five years to encourage them to make it a priority. Another important step was involving a broad range of stakeholder groups, including teacher associations and parent boards, to ensure their eventual ownership of the strategy. Key milestones in the five-year plan are shown in Figure 13.2.

The timing for developing a Personal Financial Education Framework to fit the school curriculum was ideal, as New Zealand's national curriculum was being reviewed for implementation in 2010. This meant that the Ministry of Education was able to look at how the teaching of financial literacy could contribute to achieving the outcomes set out in the curriculum's vision, principles, and values. One of the key steps in this strategy was piloting the draft framework in a mix of ten primary and secondary schools to test its effectiveness as a tool for supporting teachers. The trial was then formally evaluated and the results shared with the Ministry of Education.

The evaluation produced a number of insights and lessons to inform the wider integration of the framework into New Zealand education. These included recognition that there was a need to generate receptiveness to personal financial education; that personal financial education was a highly 'saleable' and relevant learning area; that a range of pedagogical benefits were associated with integrating personal financial education into the

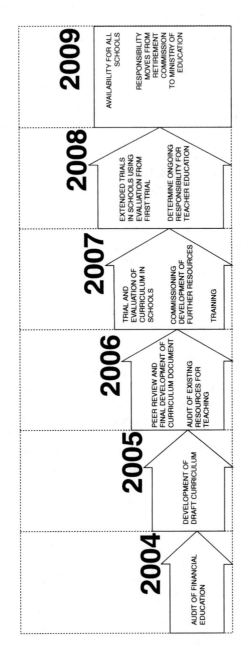

Figure 13.2 Introducing financial education into New Zealand schools

Source: Authors' calculations; see text.

curriculum; and that the trial provided an effective model for successful professional development (Martin Jenkins, 2009). Another important step, as described earlier, was drawing on private-sector support for the strategy, in the form of funding for the trial from New Zealand's banks.

In 2009, responsibility for personal financial education in schools moved from the Retirement Commission to the Ministry of Education, and teaching resources were made available to all schools. From 2011, personal financial education is being integrated into school programs in language, social studies, mathematics, and technology for years 1–10. While the framework forms part of the curriculum, it is still not mandatory, which presents a challenge. New Zealand schools are self-managing, which means they must follow the national curriculum but, within it, they are able to design learning programs to meet their students' particular needs and aspirations. It is essential that the program is now promoted, so that schools and teachers are motivated to adopt it.

Implementation of the program will be monitored by New Zealand's Education Review Office, the government agency responsible for evaluating and reporting publicly on the education in all schools. It will also be measured in the OECD's 2012 Program for International Student Assessment (PISA), which will include a financial education component to evaluate the level of mathematical literacy and skills applied to financial issues of students.

Because financial education has not been available through the school system until now, there are many young people who have left or are leaving school without the necessary skills and information to make informed and wise decisions about money. New Zealand has looked to trade or technical training and pre-employment courses (foundation education) to fill this gap. While the national qualifications framework recognized sixteen personal financial management topics (unit standards), there was a lack of teaching resources for these. The chosen strategy was to develop resources for seven topics and make them freely available to industry training organizations and tertiary institutions. A deliberate decision was made to involve all the organizations critical to the success of this strategy early on in the process and keep them involved throughout. This included the New Zealand Qualifications Authority, the Tertiary Education Commission, industry training organizations, private training establishments, unions, and employers. All could see the need for financial education, so it was a matter of turning this recognition into active participation and commitment.

With the support of all of the above organizations, various resources were launched in late 2009, linked to the seven unit standards. Considerable efforts are now being made to roll out these resources to key industry training organizations and other tertiary institutions. Take-up of the unit standards will be formally evaluated this year. Once again, promotion is a key issue.

Reaching the indigenous population

Reaching New Zealand's Māori people is a strategy still under development. Yet work carried out in recent years with Te Puni Kōkiri (the Ministry of Māori Development) and the largest South Island tribe, Ngāi Tahu, offers some directions. Māori make up around 15 percent of the population and have been a traditionally hard-to-reach audience for financial education. They are a relatively young population, with a median age of 22.7, compared with 35.9 years for New Zealanders as a whole. Only 4.1 percent of Māori are over the age of 65, compared with 12.3 percent of New Zealanders as a whole (Statistics New Zealand, 2006).

Compared to the wider population, Māori are more likely to have lower levels of financial literacy. The latest financial knowledge survey found 56 percent were in the lowest financial knowledge group, compared with 31 percent of the overall population and 24 percent of New Zealand Europeans (Retirement Commission, 2009).

Māori define themselves by their *iwi* (tribe) and *hapu* (subtribe). Whānau, or the extended family, is another important concept, embracing immediate family, relatives by marriage, and all those connected by blood ties. The initiative with the Ngāi Tahu iwi started in 2003 with the pilot of a financial education program for Māori children attending two bilingual schools. As well as focusing on the children, the program's objectives included improving financial knowledge and understanding within their whānau and providing high levels of support for personal financial education within the wider school community. The program was then extended to another five schools to further develop and test the resources, teaching methodologies, and professional development.

An independent evaluation found the program considerably raised children's knowledge about, understanding of, and interest in money. It also strengthened other components of the curriculum, such as mathematics and social studies (PricewaterhouseCoopers, 2007). Yet, engaging whānau with the curriculum and the program's concepts proved difficult. While the children gained understanding of financial concepts, there was little evidence that the program increased the level of understanding among parents and whānau. The report concluded that the nature of the community and the school, as well as the barriers for whānau, needed to be further considered, resourced, and addressed. Ngāi Tahu has since rolled out a financial independence program with around seventy whānau, focusing on investment, budgeting, goal-setting, and debt consolidation.

These programs have been an important complement to a saving plan set up specifically for iwi members four years ago. Similar to KiwiSaver, but allowing for withdrawals for tertiary education, Whai Rawa is built around Ngāi Tahu's guiding principle—'for us and our children after us'. The plan is seen as a way of securing the future of the iwi and distributing wealth that came initially from a financial settlement with the Crown for historical breaches of the 1840 Treaty of Waitangi, and from the business activities that have followed. In 2010, Ngāi Tahu plans to survey the financial knowledge of its members, possibly making it the first group of indigenous people in the world to do so. The survey will be modeled on the national adult financial knowledge survey, which will enable benchmarking against national results and, if it is repeated, comparison over time. It will also help the iwi to identify particular areas where financial education initiatives need to be focused in the future.

The challenge now is to deliver financial education to Māori throughout the country. The Retirement Commission has set up an advisory committee to develop a five-year strategy and action plan by end-2010. The committee draws together a mix of stakeholders from government agencies, financial and education sectors, and the community, balancing representation with strategic thinking skills. While many Māori do currently and in the future will access financial education via the mainstream, what is clear is that, like other groups, Māori need a pathway to information that is relevant to them and that they can trust. Traditional values, such as collectivism, are still powerful within Māoridom and could play a part in promoting modern-day financial literacy. Other concepts such as *manaakitanga* (respect for hosts or kindness to guests), *aroha* (compassion), and *whanaungatanga* (kinship) could also provide some levers.

Initial work suggests that resources will need to be further developed so that they resonate more with Māori, for example drawing on Māori paradigms and reflecting faces Māori regard as influential. While Ngāi Tahu has chosen to work through iwi groups and whānau, not all Māori are linked into these structures. This suggests that schools, community groups, and other networks (including social media) will need to play a part in delivery. The action plan is likely to start small and then build incrementally over five years.

Evaluating effectiveness

So are these and other strategies for financial education having an impact on the financial literacy of New Zealanders? Monitoring and evaluation make up the third strand of the National Strategy for Financial Literacy. These are important in finding out what has worked, or not, and why, and identifying lessons for how financial education can best be developed in future.

As noted earlier, New Zealand is one of the few countries to have measured financial literacy standards at a national level, with a benchmark survey of adult financial knowledge in 2005/6, repeated in 2009. These surveys have set the country on the track for long-term monitoring at a high level and over time will build up a valuable resource. The first survey found that while people's financial knowledge was reasonable overall, many did not understand some key financial concepts (Retirement Commission, 2006). This helped several groups develop and provide more useful information on topics such as managing debt through loan consolidation, the effect of compound interest on saving, and choosing a mortgage and managing mortgage debt. The second survey (Retirement Commission, 2009) found the population's financial knowledge had improved in the intervening three years, with more people having a high level of knowledge (43 percent compared with 33 percent). But there had been little change in the number of people with a low level of knowledge (31 percent compared with 33 percent).

One of the early indicators from these results is that it may be more difficult, and may take more time, to improve financial knowledge from a low base. Financial education and information alone may not be enough to improve the position of those with low financial knowledge. For example, basic literacy and numeracy skills may also need attention.

Evaluation is also happening at program level as noted in several places in this chapter. For example, the impact of Sorted on New Zealanders' personal financial management is gauged in a number of ways. The website's impact is measured through visits, user sessions, and demographics. These site statistics are then complemented with online surveys, general market research, and advertising cost-effectiveness measures.

In New Zealand, as in other countries, there is scope to enhance evaluation. New Zealand is an active participant in international moves to improve evaluation of financial education programs, with the Retirement Commissioner chairing the OECD's subgroup on the subject. During 2010, a set of draft guidelines, developed by the subgroup, will be sent to member countries of the International Network of Financial Education for endorsement. New Zealand will test these on three different programs with the aim of ensuring that all programs are evaluated using common standards. Having a common set of guidelines will allow comparison of what works, for which groups, in which circumstances. But as independent researcher, Alison O'Connell (2009) pointed out recently in a paper for the New Zealand Government's Capital Market Development Taskforce, evaluation is inherently difficult: 'A simple model of financial education leading to greater financial literacy leading to improved financial well-being has not been proved.'

Drawing on her work with the Retirement Commission, O'Connell suggested that three principles should be kept in mind when considering financial literacy policy and practice. First, financial literacy is complicated and multifaceted. It is likely that different types of financial education work in different ways for different people to improve different skills on the financial literacy spectrum. Second, because the effectiveness of financial education is unlikely to be proven in a simple causal way, policymakers should be realistic in their expectations about the benefits of financial education and the impacts of improved financial literacy. And finally, financial literacy is part of the policy mix, with other approaches to improving personal financial well-being.

Conclusion

Financial education is all-encompassing, touching different parts of people's lives at different times and in different settings. This means strategies for improving financial literacy must be multipronged and multilayered.

This chapter outlines five strategies that are having some success in lifting New Zealanders' financial literacy: the development of a national strategy for financial literacy, the pursuit of public–private partnerships, the choice of a website supported by ongoing promotion as a fundamental tool for lifting financial literacy, the integration of financial education into schools and tertiary training, and reaching New Zealand's indigenous Māori population. Common elements running through these include the benefits of collaborating across the public, private, and not-for-profit sectors, ensuring ownership of financial education is rooted in different parts of the community. There is also a continuous need for quality resources that people understand and can connect with. And last, it is essential to undertake promotion efforts to the general population, government ministers, teachers, employers, or unions.

Above all, financial literacy needs a champion. New Zealand is fortunate in having an independent government agency with the primary objective of promoting financial literacy.

References

Colmar Brunton (2008). 'Sorted Materials Evaluation,' Working Paper prepared for the Retirement Commission. Wellington, New Zealand: Colmar Brunton.

Martin Jenkins (2009). 'Evaluation of the Personal Financial Educational Trial,' Working Paper prepared for the Retirement Commission. Wellington, New Zealand: MartinJenkins.

Ministry of Social Development (2009). *Household Incomes in New Zealand: Trends in Indicators of Inequality and Hardship 1982 to 2008.* Wellington, New Zealand: Government Ministry of Social Development.

O'Connell, A. (2009). 'Financial Literacy in New Zealand,' Working Paper prepared for the New Zealand Government Capital Market Development Taskforce. Wellington, New Zealand: Capital Market Development Taskforce.

PricewaterhouseCoopers (2007). 'Financial Literacy Program Evaluation,' Working Paper prepared for the Retirement Commission. Wellington, New Zealand: PricewaterhouseCoopers.

Retirement Commission (2006). *ANZ-Retirement Commission 2006 Financial Knowledge Survey—Summary.* Wellington, New Zealand: Retirement Commission.

—— (2007). *2007 Review of Retirement Income Policy.* Wellington, New Zealand: Retirement Commission.

—— (2008). *National Strategy for Financial Literacy.* Wellington, New Zealand: Retirement Commission.

—— (2009). *ANZ-Retirement Commission 2009 Financial Knowledge Survey—Summary.* Wellington, New Zealand: Retirement Commission.

Statistics New Zealand (2006). *2006 Census.* Wellington, New Zealand: Statistics New Zealand. http://www.stats.govt.nz/Census/2006CensusHomePage

—— (2007). *New Zealand's 65+ Population: A Statistical Volume.* Wellington, New Zealand: Statistics New Zealand.

—— (2009). *National Population Projections: 2009 (Base)–2061.* Wellington, New Zealand: Statistics New Zealand.

—— (2010). *New Zealand in Profile: 2010.* Wellington, New Zealand: Statistics New Zealand.

The Nielsen Company (2009a). 'Sorted User Survey 2009,' Working Paper prepared for the Retirement Commission. Wellington, New Zealand: The Nielsen Company.

—— (2009b). 'Brand Awareness and Perceptions of Sorted November 2009,' Working Paper prepared for the Retirement Commission. Wellington, New Zealand: The Nielsen Company.

Chapter 14

Bringing Financial Literacy and Education to Low- and Middle-Income Countries

Robert Holzmann

The last decade has seen rising interest in financial literacy, along with public and private measures to improve it. While this interest was initially concentrated in high-income countries (HICs), the enthusiasm has now expanded to the poorer parts of the world. The common theme across all countries is the assessment that the level of understanding of financial issues by individuals is too low, with negative consequences for individuals and the economy. Providing financial education is seen as the key intervention that reduces ignorance and improves outcomes. A few rich countries have established a comprehensive national financial literacy strategy, and many others are considering doing so as well. Many poorer countries want to do so likewise, and are looking for guidance and support. While there has been progress in bringing countries and key country actors together to exchange information and experiences on concepts and practices, there has been less progress regarding convincing guidance for low- and middle-income countries (LICs and MICs) in their ambitions. Conceptual uncertainty concerns the objectives, definition, and measurement of financial understanding; empirical uncertainty concerns the effectiveness of financial education compared to other interventions to improve outcomes. Further, the translation into a low- and middle-income environment may be far from straightforward.

This chapter outlines the approach to financial literacy and education (FLE) for LICs and MICs that is currently being implemented by the World Bank under a trust fund financed by the Russian Federation. These activities focus on the development of methodologies and operational instruments for the measurement of financial literacy (actual capabilities) and effectiveness of financial education. It draws on the parallel stock-taking activities by the Organisation for Economic Co-operation and Development (OECD) in member countries that also benefit from this trust fund. The results of both activities should help countries to better design national strategies and interventions.

To motivate the World Bank-led work program, we begin with some conceptual considerations derived from the FLE discourse in HICs.

This is followed by outlining the special circumstances to consider when translating concepts and approaches to a low- and middle-income environment. Next, we present the approach and programmed implementation for LICs and MICs, that is, the focus of work program of the World Bank. We end with conclusions.

Lessons and issues from HICs

Over the last decade, major initiatives on FLE have been undertaken by a number of countries on financial literacy, in particular in the Anglo-Saxon world, and the main progress has been made in sharing that experience under the leadership of the OECD. Agencies created in New Zealand (the Retirement Commission in 1995), the United Kingdom (the Financial Service Authority in 2000), Canada (the Financial Consumer Agency in 2001), the United States (the Financial Literacy and Education Commission in 2003), and Australia (the Financial Literacy Foundation in 2005) have taken the lead on financial literacy issues, and their web sites provide a wealth of national and international information, including that on innovative studies and tools. The OECD's Financial Education project of 2003 started an international assessment on how much people know, and the 2005 study was the first stock-taking at international level (OECD, 2005). Furthermore, in 2008, the OECD created the International Network on Financial Education and the International Gateway for Financial Education, to be an international clearinghouse on financial education.[1]

A review of the policy and academic discourse on FLE for the purpose of application in LICs and MICs provides a number of lessons and issues. First, the concept of financial literacy is broadening. Specifically, the interest has shifted from financial knowledge and understanding to include financial skills, competences, attitudes, and behavior. To signal this broader concept, the United Kingdom has coined the notion of financial capability that is increasingly used by others.[2] This change in content and related definition is important, as it has a major bearing on how objectives are defined and measured, and the choice of interventions regarding how to improve them. While there is a consensus nowadays that the broader concept is relevant, it remains the case that defining, measuring, and influencing it still constitute a moving target.

The concept of financial capability we have in mind proposes that financially capable individuals should demonstrate sensible financial behaviors such as drawing up budgets and saving for old age. This requires moving from knowledge to skills to attitudes to behavior (Kempson, 2008). Knowledge includes understanding the purpose of saving and its instruments; skills refer to the capacity to make a saving plan; attitude pertains to the willingness to save; and behavior requires putting aside the savings. In this conceptualization, information and cognitive understanding is the basis of the ultimate desired financial behavior. This information-based cognitive route is also the underlying concept of much financial education, and it is also consistent with academic studies that take course participation (inputs) to measure the impact on cognitive skills (intermediate outputs) or actual behavior (outcomes). Yet, this value chain may not be needed to achieve outcomes, nor may it work the way it is often conceptualized. We say more on the latter later.

Independent of the type of interventions triggering financial capability, the issue remains of how best to define financial capability. We therefore adopted the working definition of financial capability proposed by Kempson (2008: 3): 'A financially capable person is one who has the knowledge, skills and confidence to be aware of financial opportunities, to know where to go for help, to make informed choices, and to take effective action to improve his or her financial well-being while an enabling environment for financial capability building would promote the acquisition of those skills.'

To operationalize the financial capability concept, the Financial Saving Authority (FSA) proposes five content domains explored in the UK national financial capability survey (FSA, 2005, 2006a, 2006b, 2006c): keeping track, making ends meet, planning ahead, choosing products, and staying informed. This approach was developed bottom-up through focus groups and exploratory studies, and it serves as a consensus approach for how to measure financial capability and identify capability gaps and target groups. It has been applied with adjustments in Ireland (in 2008) and Canada (in 2010), and other countries are also considering this step. Hence, it has the making of becoming the nucleus for an international methodology to measure financial literacy/capability across time and space.

While the content domains seem to have widespread appeal, the challenge is to translate them into questions and coding that take account of national and local circumstances. Ideally, questions and scores should be broadly applicable, but adjustments in questions or coding or both are likely to be required. To do so well will require substantial preparatory work and coordination across countries to achieve comparable results.

Establishing a results framework and testing

The intensive exchange across countries has favored the development of approaches answering the key questions: why and what, for whom, and how.[3] To establish and implement such a framework in a cross-national context requires: (a) a clear formulation of the objectives that a national strategy and individual components seek to achieve; (b) a clear presentation of the hypotheses to be tested and how proposed interventions (type of intervention and delivery mode) are conjectured to influence outputs and outcomes; and (c) an approach for qualitative and quantitative monitoring and evaluation. In practice, however, key elements of such a framework are often missing.

The objectives for enhanced financial understanding (literacy/capability) are relatively well articulated, and range from increased supply and complexity of financial markets instruments to the need of individuals to take better care of their own against the background of perceived low levels of financial literacy and the consequences for individuals and society (Orton, 2007). But as yet there is no broad consensus on specific outcomes. The link between objectives and proposed interventions should also be designed to test hypothesis based on prior work and measurement. In practice, however, quantitative evaluations often serve to explore potential links. As a result, intervention 'effectiveness' may only be suggestive.[4]

Another point is that the number of (financial education) interventions to improve financial literacy has increased dramatically, but a rigorous monitoring and evaluation of such interventions is still the exception, not the rule. Impact evaluations, when done, are often conducted after the fact, rather than as part of the overall intervention design, which limits quality and value of results. There are many reasons why evaluation is not included in interventions, ranging from lack of understanding by program sponsors to lack of funds.

Financial education, behavioral finance, and alternatives to impact outcomes

Recent attempts to increase financial literacy/capability have offered limited empirical evidence that they are very effective, to date. A review by Atkinson (2008: 5) concluded: 'there is little in the way of robust evidence to show the overall effect of financial training'.[5] This conclusion was valid for several different types of interventions from academic to workplace training, and in poorer countries mostly around microfinance projects. Reasons for lack of evidence included inappropriately chosen indicators, data problems and estimation issues, little attention to type and quality of the delivery mechanism, lack of control group, predominance of after-the-fact evaluations, and more. In our view, this calls for caution, rather than giving up, until better evidence is at hand. Indeed, there is a need for more and rigorous impact evaluations that are part and parcel of overall program design.

It may be that financial education may actually do very little for financial capability, at least for aspects such as planning ahead. For instance, good academic financial education could increase financial knowledge, and if linked with hands-on training, could improve financial skills—yet there could be no measurable impact on attitudes or even many behaviors.[6] This might occur, for instance, if people lack trust in financial institutions or they have cultural norms requiring interventions outside financial education to be addressed. Furthermore, even if attitudinal problems and inability to plan could be overcome by financial education, there could still be other impediments to change behavior. The behavioral finance literature provides many examples of cognitive biases with regard to attitude, as well behavior including procrastination, regret and loss aversion, mental accounting status quo, and information overload.[7] This has led some authors to question the role of financial education to enhance financial capabilities and to claim that psychology, rather than knowledge, may be key to what people actually do (e.g., de Meza et al., 2008; Willis, 2008). Working in the other direction are studies by Lusardi and Mitchell (2007), indicating that literacy actually does enhance planning and wealth accumulation.

If financial education is, in fact, ineffective, then the types of interventions to improve behavioral outcomes would need to be revised. For instance, interventions might instead be guided by behavioral finance and psychological findings, and to some extent this is already happening. In US corporate and some public pension plans (in New Zealand and the United Kingdom), lack of planning and follow-through for retirement saving has led plan sponsors to change the default option, using inertia and status quo bias to overcome behavioral shortcomings. Information overload creating indecision can be addressed by reducing the number of options, such as the number of pension funds to choose from. More broadly, the design of the (financial) choice environment can be adjusted to 'nudge' individuals toward desired behaviors, while keeping their decision autonomy (Thaler and Sunstein, 2008). Other, more direct, approaches to change behavior are also gaining prominence. In some Central European countries, saving behavior was reportedly positively influenced by a 'World Saving Day', linked to an information campaign in schools and peer pressure to take one's moneybank to school. Other efforts to directly influence financial attitude and behavior include 'edutainment' interventions with messages on behavior delivered in TV soaps, TV clips, or street theatre. To date, however, few of these efforts have been subject to rigorous impact evaluation.

Financial literacy in LICs and MICs

The last few years have also seen a rising interest in financial literacy, in LICs and MICs. This is clear from the number of countries that have started financial literacy initiatives, and held conferences and workshops, and specific initiatives of nations, as well as regional initiatives for LICs. The Partnership on Making Finance Work for Africa, established in 2008, includes a focus on financial capability; the related September 2009 Accra conference brought together some 200 participants from most African countries on the issue of financial capability and consumer protection. Rising international interest in financial literacy for the less affluent has many different motivations, of which three are worth noting here: concerns with the perceived low level of financial capability; concerns with the low level of financial access; and recognition that finance is a critical element for innovation and growth. In this section, we explore characteristics of LICs and MICs that will be important to consider when measuring the level of financial literacy and designing interventions to raise it.

Definition of LICs and MICs and common relevant characteristics

The World Bank's definition of LICs and MICs is related to their access to World Bank Group financial services, linked to income thresholds measured in Gross National Income (GNI) per capita. LICs are countries with GNI per capita below about US$ 1,100, which makes them eligible for grants and subsidized financing under the International Development Agency (IDA) (the soft lending arm of the World Bank Group). MICs have a per capita GNI between US$ 1,100 and slightly above US$ 10,000, and can access financing under the terms of the International Bank for Reconstruction and Development—IBRD (the market-based lending arm). While these limits are admittedly somewhat arbitrary, they broadly reflect the financial needs and opportunities such as the access (or their lack of) to the international capital market. Five interrelated characteristics seem to be of particular relevance for LIC countries: access, poverty, rural, informality, and risk management. Access to financial instruments in LICs is very limited for a very large share of the population. In most LICs, account accesses is 20 percent or below, while it is 80 percent and above for HICs, with MICs somewhere between. These figures are likely to overstate the access by individuals, as households are considered in the tallies. From a measurement point of view, it is difficult to differentiate financial capability from financial access, as both are interrelated but not the same.

Regarding poverty, LICs do not only have a lower income per capita, but mostly also a much larger share of poor in the population, whether measured as absolute poverty (e.g., those living on below one or two dollars a day) or as relative poverty (e.g., share of individuals having less than, say, 60 percent of the mean income) as income inequality is typically also higher. Absolute poverty induces special behavior, as physical survival gets priority. Observed behaviors may seem to indicate lack of capability, although the individual might behave differently if not poor. This is related to rural residence, as LIC populations live in rural and often sparsely populated areas with limited exposure to financial institutions and products. They tend to have limited cash needs; have assets predominantly in land, cattle, seeds, or gold; and live in larger families and tight-knit communities. This creates special features of planning and saving that may be insufficiently appreciated if behavioral outcomes are assessed only in terms of money.

Informality refers to the well-documented form of work in LICs where formal employment (i.e., with labor contract or licensed, and paying social security contributions and income taxes) is restricted to a very small share of the population (often 10 percent or less), whereas the large majority has the status of self-account workers. As a result, managing money and other resources for a large part of the population means managing jointly the accounts of a consumer and a micro-business. Furthermore, residents in LIC's often face natural, security, economic, and other risks, with limited access to formal (public and private) risk management instruments. They also suffer from incomplete financial markets and limited social transfer programs. Hence, short-term weather and other insurances, where they exist, are of primary interest. As short-term risks dominate, long-term planning and saving (e.g., retirement) is often not feasible. In this setting, lack of saving need not signal lacking financial capability or even myopia; it may be rational.[8]

By contrast, MICs may be described as countries that have the characteristics of both LICS and HICs. Some of the population in a MIC will exhibit characteristics and financial behavior as in an LIC, while others as in an HIC. Sub-Saharan Africa is mainly comprised of LICs, while in the (World Bank) regions of Central and Eastern Europe and Central Asia, there are mainly MICs that are furthermore countries emerging from economic transition. This needs to be taken into account when measuring financial capability and designing interventions. Such issues exist to a more limited extent also in HICs with presence of ethnic minorities and other subgroups.

Idiosyncratic characteristics that may matter

Besides these common characteristics, there are a number of more idiosyncratic characteristics that will also influence the why and the what, for whom, and the how of financial literacy programs, in particular in LICs. The following list is not exhaustive, but demonstrative.

- *Why and what.* Policy statements on the objectives of financial literacy in LICs often mirror that of MICs and HICs (or have been copied from there), suggesting that financial literacy should facilitate and increase access to financial services, even if they are only the most basic ones (i.e., bank accounts). Yet, two others in these countries are also important: basic business education and avoidance of overindebtedness.

As most LIC individuals are own-account workers, as mentioned earlier, their financial management typically mixes consumer and business accounts with, at times, detrimental effects for both. Hence, the frequent request of financial capability programs to strengthen basic business education. Yet, the question remains as to how to define, measure, and separate this from the financial capability of such consumers.

A related overriding concern in many (but not all) LICs is the level of debt of major subgroups of the population with formal and informal lenders. This indebtedness is linked, as in HICs, to low levels of financial capability and poverty but may also reflect, at times, cultural issues that have been little explored.

- *For whom.* As few national financial literacy (not capability) surveys have been undertaken in LICs (and MICs), the key target groups have not yet been freely identified. Gender may require a special focus and treatment in capability surveys, as well as education and other intervention programs. In some regions and countries, gender-specific differentiation with regard to financial decisions seems important, such as when women are excluded from key budgeting and planning decisions, or when women both run the day-to-day family business and manage the precautionary saving budget.
- *How.* There are indications that financial capability surveys and interventions in LICs will have to take account of country specificities, with regard to both content domain and delivery mechanism. For instance, in many countries remittances play a major role for household resources. If so, this may affect the measurement of financial capabilities. Similarly, conditional cash transfers are gaining importance on both LICs and MICs, with similar challenges as well as opportunities. A related topic is microfinance institutions in many LICs and MICs, which can influence financial behavior and deliver financial education. Similarly, mobile phones are becoming a primary instrument to provide financial access, in particular to the very poor.
- *Cultural differences.* Last but not least, there are often striking cultural factors that may explain some of the differences in saving behavior and measured differences in financial capabilities. For instance, in most African societies, it is difficult to keep liquid resources away from the

demands of the extended family. There are historic, economic, and anthropological explanations for such requests to share available resources (Platteau, 1996), but the practice leads to low holding of liquid assets in cash or accounts and preferences for illiquid assets for medium- and longer-term needs. This will not only impact measured financial capability, but could also imply that financial education may do little to help.

Measuring financial capability and the effectiveness of interventions in LICs and MICs: a work program under the Russian Federation Trust Fund

Having explored developments in the area of financial literacy, next we turn to describe the World Bank work program administering the Trust Fund (TF) on FLE sponsored by the Russian Federation. The TF origins are linked to the Russian G8 presidency of 2006, in which FLE was introduced as an important topic in the Pre-Summit Statement by the G8 Ministers of Finance (2006) and an OECD-organized conference in 2006 on the topic in Moscow, with broad international participation. The topic is close to the domestic policy agenda of Russia, as financial literacy of the population is considered much too low but crucial for its economic development. A Russia–World Bank project on FLE is under preparation and should start later in 2010.

Discussions with Russian government officials during the Moscow conference led to the idea and proposal for a TF that should assist in the implementation of the Summit Statement; the TF was established in October 2008. The TF will finance joint and individual work programs of OECD and World Bank with a total amount of $15 million over three years. The two key objectives of this work program are (*a*) to provide an operational country-tested instrument for LICs and MICs to allow them to implement national capability surveys that deliver results which are comparable across time and space; and (*b*) to develop and test a toolkit to better assess the effectiveness of financial education and related interventions to improve financial capability. The financial capability program will be tested in two stages: Stage 1 will explore the domains, questions, and coding in eight country pilots, resulting in a draft questionnaire. Stage 2 will test the questionnaire in the same and possibly other countries. A final phase is anticipated, where the results and lessons are translated into an operational survey instrument on financial capability, available as a public good.

The financial evaluation education program consists of three interrelated components: the development of an M&E toolkit for financial education and related interventions; financial support of impact evaluations for country-specific intervention projects; and financing integrated impact evaluations of financial education projects.

Specific programs to be evaluated will include the following:

- *Formal financial education* (one-to-one and classroom-based): targeting school children, people working in informal economy, or generally low-income consumers;
- *Social marketing/edutainment*: targeting people working in informal economy, generally low-income consumers, including opportunities created by significant life events, such as birth of a new child, death in family, health-related problems, etc.;
- *Financial education for micro-enterprise*: targeting people working in informal economy, farm households, or other subgroups representing low income population;
- *Opportunities provided by government-to-people transfers*:
  - Conditional Cash Transfers (CCTs)
  - matching defined contributions (MDC) saving arrangements, and
  - other government-to-people transfers.

In order to lend better for findings from the funded pilots to be generalized, all projects are expected to measure the effect of financial education programs on knowledge enhancement; measure the effect of financial education programs on changing behavior; and measure the extent to which the change in behavior improves decision-making and enhances the financial well-being of consumers. Each will require an evaluation assessing the delivery mechanisms as well as the objectives, outcomes, and impacts of the financial education programs. A combination of process evaluation and impact evaluation will be used, including qualitative research methods (in-depth interviews, focus groups, or observation techniques) and quantitative experimental studies.

Each study must determine both causality and attribution, and must be able to show to the most rigorous extent possible that the observed outcomes were caused by the intervention being evaluated. It must also control for, or otherwise dismiss, other possible explanations for the observed outcomes, and unobserved factors that might determine heterogeneity in outcomes.

Conclusion

HICs have expressed strong interest in, and supported, many FLE activities that provide a rich albeit incomplete material to guide FLE activities in low- and middle-income world. While progress has been made to move from a knowledge-based concept of financial literacy to a behavior-based concept of financial capability, more remains to be done. In LICs and MICs, there are some common as well as idiosyncratic characteristics that mitigate against a simple transfer of concepts of how to measure financial literacy/capability and how to improve it. Common characteristics for LICs include low access to finance, high poverty, rural population, high informality, and special risks profiles. Idiosyncratic characteristics include issues of trust, differential gender considerations, and cultural norms that differ across countries. MICs naturally have something in common with both the rich and poor countries, for different parts of the population. This complexity calls for adjustments in the way financial capability is defined and measured, and how financial education and related programs are provided. The Russia trust-funded World Bank activities should importantly improve the understanding of the working of FLE in LICs and MICs and assist in design and implementation of effective national strategies and programs. As this is a multiyear work program in progress, the interactions with the international research community will be crucial to participate in the work and to provide feedback and guidance.

Endnotes

[1]   See the OECD website for events and documents: http://www.oecd.org
[2]   In this chapter, we use the term 'financial literacy' interchangeably with financial capability.
[3]   For elements of such a framework, see Microfinance Opportunities (2006, 2009), Kempson (2008), Kempson and Atkinson (2009), Mundy (2009) and O'Connell (2009).
[4]   For a discussion, see Ravallion (2008, 2009).
[5]   See Orton (2007), Atkinson (2008), Mundy (2009), and O'Connell (2009).
[6]   Microfinance Opportunities (2009) suggests a measurable impact on knowledge and skills, although little is observed regarding outcomes in Bolivia and Sri Lanka; the financial crisis may be responsible for this result.
[7]   DellaVigna (2009) has a recent and excellent survey on psychology and economics.
[8]   See Holzmann and Jorgenson (2001) on the Social Risk Management framework and its implications.

References

Atkinson, A. (2008). 'Evidence of Impact: An Overview of Financial Education Evaluations,' Consumer Research No. 68. London, UK: Financial Services Authority.
DellaVigna, S. (2009). 'Psychology and Economics: Evidence from the Field,' *Journal of Economic Literature*, 47(2): 315–72.

De Meza, D., B. Irlenbush, and D. Reyniers (2008). 'Financial Capability: A Behavioural Economics Perspective,' Consumer Research No. 69. London, UK: Financial Services Authority.

Financial Service Authority (FSA) (2005). 'Measuring Financial Capability: An Exploratory Study,' Consumer Research Study No. 37. London, UK: Financial Services Authority.

—— (2006a). *Financial Capability in the UK: Establishing a Baseline.* London, UK: Financial Services Authority. http://www.fsa.gov.uk/pubs/other/fincap_baseline.pdf

—— (2006b). 'Financial Capability Baseline Survey: Methodological Report,' Consumer Research Study No. 47a. London, UK: Financial Services Authority.

—— (2006c). 'Financial Capability Baseline Survey: Questionnaire,' Consumer Research Study No. 47b. London, UK: Financial Services Authority.

G8 Ministers of Finance (2006). 'Pre-Summit Statement by G8 Finance Ministers,' St Petersburg, Russia, June 9.

Holzmann, R. and S. Jorgensen (2001). 'Social Risk Management: A New Conceptual Framework for Social Protection, and Beyond,' *International Tax and Public Finance*, 8(4): 529–56.

Kempson, E. (2008). *Financial Education Fund: Fund Management Inception Report.* Paris, France: Financial Education Fund. http://www.oecd.org/dataoecd/0/41/42271820.pdf

—— A. Atkinson (2009). 'Measuring Levels of Financial Literacy at an International Level,' OECD Working Paper. Paris, France: OECD.

Lusardi, A. and O. S. Mitchell (2007). 'Baby Boomer Retirement Security: The Roles of Planning, Financial Literacy, and Housing Wealth,' *Journal of Monetary Economics*, 54(1): 205–24.

Microfinance Opportunities (2006). 'Assessing the Outcomes of Financial Education,' Working Paper No. 3. Washington, DC: Microfinance Opportunities.

—— (2009). 'Can Financial Education Change Behavior? Lessons from Bolivia and Sri Lanka,' Working Paper No. 4. Washington, DC: Microfinance Opportunities.

Mundy, S. (2009). 'Financial Education Programs in Schools: Analysis of Selected Current Programs and Literature: Draft Recommendations for Best Practices,' OECD Working Paper. Paris, France: OECD.

OECD (2005). *Improving Financial Literacy: Analysis of Issues and Policies.* Paris, France: OECD.

Orton, L. (2007). *Financial Literacy: Lessons from International Experience.* Ontario, Canada: Canadian Policy Research Network Research Report. http://cprn.org/documents/48647_EN.pdf

O'Connell, A. (2009). 'Evaluating the Effectiveness of Financial Education Programs,' OECD Working Paper. Paris, France: OECD.

Platteau, J. P. (1996). 'Mutual Insurance as an Elusive Concept in Traditional Rural Societies,' *Journal of Development Studies*, 23(4): 461–90.

Ravallion, M. (2008). 'Evaluation in the Practice of Development,' Policy Research Work Paper No. 4547. Washington, DC: The World Bank.

—— (2009). *Should the Randomistas Rule?* Berkley, CA: The Berkeley Electronic Press Economists Voice. http://www.bepress.com/cgi/viewcontent.cgi?article=1368&context=ev

Thaler, R. and C. Sunstein (2008). *Nudge: Improving Decisions about Health, Wealth and Happiness*. New Haven, CT: Yale University Press.

Willis, L. E. (2008). 'Against Financial Literacy Education,' *Iowa Law Review*, 94: 197–285.

Chapter 15

Improving Financial Literacy: The Role of Nonprofit Providers

J. Michael Collins

In the United States, financial literacy interventions for lower-income adults are often delivered by nonprofit organizations. These interventions include financial education programs, financial counseling services, and other programs designed to increase consumers' financial capacity (Vitt et al., 2005). The provision of financial literacy interventions by the non-profit sector contrasts with services available in the for-profit sector, which provides financial planning services, and with financial literacy efforts in the public sector. The role of the nonprofit sector in the area of financial literacy is important to understand in the context of public policies and strategies designed to promote financial literacy. This chapter reviews the reasons why nonprofit organizations are involved in the provision of finan-cial literacy interventions and provides a brief overview of the development of the nonprofit sector in this field. Next, using tax records, we attempt to frame the scale of the nonprofit financial literacy industry. The chapter then turns to studies about the effectiveness of financial literacy interven-tions delivered by nonprofit entities, discusses trends in this field, and concludes with implications for the future.

Defining financial literacy, education, and counseling

The concept of financial literacy has become increasingly prevalent in research on consumers' financial capability. Financial literacy is a common-ly used term but arguably an imprecise one. The concept of financial literacy borrows from the reading literacy field, in assuming that literacy can be taught and measured. Unlike reading literacy, however, there are no broadly accepted criteria for measuring financial literacy. The President's Advisory Council on Financial Literacy (2009) defines financial literacy as, 'the ability to use knowledge and skills to manage financial resources effectively for a lifetime of financial well-being'. Thus, financial literacy is not simply a basic understanding of terms and definitions, as the Council's definition highlights the importance of being able to incorporate financial knowledge into one's decisions and behavior. For this chapter, financial literacy is defined as a set of financial skills that informs decisions, affects behavior, and ultimately leads to financial security over the life course.

The distinction between financial education and counseling is not always clear. Financial education typically means group seminars or classes in which financial information is provided to participants. Financial counseling generally refers to one-on-one advice or consulting, often provided before an impending decision or in response to a financial problem. Nonetheless, financial counseling sessions may incorporate more general educational topics and materials, and participants in financial education programs may have personal issues or questions that the educator or their peers address. The advent of telephone and Internet services further blurs the distinction between financial education and counseling. As financial education and counseling overlap in practice, this chapter refers to these modes interchangeably unless otherwise noted.

Nonprofit provision of financial literacy services

Nonprofit organizations are unusual because they are often defined by what they do not do—that is, generate profits for owners and shareholders. Even the term 'nonprofit' may cause some confusion, as nonprofit organizations may in fact generate accounting profit. The defining characteristic of a nonprofit organization is the principle of nondistribution of profits. In the United States, nonprofits are defined by the Internal Revenue Service's (IRS's) interpretations of the tax code (Internal Revenue Service, 2008). The tax-exempt status of nonprofit charitable organizations is enumerated under section 501(c)(3) of the IRS code. Nonprofit organizations are distinct from private foundations, and nonprofit entities must not benefit private interests. If a nonprofit organization engages in transactions that generate excess benefits for a person who has substantial influence over the organization, then the IRS may impose an excise tax. In addition to the prohibition against accruing excess personal benefits, nonprofit organizations are restricted but not entirely prohibited from engaging in political activities. The public's support for a nonprofit organization must be fairly broad, and must not be limited to a few individuals or families. Churches and religious organizations may operate similarly to 501(c)(3) organizations without the formal tax status designation, although some of these organizations may form other entities under the tax code to deliver services beyond religious functions.

There is an extensive literature on the role of nonprofits in the United States across a range of programs and policy contexts. Although this chapter by no means attempts to summarize all of the literature on non-profits, some insights from past research are helpful for understanding why nonprofits are engaged in promoting financial literacy. In a widely cited study, Rose-Ackerman (1996) identifies three major economic functions of nonprofits. First, nonprofit managers are not motivated by the need to return profits to owners or shareholders. Second, because nonprofit managers are not motivated to seek profits, consumers may select nonprofit goods and services because they believe that nonprofit organizations have little incentive to misrepresent their services. Therefore, an organization's nonprofit status serves as a quality signal in environments where consumers recognize information asymmetries and therefore distrust private-sector providers. Third, nonprofits may provide more diverse services than the services provided in other sectors, as the nonprofit sector allows individuals with extreme or unpopular ideas to develop and advance their ideas or services outside of the pressures of the market or political economy. In such cases, nonprofit entities may be better able to meet the needs of people who are otherwise underserved by the private market.

An alternative approach by DiMaggio and Anheier (1990) examines nonprofits from a sociological perspective. The authors review the historic development of nonprofit organizations, which arose out of the Gilded Age to confront urban problems, while also defining and protecting the boundaries of social classes. Over time, nonprofits evolved from charities that worked with the underclass to organizations that perform functions that typically fall under the purview of government. Similar to Rose-Ackerman's later insights (1996), DiMaggio and Anheier (1990) observe that nonprofits offer an avenue for pluralism in civil society by providing services to subsets of the public that are not represented by the median voter. Because nonprofits exist outside of government, they may have a greater desire and ability to test innovative policy interventions. In turn, the public sector may later adopt and expand programs and interventions that prove successful in the nonprofit sector.

Weisbrod (1997), a long-time scholar in the area of nonprofits, explores the growth in the use of nonprofits for delivering public programs and policies both domestically and abroad. His work presents a number of critiques and challenges for the nonprofit sector. As the nonprofit sector has grown, it has become more reliant on public funds, corporate grants, and program-related revenue and less reliant on charitable donations. This shift away from charitable contributions could potentially erode consumers' perceptions that nonprofits are more objective and less biased than for-profit entities. Nonprofit organizations have also increasingly entered markets in the pursuit of revenue. Nonprofits that enter new markets may potentially disrupt the sectors of the economy that were already engaged in those markets. Finally, a lack of market or public accountability may result in nonprofits interfering with public and for-profit responses to society's needs.

The nonprofit sector's involvement in the financial literacy arena reflects this literature. First, nonprofits that offer financial literacy programs are often perceived as having no vested interest in consumers' financial choices. Unlike for-profit financial institutions, nonprofits are less likely to benefit from steering consumers to particular financial decisions. The role of nonprofit organizations as unbiased and objective sources of information may serve as a quality signal for consumers and donors, and might facilitate subsidies from the public sector. Second, nonprofits can potentially serve consumers whose financial literacy needs fall outside the scope of services provided by the public and for-profit sectors. In practice, this role often takes the form of community-based organizations using geographic proximity or existing social relationships to deliver services to lower-income, minority, or culturally distinct populations. These efforts may increase the perception that nonprofit organizations are readily accessible and may lower barriers to entry into services for populations that are otherwise underserved.

Roles of nonprofits in providing financial literacy interventions

Nonprofit organizations are highly heterogeneous in terms of the services they provide and their positions in the broader economy. Nonprofits that provide financial literacy programming appear to comprise an especially diverse group of organizations. As such, making generalizations about financial literacy efforts in the nonprofit sector is infeasible. However, even stylized facts about the nonprofit field and its involvement in efforts to promote financial literacy should prove useful in understanding the potential contributions of the nonprofit sector to this field. Nonprofits engaged in promoting financial literacy range from small community-based organizations whose volunteers conduct educational workshops, to large multiservice agencies that offer intensive ongoing programs with professional staff.

Few nonprofit organizations have been established to deliver financial literacy explicitly; rather, most nonprofit agencies engaged in efforts to promote financial literacy became involved in this field over time. Furthermore, many nonprofit organizations in this field are associated with a particular funding source and/or type of service. For instance, the US Department of Housing and Urban Development (HUD) housing counseling program has existed for several decades and has funded more than 1,000 nonprofit organizations that provide financial education or counseling related to housing (Herbert et al., 2008). In addition, the Assets for Independence (AFI) program of the US Department of Health and Human Services has funded nearly 300 nonprofit organizations that provide matched saving accounts, also known as Individual Development Accounts (IDAs). Most of the organizations that administer IDAs through the AFI program provide or even require some degree of financial literacy education or counseling (Office of Community Services, 2008). With the goal of increasing consumers' capacity to utilize banking services, the Community Reinvestment Act of 1977 gives financial institutions incentives to provide financial support to nonprofit organizations that focus on bolstering consumers' banking and borrowing literacy. In terms of examples of support from entities outside of the public sector, the National Foundation for Credit Counseling has provided an accreditation system for nonprofit financial counseling agencies since the 1950s, in part to offer standards and credentials across organizations, as well as to provide a forum for collective advocacy with financial institutions and policymakers. In each of these cases, however, the financial education is linked to a particular product or industry segment, rather than to support the development of general financial education.

A growing number of government policies mandate financial education and counseling services within certain contexts. In turn, nonprofit organizations commonly provide programs that fulfill the financial education and counseling requirements enacted by the government. For instance, under the Bankruptcy Abuse Prevention and Consumer Protection Act of 2005, individuals must receive financial counseling before they can file for bankruptcy in court and must participate in financial education after filing. Approved nonprofit organizations must provide these financial counseling and education services. Housing is another area in which the government mandates financial counseling in particular circumstances. Throughout much of the 2000s, the government-sponsored enterprises Fannie Mae and Freddie Mac required financial counseling before approving mortgages that fell under certain guidelines. Fannie Mae and Freddie Mac's housing counseling requirements spurred the growth of nonprofit financial counseling providers.

Human services agencies, including agencies that provide unemployment assistance, food assistance, and family services, may also incorporate financial education or counseling into their programs. For example, in some areas nonprofit educators under contract with the Supplemental Nutrition Assistance Program, previously known as the Food Stamps Program, engage in budgeting exercises with the goal of helping clients save money and afford healthier food. Overall, nonprofit organizations that provide financial literacy services in response to government policies must deliver financial education and counseling services that fulfill the legislative mandates. However, their programs often address broader financial topics as well.

Beyond financial education and counseling programs that are tied to specific mandates or funding streams, some nonprofit organizations are engaged in the provision of more general financial literacy services. These programs are often taught in a classroom or seminar format with the goal of increasing participants' financial knowledge across a range of topics including credit, banking, taxes, and saving. Programs may be offered in a variety of contexts and settings, including public spaces, workplaces, and schools. Typically, group education seminars or workshops focus on particular financial topics. One-on-one counseling is delivered either face-to-face or via telephone, in response to an acute crisis or to address specific issues.

Costs of providing financial education and counseling services

It is tempting to assume that the nonprofit delivery of financial education and counseling services is less costly than the provision of the same services by the private for-profit sector (due to the elimination of profit margins) or by the public sector (due to increased efficiencies in service delivery, which include closer proximity to targeted populations and the use of donated labor and materials). Nevertheless, the extensive empirical literature on the costs of service delivery across the nonprofit, public, and for-profit sectors yields mixed results for an array of industries, including health-care and legal services (cf. Rose-Ackerman, 1996). While no studies have compared the costs of financial literacy services across sectors, the findings from more general analyses remain informative. Few studies conclude that nonprofit entities provide services at lower costs than the for-profit sector, although several studies indicate that nonprofits provide higher-quality services at similar costs. In some cases, the literature suggests that no discernable differences exist in cost or quality across sectors. Nevertheless, lower costs are not a primary finding in the literature on the benefits of nonprofits. Therefore, until studies specifically compare the costs of financial literacy services across sectors, the more general literature indicates that nonprofit financial education and counseling programs are likely not less expensive than the services that the for-profit and public sectors provide.

Estimating the costs of nonprofit financial literacy services is an interesting yet elusive empirical issue in search of reliable data. While evidence in this area is small in scale and unpublished, a few studies have attempted to quantify the costs of various financial education and counseling programs. As these studies tend to employ different accounting methods, comparing findings across studies is challenging (Dylla and Caldwell-Tautges, 2009; Gabriel and Todd, 2010). One method of estimating the costs of financial literacy service delivery is to refer to the standardized cost measurement systems used by public pension systems (CEM Benchmarking Incorporated, 2010). According to one summary of thirty-five state pension programs, the median cost for one-on-one counseling was $138, and the median cost for group presentations was $54 per client in 2009. These figures are consistent with estimates from the housing and credit counseling industries, as well as with estimates derived from HUD-housing counseling funding levels and the number of clients served by these funds (Mayer et al., 2009).

Prior research on nonprofit delivery of financial literacy

Few studies explicitly examine nonprofit providers of financial literacy services, and many of the studies we identified for this chapter appear only as working papers or as reports, and have not been published in peer-reviewed journals. One wide-ranging report by Vitt et al. (2000) describes over eighty financial education programs operating in the early 2000s. Primarily based on case studies, this report demonstrates the breadth of financial education activities in existence. A range of institutions, including human services agencies, housing organizations, nonprofit credit unions, and faith-based organizations, are described in this report. Most of the twenty-nine community-based financial literacy organizations they identified were founded since 1998, and local governments or public–private collaboratives established many of these organizations. Vitt et al. note that these initiatives are often organized under complex coalitions of partners, and that about one-third of the groups they identified focused on homeownership education. Consistent with the theories about the role of nonprofits in the economy, many organizations in their report served populations with special needs. The typical organization provided 9–12 hours of education per client, although some programs were much more intensive. Compared to the financial education and counseling field as a whole, the programs in their report likely provided relatively longer and more intensive services because of the high proportion of homeownership programs included in their report. Homeownership programs often include multiple sessions delivered over a number of days or weeks. Vitt et al. also describe the frequent use of lay volunteers or pro bono professionals as program instructors or guest speakers. Some of these volunteers or professionals may have a vested interest in client outcomes. For example, bankers and real estate agents may be experts on buying and financing a home, but they may also have incentives to promote particular services and service providers.

Most of the remaining studies about nonprofit financial literacy services examine particular facets of financial education or counseling programs. For instance, Herbert et al.'s paper (2008) on housing counseling tracks HUD-certified nonprofit housing counseling providers. The authors estimate that 1.7 million individuals received housing education and counseling through the 1,800 HUD-certified nonprofits in 2007. The authors surveyed a sample of these organizations and found that HUD funding represented the largest source of revenue for most of these organizations. The survey also indicated that about three-quarters of the HUD-certified nonprofit counseling agencies had fifty or fewer employees and served fewer than 1,000 clients per year. Seventy-seven percent of the HUD-approved housing counseling agencies reported offering financial literacy education.

As noted earlier, most of the organizations that administer IDAs through the AFI program provide or even require some degree of financial education or counseling. One study found that most of the nonprofit organizations (79 percent) that received AFI funding offered general financial literacy services (Office of Community Services, 2008). A survey of ninety-one AFI-funded programs documented how often the organizations covered specific financial topics. Budgeting and credit management were the most common topics the organizations covered, followed by saving and banking. It is notable that the topics covered by the AFI-funded entities extended beyond mere information and definitions. The programs also covered attitudes, goals, and even values. In fact, more organizations addressed financial values and goals (86 percent) than homeownership (66 percent) or retirement (37 percent). The typical AFI-funded program provided 5–12 hours of financial education, and 80 percent of the organizations also offered financial counseling.

Trends in nonprofit providers of financial education and counseling

In order to describe the field of nonprofit providers of financial literacy services, one can link administrative data from the IRS to data from Guide-Star, which provides information about nonprofits. Working with the National Center for Charitable Statistics, GuideStar receives images of tax forms directly from the IRS and then posts them online. Public charities with incomes in excess of $5,000 must file IRS Form 990 or 990-EZ each year. Every private foundation, regardless of income, must file IRS Form 990-PF. Data from the forms are digitized, searchable, and may be downloaded. Besides providing financial information, each organization lists its tax-exempt purposes or the mission of its four largest programs using the National Taxonomy of Exempt Entities Core Codes (NTEE-CC). This hierarchical system classifies organizational activities into ten major categories and dozens of subcategories. Along with each organization's name, its mission statement, comments from its financial statements, and descriptions of its programs, the NTEE-CC codes can also be searched.

In general, data from IRS forms are considered reliable and accurate (Froelich et al., 2000). Because the dates of nonprofit organizations' fiscal years differ, filing dates for the IRS forms vary. Organizations may have an additional six months to file their Form 990 if they receive extensions, and it may take GuideStar up to six months to digitize the IRS data. Therefore, data lags of up to two years are possible. Our analysis draws on tax records from June 2007 to May 2009. The data exclude smaller organizations (gross receipts under $5,000), which are not required to report to the IRS, and organizations with less than $25,000 in annual gross receipts that lack full financial and programmatic information. The GuideStar dataset offers little information about religious entities, regardless of size, because they are not required to file with the IRS. However, some religious organizations voluntarily choose to file with the IRS and may be represented in the data. Other challenges arise from the fact that the NTEE-CC codes may be overly broad and from the possibility that organizations with many programmatic activities may not list codes associated with their secondary activities.

The data in this analysis were downloaded for the specified date range using these search terms: 'financial literacy', 'financial education', 'financial counseling', 'credit counseling', and 'housing counseling'. These searches were designed to identify common descriptive phrases (e.g., 'financial literacy') such that the universe of organizations engaged in financial literacy services would be flagged. A total of 2,218 unique organizations were identified out of the 1.9 million tax-exempt organizations in the GuideStar dataset. By comparison, 'poverty' and 'health' generated 6,056 and 124,752 results, respectively. If more than one record for an organization was available, only the record from the most recent tax year was retained.

Table 15.1 displays the NTEE-CC codes at the highest grouping level for the 2,218 organizations. Three-quarters (74 percent) of the organizations in the dataset are classified as human services agencies. Together, education and public benefit programs account for just 16 percent of the organizations in the extracted dataset. The majority of the remaining organizations were either uncoded or health-related entities.

Table 15.2 displays the program category codes for each organization's major programmatic activities. Only the ten most frequently cited codes are included in the table, and less common codes are aggregated into the

TABLE 15.1 GuideStar records for tax-exempt organizations by National Taxonomy of Exempt Entities—Core Codes (2007–9)

NTEE-CC[a]	Number	Percentage
Arts, culture, humanities	24	1.1
Education	162	7.6
Environment	3	0.1
Health	54	2.5
Human services	1570	73.8
International affairs	7	0.3
Public benefit	188	8.8
Religion related	22	1.0
Unclassified	3	0.1
Missing	95	4.5
Total	2,128	100.0

[a] National Taxonomy of Exempt Entities—Core Codes.

Source: Author's calculations; see text.

TABLE 15.2 GuideStar records for tax-exempt organizations by program category (ten most frequent, 2007–9)

Major program category code	Number	Percentage
Financial counseling/money management	847	39.8
Housing development	97	4.6
Human services: multi	35	1.6
Community/neighborhood development	40	1.9
Human services: Other	482	22.7
Education: Other	32	1.5
Housing: Other	31	1.5
Housing rehabilitation	25	1.2
Homeless	28	1.3
Family services	25	1.2
Other	486	22.8
Total	2,128	100.0

Note: Program categories based on National Taxonomy of Exempt Entities—Core Codes.

Source: Author's calculations; see text.

'other' category. Forty percent of organizations listed 'Financial Counseling/Money Management' as a programmatic activity. Listing a code is a choice that each organization makes. Organizations with multiple activities may not list every programmatic code. This is clear when examining the remaining 60 percent of the programmatic codes. The largest share of the 1,281 organizations that were not coded 'Financial Counseling/ Money Management' listed a human services code (482 organizations, which accounts for 23 percent of the total and 38 percent of the organizations

TABLE 15.3 Financial literacy extract from GuideStar records by IRS tax status (2007–9)

Tax status	Number	Percentage
501(c)(14) Credit unions	7	0.3
501(c)(19) Post or organizations of war veterans	2	0.1
501(c)(3) Private nonoperating foundation	71	3.3
501(c)(3) Private operating foundation	20	0.9
501(c)(3) Public charity	1,990	93.5
501(c)(4) Civic leagues and social welfare orgs	25	1.2
501(c)(6) Business leagues, etc.	11	0.5
501(c)(7) Social and recreation clubs	1	0.1
501(c)(9) Employees associations	1	0.1
Total	2,128	100.0

Source: Author's calculations; see text.

that were not coded as 'Financial Counseling/Money Management'). The 'Other' category covers 486 of the 2,128 organizations (23 percent). This finding suggests that organizations with financial literacy search terms are engaged in a wide range of programmatic activities. While one might predict that the 'Financial Counseling/Money Management' code would encompass the entirety of the financial education and counseling field, relying on this code alone would not capture all of the organizations with mission statements or program descriptions that discuss financial literacy services. In the end, the NTEE-CC code alone is insufficient for capturing the extent of the financial literacy services delivered by nonprofit organizations, as approximately 60 percent of organizations do not fall under the 'Financial Counseling/Money Management' code.

Table 15.3 lists the IRS tax status of the extracted organizations. Nearly all of the organizations (94 percent) are public charities under Section 501(c)(3) of the Internal Revenue Code. Three percent of the organizations, or just seventy-one entities, are private non-operating foundations, which grant money to other charitable organizations. Only twenty organizations (1 percent) are private operating foundations, which fund in-house charitable programs, rather than making grants. Only a small number of other legal forms of organizations are identified in the dataset. Thus, most nonprofit organizations identified as financial literacy service providers are charities in the narrow legal sense, as opposed to other forms of not-for-profit organizations.

Finally, Table 15.4 displays financial data on organizations categorized by NTEE-CC program code. The data include median total revenue, median total expenses, the ratio of revenue to expenses, and the ratio of administrative expenses to total expenses. Note that data were available for only 1,426 out of the 2,128 organizations (67 percent) that were initially identi-

TABLE 15.4 Financial literacy GuideStar records median dollar value of reported revenue, expenses, and administrative cost to total expenses ratio by organization category (2007–9)

Program code	Revenue ($)	Expenses ($)	Revenue expense ratio (%)	Administrative expense ratio (%)	Number reporting
Financial counseling/ money management	260,913	594,480	44	17	394
Housing development	1,433,816	1,168,027	123	16	91
Human services: multi	893,748	938,600	95	14	24
Community/ neighborhood development	1,787,428	1,569,170	114	17	35
Human services: Other	1,102,373	1,251,253	88	15	411
Education: Other	255,450	281,096	91	10	17
Housing: Other	591,464	599,135	99	16	28
Housing rehabilitation	1,431,309	1,834,142	78	14	23
Homeless	665,780	678,046	98	15	28
Family services	528,852	486,380	109	21	24
Other	602,830	685,182	88	17	351
All codes (median)	699,699	855,583	82	16	1,426

Note: 702 organizations in data did not report selected financial variables.

Source: Author's calculations; see text.

fied—meaning the remainder of organizations failed to meet the $25,000 threshold for reporting and selected not to report detailed expenses. Median expenses exceeded median revenue in eight of the eleven program codes. Among all of the 1,426 organizations, median revenues are 82 percent of expenses—and as low as 44 percent for organizations that fall under the Financial Counseling/Money Management program code. Median administrative costs range from 10 to 21 percent of total expenses across the program codes. Housing rehabilitation, neighborhood development, and human services organizations are the largest entities in terms of median revenue and expenses. Financial Counseling/Money Management organizations are relatively small in terms of their median revenue and expenses and, as mentioned earlier, organizations with this program code have the smallest ratio of revenue to expenses (44 percent). Note also that only 394 out of the 847 (47 percent) organizations with the Financial Counseling/Money Management program code in Table 15.2 reported financial data on IRS Form 990. The fact that only 47 percent of these organizations met the minimum threshold for reporting their financial data (an annual gross revenue of $25,000) suggests that many of the Financial Counseling/Money Management organizations in the GuideStar dataset are small legal entities without significant activities.

Because of the methodology used to extract the data, the time lags associated with filing IRS forms and posting them online, and the nature of the IRS reporting requirements, one must be cautious in interpreting these findings. Nevertheless, the general patterns appear to suggest that organizations focused exclusively on Financial Counseling/Money Management have fewer resources than organizations for which financial education or counseling is a secondary activity. It also appears that Financial Counseling/Money Management organizations generate less revenue than organizations that fall under most other program codes. This finding may reflect the fact that this field is relatively new, or it may signal a lack of sustainable resources.

Literature on the impact of financial education and counseling provided by nonprofits

There is a growing literature on the impact of financial education and counseling, much of which centers on programs operated by nonprofit agencies. For example, Zhan et al. (2006) analyze financial education programs operated by ten nonprofit agencies associated with the Financial Links for Low-Income People program in Illinois. The sites provided 12 hours of financial education to individuals with incomes less than 200 percent of the poverty level. Participants completed forty-eight true–false and multiple-choice questions in pre–post surveys. The questions covered five areas the authors identified as important to low-income individuals: predatory lending, public and work-related benefits, saving and investing, banking, and credit use and interest rates. Participants' financial knowledge scores increased by 20 percentage points to a mean of 74 percent, more than a one-third marginal increase. However, the study did not utilize a comparison group, which raises concerns about the magnitude of the findings.

Another illustrative example is Sanders et al.'s evaluation (2007) of a financial education program delivered in two battered women's shelters. Women in two similar shelters with comparable populations comprised a comparison group. The financial education program consisted of four 3-hour sessions that focused on money and power, developing a cost-of-living plan, building and repairing credit, and banking and invest-ing. A thirty-five-item pre–post questionnaire was used to measure changes in financial knowledge and attitudes. The comparison group's mean score did not change from pre- to post-test, and the treatment group's mean score increased by 5 percent (at the margin). While the use of a compari-son group marks an improvement over descriptive studies that lack such a group, this study highlights another common problem with evaluations in the field—attrition. Only 57 percent of women completed the post-test; furthermore, pretest scores were significantly different between women who completed the post-test and those who dropped out of the study.

Clancy et al. (2001) use a quasi-experimental exposure model to analyze fourteen nonprofits in the American Dream Policy Demonstration. Funded programs offered IDAs, which are subsidized saving accounts available to low-income households. The number of required hours of financial education varied across the sites, which allowed the authors to estimate the effect of each additional hour of financial education on participants' deposit frequencies and average monthly net deposits. Data on these two outcomes were obtained from depository institutions up to 3 years after enrollment in the program. From 0 to 6 hours, each additional hour of financial education is associated with a $1.24 increase in monthly net deposits and from 7 to 12 hours a $0.54 increase, and diminishing and inconsistent effects occur beyond 12 hours. From 0 to 12 hours, each additional hour of financial education is associated with a 2 percent marginal increase in deposit frequency. However, clients who seek more financial education may be more motivated and likely to succeed, so these estimates may overstate financial education's causal effects.

Elliehausen et al. (2007) evaluate nonprofit credit counseling using a quasi-experimental design. Five nonprofit agencies administered counseling in person or over the telephone. All of the clients participated in an initial 60–90-minute session, and some clients participated in more than one counseling session. The comparison group comprised noncoun-seled borrowers who lived in the same zip code and had similar credit profiles as the treatment group. While the initial analysis indicated that counseling led to significant improvements in credit scores, the estimated effects decreased sharply after controlling for selection effects. Among counseled borrowers in the lowest credit score quintile, credit scores increased by less than 1 percent more than the comparison group. This evaluation design not only illustrates how researchers can use credit bureau data to assess behavioral outcomes associated with nonprofit programs, but also highlights the need for a very large sample when attempting to model selection processes.

More recently, Carswell (2009) surveyed 1,720 mortgage borrowers who had participated in nonprofit prepurchase housing counseling in Philadelphia. This evaluation is notable because the survey was administered 5 years after counseling. In view of the lengthy follow-up period, the 24 percent response rate (405 responses) is low, but still quite remarkable. Over 72 percent of respondents reported they had no difficulty paying their mortgages, 85 percent reported they prioritized mortgage payments over other bills, and 64 percent reported they had made financial sacrifices since becoming homeowners. As twenty-six counseling agencies were involved in the evaluation, Carswell analyzed whether agency characteristics were associated with the outcome measures. However, this portion of the analysis yielded few statistically significant findings, other than some evidence that borrowers with more financial problems attended more intensive services, consistent with selection effects.

Turning to postpurchase homeownership counseling, Collins (2007) analyzes nonprofit financial counseling for mortgage borrowers in default. The dataset comprised 299 clients who received face-to-face and/or telephone-based counseling. The author consulted public records to determine mortgage outcomes six to nine months after counseling. Because the number of hours in counseling could be endogenous with loan outcomes, the author constructed an instrumental variable using the number of marketing materials the city used to promote counseling in each zip code. This instrument proved correlated with the number of hours in counseling but uncorrelated with individual foreclosures. The analysis indicated that counseling reduced the probability of negative foreclosure outcomes.

One of the only studies that explicitly compares nonprofit financial counseling/education delivery to other forms of service delivery was conducted by Hirad and Zorn (2002), who evaluate prepurchase homeownership counseling's impact on ninety-day mortgage delinquency rates. Their dataset allowed them to compare a nonrandom comparison group to individuals who participated in four different modes of counseling: in person, classroom, home study, and telephone. Face-to-face counseling was associated with a 34 percent reduction in delinquency, while classroom and home study counseling were associated with 26 and 21 percent reductions, respectively. Nonprofit education/counseling resulted in even greater effects, but further analysis shows that this relationship is a result of the mode of delivery. For instance, classroom education provided by a lender, public agency, or nonprofit organization yields similar effects, regardless of which type of agency runs the program. When selection effects are modeled, only classroom education is linked with a decline in delinquency, with no effects for type of provider.

Overall, the evidence of the effectiveness of nonprofit programs is not robust. It is possible that current counseling models are delivered in such crisis moments (e.g., foreclosure) that they fail to impact behavior significantly. Likewise, education models may be too shallow and lack opportunities for practice and follow-up. The lack of robust findings may also be attributable to problems in evaluation design. Most importantly, existing studies often suffer from selection effects due to a lack of random assignment. Seeking out and completing financial education or counseling may be endogenous with outcome measures in unobservable ways. Meier and Sprenger's research (2008) has important methodological implications in this regard. The authors offered a short credit education workshop at a tax preparation site. On the basis of a time preference survey, individuals who were most future-oriented were also the most likely to agree to attend the workshop. The authors conclude that if 'the measured effects of financial information interventions do not rely on randomization, then their observed educational effects are most likely overestimated' (Meier and Sprenger, 2008: 4).

Together, the findings from the studies discussed earlier are consistent with the notion that the most motivated consumers enroll in financial literacy programs. These consumers may already be the most likely to demonstrate knowledge gains and behavior changes relative to nonparticipants, regardless of the intervention. Given that few studies use randomized designs, it seems likely that many evaluations overestimate program impacts. Furthermore, reliance on self-reported outcomes raises concerns about response bias, in which participants select desirable survey answers. Because many studies rely on self-reports collected at the point of service, service providers could overtly or subtly guide respondents to particular survey answers, which would also upwardly bias results.

To the extent nonprofit organizations are the setting for research into the effects of financial literacy services, the length of the follow-up period is important to consider. Short follow-up periods allow researchers to capture immediate effects, but they hinder researchers' ability to capture more permanent outcomes. However, longer follow-up periods can exacerbate the problem of attrition bias, as fewer baseline respondents can be traced. Lengthier follow-up periods entail higher costs, which may be a greater burden for nonprofit organizations than for the for-profit and public sectors. Nonprofit organizations often have high staff turnover rates, which can hamper tracking clients and even disrupt program implementation. Any program evaluation with two or more data collection points requires clients' cooperation, administrative procedures for following-up with nonrespondents, and in some cases incentives (sanctions) for client compliance (noncompliance) to minimize attrition.

A final consideration relates to the degree to which one expects consumers' behavior to change when nonprofits provide financial information or advice. A number of competing factors could impede even a knowledgeable consumer from making optimal financial decisions. There are several examples in which financial education is one component of a larger program, including homebuyer education and matched saving initiatives. In such programs, financial information conceptually enhances the effectiveness of the primary intervention. Alternatively, auxiliary programs could be created to complement financial education and enhance consumers' ability to act on newly gained information. For example, to the extent a lack of self-control prevents consumers from changing their behavior, an ongoing financial coach could help clients set and monitor goals. Providing services that directly complement financial education may prove more effective than the provision of financial education alone.

Components of leading programs

As the field develops and matures, best practices will emerge concerning what content is best matched to various types of learners and what modes of service delivery are well received by learners. Unfortunately, no existing research clearly documents the relative efficacy of different content areas. Discussions with community-based educators, as well as a review of widely used curricula, indicate that nonprofit financial education and counseling programs tend to cover a set of key financial topics. Currently, nonprofit organizations tend to focus on broad concepts and rules of thumb, as opposed to specific financial strategies. Content is not strictly knowledge-based but also focuses on self-awareness of financial attitudes, with an eye toward preventing or improving negative financial behaviors. Areas highlighted by existing programs include (*a*) developing goals, which helps people take control of their financial choices; (*b*) budgeting, which promotes monitoring spending in order to save and pay off debt; (*c*) managing credit, which includes repairing past problems and reconfiguring existing liabilities; (*d*) accessing financial services, which includes opening and utilizing transaction and saving accounts, as well as borrowing; (*e*) income tax preparation, which includes strategies for using a refund and ways to take advantage of tax provisions; and (*f*) saving for the future, including maximizing access to retirement and other benefits, as well as targeted saving products. Most but not all programs cover these topics. Some nonprofit programs are beginning to cover topics such as investing, insurance, disability claims, and other topics of interest to lower-income adults, but most remain focused on basic budgeting, credit, and saving. These content areas are distinct from the issues and topics covered by private financial planners. Issues such as risk tolerance, portfolio allocation, and estate planning seem more likely to be handled by private for-profit providers than by nonprofit programs. While these divisions may change over time, it does not appear that a high degree of overlap or competition exists between for-profit and nonprofit providers of financial literacy services.

The direct and indirect evidence suggest that financial literacy programs systematically attract people with specific risk and motivation profiles into particular modes and durations of education and counseling (Meier and Sprenger, 2008). For example, clients who can navigate the logistical challenges of attending lengthy face-to-face services are likely highly motivated. In contrast, clients mandated to enroll in web-based seminars may have less interest in sustained behavior change. While some practitioners may be eager to work with highly motivated clients, mandated clients will display a range of motivation levels and will include individuals who otherwise would be difficult or even impossible to reach. Nonprofit programs will be better able to tailor their outreach efforts and services as selection effects are better understood. By reviewing the characteristics of clients who enroll in each type of service, programs will be in a better position to match services to clients.

Conclusion

This chapter began with questions about the role of nonprofits in the economy and the scale of nonprofit organizations' involvement in financial literacy services. While there is little prior research in this area, we draw on analyses of related not-for-profit organizations to argue that nonprofits are less likely to have incentives to mislead consumers, and that nonprofits can meet the needs of populations underserved by public programs and the private market. Our analysis of IRS data suggests that approximately 2,100 nonprofits in the United States provide financial literacy services. Of these, about two-thirds were active enough that they had to report their revenues and expenses to the IRS. It appears that entities focused principally on financial counseling and money management are smaller and less financially viable than other more diverse organizations, for which financial literacy services are secondary activities.

Our review does not provide much evidence that nonprofit financial education and counseling services have strong impacts on financial behavior. However, in light of the scale and capacity of many programs, it should come as no surprise that few nonprofits have participated in large-scale program evaluations. Existing studies are marred by selection bias, a lack of longitudinal data, and attrition. In particular, studies using quasi-experimental approaches generally find that program impacts are modest. Yet even in nonprofit settings, randomized waitlists or other innovative research designs could allow researchers to identify comparison groups without withholding services from clients. The use of administrative or institutional data can mitigate the problems of client cooperation at follow-up. Accordingly, nonprofit programs could engage in more carefully designed and implemented evaluations in the future. If a goal is facilitating behavior change, more focused interventions may be required, including ongoing counseling, financial coaching, or peer-to-peer services.

In 2009, the US Treasury Community Development Financial Institutions Fund launched the Financial Education and Counseling Pilot Program. This is a new federal effort to award grants to nonprofits that provide financial literacy services for prospective homebuyers. The explicit focus on nonprofits and financial literacy is consistent with the continued use of this sector to deliver financial education and counseling. The continued expansion of federal subsidies will help this field build capacity over time.

References

Carswell, A. T. (2009). 'Does Housing Counseling Change Consumer Financial Behaviors? Evidence from Philadelphia,' *Journal of Family and Economic Issues*, 30(4): 339–56.

CEM Benchmarking Incorporated (2010). *Wisconsin DETF: Defined Benefit Administration Benchmarking Analysis FY 2009*. Toronto, Canada: CEM Benchmarking Incorporated.

Clancy, M., M. Grinstein-Weiss, and M. Schreiner (2001). 'Financial Education and Savings Outcomes in Individual Development Accounts,' Working Paper No. 01-2. St Louis, MO: Center for Social Development, Washington University.

Collins, J. M. (2007). 'Exploring the Design of Financial Counseling for Mortgage Borrowers in Default,' *Journal of Family and Economic Issues*, 28(2): 207–26.

DiMaggio, P. J. and H. K. Anheier (1990). 'The Sociology of Nonprofit Organizations and Sectors,' *Annual Review of Sociology*, 16(1): 137–59.

Dylla, D. and D. Caldwell-Tautges (2009). *Managing Foreclosure Counseling Caseloads and Costs*. Washington, DC: Freddie Mac.

Elliehausen, G., E. C. Lundquist, and M. E. Staten (2007). 'The Impact of Credit Counseling on Subsequent Borrower Behavior,' *The Journal of Consumer Affairs*, 41(1): 1–28.

Froelich, K. A., T. W. Knoepfle, and T. H. Pollak (2000). 'Financial Measures in Nonprofit Organization Research: Comparing IRS 990 Return and Audited Financial Statement Data,' *Nonprofit and Voluntary Sector Quarterly*, 29(2): 232–54.

Gabriel, L. T. and R. M. Todd (2010). *Minnesota Home Ownership Center Case Study Illuminates Costs of Foreclosure Counseling*. Minneapolis, MN: Federal Reserve Bank of Minneapolis. http://www.minneapolisfed.org/publications_papers/pub_display.cfm?id=4398

Herbert, C. E., J. Turnham, and C. N. Rodgers (2008). *The State of the Housing Counseling Industry: 2008 Report*. Cambridge, MA: Abt Associates.

Hirad, A. and P. Zorn (2002). 'Pre-Purchase Homeownership Counseling: A Little Knowledge is a Good Thing,' in N. P. Retsinas and E. S. Belsky, eds, *Low-Income*

Homeownership: Examining the Unexamined Goal. Washington, DC: Brookings Institution, pp. 146–74.

Internal Revenue Service (2008). *Publication 557: Tax-Exempt Status for Your Organization.* Washington, DC: Department of the Treasury.

Mayer, N. S., P. A. Tatian, K. Temkin, and C. A. Calhoun (2009). *National Foreclosure Mitigation Counseling Program Evaluation: Preliminary Analysis of Program Effects.* Washington, DC: The Urban Institute.

Meier, S. and C. Sprenger (2008). 'Discounting Financial Literacy: Time Preferences and Participation in Financial Education Programs,' IZA Discussion Paper. Bonn, Germany: Institute for the Study of Labor.

Office of Community Services (2008). *Report to Congress: Assets for Independence Program, Status at the Conclusion of the Eighth Year.* Washington, DC: Administration for Children and Families, US Department of Health and Human Services.

President's Advisory Council on Financial Literacy (2009). *2008 Annual Report to the President.* Washington: DC: The Department of the Treasury.

Rose-Ackerman, S. (1996). 'Altruism, Nonprofits, and Economic Theory,' *Journal of Economic Literature*, 34(2): 701–28.

Sanders, C. K., T. L. Weaver, and M. Schnabel (2007). 'Economic Education for Battered Women,' *Affilia*, 22(3): 240–54.

Vitt, L. A., C. Anderson, J. Kent, D. M. Lyter, J. K. Siegenthaler, and J. Ward (2000). *Personal Finance and the Rush to Competence: Financial Literacy Education in the US.* Middleburg, VA: Institute for Socio-Financial Studies. http://www.isfs.org/documents-pdfs/rep-finliteracy.pdf

——G. M. Reichbach, J. L. Kent, and J. K. Siegenthaler (2005). *Goodbye to Complacency: Financial Literacy Education in the US 2000–2005.* Middleburg, VA: Institute for Socio-Financial Studies. http://www.isfs.org/documents-pdfs/Goodbyeto-Complacency-nocover.pdf

Weisbrod, B. A. (1997). 'The Future of the Nonprofit Sector: Its Entwining with Private Enterprise and Government,' *Journal of Policy Analysis and Management*, 16(4): 541–55.

Zhan, M., S. G. Anderson, and J. Scott (2006). 'Financial Knowledge of the Low-Income Population: Effects of a Financial Education Program,' *Journal of Sociology & Social Welfare*, 33: 53–74.

End Pages

The Pension Research Council

The Pension Research Council of the Wharton School at the University of Pennsylvania is committed to generating debate on key policy issues affecting pensions and other employee benefits. The Council sponsors interdisciplinary research on private and social retirement security and related benefit plans in the United States and around the world. It seeks to broaden understanding of these complex arrangements through basic research into their economic, social, legal, actuarial, and financial foundations. Members of the Advisory Board of the Council, appointed by the Dean of the Wharton School, are leaders in the employee benefits field, and they recognize the essential role of social security and other public sector income maintenance programs while sharing a desire to strengthen private sector approaches to economic security. For more information, see http://www.pensionresearchcouncil.org

The Boettner Center for Pensions and Retirement Security

Founded at the Wharton School to support scholarly research, teaching, and outreach on global aging, retirement, and public and private pensions, the Center is named after Joseph E. Boettner. Funding to the University of Pennsylvania was provided through the generosity of the Boettner family, whose intent was to spur financial well-being at older ages through work on how aging influences financial security and life satisfaction. The Center disseminates research and evaluation on challenges and opportunities associated with global aging and retirement, how to strengthen retirement income systems, saving and investment behavior of the young and the old, interactions between physical and mental health, and successful retirement. For more information, see http://www.pensionresearchcouncil.org/boettner/.

Executive Director

Olivia S. Mitchell, International Foundation of Employee Benefit Plans Professor, The Wharton School, University of Pennsylvania.

MetLife, Inc.
Morgan Stanley Smith Barney
Mutual of America Life Insurance Company
New York Life—Mainstay
Pacific Investment Mgmt. Co. LLC
Prudential Financial
Pyramis Global Advisors
Retirement Made Simpler
Social Security Administration
State Street Global Advisors
TIAA-CREF Institute
The Vanguard Group
Towers Watson

Institutional Members:
AARP Public Policy Institute
Financial Engines, Inc.
International Foundation of Employee Benefit Plans
Loomis, Sayles and Company, LP
Ontario Pension Board
Society of Actuaries

Recent Pension Research Council Publications

Reorienting Retirement Risk Management. Robert L. Clark and Olivia S. Mitchell, eds. 2010. (ISBN 0-19-959260-9).

Fundamentals of Private Pensions. Dan M. McGill, Kyle N. Brown, John J. Haley, Sylvester Schieber, and Mark J. Warshawsky. 9th Ed. 2010. (ISBN 0-19-954451-6).

The Future of Public Employees Retirement Systems. Olivia S. Mitchell and Gary Anderson, eds. 2009. (ISBN 0-19-957334-9).

Recalibrating Retirement Spending and Saving. John Ameriks and Olivia S. Mitchell, eds. 2008. (ISBN 0-19-954910-8).

Lessons from Pension Reform in the Americas. Stephen J. Kay and Tapen Sinha, eds. 2008. (ISBN 0-19-922680-6).

Redefining Retirement: How Will Boomers Fare? Brigitte Madrian, Olivia S. Mitchell, and Beth J. Soldo, eds. 2007. (ISBN 0-19-923077-3).

Restructuring Retirement Risks. David Blitzstein, Olivia S. Mitchell, and Steven P. Utkus, eds. 2006. (ISBN 0-19-920465-9).

Reinventing the Retirement Paradigm. Robert L. Clark and Olivia S. Mitchell, eds. 2005. (ISBN 0-19-928460-1).

Pension Design and Structure: New Lessons from Behavioral Finance. Olivia S. Mitchell and Steven P. Utkus, eds. 2004. (ISBN 0-19-927339-1).

The Pension Challenge: Risk Transfers and Retirement Income Security. Olivia S. Mitchell and Kent Smetters, eds. 2003. (ISBN 0-19-926691-3).

A History of Public Sector Pensions in the United States. Robert L. Clark, Lee A. Craig, and Jack W. Wilson, eds. 2003. (ISBN 0-8122-3714-5).

Benefits for the Workplace of the Future. Olivia S. Mitchell, David Blitzstein, Michael Gordon, and Judith Mazo, eds. 2003. (ISBN 0-8122-3708-0).

Innovations in Retirement Financing. Olivia S. Mitchell, Zvi Bodie, P. Brett Hammond, and Stephen Zeldes, eds. 2002. (ISBN 0-8122-3641-6).

To Retire or Not: Retirement Policy and Practice in Higher Education. Robert L. Clark and P. Brett Hammond, eds. 2001. (ISBN 0-8122-3572-X).

Pensions in the Public Sector. Olivia S. Mitchell and Edwin Hustead, eds. 2001. (ISBN 0-8122-3578-9).

The Role of Annuity Markets in Financing Retirement. Jeffrey Brown, Olivia S. Mitchell, James Poterba, and Mark Warshawsky, eds. 2001. (ISBN 0-262-02509-4).

Forecasting Retirement Needs and Retirement Wealth. Olivia S. Mitchell, P. Brett Hammond, and Anna Rappaport, eds. 2000. (ISBN 0-8122-3529-0).

Prospects for Social Security Reform. Olivia S. Mitchell, Robert J. Myers, and Howard Young, eds. 1999. (ISBN 0-8122-3479-0).

Living with Defined Contribution Pensions: Remaking Responsibility for Retirement. Olivia S. Mitchell and Sylvester J. Schieber, eds. 1998. (ISBN 0-8122-3439-1).

Positioning Pensions for the Twenty-First Century. Michael S. Gordon, Olivia S. Mitchell, and Marc M. Twinney, eds. 1997. (ISBN 0-8122-3391-3).

Securing Employer-Based Pensions: An International Perspective. Zvi Bodie, Olivia S. Mitchell, and John A. Turner, eds. 1996. (ISBN 0-8122-3334-4).

Available from the Pension Research Council web site: http://www.pensionresearchcouncil.org/

Index

absolute poverty 260–1
abusive sales practices 116
Accra 260
ADD (American Dream
    Demonstration) 238 n. 13
Affinity Plus Federal Credit Union 232
AFI (Assets for Independence)
    program 272, 275
AFP (Chilean Asociación de Fondos de
    Pensiones) 102, 103–10, 113 nn.
    1–3, 6
African countries 260
Agarwal, S. 6–7, 76, 146, 181, 186, 194,
    199 n. 1
Agnew, J. 6, 36 n. 5, 42, 158, 159,
    160, 161, 162, 163, 165, 169, 170,
    176 n. 3
Alexandria 136
ALP (RAND American Life Panel) 4,
    76–97, 120, 136, 138–41, 186, 187
American Finance Association 101
American Money Market Accounts 221
Ameriks, J. 27, 56 n. 3, 162
Anderson, T. W. 90, 94 n. 6
Anheier, H. K. 270
annuities 1, 49, 50, 51, 57 n. 4, 136
    choosing between lump sums
        and 41–7, 52, 56 nn. 2, 3, 160
    information overload and 158–78
    voluntarily purchased in open
        market 40
Arenas de Mesa, A. 102, 103, 107,
    113 n. 8
Argentina 223
Ariely, D. 209
ARMs (adjustable-rate mortgages) 1,
    186–7
Asians 136
Atkinson, A. 258, 265 nn. 3, 5
Attanasio, O. P. 77

Australia 256
Avanzi, B. 57 n. 4

Baby-Boomers 25, 32, 242
Bakken, R. 199 n. 3
Banco Bilboa Vizcaya 223
Bankruptcy Abuse Prevention and
    Consumer Protection Act
    (US 2005) 272
barriers to entry 76
    economic and psychological 159
Barron, J. M. 196, 200 n. 13
Barsky, R. B. 79, 91, 94 n. 3,
    95–6 nn. 11
basic knowledge index 95 n. 10
Bayer, P. J. 76, 78, 89–90, 190
BD (Becton, Dickinson and Company)
    42–3, 45, 49, 51, 57 n. 9
    Saving Incentive Plan 44
behavioral decision research 207, 211
behavioral economics 207, 211, 220
behavioral finance 258, 259
behavioral mechanisms/outcomes
    208, 216, 259, 261, 281
Benartzi, S. 212
Bergstresser, D. 11 n.
Bernheim, B. D. 21, 76, 89, 101, 185,
    189, 190, 191–2
Bertaut, C. C. 22, 34, 77
Beshears, J. 11 n.
best practices 116, 243, 284
Blacks 22, 136, 220, 231
BLS (US Bureau of Labor Statistics)
    56 n. 1, 220
Bolivia 265 n. 6
bond pricing knowledge 87–8, 90
Boyce, L. 200 n. 11
Britain, see United Kingdom
broker-dealers 116–44
Brown, J. 57 n. 5, 159–60, 176 n. 4

Bubb, R. 145–6
Bucks, B. 11 n., 186
budget constraint 18

Calvert, L. 17
Campbell, J. 36 n. 1, 77, 101, 158, 188
Canada 256, 257
canonical correlations test 90, 94 n. 6
Carswell, A. T. 281–2
Carter, S. 6
Cary 214
Caskey, J. P. 189
CCTs (conditional cash transfers) 264
    CDs (certificates of deposit) 136, 234
Center for Financial Services
    Innovation 232
Centra Credit Union (Indiana) 232,
    233, 234, 235
Central Asia 261
Central/Eastern Europe 259, 261
CFA (Consumer Federation of
    America) 118, 221
CFA/AMEX (CFA/American Express)
    199 n. 3
Chan, S. 36 n. 8
Chao, C. N. 120
Chen, H. 183–4
Chicago 7, 186–7, 194
Chile 5, 6, 101–15
Chilean Social Protection Survey,
    see EPS
Choi, J. J. 175
Christelis, D. 36 n. 6, 77, 158
churning 116
Clancy, M. 196, 281
Clark, R. L. 3, 35, 57 n. 7,
    200 n. 10
Clarksville 232
cognitive ability 77, 199 n. 1
    IQ and 176 n. 5
cognitive biases 259
Cole, S. 76, 192, 231, 238 nn. 6, 8
Collins, J. M. 9, 35, 188, 196, 197, 282
Colombia 223
Community Reinvestment Act
    (US 1977) 272

company benefits 43–4
Constantinides, G. M. 77
construal level theory 210–11, 215
Consumer Federation of America 221
consumption 228
    current/present 57 n. 6, 70, 71
    delayed 208, 209, 210, 211
    financing in retirement 42
    future 70, 158
    immediate 208–9
    low-literacy respondents use loan
        proceeds for 72
    rational and foresighted consumers
        derive utility from 17–18
costs and benefits 112, 206, 215
    tradeoff between 207
Cragg-Donald *F*-statistic 94 n. 6
credit cards 1, 63, 112, 146, 148
    failure to repay debt each month 60
    outstanding balances 70, 71, 73, 181
    teaser rates 101
credit constraints 77
credit unions 6, 145–57, 274
    prize-linked saving products 8, 232,
        233, 234, 235
Cronqvist, H. 176 n. 2
Crossan, D. 8
Current Population Survey (2007)
    143 n. 2

D2D (Doorways to Dreams) Fund 232,
    238 nn. 9, 14
D'Ambrosio, M. 35, 200 n. 10
Danes, S. M. 199 n. 3, 200 n. 11
Davidoff, T. 57 n. 5
Davis, S. J. 77
DB (defined-benefit) plans 1, 3, 52,
    158, 160
    alternative forms of distributions
        from 40
    default option for 45
    distribution choice in 43
    lump sum 4, 41, 42, 43, 46, 47, 49, 50,
        51, 56 n. 1, 57 n. 6
    mandatory, collective 90
    see also annuities

DC (defined-contribution) plans 1, 3,
  59, 102, 160
  alternative forms of distributions
    from 40
  DB shift to 158
  distribution choice in 43, 52
  how pension benefits are computed
    113 n. 5
  mandatory 5
  see also annuities
De Meza, D. 259
DellaVigna, S. 265 n. 7
demographic characteristics 32, 33,
  160, 185, 186, 187
demographic groups:
  financial literacy rates vary
    consistently by 182
  lottery participation fairly evenly
    distributed across 231
  PLS product holds appeal for 234
demographic variables 51, 66, 113, 171
  statistically significant 172
demographics 1, 34, 42, 69, 85, 90, 103,
  111, 170, 184, 197, 198
  how related to tested financial
    knowledge 168
  influence of 164
  literacy relative to 167, 182
dependent variables 30–2, 49, 66, 84,
  107, 169
  binary 85, 172
Detroit 234
DHS (Dutch Household Survey) 77,
  94 n. 4
Dickemper, J. 17, 27
DiMaggio, P. J. 270
Ding, L. 195, 196
discount rates 18, 56 n. 2
  high (er) 60, 70–1, 73, 207, 208,
    209, 214
  low 71
discounting models:
  hyperbolic 208, 209, 212, 213
  normative 207
  time-based/temporal 206, 207, 212,
    214, 215

disposition choice 47–51
distribution choice 43–7
DKs (don't-knows) 20–1, 25, 83–4, 85,
  94 n. 5
Dominitz, J. 83
Duarte, F. 112, 113 n. 8
Duflo, E. 36 n. 8, 76, 191, 197
dummy variables 32, 86, 155–6, 187,
  192, 200 n. 12
Durbin-Wu-Hausman test 91, 95 n. 9

Ebert, J. 212
EBRI (Employee Benefits Research
  Institute) 19, 199 n. 3
economic/financial crisis 1, 2, 10, 206,
  246, 265 n. 6
economics education:
  exogeneity of 78
  self-reported 89–90
Education Review Office (NZ) 249
educational attainment 22, 25, 32, 33,
  62, 231
  Social Security payments increase
    with 160
  see also economics education;
    financial education
Edward D. Jones 118
Elliehausen, G. 195, 281
endogeneity 90, 196, 282, 283
  eliminating 187, 189
  many program evaluations suffer
    from 197
  potential 91
endogeneity bias 77, 88
Enron 137
Eppler, M. 161
EPS (Chilean Encuesta de Protección
  Social) 102, 103, 104, 107, 109,
  113 nn. 4, 6
ethnicity 22, 118, 136, 261
European financial markets 223
exogeneity 78, 88, 89, 90, 91, 94 n. 6,
  192, 198
expectations 18, 49, 253
  confirmed 22
  investor 117, 118

expectations (*cont.*)
  optimistic 210
  subjective 92
  see also Index of Consumer
    Expectations
expected utility 80
  lifetime 18
  maximization 77
explanatory variables 66

F-statistics 94 n. 6, 95 n. 9
Facebook 246
factor analysis 94 n. 5, 95 n. 10
Fang, X. 119–20
Fannie Mae 193, 272
FDIC (Federal Deposit Insurance
  Corporation) 184, 231
Federal Credit Union Act (US 1934)
  145
Fedorikhin, A. 209
fees 102–4, 105, 109, 110, 112,
  113 n. 7
FICO (Fair Isaac Co.) scores 147, 150,
  151, 153, 154–6
fiduciary duty 141, 142, 143 n. 2
Filene Research Institute 232
financial capability 256, 258, 259, 260,
  262, 268
  behavior-based concept of 265
  enabling environment for
    building 257
  measuring 261, 263–4
financial counseling 6–7, 181–205,
  269, 272
  nonprofit providers of 275–84
  see also Financial Education and
    Counseling Pilot Program; HUD;
    NFCC
financial education 9, 60, 73, 77,
  160, 174, 181–2, 194, 197, 241–7,
  268, 286
  access via the mainstream 251
  benefits of 247, 253
  breadth of activities in existence 274
  classes for low-income participants
    196

costs of providing 273
distinction between counseling
  and 269
employer-provided 42, 76, 78, 188
empowering investors through 175
evaluation of programs 189, 193,
  198, 199, 252
evaluation of specific programs and
  policies 76
important source of 3
initiative to identify those most in
  need of 2
integration into schools and tertiary
  training 254
literature on the impact of 280–4
low- and middle-income
  countries 255–67
nonprofit providers of 275–84
programs to spur 35
recent proliferation of programs 199
related to housing 271–2
school-based 89, 90, 191, 245, 247, 249
state 191–2
traditionally hard-to-reach audience
  for 250
virtually no access outside formal
  schooling 78
workplace programs 89, 90, 189–90,
  191, 200 n. 9
see also FLE
Financial Education and Counseling
  Pilot Program 286
financial illiteracy 2, 6, 21, 22–5, 102,
  181, 186, 188
major initiatives to address 3
pervasiveness understated 184
poor planning and 17, 32
private costs of 11
pronounced among those with
  low income/education/wealth
  holdings 33
stock-market participation and
  76–97
suboptimal/welfare-reducing
  financial behavior and 181, 182–3
widespread 3, 10, 34, 35

Financial Planning Association
221
financial security 1, 6, 269
fixed costs 77
FLE (financial literacy and education)
255–67
Flint 234
FNB (First National Bank of South
Africa) 8, 230, 231–2
foreclosure 195, 196, 282
Fort Wayne 136
Freddie Mac 272
Frederick, S. 207, 208
FSA (UK Financial Services Authority)
257, 256
Fusilier, M. 119

G8 Ministers of Finance Pre-Summit
Statement (2006) 263
gambling behavior 219, 220, 223, 228,
238 n. 3
Gardnerville Ranchos 214
Garman, E. T. 200 n. 10
Garrett, D. 189, 190, 192
Gelb Consulting Group 119
gender 32, 33, 231, 262
Gerardi, K. 11 n.
Germany 223–7
GMM (generalized-methods-of-
moments) estimator 95 n. 8
GNI (Gross National Income) per
capita 260
Gonzalez-Vega, C. 193–4
gratification delay 209
Green, L. 207
Green, R. 238 n. 5
Gross, D. 146
GuideStar dataset 275, 276, 280
Guillen, M. 223, 227
Guiso, L. 77, 92
Guryan, J. 238 n. 12
Gustman, A. 27, 185

Haliassos, M. 22, 34, 77
Hartarska, V. 193–4
Harvard Law School 238 n. 14

Hastings, J. 5, 101, 103, 104, 107, 112,
113 n. 8
Hathaway, I. 188–9, 199
Herbert, C. E. 272, 275
heteroskedasticity 95 n. 8
Heywood solution 95 n. 10
HICs (high-income countries) 255,
256–7, 260, 261, 262, 264
Hilgert, M. 17, 21, 77, 101, 181
Hira, T. K. 191, 199 n. 3
Hirad, A. 193, 196, 200 n. 13, 282
Hispanics 22, 136, 220
low-income immigrants 198
Hogarth, J. 21, 22, 188
Holland, J. H. 200 n. 10
Holt, C. A. 91, 95–6 nn. 11, 161
Holzl, A. 238 n. 11
Holzmann, R. 9, 265 n. 8
Hong, H. 77, 92, 93
House of Representatives 143 n. 2
Housing Action Illinois 200 n. 7
HRS (US Health and Retirement
Study 1992/2004) 17, 19, 26–8, 34,
36 n. 3, 44, 77, 83, 104, 160,
185–6, 187, 190–1, 200 n. 8
Hu, W. 41, 42
HUD (US Department of Housing and
Urban Development) counseling
program 7, 9, 271–2, 274, 275
Hung, A. 5, 35, 83, 122, 128, 143 n. 1
Hurd, M. 44

IBRD (International Bank for
Reconstruction and
Development) 260
IDAs (Individual Development
Accounts) 196, 219, 234, 238 n. 13,
260, 272, 275, 281
Illinois 7, 200 n. 7, 280
see also Chicago
income inequality 260
Index of Consumer Expectations 78
Indiana 7, 136
see also Centra Credit Union; INHP
Indonesia 223, 227
inertia 77, 162, 259

inflation 10, 18, 19, 20–1, 22, 28, 30, 32, 80, 104–5, 110
  adjustment for 242
  comprehension of 34
  consequences of 186
  consistent series 238 n. 4
  leading edge of Baby-Boomers not very knowledgeable about 25
  limited historical exposure to 25–6
INHP (Indianapolis Neighborhood Housing Partnership) 194–5
instrumental variables 77, 88–91, 95 n. 8, 187, 189, 282
interest rates 19, 22, 25, 28, 104–5, 146, 148, 151, 153–4, 187, 280
  astronomical 181
  calculations related to 20–1, 30, 34, 56 n. 2, 188
  comprehension of 34
  facility with 186
  fixed by state law 149
  lack of knowledge about 32
  nominal 230–1
  per-period cap on changes 199 n. 6
  poor understanding of 36 n. 6
  prices and 80, 83, 87, 163
  prize fund 228
  stochastic 227
  unusually low 194
  wedge between borrowing and lending 77
International Gateway for Financial Education 256
International Network of Financial Education 252, 256
Internet 78, 83, 120, 137, 196, 269
intertemporal choice 207, 208, 215
investment advisers 116–44
Investment Advisers Act (US 1940) 116–17
Investment, Savings, and Insurance Association (NZ) 244
IRAs (Individual Retirement Accounts) 33, 43–4, 50, 219
Ireland 257

IRS (US Internal Revenue Service) 269, 275–6, 278, 280, 285
IXI company 74 n. 4

Jackson, H. 238 n. 14
Japan 223, 227
Jappelli, T. 77
job tenure 45, 60, 62, 66
Johnson, R. 57 n. 5, 160
Jonan Shinkin Bank 227
Jorgenson, S. 265 n. 8
JPMorgan Chase 235
  Jump$tart Financial Literacy Survey 183, 184

Kaestner, R. 197
Kang, A. S. 238 n. 14
Kaufmann, A. 145–6
Kearney, M. 8, 220, 238 n. 7
Kempson, E. 256, 257, 265 n. 3
Kenya 227
Keoghs 33
Khatiwada, S. 188–9, 199
Killeen, P. R. 212
Kim, B. K. 7, 206, 207, 212, 213–14
Kim, J. 200 n. 10
Kirby, K. N. 207, 209
KiwiSaver 243, 251
KPMG Peat Marwick 199 n. 3
KYC (know-your-customer) accounts 231

labor markets 1, 104
Langrehr, F. W. 199 n. 3
Latin America, *see* Argentina; Bolivia; Chile; Colombia; Mexico; Venezuela
Laury, S. K. 91, 95–6 nn. 11, 161
least squares 90
  see also OLS
leisure 17–18
Levitt, A. 116
Liberman, N. 206, 210
LICs (low-income countries) 255–67
life expectancy 45, 51

better information concerning
57 n. 5
longer than average 50
likelihood 116, 121
likelihood-ratio test 90
linear probability models 49, 85
liquidity 146, 147, 148, 184, 262–3
access to 152, 153
constrained 60, 70
ease of providing 222
emergency savers demand 221
minimum levels of 149
loan-taking behavior 60, 66, 70, 72,
74 n. 3
Lobe, S. 238 n. 11
LOCs (line of credit) accounts 147,
148–9, 150–1, 153–4
Loewenstein, G. 208–9
logistic regression models 66
Loibl, C. 191
lotteries 8, 104, 186, 218, 222, 223, 227,
232, 237
choice experiment 161
essential components of 234
hypothetical, over lifetime income 79
jackpot games 228
participation evenly distributed
across demographic groups 231
PLS programs deemed 234–5
safe 95 n. 11
spending in 231, 233, 234, 238 n.
see also state lotteries
lump sums 1, 4, 40, 49, 50, 51, 56 nn.
1–3, 57 nn. 4–6
choosing between annuities and
41–7, 160
Lusardi, A. 3, 17, 21, 22, 25, 27, 30, 32,
35, 36, 76, 77, 78, 83, 94 n. 4, 101,
104, 145, 146, 158, 159, 160, 163,
176, 181, 186, 187, 190–1, 200, 259
Lynch, J. G. 206, 209, 212

Macmillan, Harold 227
Malkoc, S. A. 206, 211
MaMA (FNB *Million-a-Month Account*)
8, 230–2, 236

Mandell, L. 21, 199 n. 4, 200 n. 11
Māori people 241, 242, 244, 250–1, 253
Martin, M. 188
Maryland 119, 235, 236
see also University of Maryland
Mastrobuoni, G. 36 n. 8
maximum-likelihood methods
95 n. 10
Mazumder, B. 199 n. 1
MDCs (matching defined
contributions) 264
measurement error 88
Medicare 112
Meier, S. 283, 285
Mengis, J. 161
Merrill Lynch 118, 189, 192
Metcalfe, J. 209
Mexico 113 n. 8, 223
Michigan 232, 233, 235
see also University of Michigan
microfinance lending 227, 258, 262
Microfinance Opportunities 265 nn.
1, 6
MICs (middle-income countries)
255–67
Miles, D. 36 n. 6, 199 n. 2
Million Adventure bonds (1694) 8, 223
Ministry of Education (NZ) 244,
247, 249
Mischel, W. 209
Mitchell, O. S. 3, 17, 21, 25, 27, 30, 35,
36, 57, 59, 76, 77, 78, 83, 94 n. 4,
101, 103, 104, 145, 146, 158, 159,
160, 163, 176, 181, 185, 186, 187,
190–1, 200, 259
MMAs (money-market accounts) 136
Moore, D. 188
Moore, J. 21, 35, 56 n. 1
Morgan Stanley 118
mortgages 21, 60, 189, 242, 252, 281
adjustable-rate 1, 186–7
counseling programs 6–7, 188,
193–6, 272, 282
delinquency rates 193, 195, 196, 282
failed/poor understanding of 11,
36 n. 6

mortgages (*cont.*)
  inferior product choices 188
  no-income-no-down-payment 101
  refinancing 158, 181, 188
  risky products 7
  shocking ignorance of terms 186
Moscow 263
Mottola, G. R. 59, 160, 171
Muller, L. 56 n. 1
multiple price list method 91
multivariate analysis 20, 30–2, 47, 84–5, 228, 233
Mundy, S. 265 nn. 3, 5
Murphy, A. L. 223
myopia 261
myopic decisions:
  affective and visceral influences on 208
  cognitive processes explaining 209
  role of construal in 211

National Bank Act (US 1863/64) 234, 235
National Center for Charitable Statistics 275
National Compensation Survey 56 n. 1
National Foundation for Credit Counseling 272
National Savings bonds (UK) 228, 229
National Strategy for Financial Literacy (NZ) 244, 251
NCEE (National Council on Economic Education) 21
Neale, Thomas 223
Netherlands 77, 78, 90
  see also DHS
New Zealand 3, 8–9, 241–54, 256, 259
NFCC (National Foundation for Credit Counseling) 195
Ngāi Tahu tribe 250–1
NGOs (nongovernment organizations) 245
Nine Years' War (1689–97) 223
NLSY (National Longitudinal Survey of Youth) 200 n. 8

nonlinear functions 213
nonprofit providers 35, 76, 232
  grants to 10
  role in improving financial literacy 9, 268–87
NORC (National Opinion Research Council) 220, 238 n. 3
NSAI (UK National Savings and Investments) 227, 228
NTEE-CC (National Taxonomy of Exempt Entities Core Codes) 276, 278
null hypotheses 86, 90, 94 n. 6
numeracy 21, 36 n. 6, 104, 252
  simple/basic 10, 32, 33, 34
NZ Super (New Zealand Superannuation) 242, 243

Obama, Barack 10
O'Connell, A. 242, 245, 252–3, 265 nn. 3, 5
O'Donoghue, J. 238 n. 4
OECD (Organization for Economic Co-operation and Development) 2, 199 n. 2, 252, 255, 263, 265 n. 1
  Financial Education project 256
  Program for International Student Assessment 249
Office of the Comptroller of the Currency 235
Office of Thrift Supervision 235
old-age pensions 242
OLS (ordinary least squares) 85–8, 91, 150
Oppenheimer Funds/Girls Inc. 199 n. 3
O'Rourke, C. M. 188
Orton, L. 258, 265 n. 5

PACFL (US President's Advisory Council on Financial Literacy) 2, 268
Pagan-Hall test 95 n. 8
Pakistan 227
Panis, C. 44

PARS (Participants Attending
    Retirement Seminars) 42
Partnership on Making Finance Work
    for Africa 260
payday loans 6, 60, 145–57
PCA (principal components analysis)
    83, 84
  important caveat to straightforward
    application of 95 n. 10
Pence, K. 11 n., 186
Peng, T. M. 200 n. 11
pension manager fees 101–15
pension plans 4, 27, 181, 189, 259
  characteristics of 185, 190
  importance of financial literacy in
    distributions 40–58
  spread of DC 76
Philadelphia 214, 281–2
PISA (OECD 2012 Program for Inter-
    national Student Assessment) 249
PLS (prize-linked saving) accounts
    218–40
preferences 7, 40, 51, 52, 120, 138, 160,
    206, 213, 233, 263
  ambiguity 93
  distributional 44
  intertemporal 207, 210
  observed for uncertain payoffs 220
  present-biased 212
  risk 77, 104, 161
  social 78
  substantial differences in 35
  unobservable 77
  see also time preferences
Prelec, D. 212
Premium Bonds (UK) 8, 218, 227–30,
    231, 236, 238 n. 11
Previtero, A. 160
Preysman, D. 238 n. 14
probability 60, 66, 73, 107, 120, 146,
    159, 186, 192
  low 219, 220
  positive 134
  reduced 51, 196, 282
  subjective 92

taking a lump sum 49
  see also linear probability models;
    survival probability
Progress Energy 42–4, 45, 49, 51, 52
propensity to save 76
  factors that influence 70, 73
PSRA (Princeton Survey Research
    Associates) 199 n. 3
psychology 259

Qualifications Authority (NZ) 249
Quercia, R. 193–4, 196, 200 n. 13

race 22, 32, 33, 118, 136, 199 n. 4,
    220, 231
Ramamonjiarivelo, Z. H. 145
RAND Corporation 117
  see also ALP
randomization 197, 283
rational choice models 146
Rauterkus, A. 145
Ravallion, M. 265 n. 4
Read, D. 212
regression discontinuity approach
    151, 154
regressions 32, 45, 150, 155, 156,
    168, 193
  first-stage 90, 94 n. 6
  instrumental variable 95 n. 8
  linear 88
  post-game 173
  probit 86, 169, 172
  see also multivariate analysis
relative poverty 260
Reserve Bank of India 2
Reserve Bank of New Zealand 244
resource slack theory 206, 209–10,
    211–12, 215
Restoring American Financial Stability
    Act (2010) 143 n. 2
Retirement Commission (NZ) 8,
    241–2, 243, 244, 245–9, 250, 251,
    252, 253, 256
retirement planning 1–3, 6, 44, 49, 76,
    102, 187

retirement planning (*cont.*)
  advanced financial knowledge
    related to 159
  assistance with 135
  company-provided programs 52
  consultation with financial
    planners 91
  factors associated with disposition
    choice 47–51
  findings for 26–30
  implications for well-being 17–39
  literature on relationship between
    financial literacy and 184–5
  saving and 8, 17–20, 206–17
  seminars on 28, 35, 41, 42, 46,
    51, 188
  special module to assess financial
    literacy 18–19
  successful 34
  tax-deferred accounts 73
  widespread lack of 27
returns on assets 18, 87
rewards 208, 209, 213
  delayed 207, 214
RHS (Social Security Retirement
  History Survey) 185
risk aversion 34, 50, 78–9, 80, 85, 86, 91,
  95 n. 11, 176
  controls for 171
  relative 94 n. 2
  strong 40
risk diversification 28, 30, 32, 33, 80,
  104, 105
  many respondents do not
    understand 34
  women less likely to respond
    correctly 25
Rose-Ackerman, S. 270, 273
Russian Federation 2, 255, 263–4, 265
Ryan, A. 238 n. 14
Rydqvist, K. 238 n. 5

Saez, E. 36 n. 8, 76, 191, 197
Sanders, C. K. 198, 280
Sargan-Hansen test 94 n. 6
Save to Win project 233, 234, 235

Saver's Credit initiative 219
saving 8, 17–20, 104, 105, 107, 112, 256
  behavior linked to information
    campaign in schools 259
  cost-effective decisions 102
  education and 196
  framing of decisions 101
  groups most at risk of falling short
    of 103
  often not feasible 261
  prize-linked products 218–40
  tax incentives attached to 243
  time perception and 206–17
  understanding the purpose of 256
  see also IDAs
SCA (Survey of Consumer Attitudes) 78
scandals 137
SCF (Survey of Consumer
  Finances) 185, 238 n. 3
Schaub, M. 119
Schneider, D. 219, 222, 237 n. 1
Scott, J. 41, 42
SEC (US Securities and Exchange
  Commission) 116, 117, 119,
  143 n. 2
  registered investment advisers 128,
    143 n. 8
Securities Commission (NZ) 244
Securities Exchange Act (US 1934) 116
Senate Banking Committee 143 n. 2
Servon, L. J. 197
sexually-arousing stimuli 213–14
Shamosh, N. A. 207
SHARE (Survey of Health, Ageing,
  and Retirement in Europe)
  36 n. 6, 77
Shastry, G. K. 76, 192
Shiv, B. 209
Siegel and Gale, LLC 119
Simple Planners 26, 28, 30
Sinha, A. C. 238 n. 14
soap operas 198, 259
social interaction 77
  trust and 92–3
social marketing 9, 264
Social Security 18, 27, 36 n. 8, 41, 160

entitlements and pensions 185–6
Sorted approach (NZ) 242, 245–7, 252
Souleles, N. 146
South Africa 222, 230–2, 236, 238 n. 9
    see also FNB
Spader, J. 193–4, 196, 198, 200 n. 13
Spain 223
Sprenger, C. 283, 285
Sri Lanka 265 n. 6
SROs (self-regulating organizations)
    116
standard deviation 86, 88, 151, 159
Stango, V. 188
state lotteries 220, 221
    consistent mandate of 235–6
    demand for products 238 n. 7
    propensity of low- and middle-
        income families to gamble on 219
Staten, M. E. 196, 200 n. 13
statistical significance 32, 50, 51, 66,
    72, 88, 110, 121, 172, 176, 195,
    200 n. 12, 221, 282
Steinmeier, T. 27, 185
Stevens, A. H. 36 n. 8
stockbrokers, *see* broker-dealers
stockmarket participation 76–97
    financial sophistication fosters 159
Stock-Yogo critical values 94 n. 6
Sub-Saharan Africa 261
Successful Planners 28
Sunstein, C. 259
Supplemental Nutrition Assistance
    Program 272
Survey of Consumer Finances 34, 146
survival probability 49
    identical 162
    prospective 18
    subjective 50
Sweden 176 n. 2, 223, 227
sweepstakes 232, 233, 235
Switzerland 57 n. 4, 223
Szykman, L. 6, 36 n. 5, 42, 158, 159,
    161, 163, 165, 169

tax-deferred accounts 73
tax-exempt status 9, 147, 269, 276

TD Ameritrade 119
Te Puni Kōkiri 250
Tejeda-Ashton, L. 101, 103, 104, 107,
    112, 113 n. 8
Tennessee 119
Tertiary Education Commission
    (NZ) 249
tetrachoric correlation matrix 95 n. 10
Thaler, R. H. 176 n. 2, 212, 259
TIAA-CREF (Teachers Insurance and
    Annuity Association-College
    Retirement Equities Fund) 19,
    56 n. 3
time preferences 60, 283
    high discount rates in 73
    unobserved 70
Treaty of Waitangi (1840) 251
Trope, Y. 206, 210
trust:
    and culture 77
    and social interaction 92–3
Tschoegl, A. 223, 227
Tufano, P. 145, 163, 219, 222, 228, 233,
    237 n. 1, 238 nn. 10–11, 14
Tully Report (US 1995) 116
Twitter 246

undersaving 208, 214, 215
    important implications for 213
United Kingdom 222, 256, 259
    Premium Bonds 8, 218, 227–30, 231,
        236, 238 n. 11
    see also FSA
University of Auckland Business
    School 244
University of Chile 104
University of Maryland 238 n. 11
University of Michigan Survey Research
    Center 78
US 401k environment 4, 40, 43–51,
    59–75, 89, 189–90, 219
    automatic and voluntary
        enrollment 159
US Department of Health and Human
    Services 272
US Treasury 227

US Treasury (*cont.*)
  Community Development Financial
    Institutions Fund 9–10, 286
Utkus, S. P. 4, 59, 160, 171

Van Rooij, M. 77, 78, 79, 80, 83, 87, 88,
    90, 94 n. 5, 95 nn. 7, 10, 158, 159,
    163, 176
Vanguard Group/*Money Magazine* 199
    n. 3
variance estimates 95 n. 10
Venezuela 223
vices and virtues 209
Virginia 136
visceral states 208, 209, 213
Vissing-Jorgensen, A. 77
Vitt, L. A. 268, 274
Volpe, R. P. 183–4, 199 n. 3
Volpp, K. G. 221

Wal-Mart customers 232
Washington State 188
weak instruments 90, 94 n. 6
wealth accumulation 30, 32–4, 60, 259
    long-term 76, 77
      risk to 72

Web TV 78, 120
Weinstein, J. M. 112
Weisbrod, B. A. 270
Willis, L. E. 188–9, 191, 259
World Bank 9, 256, 261
    International Development
      Agency 260
    Russian trust-funded activities 2, 255,
      263–4, 265
World Values Survey 92
WorldCom 137
Wu-Hausman test 91, 95 n. 9

Yakoboski, P. 17, 27
Yang, Z. 119–20
Yoong, J. 94 n. 1
Young, J. A. 4

ZAG (Zero Alpha Group) 118
Zauberman, G. 203, 206, 207, 209, 211,
    212, 213–14
Zeldes, S. P. 162
Zhan, M. 280
Zinman, J. 146, 188
Zorn, P. 193, 196, 200 n. 13,
    282

CPSIA information can be obtained at www.ICGtesting.com
Printed in the USA
BVOW05*1255300315

393685BV00010B/32/P

9 780199 696819